W9-CRK-702

THE CENTER FOR CHINESE STUDIES

at the University of California, Berkeley, supported by the Ford Foundation, the Institute of International Studies (University of California, Berkeley), and the State of California, is the unifying organization for social science and interdisciplinary research on contemporary China.

PUBLICATIONS

Wakeman, Frederic, Jr. *Strangers at the Gate: Social Disorder in South China, 1839–1681* (1966)

Townsend, James. *Political Participation in Communist China* (1967)

Potter, J. M. *Capitalism and the Chinese Peasant: Social and Economic Change in a Hong Kong Village* (1968)

Schiffrin, Harold Z. *Sun Yat-sen and the Origins of the Chinese Revolution* (1968)

Schurmann, Franz. *Ideology and Organization in Communist China* (Second Edition, 1968)

Van Ness, Peter. *Revolution and Chinese Foreign Policy: Peking's Support for Wars of National Liberation* (1970)

Larkin, Bruce D. *China and Africa, 1949–1970: The Foreign Policy of the People's Republic of China* (1971)

Ku Chieh-kang and China's New History

This volume is sponsored by the
Center for Chinese Studies,
University of California, Berkeley

Ku Chieh-kang and China's New History

NATIONALISM AND THE QUEST FOR ALTERNATIVE TRADITIONS

Laurence A. Schneider

UNIVERSITY OF CALIFORNIA PRESS
BERKELEY, LOS ANGELES, LONDON, 1971

University of California Press
Berkeley and Los Angeles, California
University of California Press, Ltd.
London, England

Library of Congress Catalog Card Number: 73-129608
International Standard Book Number: 0-520-01804-4
Printed in the United States of America

For My Wife Leslie

Please tell me who the Chinese are,
Teach me how to cling to memory.
Please tell me the greatness of this people
Tell me gently, ever so gently.

Please tell me: Who are the Chinese?
Whose hearts embody the hearts of Yao and Shun?
In whose veins flow the blood of Chin K'o and Nieh Cheng?
Who are the true children of the Yellow Emperor?

Wen I-to, 1927*

* "Prayer" from TWENTIETH CENTURY CHINESE POETRY by Kai Yu Hsu. Copyright © 1963 by Kai Yu Hsu. Reprinted by permission of Doubleday & Company, Inc.

Contents

Acknowledgments

The main protagonist of this book, Ku Chieh-kang, was suggested to me as a subject of study by Professor Chen Shih-hsiang, five years ago and in quieter times. With Professor Chen's continuous encouragement, the present work has evolved out of the original doctoral thesis. Professor Wolfram Eberhard, with his usual generosity and energy, read the latter and offered me detailed suggestions for developing it; it was he who first brought to my attention the Chinese Folklore Movement and Ku Chieh-kang's role in it. I had the pleasure of spending many hours of fruitful conversation with the late T. A. Hsia on various topics related to this study, and was fortunate enough to profit from his incisive, thorough knowledge of the literature of modern China. My colleague Ralph Croizier read parts of the earlier manuscript and made useful and encouraging suggestions. My wife knows the various stages of this book better, I suspect, than she cares to; nevertheless, her dedicated help, with typewriter and blue pencil, has been persistent and indispensable.

The last stages of the book were completed partly under a faculty research fellowship from the Research Foundation of the State University of New York and a Younger Scholars' Fellowship from the National Endowment for the Humanities, for which I am grateful.

My very great debt to and respect for Joseph R. Levenson (1920–1969) can be only partly expressed here. His gentle humanity, his wit and charm, his exquisite sense of history and of the word were a source of pleasure and inspiration to his students. Everywhere I have gone in this book, I have met him coming back.

Berkeley, Calif.
July, 1970

L.A.S.

Footnote Abbreviations

ACH	*The Autobiography of a Chinese Historian,* A. Hummel, trans.
BDRC	*Biographical Dictionary of Republican China*
BMFEA	*Bulletin of the Museum of Far Eastern Antiquities*
BSCS	"Biographical Sketches of 29 Classical Scholars of the Late Manchu and Early Republican Period," Wang Yi-t'ung
CCMF	*Confucian China and Its Modern Fate,* J. R. Levenson
CHFSJS	*Ch'in Han te Fang-shih yü Ju-sheng,* Ku Chieh-kang
CKLSYCF	*Chung-kuo li-shih yen-chiu fa,* Liang Ch'i-ch'ao
ECCP	*Eminent Chinese of the Ch'ing Period,* A. Hummel, ed.
FSNHC	*Fu Ssu-nien hsüan-chi*
HC	*Hsin-ch'ao*
HPKCJC	*Hsi-pei k'ao-ch'a jih-chi,* Ku Chieh-kang

HSWT	*Hu Shih wen-ts'un*
KKTLC	*Kuo-ku t'ao-lün chi*
KSP	*Ku-shih pien,* Ku Chieh-kang, *et al.,* eds.
KTHP	*Kuo-ts'ui hsüeh-pao*
MFM	*The May Fourth Movement,* Chow Tse-tsung
MS	*Min-su*
SHK	*San Huang k'ao,* Ku Chieh-kang and Yang Hsiang-k'uei
SJCMC	"Shang-jang ch'uan-shuo ch'i yü Mo-chia k'ao," Ku Chieh-kang
SLTC	*Shih-lin tsa-chih,* Ku Chieh-kang
SSYCCI	*Shang-shu yen-chiu chiang-i,* Ku Chieh-kang, ed.
TS	*Tse-shan pan-yüeh-k'an*
TTPIS	*Ts'ui Tung-pi i-shu,* Ku Chieh-kang, ed.
WTCSS	"Wu te chung-shih shuo hsia te cheng-chih ho li-shih," Ku Chieh-kang
YK	*Yü Kung pan-yüeh-k'an*

Introduction

> *We should beware of supposing that the criticism of tradition by those in search of an alternative basis for authority necessarily leads them into ideological postures, so that every dialogue between the conservers and the critics of a tradition is like that between Burke and Paine. . . . The range of strategies open to both the conservative and the radical is greater than we have so far allowed, and . . . in confrontations between them the awareness of history is by no means all on one side. If the abridgement of tradition is ideology, the criticism of tradition may be history—the ascription to the past of a relation to the present more complex than mere transmission. The ideologist and the historian may be closer partners than seemed likely at first.*—J. G. A. Pocock[1]

An evolving Chinese nationalism has unrelentingly demanded the abandonment or destruction of those traditional intellectual attitudes and those traditional institutions which seem to have brought China, defenseless and moribund, to the brink of destruction in the nineteenth and twentieth centuries. Simultaneously, there has been a demand to retain for the new Chinese nation a culturally unique identity, distinct from other (and particularly Western) nations—separate but equal. In the radical modern transformation of Chinese society, there has been a persistent conservatizing force dedicated to constructing

1. J. G. A. Pocock, "Time, Institutions and Action: An Essay on Traditions and Their Understanding," in *Politics and Experience: Essays Presented to Professor Michael Oakeshott on the Occasion of His Retirement* (Cambridge, England, 1968), p. 223.

this unique cultural identity out of indigenous materials that are deemed appropriate to and viable in the modern world. In their attempt to implement the formula "Chinese *and* modern," concerned nationalists have been more able to specify the 'modern' factors than to identify the 'Chinese' factors.

The present study is devoted to a professional scholar, Ku Chieh-kang[2] (b. 1893), and his associates, whose work was directly or indirectly devoted, in effect, to redefining the idea of 'Chinese' through a process of reordering the relationship of past and present. These scholars believed that in China's past there were sources of radical inspiration both for destroying the old traditions and for creating and authorizing new ones. While they were not themselves uninfluenced by Western thought, these scholars significantly differed from the Westernizing intellectuals who could find no inspiration for change and reconstruction within their own history. Historical studies were the chief instruments for razing unviable traditions and for finding indigenous alternatives to what was thus rejected as unsuitable for modern China. The present analysis uses this historiography as a source of intellectual history; historical writing and ideas about history are taken as historical evidence for the nature and direction of some of the basic transformations of twentieth-century China.

Ku Chieh-kang, the main protagonist here, has been one of modern China's most prominent historians. He is a post-Confucian iconoclast and historical revisionist. In the 1920s he was the protégé of Hu Shih (1891–1962), who had studied with John Dewey at Columbia University and became his disciple in China. By the end of the decade, Ku had become one of the most eloquent publicists and imaginative scholars of China's anti-traditional 'New Thought.' His intellectual milieu was characteristically evolutionist in its historiography, pragmatic in its philosophy, gradualist and optimistic in its attitudes toward reform. Politically, his milieu was liberal democratic, and though he and his colleagues tended to remain aloof from direct

2. The Wade-Giles method of romanization is used throughout the text. Ku Chieh-kang should be pronounced "Goo Jyeh-gäng."

political involvements, they sometimes played back-bench critics to the policies of the central government.

During the more-than-thirty-year segment of his career which is examined here (ca. 1913–1945), Ku Chieh-kang was continuously and hyperactively involved with Chinese historical scholarship. Through his scholarship he hoped to correct distorted views of China's past and to right a variety of intellectual attitudes which he believed were inimical to the proper growth of a modern Chinese nation. It was not only for the nation that he showed concern, and sometimes despair; it was also for that class, the intelligentsia, with which he identified himself and with which he sometimes identified the ultimate fate of China. Proper study of the past; the intelligentsia; his own career and the future of China—all these were subjects of his most somber speculations. More often, they were targets of his boundless creative energies, guided by a cautious faith in the ameliorative powers of the 'scientific' intellect, properly employed.

A central concern of this study is to reveal and explicate the intellectual symptoms of modernity which express themselves in Ku Chieh-kang's scholarship and polemics—to determine to what degree his self-proclaimed scientific scholarship has torn away from the outlooks of pre-modern Chinese thought, and to discover where this scholarship is engaged with the problems of post-Confucian Chinese life. His thought has achieved its vitality and stature from his refusal (perhaps inability) to dismiss the Chinese past without complex reservations. His thinking has been directed by China's cultural crisis, a crisis resulting from the fact that the rejection of Chinese tradition by Chinese moderns has been perilously near to being a European or an American rejection—a dismissal of tradition on the grounds of truly alien criteria. The obvious dangers here, which were repeatedly acknowledged by Ku Chieh-kang, were the severance of historical continuity, the obliteration of a Chinese identity, and the inundation of China by Western culture. Clearly, Ku was a destroyer of traditional conceptions of the past and, concomitantly, the values for which these conceptions acted as vessels. However, implicit in all of his wide-ranging work has been a persistent drive to reconstruct a past which is consistent with his twentieth-century epistemology and sense of history and, at the same time, consistent with his will to retain a Chinese identity for a twentieth-century China.

Ku Chieh-kang was educated deeply within the Chinese traditions of higher criticism, while his familiarity with Western thought was indirect and fragmentary. When he studied at National Peking University, the apex of the educational system, from 1917 to 1921, it was the epicenter of those political and intellectual upheavals called respectively the May Fourth and New Culture movements. The former was a student-led anti-imperialist reaction to China's mistreatment at the Versailles treaty negotiations; the latter, a multifaceted attempt to find the internal sources of China's weakness. Ku's distinguished teaching career began at Peking University in the early 1920s. Thereafter, he was chairman of various history departments and advanced research institutes at other national centers of learning. During the twenties and thirties, he lectured and published widely and energetically promoted a wide range of research projects, not only in the area of ancient history but also in new areas such as folklore, historical geography, and the ethnography of China's inner Asian frontiers. He founded, edited, or sat on the editorial boards of many of the most important scholarly periodicals of the time, and he guided these publications toward the goals of his sundry projects. While there were no final arbiters in the fragmented Chinese intellectual world of these decades, the weight of Ku's personal scholarship plus the influence he achieved through his key administrative positions made him one of the central figures of non-Marxist historical scholarship during the Republican era.

During the Japanese invasion and occupation of China, Ku continued to occupy this role within the academic community that was exiled in China's far west. I stop my study of Ku's life and work with this period, ending in 1945, primarily because I lack data on his later personal life and professional activities, his political sentiments and his reactions to the civil war and the Communist regime. His scholarly publications available from the 1950s and 1960s show a distinct continuity with his work of the previous decades, and some of his work from the Republican period has been re-published under the People's Republic. In the Epilogue, I discuss, in general terms, the significance of Ku's work in a broad context that includes post-1949 China.

Scholarship and Politics

Ku Chieh-kang's pursuit of his goals during the 1920s and 1930s was characterized by two interacting themes which, in his mind, linked his own life as a scholar with the life of scholars in the past, and linked both of these with the course of Chinese history. His understanding of the relationship of scholarship to politics (the first theme) and of intellectuals to society (the second theme) lies at the foundation of his interpretations of China's formative ages and his prescriptions for contemporary society. His thesis was that scholarship and politics should remain distinctly separate. Their connection in the past had obviated a tradition of 'pure scholarship,' the subsequent growth of science, and hence the progress of Chinese civilization. Ku accused the intellectuals, whose role it should have been to protect and perpetuate pure scholarship, of selling out to the ruling class. For material profit and status, the intellectuals became the parasitic ideologues of the aristocracy.

Ku Chieh-kang's own career began with active involvement in politics and came by 1945 to an active though very different kind of political involvement. In the interim, from 1914 to 1935 and especially during the 1920s, he vigorously crusaded for an ethos of pure scholarship and the separation of knowledge from action and of scholarship (and scholars) from politics. As a youth he had been an active member of the Socialist party, but by the time he entered Peking University he had disavowed any formal political affiliations. For a short time these sentiments found considerable support among Chinese intellectuals, who were widely discouraged with the major political events following the 1911 Revolution; but by the time of the May Fourth Movement of 1919, there had begun a distinct shift back toward political activism, and Ku found himself with fewer and fewer sympathizers as he persisted in advocating political nonalignment. However, when the Japanese began their move into north China, in the mid-thirties, Ku unapologetically began to divide his energies between anti-Japanese propaganda and his normal academic activities. During the Japanese occupation, most of his publications were devoted to what he euphemistically called "popular history"—that is, propaganda, in the form of historical pieces on the themes of national unity and survival in a time of crisis. He made no pretense that this propaganda was serious scholarship, and he never expressed the feeling that he was contradicting his earlier position (which he stopped promoting from the mid-thirties). Even in these activities, he remained aloof from political party affiliation and acted very much as a maverick, his favorite persona.

From the sidelines, Ku had supported the Nationalist party (allied with the Chinese Communist party) in its efforts to unify China from 1924 to 1927 and to govern China from 1928 onward. During the latter period, however, he repeatedly clashed with the regime and discovered the sharp political implications of many of his enterprises in pure scholarship.

Intellectuals and Society

When the traditional examination system was abolished in 1905 it in effect destroyed a class, an educated elite, which not only served vital political functions but played a crucial cultural role as well. Not merely bureaucrats and officials, this elite was the keeper of intellectual orthodoxy, the interpreter of scripture, and the formulator of history and tradition. The examination system institutionalized the high status and complex function of this elite, and when the system was abolished in 1905 it signaled the fragmentation of functions and the removal of grounds for status. China's young, educated elite was then left to redefine itself, in response partially to evaluations of the traditional literati and partially to contemporary social pressures. Social functions, intellectual obligations, and political roles were all open to speculation.

In Ku Chieh-kang's circles, the speculation began with evaluations of past scholars whose individual experiences seemed to hold lessons for their modern counterparts. Next, under the expanding influence of Marxist rhetoric, past scholars were no longer evaluated as individuals, but as 'intellectuals' who were members of a larger social class, the intelligentsia. The old intelligentsia were ordinarily characterized by Ku as parasites of the aristocracy, but neither he nor his colleagues readily agreed on how to assess themselves as a group. They did not know exactly who comprised this new intelligentsia, and they were not sure to what degree the new intellectuals continued to foster the evils of their predecessors. Finally, over the 1920s, there was a marked tendency in Ku's circles (and throughout the new educated elite) to create a modern identity for the intelligentsia, based on the relationship of intellectuals to the common people.

The 'people' were considered by this group to be the great unwashed and untutored (but vital and spontaneously creative) body of the new nation. The intellectuals' obligation was to go to the people and study their situation in order to learn what areas of life needed reform. The intellectuals' role here was primarily investigative and educational, and their goal was to remove those outdated institutions and ideas which were the by-product of aristocratic oppression. Ultimately, the intellectuals would educate and reform the people to the point where the people could govern themselves along some kind of democratic lines. Not only would the intellectuals bring the new culture to the masses, but within the suppressed traditions of the people, it was hoped, there would be sources of inspiration for certain aspects of the new culture.

Clearly, China's post-examination-educated elite were not satisfied with being mere 'intellectuals' according to the definition that Ku Chieh-kang usually gave to that term. It was not that the persona of an olympian scientist was unattractive; it was rather that few could keep that persona clear of the compulsion to serve society. That traditional compulsion, now rationalized on new grounds, was obviously pervasive in the Republican period, and it was frustrated at every turn by social chaos and brute politics. Various movements 'to the people' seemed to provide dramatic means both to serve society and to satisfy a craving for political fulfillment. Populism also opened a broad avenue to the reintegration of those new intellectuals who felt themselves not merely deprived of their former status and political potential but, moreover, alienated from the total society.

The Role of History

According to Ku Chieh-kang, the masses and the new nation as a whole could only be helped by a thorough evaluation of the institutional and intellectual legacies of the past. What was not relevant to the needs of the modern nation would be disposed of; what was appropriate would remain and be updated or developed. Judgments of relevancy relied mainly on historical investigations which applied a genetic method to determine how a particular institution or idea was first developed. Knowing the original conditions and comparing them to the conditions of China in the twentieth century, it would be possible to make practical decisions. In a word, anachronisms were the chief evil; historical investigations were the means of exposing them.

The old historiography, however, would not serve to make these discoveries and decisions. Traditional historical outlooks, Ku argued, were themselves anachronisms; these failures to keep up with the times were ultimately ascribed to the ruling class, which had guarded its economic and political position by imposing a stasis on the whole society. If the old histories and historical attitudes were useless and even inimical to modernization, it was because they had been tools for imposing and perpetuating this condition of stasis and for conveying the narrow political values of the ruling class. When a modern historical outlook supplanted the traditional attitude, it was argued, the ideas of evolution, historical relevance, and progress would put the Chinese into a frame of mind, once and for all, to adapt themselves to changing circumstances. In addition, the truth could finally begin to be revealed about China's past, the reality of which had been so long obscured and distorted. With accurate knowledge about the past, the 'real' identity of China, past, present, and future, could then be determined.

From Validity to Origin and Function

Wrestling with the sociology of knowledge, Robert K. Merton suggested that "on the social level, a radical difference of outlook of various groups leads not only to *ad hominem* attacks, but also to 'functionalized explanations' "; and he pointed to a tendency, under such social conditions, "to seek out the origins rather than test the validity of statements which seem palpably absurd to us." [3] Ku Chieh-kang and his colleagues found themselves confronted with an array of historical notions rooted in broad social values, many of which seemed palpably absurd to them; however, they did not as a rule confront past historians, or the vestigial keepers of historical orthodoxy, or the neo-traditionalists, with arguments of validity. They accused the latter two groups of personal or class bias, of cynicism or stupidity; and when old social values and historical notions were considered, they were looked at from the point of view of 'origins' and 'functions.'

Ku Chieh-kang's historiography arrived at this point of view early in its development. It did begin, however, with efforts directed at undermining the credibility and authority of the orthodox histories and the historiographical foundations of scripture. This was done by using conventional textual critical devices to reveal contradictions within revered texts and to expose their spurious elements. His most mature work focused on the mechanisms characteristic in the creation of this literature, on the social-political motivations for creating spurious history, and on the patterns of abuse of historical writing. Ku Chieh-kang was an eclectic, in the best sense of the word, and in his creative treatment of textual and historiographical problems the direct influence of K'ang Yu-wei (1858–1927) and Liang Ch'i-ch'ao (1873–1929), as well as indirect influence of the American New History (via Hu Shih), is clearly evident. In his synthesis, Ku preserved the intellectualist (or idealistic) bias of all of these streams, for his primary concern was the idea of

3. Robert K. Merton, *Social Theory and Social Action,* rev. and enl. ed. (New York, 1964), p. 458.

history in the minds of the men of antiquity. He determined that writing history was itself a historical act, and that written history was valuable evidence about the times in which it was written, whatever its value for understanding the times it purported to describe.

The skepticism and sense of absurdity evoked by the clash of generations and social groups, and by the collapse of traditional social structures, are evident in Ku Chieh-kang's research attitudes. From his earliest writings, he considered the historicity of the Golden Age (the model for proper governance and social virtue) a patently absurd idea, just as he considered the notion of Confucius as semi-divine prophet to be absurd. The validity of these notions was not really at issue for him; he was devoted, rather, to the question of their origin and function. It is no accident, then, that very early in his career Ku was enthralled with the problem of myth-making processes. He was guided in part by Hu Shih and by the thoughts of some Sung (960–1280) and Ch'ing (1644–1911) dynasty critics.

It is more revealing, however, to know that his understanding of these processes was initially derived from his acquaintance with Peking Opera. By collating personae within the vast repertoire of these popular operas, he detected patterns of change, and he was early convinced that similar processes affected the growth of reputedly historic personages in ancient Chinese history. When we view these reputedly historical figures as actors in a drama, he wrote, it is readily understandable why traditional histories depict the first kings of a dynasty as sage and good, the last kings as evil. The diametrically opposite characters of these kings functioned didactically, quite like the *good* and *evil* personae in popular drama. Likewise, Ku said, he studied folktales because the processes of their creation, transmission, and transformation were similar to the processes characterizing the development of traditional Chinese historiography.

Thus Ku cast a very disconcerting aura of insubstantiality over the once sacred reaches of high antiquity that had authorized many areas of political and social behavior. "We have been as though in a dream in regard to our past, the Golden

Age," he wrote in 1936, still trying to awaken his countrymen. By that time he had repeatedly asked who or what had been responsible for the legends, the spurious history, the forged texts? How and why had this 'dream' been perpetuated so long?

Sources of Traditional Historiography

In his first answers to these questions, Ku pointed to the schools of scholarship that had dominated antiquity. For their own political goals and for the status of their own identifying philosophy, these schools shaped truth to their preconceived notions and whimsically distorted the realities of the past. This was a tack Ku did not develop, and he notably did not identify these schools of scholarship with class interests in general or with the specific interests of an intelligentsia. In his second position, however, he made an attempt to relate distortions of historical reality to the social needs of specific eras. He saw the legends and counterfeit histories of antiquity as reflections of concrete social problems. This was not intended to be an indictment; rather, it was an attempt to relate ideas and social forms in some kind of organic, functional relationship. This approach soon gave way to his final position, in which he laid heavy emphasis on the notion of social class and, in particular, the intellectual class. Here, ideas about the past were deemed to be masks for invidious class interests, and China's Golden Age legends were considered to have been ideological weapons designed by a parasitic intelligentsia serving the political needs of the ruling class. In his final telling, it was the intelligentsia who were responsible for the creation and perpetuation of spurious history, the idea of the Golden Age, and all the other apparatus that straitjacketed traditional Chinese historical consciousness

Historical Continuity and Cultural Alternatives

From Ku Chieh-kang's point of view, it was the intelligentsia of antiquity and their successors who were ultimately responsible, as well, for China's precarious perch on the threshold of the twentieth century. To the new intelligentsia he assigned the task of bringing China, and Chinese history, safely across it.

Armed with their new historical consciousness, the new intelligentsia were obliged, Ku argued, to supply not only correct ideas about the nature of China's past but, concomitantly, to establish lifelines between past and future. To this end, over the course of his career, he unsystematically formulated four alternatives to the various 'aristocratic' intellectual traditions which he sought to dissolve. He did not explicitly relate the four to each other; however, they can be related precisely on the grounds that he saw them all as alternatives, supplanting fundamental areas of the old culture and pointing the direction for the new culture—Chinese bedrock for a modern China. These four alternatives were: the tradition of proto-scientific scholarship; popular culture; barbarian culture; and the ancient rival traditions of Confucianism.

PROTO-SCIENTIFIC SCHOLARSHIP

This was a tradition of thought, in Ku's description of it, parallel to and in conflict with the mainstream of Confucian orthodox scholarship. The 'scientific' thought of this tradition was undeniably Chinese, yet at the same time it was antagonistic to what he described as the shallow, inflexible, aristocratic thought that had prevented the development of a progressive intellectual tradition in China. Not only did this scientific tradition fill the void left by the rejected orthodoxies and unacceptable heterodoxies, it served as an indigenous precedent for the New Thought. The latter was sometimes depicted as an organic evolution out of the thought of these proto-scientific thinkers, all of whom were made to appear to be part of a coherent convention of protest. However, the more closely the thought of these proto-moderns was scrutinized, the more conventional their thought was seen to be. The more Ku Chieh-kang tried to identify with his scholar heroes, the greater was his need to stress the distance between his thought and theirs. Ultimately, there was the danger of being a mere imitator of the past and of trying to employ thought and values inappropriate for moderns, however advanced that thought might have been in its own time. To avoid this dilemma, the proto-scientific scholarly tradition was made safe for the New Thought by being transformed into a mere symbol of something intellectually Chinese that was not Confucian; something that was not Western which pointed the way toward intellectual modernity.

POPULAR CULTURE

The problem of defining and evaluating popular culture was for the New Thought intellectuals a problem of self as well as national definition and evaluation. The political and social implications of Ku Chieh-kang's contributions to the New Thought were most fully dramatized here. For in defining their new social role, the intelligentsia (quite often with the earlier experience of the Russian intellectuals in mind) relied heavily on their relationship to the common people. The intellectuals whom Ku exemplified stiffly embraced the peasantry, but they eschewed the possibility of merging with them, or leading them on to militant social revolution, or patronizing them, as did the sages of old. Instead, they chose to go to the people and patiently educate them.

At the same time, Ku Chieh-kang led his associates in a serious campaign to substitute the culture (in the sense of literature, poetry, and song) of the people for that of the aristocrats. It was decided that the popular tradition was the proper Chinese tradition, usurped and suppressed by the upper classes and their intellectual accomplices. The new intelligentsia would set things aright through the dual process of simultaneously educating and being educated by the long-suffering masses. They would bring the society of the people up to date; and the people's literature would provide the substance for an acceptable tradition and the inspiration for a future New Culture. The alternative of the popular tradition was seldom related in any direct manner to the proto-scientific tradition in Ku Chieh-kang's writings. I link the two by suggesting that the latter functioned to undermine and destroy the authority of the old aristocratic culture; the popular was meant to supplant the aristocratic tradition of the past and to take over its place in the future. The 'scientific' and 'democratic' attitudes which these two new alternatives represented were assumed to be compatible, because they were considered to be fundamental aspects of modernity.

BARBARIAN CULTURE

The least elaborated and the most emotionally espoused of Ku Chieh-kang's cultural alternatives was derived from the peoples of China's inner Asian frontiers. Ku's erratic and multiple usage of the concept of the barbarian revolved around his growing fear for the viability of Chinese civilization under the pressures of the West and Japan. Ku wrote of the barbarians, historically, as the perennial resuscitators of a cyclically decrepit Chinese culture; and in moments of despair, he entertained the possibility that they could do the trick again in China's twentieth-century cultural crisis. The non-Chinese peoples were thus seen as a primary source of historical continuity for China, past and present. But there was an ambiguity here which did not seem to trouble Ku. If a periodically failing *Chinese* civilization was revived by infusions of barbarian blood or culture, then how could it be said that the subsequent product was Chinese? How could it be said that it was a continuous, coherent tradition? Could it not be said, instead, that there were a series of new peoples and new cultures following each cycle of barbarian influence? These questions were not directly confronted by Ku Chieh-kang in his writings. They evoke the major intellectual problems facing Ku as a twentieth-century Chinese—that is, how best to balance and employ the ideas of historical persistence, survival, continuity, and change.

In Ku's historical treatment of the barbarians, these ideas were more blurred than usual, but it is at least evident that for him *continuity* did not denote *persistence,* but a kind of gradual, evolutionary, organic change. In his discussions of the formation of the Chinese people in antiquity, it is quite clear that Ku wanted to destroy at its root the idea that from time immemorial there was a transcendent, unchanging Chinese essence. Just as there were many ethnic stocks and local cultures which contributed to the gradual development of the first 'Chinese' tradition (called *Hua* or *Hsia*), so did the barbarians contribute to that tradition's later developments (through Buddhism, for example). The content of Chinese identity, in Ku's telling, was thus always in a state of change. It had to be, according to his evolutionary point of view, for only in change (in the sense of innovation and adaptation) is there survival. Ku sought no metaphysical answers for the problem of how something could be the same and yet always be changing; but the scheme of his logic was that cultural continuity depends on physical survival, and therefore continuity depends on change.

ANCIENT RIVALS OF CONFUCIANISM

According to Ku Chieh-kang, the intellectuals of antiquity, serving bigoted political leaders, obscured the positive role the so-called barbarians had played in developing and sustaining Chinese culture. It was the same intellectuals, and for similar motives, who formulated 'Confucianism'—a historiography and a social philosophy whose ultimate function was to aid the aristocracy in suppressing and exploiting the common people. A fourth partial alternative which Ku offered to replace this Confucian tradition was the teachings of the social philosophers Mo Tzu (480–390 B.C.) and Tsou Yen (fourth century B.C.), which Ku described as having once been potential antidotes to an inimical class system and despotic government. Ku argued that these rivals of the anti-popular aristocratic tradition were proofs that Chinese history was not merely the history of Confucianism. The destruction of Confucian culture would make it possible to liberate these ancient (and proper) tendencies toward an egalitarian and responsibly governed society in China.

Thus, each of the four alternatives was in itself only partially sufficient to create a new concept of the past and new roots for modern Chinese civilization. Together, the four formed the outlines of a new culture, continuous with an acceptable past, viable in the foreseeable future: The as-yet-youthful vitality of the great Chinese masses and the border peoples would be the vital life source of the new nation; and the People's Culture—spontaneous, fresh, and elastic—would inform the arts of the new civilization. The new intellectuals would be guided by democratic values and scientific methods of understanding (derived from Chinese as well as Western traditions). Their job would be to continue to purify Chinese civilization of its moribund elements, using its scientific intellect, and to help the masses purify their own traditions and institutions, so long corrupted by the ruling class.

There were other intellectuals, contemporaries of Ku Chieh-kang, who, with equal passion, were concerned with the continuity of Chinese history into the modern era. These men, whom I deal with under the rubric of National Essence, also promoted historical studies and tried to direct their contemporaries' attention to specific aspects of the past. However, their intent was to preserve what they believed to be a historically transcendent Chinese identity (conveyed, for example, in some traditional aesthetic forms) that from time immemorial had remained unchanged. Where National Essence was primarily concerned with the recognition of an 'essential China' and its persistence, Ku was devoted to fostering the evolution of a new Chinese identity altogether. Advocates of National Essence, and their many conservative offshoots, could not agree that China's identity, past or future, was bound up with those four areas in which Ku sought his cultural alternatives.

It is in juxtaposition to the conservators of National Essence and their predecessors that Ku's role as anti-traditional thinker is set into deepest relief. He was not one who specifically set about to abolish the authority of the past or to impose a new conception of authority on society. Rather he was, in effect, one who, "having denied that the past authorizes the present by vesting it with continuity, is obliged to create a new past and invest it with an authority which easily abolishes the necessity of referring to a past at all." [4] And although Ku Chieh-kang may easily be considered, by Western criteria, among China's first modern historians, his thought tends to become unhistorical, in the sense "that it devises a mode of authority independent of social continuity." [5]

4. Pocock, "Time, Institutions and Action," p. 228. Pocock's referent is general; I apply the characterization to Ku Chieh-kang.

5. *Ibid.*

Ku's anti-traditionalism is of revolutionary proportions, and his contributions to Chinese scholarship are likewise contributions to the revolutionary processes of twentieth-century China. If we consider an outline of the Chinese revolution such as the one provided by Franz Schurmann,[6] it becomes easier to assess as 'revolutionary' a man like Ku Chieh-kang, who espoused neither Marxism nor Communism, who advocated gradual reform, and whose life and thought were devoted to history and the past. Schurmann's scheme suggests that a revolution, properly called, involves the destruction (and perhaps replacement) of a social system's traditional polity, its economic class structure, its mode of production, and most essentially, its elite, and the ethos of that elite. In China, because of quantitative and qualitative characteristics of the traditional social system, these facets of the system have had to be destroyed over a long span of time and, seemingly, independently of each other. When Ku began his career, the traditional polity and the traditional scholarly elite had largely disintegrated. His thought, in effect, was devoted to that aspect of the revolution which collapsed or transformed the ethos of the traditional upper class and the scholarly elite. It was an ethos which had been formulated, to a large extent, in conceptions of the past and of the nature of history. When we understand Ku and his apparently nonrevolutionary milieu within the evolving, long-range processes of revolution in China, I believe we can then see the pertinence here of Michael Gasster's recent observation that "It is sometimes thought that revolutionaries who look at all traditionalistic cannot be revolutionary; now we begin to understand that *only* revolutionaries who are intelligently traditionalistic can be successful revolutionaries." [7]

6. Franz Schurmann, *Ideology and Organization in Communist China* (Berkeley and Los Angles, 1966), esp. Prologue and Introduction.

7. Michael Gasster, *Journal of Asian Studies,* XXXIX:2 (Feb. 1970), 435.

Part One: The Scholars

I

Setting for a Skeptic: New Tides and National Essence

> *The propositions I make* [*about Chinese history*] *are the product of an agreement between my times, my individual nature, and my circumstances. . . .* [*My ideas*] *are quite in the ordinary course of things, what is necessitated by circumstances; I merely obeyed my spontaneous inclinations.*—Ku Chieh-kang, *Autobiography,* 1926.

In 1926, at the age of thirty-three, Ku Chieh-kang felt it was time to analyze publicly the validity of his provocative reinterpretations of China's ancient history and China's traditional historiography. He argued the soundness of his ideas from the previous five years not only on grounds of scholarship, but on pragmatic grounds as well. The most dramatic case he felt he could make for his thought was its appropriateness for his place in the stream of history and for the actualities occurring at that time. But he was no mere vessel of history; his writing no mere response to social demands; there was, rather, a happy coincidence between his spontaneous intellectual urges and the pressures of twentieth-century China.

These observations about his thought are drawn from the autobiographical preface to the first volume of the *Critiques of Ancient History* (*Ku-shih pien*), a weighty collection of scholarly writings that marks the path, during the 1920s and 1930s, along which scholars rejected or reinterpreted most of the traditional conceptions of China's classical antiquity. The kind of scholarship brought together in the collection led appreciative scholars to praise Ku Chieh-kang (in the effusive fashion of the day) as "the Newton and Darwin of Chinese Ancient History," [1] or to compare him favorably with Fustel [2] and Niebuhr.[3] With quiet modesty, Ku claimed only to be doing what came naturally and that which, as it turned out, was best for China.

The *Autobiography* (as we shall call the preface to Volume One of the *Critiques*) is a highly personal narrative which was meant to give the reader an insight into the life behind the ideas. More interesting than the facts that it gives us about Ku's life is the image he wished to convey of himself: as the independent, the challenger, the doubter, the iconoclast. In his youth he was "by nature uncommonly independent and intractable." "Outwardly gentle and submissive," he wrote, "my inner spirit refused to submit even to the mildest compulsion." [4] He "was unwilling to follow blindly the conclusions of [his] predecessors." [5] It was during the germination of the New Culture movement (ca. 1916–1921), that he had first brought his "haughty

1. Fu Ssu-nien's appraisal in "T'an liang-chien *Nu-li chou-pao* shang te wu-chih" [A Discussion of Two Kinds of Errors in the *Endeavor*] in Ku Chieh-kang *et al.*, eds., *Ku-shih pien* [Critiques of Ancient History]—hereinafter referred to as *KSP*—7 vols. (Shanghai, 1926–1941), II, 298.

Fu Ssu-nien (1896–1950) was a leader of the intellectual ferment accompanying the May Fourth movement, and later, in his position as director of the Academia Sinica's Historical and Philological Research Institute (1928–1949), he was a leading historian and an important arbiter of historical scholarship. He was an intimate friend of Ku when the aforementioned essay was written. They had been roommates at Peking University in 1917.

2. Tung Shu-yeh, preface to Ku Chieh-kang and Yang Hsiang-k'uei, *San Huang K'ao* [A Study of Three Emperors]—hereinafter referred to as *SHK*—(Peking, 1936); reprinted in *KSP*, VII, part 2, pp. 22–23.

3. Ch'i Ssu-ho, "Chin pai nien lai Chung-kuo shih-hsüeh te fa-chan" [The Development of Chinese Historical Scholarship in the Past Century], *Yen-ching she-hui k'o-hsüeh* [Yenching Journal of Social Science], II (1949), 29.

4. Arthur Hummel, trans., *The Autobiography of a Chinese Historian*—hereinafter referred to as *ACH*—(Leyden, 1931, and Taipei, 1966), p. 10. Hummel's book is a translation of Ku's autobiographical preface to *KSP*, I. Unless otherwise indicated, all of my citations from this preface will be from Hummel's translation.

5. *ACH*, p. 1.

and independent nature" and his "smoldering and unsubmissive spirit" to the career described in the *Autobiography*.[6] For almost a decade before the publication of the *Critiques*, he poured himself into a variety of projects centering around the study of ancient Chinese history and the lore of China's Golden Age of Sage Kings. While many of his colleagues traveled outside of China, he remained during this period in Peking, obtaining his degree from and doing advanced research at Peking University, the hub of academe and the fulcrum of revolution. While most of his associates submitted themselves directly to the intellectual milieux of America, Germany, or Japan, he received the jarring influences of those cultures indirectly if at all, and then blended them in a desultory manner with the indigenous intellectual traditions to which he found himself heir and which were always his major concern.

If the *Autobiography* claimed Ku's thought to be harmonious with modern China, modern China was not very harmonious with itself. As a young man, Ku had watched the old polity challenged; he saw the traditional examination system abolished in 1905, and when he was eighteen, the monarchy itself was dissolved. The New Culture movement continued the concerted destruction of the old order by 'liberating' the new generation from the values and modes of thought which supported traditional institutions. While Ku Chieh-kang attempted to dissolve the legends and myths which lodged those values and modes of thought, anti-imperialist sentiment and attempts to find a source of national unity followed an erratic, tumultuous course throughout the 1920s. During the months he wrote the *Autobiography*, the massive general strike, the demonstrations, and the anti-imperialist sentiment that comprised the May Thirtieth Movement gave new life and direction to Chinese nationalism; at the same time, Chiang Kai-shek's Northern Expedition set out to unify a fragmented nation and to see to it that the Communists would have no role to play in the new order. And as Ku put the finishing touches on his *Autobiography*, his brush was accompanied by Warlord cannonades just outside the gates

6. *Ibid.*, p. 18.

of Peking and the explosions of their bombs, dropped within that city of Emperors and scholars, academies and libraries, museums and memories.[7]

Though Ku Chieh-kang insisted upon the relevance of his own thought to China's modern needs, he felt no compulsion to identify himself with some Western school of scholarship, nor with a Chinese variant. He apparently felt a strong urge, however, to detail his filiation with past Chinese scholars and with the rich tradition of scholarship which he meanwhile subverted at every turn. He was born in 1893 in the eastern Soochow village of Tao-i, in Kiangsu province—a locale, he noted in reminiscences, which was the center of the most productive school of scholarship in the Ch'ing dynasty[8] and the home of many renowned eighteenth-century scholars whose legacy played an important role in his own work.[9] His own family "had for generations been interested in literary pursuits," and he was expected to "advance in life by the same path." [10] His father was a scholar, private tutor, and advanced-degree holder; his grandfather, from whom he received his early education, a competent guide to classical literature and textual criticism.[11] Ku considered himself fortunate that the old examination system was still in operation when he was a youth, so that he "could be trained from childhood in the classics and histories." [12] His middle-level education was a mixture of old-style tutorial in traditional subjects and 'modern' school instruction, wherein he received his "smattering" of the scientific method.[13] Except for his grandfather's guidance, he had little but contempt for his

7. *Ibid.,* pp. 182–183.

8. Preface to Ku Chieh-kang, *Ch'in Han te Fang-shih yü Ju-sheng* [The Alchemists and Confucianists of the Ch'in Han Era]—hereinafter referred to as *CHFSJS*—(Shanghai, 1955), p. 4. This book was originally published as *Han-tai hsüeh-shu shih-lüeh* [An Outline History of the Scholarship of the Han Era] (Chengtu, 1935).

9. Preface to Ku Chieh-kang, *Hsi-pei k'ao-ch'a jih-chi* [Northwest Studies Diary]—hereinafter referred to as *HPKCJC*—(Peking, 1949), p. 1a.

10. *ACH,* p. 5.

11. *Ibid.,* p. 16.

12. *Ibid.,* p. 153.

13. *Ibid.*

early education—the "paltry and vulgar" teaching in the Soochow grammar school,[14] the classroom stupidities of the middle and preparatory schools "where Chinese youth is slaughtered." [15]

Autobiographical observations on his childhood always cast him in the role of intellectual upstart, precocious skeptic, and mini-critic of traditional scholarship.[16] Consistent with this persona, in the *Autobiography* Ku depicted himself as completely caught up in the revolutionary fervors preceding the Republican Revolution in 1911. Enthralled by the writings of anti-Manchu spokesmen such as Liang Ch'i-ch'ao (1873–1929) and Chang T'ai-yen (1868–1936), Ku "came to regard self-sacrifice for the salvation of others as the sole aim of heroes; and politics and social service as the sole duty of scholars." [17]

After the 1911 Revolution, he recalled in the *Autobiography*,

> my zeal for the cause mounted yet higher. I fancied that there is nothing under the sun too difficult for men to accomplish; that the good, the true and the beautiful need only to be advocated, and they will become actualities. A race-revolution was only an insignificant part of our program. We would not consider our revolutionary task accomplished until we had abolished government, had discarded the family system, and had made currency unnecessary! [18]

At the end of 1911 his political zeal led him to join the Socialist party, through which he hoped to realize this program. He was an active member of the party for a year and a half, that is, down to the collapse of the Republic under the weight of Yüan Shih-k'ai's monarchical pretensions and the Republic's subsequent political fragmentation. Ku recalled being one of the Socialist party's most devoted members,

> often not getting to sleep until far into the night in order to perform some public service. Not a few relatives or older friends cautioned me, saying, "Why do you associate with those vagabonds and ne'er-

14. *Ibid.*, p. 20.
15. *Ibid.*, p. 163.
16. For examples see *ibid.*, p. 21, and Ku's preface to his *Shih-lin tsa-chih* [A Historical Miscellany]—hereinafter referred to as *SLTC*—(Peking, 1963), p. 1
17. *ACH,* p. 17.
18. *Ibid.*, p. 28

do-wells? Their business should be no concern of yours." But criticism, so evidently motivated by prejudice, made very little impression upon me. I had already come to the conclusion that gentry, as well as vagabonds, are the products of an evil social order. I felt that the [gentry] especially were the means of blocking many a program of reform and I could not be content until this class was eliminated.[19]

Ku Chieh-kang, like many of his contemporaries, soon realized the disparity between programs and realities. The gulf that now showed itself between "thought and the possibilities for action" was no doubt a source of frustration for him as well as for other Chinese intellectuals.[20] When institutional changes "lagged ever farther behind the intellectuals' galloping ideals," [21] a pall of disappointment and pessimism replaced the earlier fervor. The melee of politicians, bureaucrats, and warlords that followed the first year of the Republic inaugurated among the members of China's newly emerging Westernized intelligentsia a period of withdrawal from or refusal to enter public life.[22] Ku Chieh-kang reacted typically:

After the tide of revolution had somewhat receded, not much time had elapsed before we were again subjected to the dictatorship of Yüan Shih-k'ai's government, and the revival of old practices under the leadership of the surviving literati of the preceding dynasty. Of all the joyous emotions and fervent hopes that we had heaped up in previous years, we now had left to us only melancholy memories.[23]

From 1913 to 1916 Ku attended the preparatory department of Peking University, and there, on a steady diet of classical studies, his passion for political commitment was rechanneled into scholarship. Now his leisure was devoted to intensive reading in recent classical scholarship, and the more he read, the more con-

19. *Ibid.*

20. See Michael Gasster, "China's Political Modernization," in Mary Wright, ed., *China in Revolution: The First Phase, 1900–1913* (New Haven, 1968), p. 93.

21. *Ibid.*

22. See Maurice Meisner, *Li Ta-chao and the Origins of Chinese Marxism* (Cambridge, Mass., 1967), p. 9.

23. *ACH,* pp. 59–60.

tempt he felt for those contemporary scholars who advocated 'practical' ends for scholarship and who, in Ku's estimation, compromised the integrity of their thought for political reasons.

He became more engrossed in studies of antiquity, and began to formulate a personal ethic revolving about a commitment to 'pure' scholarship, to 'science.' [24] His college friends, he wrote, warned him about the dangers of such a devotion to scholarship, especially to study of the past. His answer was simply that each man must follow his own inclinations; he had lost his taste for "contemporary affairs." [25]

In Ku's first year in the upper division at Peking University, 1916–17, his withdrawal was arrested by a series of events, not within the political world but within the intellectual community itself. From the energetic optimism of the first issues of the revolutionary magazine *New Youth* (*Hsin ch'ing-nien*) he took immediate encouragement.[26] The comprehensive curriculum and faculty reforms initiated by Peking University's new chancellor, Ts'ai Yüan-p'ei, promised an exciting, fresh intellectual milieu. And new associates and friends like Fu Ssu-nien and Hu Shih, direct from study in America, exposed him to new areas of thought, gave him direction, and spurred him on toward intellectual rebellion.[27] However, Ku's enthusiasms were dampened in 1917 when his young wife grew seriously ill, and he was forced to return to Soochow to care for her. She died of tuberculosis in 1918, and Ku was left in ill health and quite depressed.[28]

24. *HPKCJC,* p. 1a.

25. *Ibid.*

26. *ACH,* p. 64.

27. *Ibid.,* pp. 67, 154; and Fu Ssu-nien, "*Hsin-ch'ao* chih hui-ku yü ch'ien-chan" [A Retrospective Look at the New Tide], *Hsin-ch'ao* [New Tide]—hereinafter referred to as *HC*—II:1 (Oct. 1919). This article was reprinted in Fu Ssu-nien, *Fu Ssu-nien hsüan-chi* [Selected Works of Fu Ssu-nien]—hereinafter referred to as *FSNHC*—7 vols. (Taipei, 1967), III, 343–353.

28. *ACH,* p. 66. Ku does not seem to have mentioned his first marriage anywhere in detail, in his published writings. He was apparently married again sometime between 1919 and 1924, for the *ACH* speaks of a wife at the latter date (*ACH,* p. 194). He had two daughters as of the writing of the *ACH,* but their names are not given; it is not clear which of the two wives bore which of the daughters (*ACH,* p. 181).

The New Tide

SCHOLARSHIP AND POLITICS

At the end of 1918, as Ku completed his recuperation in Soochow and then returned to Peking, the flood of periodicals and student societies that characterized the May Fourth period had already begun to emerge. Thus, his last year as a student at Peking University was one in which young Chinese intellectuals acted out their renewed faith in China's future with melodramatic verve. Ku Chieh-kang was a founding member of one of the most important student associations of the day, the New Tide Society (Hsin-ch'ao hui), along with his roommate, Fu Ssu-nien, and their close associates at Peking University. They originally hoped to produce a special journal representing the 'new' student; a periodical to rival *New Youth*. Fu Ssu-nien recalled that the little coterie planning the new magazine had the "spirit of children," and he repeatedly emphasized the centrality of spontaneity to the values that lay at the foundation of the society.[29]

On January 1, 1919, the first issue of *New Tide* (*Hsin-ch'ao*, subtitled in English *Renaissance*), the society's journal, appeared under the editorship of Fu Ssu-nien and Lo Chia-lun.[30] Among the charter members of the society were Ku Chieh-kang's close friends Yü P'ing-po, Yeh Shao-chün, and Mao Tzu-shui.[31] Fung Yu-lan was an early member, and late in 1920 Chou Tso-jen became editor-in-chief of the journal.[32] As a

29. Fu Ssu-nien, "*Hsin-ch'ao* chih hui-ku," pp. 348–349.

30. Lo Chia-lun (b. 1896) was a folklorist, historian of modern China, and an academic administrator. See Howard L. Boorman, ed., *Biographical Dictionary of Republican China*—hereinafter referred to as *BDRC*—2 vols. (New York, 1967–1968).

31. Yü P'ing-po (b. 1899) is the grandson of the prominent scholar Yü Yüeh (1822–1906) and a literary critic in his own right. A college and university teacher since the 1920s, he has been a leading figure in the a native of Soochow. He is a novelist of repute and was editor of the Kaiming Press during the 1930s. Mao Tzu-shui, also a contemporary of Ku, was a university teacher, textual critic, and historian.

32. Fung Yu-lan (b. 1895) is a philosopher particularly prominent for his historical studies of Chinese philosophy. He studied with John Dewey criticism of the eighteenth-century classical novel *Hung lou meng* [Dream of the Red Chamber]. Yeh Shao-chün (Sheng-t'ao) (b. 1893) was, like Ku,

faculty member at Peking University, Hu Shih sponsored the society and helped it shape its policies toward politics, scholarship, and Chinese history.

The trauma of 1913 had not had time to heal before the Chinese intellectual community received shock after political shock; but now the retreat from politics that had characterized the intellectuals after the collapse of the Republic became institutionalized at Peking University under Ts'ai Yüan-p'ei's dispensation. As chancellor, he demanded in January 1917 that "students should not regard the university as a substitute for the old government examination and recruitment system." [33] So strongly was participation in politics discouraged that in 1918 a large group within the university's Society for the Promotion of Virtue vowed (in addition to social purity) not to hold government office or to become members of the parliament.[34] Chow Tse-tsung suggests that "the agreement to refrain from holding office or becoming parliamentary members reflected both the influence of anarchism and nihilism, and the contempt the new intelligentsia felt for the old bureaucrats." In the eyes of the new intellectuals, "the old bureaucrats and warlords were the sources of all vice." [35]

The platform of *New Tide* reflected these sentiments. Neither Fu Ssu-nien nor Ku Chieh-kang, at the time of planning the society and the journal, had any desire to study "social problems"; therefore the society, during its three years of activity, stressed scholarship above political activism.[36] Further, the society advocated that the subject of study should be a function of the scholar's personal interests, not of its practical, immediate importance. Over the course of the journal's publication, its no-

---

and F. J. E. Woodbridge at Columbia University from 1919 to 1923. Chou Tso-jen (b. 1885) was during the May Fourth period and the twenties and thirties a prominent essayist, folklorist, and translator of foreign literature.

33. Chow Tse-tsung, *The May Fourth Movement*—hereinafter referred to as *MFM*— (Cambridge, Mass., 1969), p. 50.

34. *Ibid.*, p. 49.

35. *Ibid.*

36. Fu Ssu-nien, "*Hsin-ch'ao* chih hui-ku," p. 352; *Wu-ssu shih-chi chi-k'an chia-chao* [An Introduction to the Periodicals of the May Fourth Period] (Peking, 1958–1959), I, 89–90; and *MFM*, p. 251.

politics policy was reinforced by the mood at Peking University, in spite of the apparent successes of the impressive May Fourth demonstrations against the handling of Chinese affairs at the Versailles conference. John Dewey, touring China in 1919 and 1920, commented that the "hopelessness of the political muddle, with corrupt officials and provincial military governors in real control, is enough to turn the youth away from direct politics." [37] Fu Ssu-nien and Yü P'ing-po, for example, were so little taken by the May Fourth Movement that they went to England to study before there was even a chance to observe the movement's political repercussions.[38] Ku Chieh-kang did not even mention the demonstrations in his writings.

In his preface to the first issue of *New Tide*, Fu Ssu-nien, speaking editorially for the New Tide Society, tried to explain the policies of the group. He wrote that Peking University, the model new Chinese university, was really an embodiment of the idea of Chinese National Studies (*Kuo hsüeh*), in spite of the European models after which it fashioned itself. The overall purpose of National Studies was to get Chinese society out of its old ruts; but entry into the contemporary world, Fu cautioned, had to be gradual. The New Tide Society believed that the university had ameliorative duties within society, but social action per se simply was not a good thing under present conditions, even though it was undesirable for the university to separate itself from the community. National Studies, through the university, should devote itself to learning what stage world culture had reached in the present and to determining the tendencies of the "contemporary thought tide." Once the historical degrees and tendencies became clear, then China could achieve self-awareness and (gradually) a stance independent of the Western world. In brief, Fu Ssu-nien suggested that the assignment of the new intellectuals of China must be to discover and then support the implementation of what was appropriate for contemporary society.[39]

37. John Dewey, "The Sequel of the Student Revolt," *The New Republic,* XXI:273 (March 3, 1920), 380–381; cited in *MFM,* p. 224.

38. Fu Ssu-nien, "*Hsin-ch'ao* chih hui-ku," p. 350.

39. *HC,* I:1 (Jan. 1, 1919); reprinted in *FSNHC,* I, 81–85.

Lo Chia-lun, co-editor of *New Tide* at the beginning, complemented Fu's introductory editorial with one of his own that emphasized the idea of historical tides or tendencies and their importance to an understanding of the directions modern China should take. Almost every significant period in world history, he wrote, has had its tide, which could not be stopped—the Renaissance, the French Revolution, and now, the new world tide of the twentieth century, heralded by the Russian October Revolution. While his editorial spoke in adulatory terms of Russia, the new exemplar, and while it asked its readers to look forward optimistically to new social revolutions, it tempered this potentially radical sentiment with the belief that democracy and socialism would coexist, and that socialism would ultimately produce individualism. Finally, Lo's editorial rejected the idea of reform by way of violence.[40]

In all cases, whether in its attitudes toward independent, pure scholarship or toward the politics of the new society, *New Tide* emphasized the need to protect individualism. Fu Ssu-nien argued that old China was just a mass, not really a society. There was no opportunity in the old China (a "sheet of loose sand") for individuals to develop; but in a proper social environment, in a true nation, individualism would be fostered.[41] The New Tide intellectuals, quite typical of the New Culture period, saw no conflict between the potential demands of nation-building and individual freedom, indeed, they looked forward to the new nation-state as a force capable of liberating the individual from oppression of family, clan, and class.

THE NEW TIDE AND THE NATIONAL HERITAGE

Of all the preoccupations of the New Tide Society, none was more important for Ku Chieh-kang's intellectual development than its concern with the configuration of history, with historical processes, and with the relation of these to a new scholarship for China and a new China for scholars. The central concept was

40. "The New Tide of the World of Today," *HC,* I:1 (Jan. 1, 1919), 19; cited in *MFM,* pp. 60–61.

41. Fu Ssu-nien, preface to *HC,* I:1; and Fu Ssu-nien, "She-hui, ch'ün-chung" [Society, Mass], *ibid.,* I:2 (Feb. 1, 1919). Also see *Wu-ssu shih-chi chi-k'an,* I, 91–92; and *MFM,* p. 251.

appropriateness (or *suitability*), and its use indicates both the residual influence of nineteenth-century Social Darwinism and the expanding influence of American Pragmatism under the direction of John Dewey's disciple, Hu Shih. Here is how Fu Ssu-nien expressed the concept in *New Tide* in 1919:

Beliefs completely ought to be suited to the conditions of contemporary circumstances. Let us say that some transmitted beliefs persist for a number of years, while social conditions change, and man's view of life is no longer compatible with them. If we contrarily protect these historical beliefs, is this not the same as believing in ghosts, or worshipping [a Buddhist deity]? Yet, the beliefs of contemporary Chinese society of the past century are ninety-nine percent dead ghosts and Buddhist deities.[42]

Determining whether or not beliefs were suitable was thus very much a historical problem, and historical research was the province of National Studies.

Mao Tzu-shui, whose intellectual rigor Ku Chieh-kang greatly admired,[43] was a major New Tide Society advocate of studying China's heritage to determine the direction China must take in the modern age. In *New Tide*, he argued the need and the feasibility of applying the 'scientific method' to an understanding and evaluation of the heritage. There were three historical ideas germane to the problem, he said. The first, the National Present (*Kuo hsin*), embodied the notion that China's history—any nation's history—consists in reality of a series of changing 'nows.' National-past Studies (*Kuo ku hsüeh*), the second concept, was the mode of looking at the past, which ought to be relative to each particular National Present. Finally, there was the National Past itself, a body of materials, merely data, which are interpreted variously (or should be) for each National Present.[44]

Emphatically, Mao Tzu-shui identified China's current National Present with Western culture; but he refused to be intimi-

42. Fu Ssu-nien, "She-hui te hsin-t'iao" [Social Beliefs], *HC,* I:2 (Feb. 2, 1919); reprinted in *FSNHC,* II, 182.

43. *ACH,* pp. 38–39.

44. Mao Tzu-shui, "*Kuo-ku* ho k'o-hsüeh te ching-shen" [The Spirits of the *National Heritage* and of Science], *HC,* I:5 (April 19, 1919).

dated by the potential loss of Chinese identity that had concerned Chinese intellectuals for over a generation. The Chinese will internalize and make their own whatever aspects of Western culture they adopt, he claimed. Mao's historical point of view here suggested a global, organic, evolutionary scheme in which the modern era was the property of no nation, but an inevitable stage through which all nations could pass, when they were in a position to do so.[45]

The National Past, as Mao Tzu-shui formulated it, thus had a dual meaning: on one hand, it meant simply what happened in the past, and on the other, it meant how Chinese had thought about their past, in the past. It was important for the New Tide intellectuals, and for the National Studies movement which they developed, that thought about the past, and one's historical attitudes, could become mere relics, mere historical data themselves. The problem was that Chinese National-past Studies had employed an ossified historical attitude for many epochs, and had remained narrowly concerned with the same subject—studies of the Classics—thus showing itself to be quite nonprogressive. Mao urged his readers to create a National Present that was abreast of European culture. And the way to begin was to employ science in the study of the nation's past, and to dismiss previous Chinese studies of the past as expressions of viewpoints no longer appropriate to the present.[46]

But there was a small loophole to the past that Mao Tzu-shui and the New Tide thinkers left for themselves. Mao wrote that just as modern Chinese scholars could make Western thought their own, so could they co-opt the thought of past Chinese scholars: "When we think or develop the thought of former [Chinese] scholars, this is *our* thought, *not* theirs; they are dead—so is their thought." [47] That thought was 'dead' because it had failed to serve the purposes of day-to-day needs in China; if it again became useful, it would have become something other

45. *Ibid.*
46. *Ibid.*
47. Mao Tzu-shui, "Po *Hsin-ch'ao, Kuo-ku* ho k'o-hsüeh te ching-shen pien ting-wu" [Arguments Against a Critique of *New Tide, National Heritage,* and the Spirit of Science], *HC,* II:1 (Aug. 1919), 40.

than what it was originally, and its use would not be a mere repetition of the past.[48]

When the New Tide Society disbanded in 1921, its serious concern with historical problems was expanded and developed in diverse ways by many of its members. The society's early notions about the rationale, scope, and methods of a new National Studies were matured and put into practice by many; but Hu Shih and Ku Chieh-kang were central. We should not consider the short span of *New Tide* as a mark of failure, for at this time the typical career of intellectual societies and periodicals was meteoric, and the Chinese intellectual firmament of the 1920s was a continually sparkling crisscross of bright and dying lights. When a periodical like *New Tide* folded, it was more likely a result of academic or ideological realignments than anything else.

In 1921, the demise of *New Tide* was part of a crucial development within the Chinese intelligentsia. That year the rather heterogeneous group that had initiated the New Culture movement, and had used *New Youth* as their primary forum, split into a number of factions. The intellectual leaders who had been allied for the four previous years moved, broadly speaking, in the direction of political activism, Marxism, and the Communist party (following Ch'en Tu-hsiu), or remained within the orientations of the New Tide Society (following Hu Shih). Ku Chieh-kang, who had become one of Hu Shih's protégés by 1920, followed his lead into the development of National Studies and yet further from politics.

The spirit of *New Tide* was reborn in the *Endeavor* (*Nu-li chou-pao*) in 1921. The magazine was founded by Hu Shih and a few associates, and while it continued to advocate virtually the same policies as *New Tide*, this new periodical and the clique associated with it found that they could no longer lay claim to youthful radicalism. The founding of the Communist party, and the espousal of Marxist thought by former colleagues who were prominent members of the scholarly community, quickly obviated that. From this point on, Hu Shih and his associates occupied that uncomfortable position 'in between': to the left

48. *Ibid.*

were the Marxist intellectuals, whose extensive critiques of Hu Shih's and Ku Chieh-kang's thought did not reach its stride until the late twenties; and to the right were a series of very colorful individuals and factions, ranging from vestiges of nineteenth-century reformers to the neo-traditionalists of the Nationalist party.

Ku Chieh-kang's most important work during the first half of the twenties focused on a reinterpretation of China's ancient history and an analysis of the ways in which the Chinese had (mistakenly) viewed their past. In the form of correspondences between himself, Hu Shih, Ch'ien Hsüan-t'ung, and others, these historical studies were ultimately published as the first volume of the *Critiques* after appearing serially in a supplement to the *Endeavor*.[49]

The Peking University group which published the journal and its supplement called itself the Society for Unadorned Learning, after the great seventeenth- and eighteenth-century school of historical scholarship that used that name.[50] The intent of course was not to suggest atavism but, rather, continuity. For all their desire to adjust modern Chinese thought and society to one another and to the times, Hu Shih and Ku Chieh-kang still bore the nagging burden of finding a way to make Chinese history in the twentieth century somehow continuous with what had come before in China; the fear of cultural annihilation often lay just below the surface of their usually confident proposals.

National Essence: Conservative Approaches to Cultural Continuity

The concepts of National Past and National Studies, one of Hu Shih's associates observed, did not derive from the tradi-

49. The Supplement was entitled *Tu-shu tsa-chih* [Study Journal].

50. The name is a translation of *P'u she* (a variation on *P'u hsüeh*). It was another name for Ku Yen-wu's School of Han Learning (*Han hsüeh*) and was used by Chang T'ai-yen's mentor Yü Yüeh and by Chang himself. See Fang Chao-ying's entry in Arthur Hummel, ed., *Eminent Chinese of the Ch'ing Period*—hereinafter referred to as *ECCP*—2 vols. (Washington, D.C., 1943), I, 423. Also see Kuo Chan-po, *Chin wu-shih nien Chung-kuo ssu-hsiang* [Chinese Thought in the Last Fifty Years] (Hong Kong, 1965), pp. 66–67.

tional lexicon; they were of recent vintage and had come about as a response to the incursions of the West and the subsequent issue of Westernization.[51] In the twentieth century, during Ku Chieh-kang's early years, the concepts were first developed by a group of scholar-revolutionaries, many devoted to anti-Manchu nationalism, who came to be loosely characterized as the National Essence clique (*Kuo ts'ui p'ai*). The trajectory of this clique's history and its ideas throughout the first three decades of the century fairly well defined the development of that cultural conservatism with which Ku Chieh-kang's thought constantly interacted. It led from anti-monarchical preoccupations before 1911 to the pseudo-monarchical restorationism five years later. And from there it led to reactions against Westernization during the First World War and, thereafter, to reactions against the iconoclastic New Culture movement. National Essence came to rest, in the late twenties, in the cultural conservatism of the Nationalist (*Kuomintang*) regime.

The National Studies movement of Hu Shih and Ku Chieh-kang shared much in terms of form and content with the pre-1911 National Essence clique, and in the person, among others, of Chang T'ai-yen, a leader of that clique, there was a direct line of pedagogical filiation. Mao Tzu-shui, Ch'ien Hsüan-t'ung, and Ku Chieh-kang himself (for a short time) had studied at the feet of Chang, and Chang's writings and influence were everywhere in the Peking University intellectual community.[52] Because the earlier and later groups were often so close, they were sometimes evaluated as if they were one; and perhaps it was for this reason that Ku and Hu Shih so explicitly condemned and disowned the pre-1911 group.

51. Ts'ao Chu-jen, "Kuo ku hsüeh chih i-i yü chieh-chih" [The Idea of National Studies], in Hsü Hsiao-t'ien, ed., *Kuo-ku t'ao-lün chi* [An Anthology of Discussions on the National Heritage]—hereinafter referred to as *KKTLC*—4 vols. (Shanghai, 1927; 1st printing, 1926), I, 51.

52. Chow Tse-tsung reports that in 1907 Chang, then editor of *Min-pao,* was invited to become director and mentor of a Society for the Promotion of National Learning (*Kuo-hsüeh chen-ch'i she*) in Tokyo. Among the members of this society were Ch'ien Hsüan-t'ung, Lu Hsün, and Chou Tso-jen (*MFM,* p. 53). This is merely an early example of Chang's prominence. At Peking University, Ma Yü-ts'ao and Shen Chien-shih, under whom Ku studied, were disciples of Chang. (*ACH,* p. 48.)

Intellectually, what set the new National Studies apart from the early National Essence clique was a changed sense of the meaning of historical continuity. The National Essence group and its conservative successors came to understand *continuity* primarily as persistence (of values or aesthetic and social forms). The National Studies scholars understood continuity as *gradualness of change,* even though the preservation of some semblance of a unique Chinese cultural identity was central to their thought.[53] It was not that the former group had not been affected by the evolutionary concepts recently introduced to China; it was rather that they saw applied Social Darwinism as a means of insuring the persistence of the vitals of Chinese civilization, the National Essence. Nor was it that the New Culturalists did not wish to preserve any of the past culture; it was rather that they wanted to preserve a very different part of the old culture than did the National Essence advocates. While National Essence was devoted to preserving traditional forms of Chinese cultural identity, Ku Chieh-kang's National Studies was devoted to shaping a new meaning for 'Chinese.'

THE JOURNAL OF NATIONAL ESSENCE

National Essence became formalized in 1904 when a small coterie of classical scholars founded the Society for the Preservation of National Essence (*Kuo-ts'ui pao-ts'un hui*), and the next year began publication of their journal, the *Journal of National Essence* (*Kuo-ts'ui hsüeh-pao*). These were years jammed with radical developments in the growth of Chinese nationalism and revolution. With the triumph of the Japanese over the Russians as their backdrop, young anti-Manchu radicals, smarting from China's inability to regain her national sovereignty, founded the Revolutionary Alliance (*T'ung-meng-hui*) and its forum, the *Min-pao* (*People's Journal*). Chang T'ai-yen and the politically erratic Liu Shih-p'ei (1884–1919), who were important participants in the Alliance and the *Min-pao,* were also founding fathers of the National Essence Society and its publication. Ac-

53. For a discussion of the concept of 'historical continuity' pertinent to its use here, see John Herman Randall, Jr., *Nature and Historical Experience.* (New York, 1962), pp. 66–67.

companying them as charter members in the latter ventures were Huang Chieh (1874–1935) and Ma Hsü-lün (b. 1884), men who did not fully share their pungent political sentiments.[54]

The leitmotif of the National Essence Society's activities was the idea that a civilization has a vulnerable physical aspect (the *kuo,* nation) and a potentially enduring spiritual aspect (*ts'ui,* essence) which is capable of resuscitating the civilization after it has become moribund or physically destroyed. It would seem from the pages of the *Journal of National Essence* that this 'essence' was conveyed in literary culture—textual and historical scholarship, *belles lettres,* and poetry. Thus, the Chinese nation was to be preserved from extinction at the hands of foreigners (on the throne and at the gates) primarily through a discriminating continuation and cultivation of the great literary traditions of China's past. Reflecting the major and widespread fear of China's first decade of the twentieth century (annihilation of the nation and racial extinction), this defense of Chinese traditional essence went hand in hand with political revolution, which itself was meant to provide a new means of protecting the old culture.[55]

The platform of the Society for the Preservation of National Essence dedicated the group primarily to the "clarification of National Studies and protection of the National Essence" by

54. Huang Chieh (P'ei-wen) was a student-disciple of the scholar Chu Tz'u-ch'i. He was a co-founder of the Southern Society (*Nan she*) in 1908 (for which, see text below). Though he displayed strong nationalistic sentiments, he did not join the T'ung Meng Hui.

Ma Hsü-lün was later, in 1917, brought to Peking University by Ts'ai Yüan-p'ei. From 1919 to 1928 Ma held important administrative positions there; and as a leader of the teachers' union, he was central in the university-government clashes during the period. (See Wang Yi-t'ung, "Biographical Sketches of 29 Classical Scholars of the Late Manchu and Early Republican Period"—hereinafter referred to as *BSCS*—(mimeo, Pittsburgh, 1963), pp. 31–32, 49–53; and see *BDRC,* II, 465–468.

55. See Joseph R. Levenson, *Confucian China and Its Modern Fate*—hereinafter referred to as *CCMF*—3 vols. (Berkeley and Los Angeles, 1958–1965), I, 89. Also see Harold Z. Schiffren, *Sun Yat-sen and the Origins of the Chinese Revolution* (Berkeley and Los Angeles, 1968), pp. 282, 289. And for Chang T'ai-yen's thoughts on National Essence, see summary in Michael Gasster, *Chinese Intellectuals and the Revolution of 1911* (Seattle, 1969), pp. 200–201.

way of a number of literary channels.[56] Its journal claimed it would use the purest and most outstanding forms of China's literature, and would make all efforts to "wash away the [current] evil practices [in Chinese intellectual circles] of [employing] Japanese literary crudities." [57] Further, by employing a division of responsibilities and applying specialized knowledge, a careful examination of the sources and origins of National Scholarship would be pursued in order "to know the gateway and path of learning." [58] Contributors to the *Journal of National Essence* would employ Western learning to illuminate Chinese learning, and would try to become liaisons between Chinese learning and Western science.

The platform also set out for the society and journal two other scholarly functions in the realm of publication. Since respectable textbooks did not yet exist in the middle schools, according to the platform statement, the National Essence scholars would see to it that this lack was remedied with new, clearly-written texts. Finally, under the heading of "preserving family heirlooms," valuable literary fragments and unpublished writings of famous Confucianists would be printed and circulated. While the journal itself performed these functions at first, within a year or so the society was publishing numerous other titles, in keeping with the goals of its platform.

The journal was published openly in China, but the anti-Manchu sentiments of the National Essence Society were expressed clearly enough. For example, Huang Chieh's first efforts on joining the society were devoted to searching out and re-publishing books earlier interdicted by the Manchus.[59] Or again, the political sentiment of the society was conveyed in the biographical section of the first issues of the journal, which celebrated the lives of a group of scholars who were directly or indirectly associated with the Ming loyalists—men who resisted the Manchu takeover of the Ming in the seventeenth century

56. *Kuo ts'ui hsüeh-pao* [Journal of National Essence]—hereinafter referred to as *KTHP*—I:1 (Jan. 1905).

57. *Ibid.*, item 2.

58. *Ibid.*, items 3, 4.

59. *BSCS*, pp. 31–32; also see L. C. Goodrich, *The Literary Inquisitions of Ch'ien-lung* (Baltimore, 1935).

and refused to recognize the political legitimacy of the Ch'ing dynasty. Some of these biographies, like those about the seventeenth-century Chu Chih-yü and Chang Fei, told of loyalists who were forced to become expatriates and live in Japan.[60] The allusions here to twentieth-century anti-Manchus are obvious.

The journal was, however, less concerned with the Manchus in particular than the problem of Chinese survival in general. Huang Cheih wrote in his editorial in the first issue of the *Journal of National Essence* that China's history was a long history of decline: 'nationhood' had declined ever since the corrupting influences of the first emperor of Ch'in (third century B.C.) and the imperial ideologue Liu Hsin (first century A.D.). Huang warned his readers that because of this, China might suffer the fate of India and Poland, and he lamented that China was already no more than a slave nation with a slave culture. To those of his colleagues who were awed by Japan's recent successes, he cautioned that Japan was as inimical to the Chinese nation as any Western state. Huang Chieh's somber, urgent essay again and again expressed that terrible fear of national extinction compressed in the words "the nation perishes" (*kuo wang*).[61]

During the 1898 reform movement, the great scholar official, Chang Chih-tung, had written a treatise which rationalized China's need to adopt aspects of Western culture. The essentials of Chinese culture, he argued, were of the highest spiritual nature and hence incorruptible by Western culture, which was basically material and functional. Chang wrote that the "substantial" Chinese culture could profitably employ, for its own protection, the Western cultural functions.[62] Polemics in the *Journal of National Essence* perpetuated Chang's attitude toward Westernization. One argument in its pages suggested that the Chinese had always welcomed thought from 'the outside.' (For example, Confucius drew on the thought of many states outside of his own; the Neo-Confucian philosophers drew on

60. *KTHP,* I:12 (1905).

61. Huang Chieh, preface to *KTHP,* I:1 (Jan. 1, 1905).

62. See English translation by S. I. Woodbridge, *China's Only Hope* (New Jersey, 1900); and see *CCMF,* I, chap. 4.

Buddhism.)[63] National Essence, the argument continued, is basically the study of spirit; 'Europeanization' is basically the study of form. "Without form, how can the spirit survive? Without spirit, how can form establish itself?" Review the old, the essay concluded, learn the new; the so-called materialism of the West is not inherently evil; indeed, it accomplishes things which the Chinese strongly desire for their own nation but have shown themselves incapable of implementing. "National Essence aids with Westernization; Westernization protects National Essence." [64]

Westernization could only give protection; survival and maintenance of cultural identity, according to the pages of the *Journal of National Essence,* depended ultimately on the successful preservation of National Studies (that is, traditional literary culture, or what Westerners call the "great tradition"). As proof of this proposition, the examples of Egypt and India were cited: once destroyed by England, they never restored themselves, because they failed to keep their national studies alive.[65] On the other hand, it was argued that the Chinese nation had been destroyed in the past, but the strength of her national studies had made it possible for her to restore and revive herself. Japan was yet another example in more recent times of successful revival; and Western Europe itself had experienced destructions and rebirths for the same reasons.[66]

Teng Shih, an active member of the National Essence Society, lodged these ideas about survival in a complex trans-national historical framework centering on the concept of "renaissance." He argued, in a fashion not alien to the minds of the New Culture movement, that China and Western Europe had parallel

63. Hsü Fu-ch'eng, "Lün Kuo-ts'ui wu tsu yü O-hua" [National Essence Is Without Obstruction from Westernization], *KTHP,* I:7 (July 1905), 2b–3a.

64. *Ibid.,* p. 4b.

65. *Ibid.*

66. See "Ni she kuo-ts'ui hsüeh-t'ang ch'i" [An Explanation of the National Essence Academy], *KTHP,* III:1 (Jan. 1907); Teng Shih, "Kuo-hsüeh chen lün" [A True Critique of National Studies], *KTHP, III*:2 (Feb. 1907), and Teng Shih, "Kuo-hsüeh wu-yung pien" [A Critique of the Idea that National Studies Are Useless], *KTHP,* III:5 (May 1907).

historical developments in the past and would (with the help of National Learning in China) have equal stages of development in the twentieth century. Teng Shih wrote that the golden ages of classical antiquity in China and the West were analogous; in all areas of life, the ancient Chinese were equal to the Greeks and Romans; therefore, the revivals of these ancient cultures should result in analogous societies. Asia's twentieth-century renaissance should yield the same quality of society as the European Renaissance in the fifteenth century. And, according to Teng, the former was as inevitable (if the right steps were taken) as the latter.[67]

To insure this renaissance, the National Essence Society, over its eight-year span, increasingly engaged in pedagogical activities. A National Essence Academy was established in Shanghai, and the society sponsored the publication of a considerable number of scholarly monographs on classical literary subjects, as well as textbooks for middle-school use.[68] In the pages of the journal, not only were readers exhorted to engage in National Learning; there were study charts as well, devoted to the basic bibliography and sequence of study of classical literature.[69] Even religion was advocated as a means of preserving National Essence. "We must be the Martin Luthers of the Confucian religion," one contributor wrote.[70] He believed that a religious movement in China was valid, because in the West, religion had been the mother of democracy—indeed, every important Western institution ultimately derived from religion: "Westerners use religion as the essence (*t'i*) and science as the form (*yung*)." Chang T'ai-yen himself argued the usefulness of religion to National Essence; he explicitly rejected Confucianism as the religion to use, because it was linked to ideas of status and privilege. Chang agreed that Christianity was central to the

67. Teng Shih, "Kuo-hsüeh fu-hsing lün" [The Revival of National Studies], *KTHP,* I:9 (Sept. 1905).

68. See sample bibliography of these publications in *KTHP,* II:1 (Jan. 1907).

69. For example, "Ni she kuo-ts'ui hsüeh-t'ang ch'i."

70. Hsü Chih-heng, "Tu *Kuo-ts'ui hsüeh-pao* kan-yen" [On Reading the *Journal of National Essence*], *KTHP,* I:6 (June 1905).

development of the West, but he rejected it, too, as an inherently inferior religion.[71] He chose Buddhism as the best religion for Chinese National Essence.

Before the 1911 Revolution, this 'religious' approach to National Essence was also finding support among intellectual factions with pro-Manchu sentiments, and later it became associated with Yüan Shih-k'ai's attempt to restore the monarchy in his person. It was at this point, in 1909, that Liu Shih-p'ei broke with Chang T'ai-yen (though not with the *Journal of National Essence*) and gave his support to the Manchus. In 1915, Liu was one of the six original founders of the Society to Plan for Stability, which was devoted to making Yüan monarch.[72] And so National Essence took on new political connotations.

There were yet other ramifications of National Essence that were pertinent to the background of Ku Chieh-kang's work in National Studies. One of the purest expressions of the premises of the National Essence Society was a literary club, the Southern Society (*Nan she*), founded in 1908. These two organizations had an overlapping membership, Huang Chieh being a co-founder of the Southern Society along with its leader, Liu Ya-tzu (1887–1958). The society was devoted to the study and practice of traditional literary art forms, especially poetry, and it was "the last important rallying point of traditional literature in the Republican period." [73]

During the First World War, the idea of National Essence was given special emphasis by a number of prolific, articulate writers including Liang Ch'i-ch'ao and Liang Shu-ming (b. 1893).[74] The war was interpreted by these men as a sign of the inherent weakness and lack of moral content of Western civilization—whose crass materialism, they argued, was now manifest.

71. See Gasster, *Chinese Intellectuals* (n. 55, above), p. 199.

72. *BDRC,* II, 411–413; and H. Boorman, ed., *Men and Politics in Modern China* (New York, 1960), I, 98–100.

73. *BDRC,* II, 421; and *Nan she ts'ung-hsuan* [Anthology of the Southern Society], 3 vols. (Taipei: Wen-hai reprint, n.d.; 1st ed., 1924 [Shanghai?]).

74. See, respectively, Joseph R. Levenson, *Liang Ch'i-ch'ao and the Mind of Modern China* (Cambridge, Mass., 1953), and Jerome Grieder, "Hu Shih and Liberalism: A Chapter in the Intellectual Modernization of China, 1917–1930," doctoral thesis (Harvard University, 1963), chap. 5.

This they took as solid evidence for the inferiority of Western civilization to the 'spiritual' civilization of China. By 1919, this argument for National Essence became the foundation for those who opposed the New Culture movement, which, among other things, demanded a new, vernacular literature to replace the classical tradition; and of course, it advocated the adoption of aspects of European culture, thus flying in the face of a highly emotional reaction against any kind of Westernization and any suggestions that the traditional culture be further altered.

Again Liu Shih-p'ei took up the defense of National Essence; but this time, more than a decade after his original efforts, his defense was little more than an outburst of nostalgia. Liu had been brought to Peking University by his old friend, Ts'ai Yüan-p'ei, and there he assumed leadership of a group of scholars from Kiangsu and Chekiang provinces. Most of these men were disciples or friends of Chang T'ai-yen, and they were associated with the university's School of Letters. The professors of this *Kiang-Che* faction (which included Huang Chieh and Ma Hsü-lun) were reportedly a major source of opposition to the young intellectuals who participated in such groups as the New Tide Society.[75] Their short-lived journal, *National Heritage* (*Kuo-ku*), advocated traditional literature, language, and style, "Confucianism and the old ethics." [76] Within the four issues it published, it specifically attacked the policies of the *New Tide*.[77]

Appropriately, Liu Shih-p'ei died in 1919, but the conservative responses to the literary and scholarly work of the New Culture movement continued in scattered criticism: Lin Shu (1852–1924), Yen Fu (1854–1921), and Chang T'ai-yen each refused to condone the new literature, the new thought, and the new scholarship to which they had indirectly contributed a very short generation earlier. During the twenties, however, it was the group of scholars gathered at Southeastern University in Nanking that posed the most concerted conservative criticism of the historiographical and literary aspects of the New Culture movement exemplified in the thought of Ku Chieh-kang and

75. *MFM*, pp. 62–63.
76. *Ibid.*
77. See Mao Tzu-shui, "*Po Hsin-ch'ao, Kuo-ku*" (n. 47, above).

Hu Shih. Most representative of this conservatism was the journal *Critical Review* (*Hsüeh Heng*), founded in 1922. The journal (which employed the classical idiom, though poorly) had direct bonds with the *Journal of National Essence* and with the Southern Society. Wu Mi, founder of the *Critical Review,* was a disciple of Huang Chieh, whose poems were published in the journal.[78]

But now, to the influence of the old National Essence conservatism there was added a Western touch. The *Critical Review* group was deeply influenced by the thought of Irving Babbitt, under whom Wu Mi and his associate Mei Kuang-ti had studied at Harvard. Because of this, from the point of view of the transformation of traditional society, the tension between the New Culture iconoclasts and the *Critical Review* is somewhat misleading. If New Culture intellectuals undermined Chinese identity by rejecting the past according to the principles of John Dewey at Columbia University, conservatives contributed no less to the subversion and transformation by retaining the past a la Irving Babbitt at Harvard University.

The cultural conservatism initiated by the National Essence group in the days before the 1911 Revolution found its last variation within the neo-traditional, anti-Communist ideology of the Nationalist party under the guidance of Chiang Kai-shek and Ch'en Li-fu.[79] Formalized as the New Life Movement in the early thirties, the Nationalists' attitude toward the New Culture was usually hostile and, toward New Culturalists, often manipulative and repressive. Ku Chieh-kang clashed on a number of occasions with the Nationalist government when, on grounds of national interest, it attempted to censor his writings, inhibit his research, or dictate his educational practices. And Hu Shih, piqued by confrontations with the Nationalists in the realm of scholarship and politics, decried them as a perennial source of cultural conservatism. He charged that the "reactionary" nature of the Nationalists, seen in their policies and practices after

78. *BSCS,* pp. 31–32.

79. See Mary Wright, *The Last Stand of Chinese Conservatism* (Stanford, 1957), chap. 12.

1927, was merely a revival of tendencies inherent in their thought from the early Republican period.

Hu Shih noted that Sun Yat-sen's 1924 lectures, called collectively the "Three Principles of the People" (*San Min Chu-i*), exhibited many of the basic attitudes of the earlier National Essence advocates. For example, the lectures had disparaging words for foreign culture and those Chinese interested in it, and they said that China had preserved her ancient spiritual superiority, against which the West could only muster temporary material advantage. And, closer to home, Sun's lectures had condemned the new literary departures characteristic of Hu Shih's vernacular literature movement. The "Three Principles of the People" was canonized by the Nationalists in the late twenties, and, according to Hu Shih, the lectures helped to crystallize the party's conservative nature, kept dormant during the period of the alliance with the Chinese Communist party, from 1924 to 1927. Hu Shih also cited as one cause and symptom of the Nationalists' conservatism the fact that old members of the National Essence clique had come to comprise the "intelligentsia of the Kuomintang." Among those he cited was Liu Ya-tzu, founder of the Southern Society.[80]

There had been a lot of water under the bridge since the founding of the *Journal of National Essence*, but by the beginning of the thirties there were distinct, if clumsy, attempts to ape the earlier conservatisms: boycott Western culture; restore Confucianism; revive the old virtues and the old aesthetic and scholarly forms. Hu Shih's analysis of this last major stage of conservatism is valuable, and not merely because it gives insight into his understanding of his own world. However, he has emphasized a persistent conservative nature at the cost of a changing political context. And he has ignored the tendency of the earlier twentieth-century cultural conservatism to use political forms to protect the National Essence, while the latter-day conservatism invoked National Essence to defend political forms.

80. Hu Shih, "Hsin wen-hua yün-tung yü Kuo-min-tang" [The New Culture Movement and the Kuomintang], *Hsin-yüeh* [The Crescent Moon], II:6–7 (Sept. 10, 1929), 1–15.

Anti-Manchuism, and the debates over new political institutions that followed, were for some earlier conservatives functions of the broader motivation to protect what they deemed the most important aspects of tradition. Kuomintang advocates of tradition used National Essence as a symbol of their political legitimacy, as a rallying point for precarious national unity, and, perhaps most important, as a sign that they were drawing the limits of revolution well within the inherited socioeconomic structure.

I suspect that the Kuomintang's conservatism was not at all a result of pressures from old-time conservatives within its intelligentsia, but, on the contrary, that these old-timers were attracted to support the Kuomintang after its conservatism had evolved in the context of internal politics and international relations of the late 1920s. The presence of former members of the National Essence clique in the ranks of the Kuomintang is considerably less a symptom of the former's political influence than of their nostalgia and cultural despair.

THE OLD TEXT AND NEW TEXT SCHOOLS

Cutting across the earlier groups of National Essence advocates, and much more pertinent in Ku Chieh-kang's intellectual development, were the Old Text and New Text schools of scholarship. From the point of view of Ku's personal experience, the two schools were personified, respectively, by Chang T'ai-yen and K'ang Yu-wei (1858–1927), the last great exponents of these scholarly traditions. They contributed considerably to the subject matter of Ku's scholarship, to his methodology, and—usually by negative example—to his social values as a scholar.

The Old Text school, as we might expect from Chang T'ai-yen's association with it, was preoccupied with the problem of cultural persistence. This was expressed most succinctly in the guiding idea of the *Tao T'ung*. The *Tao*, a concept of hoary vintage, signified a trans-historical body of absolute values, potentially imminent in the everyday operation of society. While the *Tao* had been active in man's world during the Chinese Golden Age in misty antiquity, there had been a moral devolution ever since, and the *Tao* (that is, proper social behavior and government) was no longer manifest. Where a knowledge of the *Tao* persisted, and where there persisted an attempt to educate mankind to its contents, and where there was an effort to recover obscured knowledge of the *Tao*—there was a tradition of sages and scholars called the *Tao T'ung.*

By contrast, an exemplary idea in K'ang's New Text school was the Three Stages (*San T'ung*), which also had a long pedigree of its own. The Three Stages was a description of the configuration and process of history. In its simplest terms, the scheme suggested that all societies developed progressively upward through the stages, at different paces, and all societies would ultimately reach the final level which was (according to K'ang's utopian *Book of the Great Harmony* [*Ta-t'ung shu*]) a unified world in which all barriers to communication, commerce, and humanity were down. Though K'ang claimed that this scheme had been heralded in the past by Confucius, it was patently concerned with an evolutionary process, with contemporary change, and with the future.

The textual concern of the two schools, in its nontechnical aspect, revolved about the question of the relationship of Confucius to the Classical canons of traditional Chinese orthodoxies. For the Old Text school, Confucius was a flesh-and-blood mortal; a wise, morally sensitive individual who was capable of passing down knowledge of the *Tao* by transmitting the historical records of the Golden Age. These records that he compiled, and certain commentaries on them, became the Old Text canon. The *Tao T'ung* was the path leading from Confucius to his immediate disciples, to Mencius (3rd century B.C.), and on into later times; a line of philosophers and scholars devoted to propagating the values of the *Tao* and removing the obscurities resulting from mishandling and misunderstanding the Classics. Textual criticism and historical studies were thus important tools for the recovery and continuation of the *Tao T'ung.*

The New Text tradition, vis-a-vis the Old Text, was esoteric. In its scheme, Confucius was a semi-divine sage-prophet who had the powers to perceive the historical scheme which would unfold in the future—that is, the Three Stages. In addition, Confucius was no mere passive transmitter, no mere chronicler of Golden Age manifestations of the *Tao*; he was, rather, a political reformer who used the device of factitious historical precedents for his reform programs. This was the burden of K'ang's book *A Study of Confucius as a Reformer* (*K'ung-tzu kai-chih k'ao*). Those texts which the New Text scholars claimed as the legitimate canon were, they said, written by Confucius himself. This canon had served Confucius in two ways: he could cite it for authoritative precedents for his proposed reforms; and he could convey, in code and opaque symbol, his unique knowledge about the nature of the historical process. As for the texts in the Old Text canon, K'ang Yu-wei attributed virtually all of them to the malicious forgeries of an ideologue of the first century A.D. who had successfully fooled generations of Chinese scholars thereafter. (This thesis K'ang argued in his *The False Classics of the New School* [Hsin-hsüeh wei-ching k'ao].) Here again, in order to demonstrate the spuriousness of the rival canon, textual criticism and a comprehensive knowledge of traditional historical literature were instrumental.

Ku Chieh-kang's contact with these schools of thought was episodic and continuously influential over his formative years. He recalled that as a child in middle school he told his instructors that he would like some day to follow in the footsteps of the famous Chang T'ai-yen and become a scholar of the classics, pursuing Chang's motto, "Reorganize the Documents of Antiquity." [81] In the same period of his life, he wrote in the *Autobiography*, he had made great efforts to obtain a set of the *Journal of National Essence*, but

> The learned articles by men like Liu Shih-p'ei and Chang T'ai-yen rather overwhelmed me, for they contained many abstruse passages that I could not understand. The chief thing that I learned from these, aside from certain new ideas about racial revolution, was the fact that Chinese scholarship had been carried on by many conflicting schools of thought.[82]

A pilgrimage to the Shanghai library of the National Essence

81. *HPKCJC*, p. 1a.
82. *ACH*, p. 20.

Society in 1909 did little to enhance his understanding of Chang's thought.

Five years later, now a student in the preparatory department at Peking University, Ku was personally introduced to Chang T'ai-yen by Mao Tzu-shui at a series of evening lectures which the Old Text scholar was giving to his recently established and short-lived National Studies Society.[83] Earlier in the year, Chang had resigned a token political position given to him by Yüan Shih-k'ai, who sought his support. Chang had come to Peking after the failure of the Second Revolution[84] in order to reorganize a political party he had once headed,[85] but his political activities and his lectures were cut short after a month. Yüan put him under house arrest and he was kept out of circulation until Yüan's death in 1916.[86]

In spite of his short personal contact with Chang T'ai-yen, Ku was very strongly influenced by him. Or perhaps it would be better to say that Chang crystallized for Ku an ethic which he had been in the process of formulating since his distasteful experience with the Socialist party. Ku wrote that Chang's lectures on the integrity of the scholar, and on the problem of 'practical' scholarship, made Chang the first scholar for whom he had any respect. That winter, Ku decided to become Chang's disciple.[87]

Ku was endeared to Chang at this time primarily because of Chang's belief that scholarship and politics should remain apart, a philosophy he expressed repeatedly in his criticisms of the members of the New Text School. Chang, as a defender of the Old Text tradition, did what he could to counter the New Text efforts, under the direction of K'ang Yu-wei, to apotheosize Confucius and to establish Confucianism as a state religion. Yüan

83. *Ibid.*, pp. 40–41.

84. The Second Revolution was the name given to the abortive revolt of seven provincial governments against Yüan Shih-k'ai's political policies. The provinces declared their independence of Peking during the autumn of 1913, but they were brought back into the fold quickly and by force.

85. Wang Yi-t'ung, "A Biographical Sketch of Chang Ping-lin," in Chang T'ai-yen, *T'ai-yen hsien-sheng tzu-ting nien-p'u* [Autobiographical Sketch] (Hong Kong, 1965), p. 5.

86. *Ibid.*, and *ACH*, p. 42.

87. *ACH*, pp. 40–41.

Shih-k'ai's government supported K'ang's program, assured that it would enhance its power and buttress Yüan's throne.

K'ang's essays about Confucius and the need for a Confucian religion began to appear in his periodical *Pu-jen tsa-chih* from February of 1913.[88] By the time Ku began to attend Chang's lectures, Chang was so irate that he refused admission to his lectures to students who had supported K'ang's crusade. In the classes which Ku attended, Chang T'ai-yen preached that in the cynical machinations of the New Text scholars could be seen the basic conflict which existed between religion and true learning. And he denounced the Confucian religious movement as a transparent political maneuver.[89]

Most shocking for Ku Chieh-kang was Chang's revelation of the manner in which the New Text scholars propounded their weird theories on the interpretation of the Confucian Classics. Chang demonstrated how Wang K'ai-yün,[90] Liao P'ing,[91] and K'ang Yu-wei had manipulated ancient textual materials for purposes of political reform (in a manner reminiscent of Confucius in K'ang Yu-wei's telling). Ku "could not comprehend how, in an age of scientific enlightenment, the Modern Text school dared to come out with doctrines so manifestly absurd" as the miraculous birth of Confucius and the prophetic nature of the Classics.[92]

These experiences during his first years at Peking University, a time when he was already quite discouraged with political involvement, enhanced his introverted mood and helped him to formulate the rudiments of his 'anti-practical' attitude. In the

88. See C. J. Liu, *Controversies in Modern Chinese Intellectual History* (Cambridge, Mass., 1964), pp. 102–105, for summary of articles.

89. *ACH*, p. 47.

90. Wang K'ai-yün (1833–1916) was a Hunanese New Text scholar, literary eccentric, and sometime supporter of the Manchu house as well as of Yüan Shih-k'ai. (*BSCS*, pp. 75–78.)

91. Liao P'ing (1852–1932) was a disciple of Wang K'ai-yün and the recognized authority on the New Text school in his day. K'ang Yu-wei's scholarship is a direct derivative of Liao P'ing's. However, Ku Chieh-kang never acknowledges a debt to Liao. (For Liao, see *BSCS*, pp. 44–45; Fung Yu-lan, *A History of Chinese Philosophy*, 2 vols. (Princeton, 1953), II, 705–722; and *CCMF*, III, chap. 1.)

92. *ACH*, pp. 41–42.

Autobiography, he recalled his earliest thoughts on this theme, so central to his life and scholarship:

While in practical matters it is necessary to differentiate between what is utile and what is theoretical, in the realm of knowledge we are concerned only with whether a thing is true, and not with whether it is useful. While it is right that knowledge should be useful, utility is only a by-product of knowledge and is not the end for which we pursue it. . . .

The realization of this truth constitutes the most memorable experience of my life.[93]

Ku felt that the most powerful incentive leading him to such a position was "the argument that Chang T'ai-yen launched against the slogan of the Modern Text school, that the Classics must be studied from a practical point of view." [94]

When the effect of Chang T'ai-yen's charisma began to wear off, Ku Chieh-kang, early in 1914, started to read the writings of K'ang Yu-wei for himself. In spite of the 'practical' purpose of K'ang's study of spurious classics, Ku now concluded that, all of Chang's sermons notwithstanding, K'ang Yu-wei could be a first-rate textual critic and historian, who offered solid arguments and intriguing materials for the study of ancient history.[95] Before the year was over, Ku had read K'ang's second major work, dealing with Confucius as a reformer. It was an even more transparent political device than the first book, but its intellectual appeal to Ku was immediate and indelible, although Ku recalled he did not fully appreciate its value nor assimilate its research techniques until he read it for the second time in 1921.[96] "The influence [of the book]," he wrote in the *Autobiography,* "which so clearly pointed out the vagueness and confusion that characterize our knowledge of ancient Chinese history, was the motive that inspired me to overturn all our [so-called] ancient history." [97]

94. *Ibid.* The phrase "the Classics must be studied from a practical point
93. *Ibid.,* p. 35.
of view" is my translation of "t'ung ching chih-yung." Hummel uses the more ambiguous word 'utilitarian' instead of 'practical.'

95. *ACH,* pp. 44–45.

96. *Ibid.,* p. 45; and see Ku's preface to *KSP,* III (1931).

97. *ACH,* p. 78.

Ironically, the key to K'ang's argumentation in both of his books was the concept of *t'o-ku kai-chih,* which roughly means "manipulate the facts about antiquity in order to find precedents for contemporary political reform." If Chang T'ai-yen demonstrated, to Ku's horror, that K'ang was 'practical' (in the sense of *t'o-ku kai-chih*), K'ang demonstrated, to Ku's intellectual fascination, that the scholars of antiquity (Confucius included) were equally 'practical.' While he could never accept K'ang's thesis that Confucius composed the Six Classics, still he "found it essential to acknowledge the thesis that in the Classics are many admixtures of the ideas of Confucianists, who tried to base themselves on antiquity in order to justify reform." [98]

The more Ku studied K'ang during his first years at Peking University, the more he realized that Chang T'ai-yen's criticism of K'ang was partially a partisan affair, inseparable from their antagonistic political views. When Ku submitted Chang's scholarship to closer scrutiny, he found it unforgivably old-fashioned and stubbornly immune to the most recent and advanced Chinese thought on antiquity. Reluctantly, Ku abjured his Old Text hero and took a vow of nonpartisan (neither Old nor New Text) eclecticism from that time forward.[99] Still, throughout his essays of the late 1930s in which he reflected on his intellectual lineage (in his prefaces to the *Critiques,* for example), we find Ku at one time claiming in sentimental tones to be a 'Old Texter' at heart and, at another, pointing to the New Text heritage of his technical skills.[100] (What is interesting for us is that he persisted in identifying with them at all.) He did not seriously begin to explore the New Text–Old Text controversy as a historical problem—that is, as a part of Han intellectual history—until the late 1920s. His experience with the controversy in its modern form at Peking University colored his later historical interpretations considerably.

Ku had joined the Old Text ranks at first because he saw Chang as a "true political revolutionary" and "considerably

98. *Ibid.*

99. For example, see Ku's preface to *KSP,* III.

100. For an example of his claim to a New Text heritage, see his Preface to *KSP,* II (1930), 6–7.

more progressive than the 'emperor-protecting' New Text advocates such as K'ang Yu-wei." [101] In addition, Chang's command of the ponderous materials of Classical studies was legendary, and his students were legion; Ku could hardly escape their influence. In addition to Mao Tzu-shui and Ch'ien Hsüan-t'ung (who had once been a follower of K'ang Yu-wei), Ku interacted with even more devoted disciples of Chang T'ai-yen on the faculty at Peking University.[102] Further, the Old Text treatment of Confucius as a mortal historical figure appealed to him over the New Text Confucius; and Ku was, at best, amused by the magical and prophetic texts which the New Text school claimed for their canon. Over the next decade Ku became an ardent student of K'ang's critical scholarship, and this was his sole, cautious bond with the New Text school. Although his understanding and appreciation of K'ang's methodology was enhanced at Peking University in the classroom of K'ang's disciple, Ts'ui Shih (1851–1924), Ku continued to make known his abhorrence of K'ang's attempts to establish the New Text Classics as a new canon.[103]

Thus, the Old Text and New Text advocates traced a complex pattern across the developing idea of National Essence, and in doing so, bequeathed a very ambiguous legacy to Ku Chieh-kang. Chang T'ai-yen had been a founder of the National Essence Society and an unwavering anti-Manchu revolutionary. But he parted company with 'National Essence' when that idea became associated with betrayal of the 1911 Revolution; and he parted company with revolution when, looking at the New

101. Introduction to *CHFSJS* (dated 1955), pp. 4–5.

102. Ma Yü-yü (Ma Yü-tsao) (b. 1880), was the chairman of the department of literature while Ku was in the preparatory department. Ma was one of the editors of Chang T'ai-yen's collected works. See *Chang Chih ts'ung shu* [Collected Works of Chang T'ai-yen], 2 vols. (Taipei: Shih-chieh, 1959). Shen Chien-shih was another editor of that collection; his academic specialty was epigraphy. *See ibid.*; also see *ACH,* p. 48.

103. For example, see Ku's "Lün K'ang Yu-wei pien-wei chih ch'eng-chi" [On the Contributions of K'ang Yu-wei's Critiques of Spurious Literature], *Chung-shan ta-hsüeh yü-yen li-shih hsüeh yen-chiu-so chou-k'an* [Journal of the National Sun Yat-sen University Institute of Advanced Philological and Historical Studies]—hereinafter referred to as *Chung-ta chou-k'an*—XI:123 (May 26, 1930), 13.

Culturalists, Chang associated that idea with a betrayal of tradition and the *Tao T'ung*. K'ang Yu-wei, whose thought was devoted to notions of progress and change, nevertheless was comfortable with the same group of intellectuals which Chang T'ai-yen abandoned; the group that supported Yüan Shih-k'ai and the Confucian religious movement under the banner of National Essence. Both Chang and K'ang ultimately relied on the study of antiquity, and on historical and textual criticism, to avert the destruction of China by the West. By doing so, they were exemplars, in spite of themselves, for Ku Chieh-kang's efforts to reorganize China's past.

II

The National Studies Movement and China's New History

Imaginative recovery of the bygone is indispensable to successful invasion of the future, but its status is that of an instrument.—John Dewey[1]

The Manchus were gone, leaving hardly a trace of themselves; so was the institution of the monarchy. The traditional examination system and the educational institutions that supplied it with candidates were gone too; but the political and cultural dangers feared by Chinese intellectuals during the first decade of the twentieth century seemed just as imminent. In the early twenties, Ku Chieh-kang and his National Studies associates were no less concerned for the continuity of Chinese society; however, they were educated in what was already a post-Confucian era, a time when a good deal of the superstructure of the traditional culture had been razed. The values of Confucianism, the classical writings, the ritual and institutions could all be viewed from an increasing distance now and evaluated with considerably less ambiguity than a Chang T'ai-yen, or even a Liang Ch'i-ch'ao, could manage. These elements of the traditional order had never played any significant role in the lives of Ku Chieh-kang and his contemporaries; they had little or

1. John Dewey, "The Need for Recovery of Philosophy," in John Dewey *et al., Creative Intelligence: Essays in the Pragmatic Attitude* (New York, 1917), p. 14.

no emotional commitment to them based on personal experiential involvement. Many had lived and studied abroad, in the West or Japan, and thereby gained an even greater opportunity for perspective. They could reject what they chose to more fully and confidently because they sensed, and took pains to demonstrate, that these rejected things had no relevance to their own lives and experience.

Continuity with the past and the survival of a Chinese civilization distinct from Europe and America were possible, however. At least Hu Shih and Ku Chieh-kang thought it possible, as long as indigenous cultural alternatives were sought out to replace what was rejected; as long as it was recognized that not all of China's past was corrupt or irrelevant to the twentieth century. Finding the cultural alternatives, making the tests of value and relevance, and generally determining the most viable filiation between the past and present were the self-assigned tasks of National Studies advocates during the 1920s.

Primarily through the influence of Hu Shih, National Studies' rhetoric and methodology resounded with echoes of American Pragmatic Philosophy and Progressive History. Hu Shih had taken his doctorate in philosophy under John Dewey at Columbia from 1915 to 1917. He participated in an ambiance there created not only by Dewey but by J. H. Robinson, F. J. E. Woodbridge, H. E. Barnes, Carl Becker, and Charles Beard, as well. Dewey himself personally toured and lectured throughout the Chinese academic world in 1919 and 1920 (after he had prepared *Reconstruction in Philosophy,* for a lecture series in Japan), and over the next decade many works representing the Columbia school were translated into Chinese.[2] In our discussion here of National Studies, reference is made to American thought not merely to explain the unfamiliar in terms of the familiar. There was actual contact between the two cultures,

2. See Ch'i Ssu-ho, "Chin pai nien lai Chung-kuo shih-hsüeh te fa-chan" [The Development of Chinese Historical Scholarship in the Past Century], *Yen-ching she-hui k'o-hsüeh* [Yenching Journal of Social Science], II (1949), 23–24. Also see O. Briere, *Fifty Years of Chinese Philosophy, 1898–1950* (London, 1956), pp. 119–121. For Dewey's general influence on Chinese intellectuals at this time, see *MFM,* p. 176.

and there was at work a process of cultural diffusion which is only now beginning to be studied.

This American influence raises a problem for the intellectual historian in general, and special problems for a study of someone like Ku Chieh-kang. The general issue is the nature of the *influence:* Were Chinese intellectuals actually moved onto new paths by American Pragmatism? Did American ideas have a momentum of their own which enabled them to force their way into the thoughts of the New Culturalists and impart new directions? Or is it more accurate and useful to say that some Chinese intellectuals, responding to the realities of their own environment as they perceived them, used the American ideas as intellectual vehicles, modes of expression and reinforcements for their own feelings, not yet fully formulated in a coherent intellectual pattern? Very few of the New Culturalists were as steeped in the American environment as Hu Shih, who no doubt was directly shaped and given definite direction by it. But what of Ku Chieh-kang, who had never left China, who read English quite poorly, and who (to my knowledge) never attributed his ideas to anyone other than Chinese scholars? Ku seems to have adopted some of the ideas and attitudes of Pragmatism and the American 'New History,' not because of Hu Shih's insistence or example but because the ideas seemed to him so suitable to his real needs. Ku certainly did acknowledge Hu Shih as a major influence on his thought, but so did he acknowledge Chang T'ai-yen and K'ang Yu-wei, with whose legacies he fused the teachings of the Chinese Pragmatist.

In the experience of Ku Chieh-kang, it seems clear, his political orientations were based on choices which he made before his full encounter with American influences, and his contact with Hu Shih served to reinforce them and help him to express them more cogently. This seems to hold true for the other New Tide Society intellectuals as well. Pragmatism did not direct their behavior, but served to help them explain it. As for the historical attitudes and techniques of National Studies—whether or not the American ideas seem *appropriate* for them, in retrospect, they were in fact found most useful at the time.

National Studies as a Historical Attitude

Generally, the American Pragmatic orientation, reflected in Chinese National Studies, perceived history as process, an evolutionary process moving from change to change, potentially in the direction of progress. Thought, beliefs, and philosophic systems were considered to be instruments that made it possible for humans to adjust to the changing circumstances of their physical and social environment. *Historical* thought was considered a very special instrument, for it was central to knowledge of whether or not, to what degree, and in what fashion there might be a maladjustment between the trends of change and persisting institutions or values. Accurate historical knowledge was the means of guarding against anachronism: If it were understood how a set of values originated, and under what circumstances, then it would be possible to compare present circumstances with those of the past to determine whether they had changed, and thereby to see if the values were still appropriate.

This was the general orientation of Dewey's idea of philosophical reconstruction, which he summarized as

> strictly an intellectual work demanding the widest possible scholarship as to the connections of the past systems [of thought] with the cultural conditions that set their problems and a knowledge of present-day science which is other than that of 'popular' expositions. [It is] a systematic exploration of the values belonging to what is genuinely new in the scientific, technological and political movements of the immediate past and of the present, when they are liberated from the incubus imposed on them by habits formed in a pre-scientific, pre-technological-industrial and pre-democratic political period.[3]

Under the sponsorship of Hu Shih, James Harvey Robinson's book of essays, *The New History,* was translated into Chinese in 1921 by Hu's pupil, Ho Ping-sun, and then published by

3. John Dewey, *Reconstruction in Philosophy* (Boston: Beacon paperback ed., 1957; orig. pub. 1920), 1948 Introduction, p. xxxvii.

the Commercial Press in 1925.[4] Robinson's apologia for the New History of Progressivism was merely his own version of Dewey's 'reconstruction.' For example, he wrote in the *New History* that we are in constant danger

> of viewing present problems with obsolete emotions and of attempting to settle them by obsolete reasoning. This is one of the chief reasons why we are never by any means perfectly adjusted to our environment.[5]

"Only a study of the vicissitudes of human opinion can make us fully aware of this," Robinson warned,

> and able to readjust our views so as to adapt them to the present environment. If . . . opinion tends, in the dynamic age in which we live, to lag far behind our changing environment, how can we better discover the anachronisms in our views and in our attitude toward the world than by studying their origin? [6]

There are several issues in our outline here that need emphasis: the tone of these Americans' attitude toward the past (*their* past, it must be stressed) and how they viewed the problem of historical continuity; what aspects of the past and present they tended to examine as part of their efforts to 'adjust' or reconstruct; and finally, how sanguine they were about their ability to make the proper adjustments and reconstructions.

The New Historians and the Pragmatists were of a very present-minded orientation and often bore little more than contempt and a feeling of aloofness toward the past, the study of which was merely a means of aiding the present.[7] Dewey wrote that "We do not merely have to repeat the past, or wait for accidents to force change upon us. We *use* our past experiences to construct new and better ones in the future." [8] Robin-

4. See Ho Ping-sun, trans., *Hsin Shih-hsüeh* [The New History] (Shanghai, 1925; original Prefaces by translator dated 1921, 1923).

5. James Harvey Robinson, *The New History* (New York: Free Press paperback ed., 1965; orig. pub. 1912), p. 22.

6. *Ibid.*, p. 103.

7. See John Higham's account in Higham *et al.*, *History* (Englewood Cliffs, N. J., 1965), pp. 171–198.

8. *Reconstruction in Philosophy*, p. 95.

son enjoyed demonstrating the manner in which "modern thought far transcends that of the Greeks," [9] and H. E. Barnes, chronicler of the New History, summarized the attitude in this fashion:

> It is obvious to all thoughtful persons that social and cultural situations in the past were so different from those of the twentieth century that we can draw little of value for ourselves from the experiences of remote historic ages. Yet, by tracing back to their beginnings our own culture and institutions, we can not only better understand our own age but can also destroy that reverential and credulous attitude toward the past which is the chief obstacle to social and intellectual progress and the most dangerous menace to society.[10]

In spite of this kind of attitude toward the past, the new historians were emphatic about the "scientific truth," in Robinson's words, of historical continuity. It was a conception to which they brought a good deal of confusion,[11] but which they seemed to understand primarily as gradual change.[12] Consonant with their idea of evolution, their idea of 'continuity' seemed not at all to connote the necessary continuance or persistence of anything. "A somewhat abrupt change may take place in some single institution or habit," Robinson wrote, "but a sudden general change is almost inconceivable." [13] For the Progressives, then, the idea of historical continuity emphasized the gradual process which brings us beyond and away from our past, in contrast to Chinese like Hu Shih and Ku Chieh-kang, who spoke of rapidly getting away from *one part* of the past and affiliating the present with another part.

In order to implement 'reconstruction' and in order to adjust us to our environment as closely as possible, the American New History emphasized the need to examine 'thought' (in the sense

9. *The New History,* p. 129.
10. Harry E. Barnes, *A History of Historical Writing,* 2nd ed., rev. (New York: Dover, 1962; orig. pub. 1937), chap. 15, p. 385.
11. John Herman Randall, Jr., *Nature and Historical Experience* (New York: Columbia University paperback ed., 1962; orig. pub. 1958), chap. 3.
12. See, for example, *The New History,* p. 65.
13. *Ibid.,* p. 64.

of philosophical systems, social values, and general popular beliefs). Even though American Progressive Historians certainly dealt with social and economic problems (Beard and Seligman, for example), the Chinese New Historians perpetuated the intellectualistic bias of Robinson and Dewey. In his preface to the Chinese translation of the *New History,* Ho Ping-sun expressed the attitude that guided a large segment of the Chinese intelligentsia during the 1920s: "If you want to reform society, you must first reform thought; it you want to reform thought, you must first understand the evolution of thought." [14]

Typical of their ambiance, Dewey and Robinson were decidedly optimistic about American historians' and philosophers' abilities to help society continue to progress. "Progress," the very word itself, Robinson wrote, "is the greatest single idea in the whole history of mankind in the vista which it opens before us." [15] In the *New History* he went so far as to list the factors in the modern outlook which were definite signs of the progress men had made in recent times,[16] and he declaimed that

> historical mindedness . . . will promote rational progress as nothing else can do. The present has hitherto been the willing victim of the past; the time has now come when it should turn on the past and exploit it in the interests of advance.[17]

Dewey designated his optimism "meliorism," a belief, he wrote,

> that the specific conditions which exist at one moment, be they comparatively bad or comparatively good, in any event may be bettered. It encourages intelligence to study the positive means of good and the obstructions to their realization, and to put forth endeavor for the improvement of conditions.[18]

Historical-mindedness, or the "genetic method" in Dewey's formulation, was the chief instrument with which intelligence went about its task of improving society, and it was this genetic

14. Preface to *Hsin shih-hsüeh,* p. 11.
15. *The New History,* p. 247.
16. *Ibid.,* p. 123.
17. *Ibid.,* p. 24; see also Frederick J. E. Woodbridge, *The Purpose of History* (New York, 1916), pp. 4, 74.
18. *Reconstruction in Philosophy,* p. 178.

method that formed the core of Chinese National Studies. When Hu Shih wrote about Dewey's intellectual gift to the Chinese, he stressed that Dewey avoided all 'isms' (that is, ideology) and concentrated solely on the fundamentals of scientific method. Hu Shih wrote that this scientific method was essentially a historical or genetic one, based on the premise that value is a function of situation. The method, he said, demanded that decisions of value must begin with "actualities and real situations," and it assumed the hypothetical nature of all knowledge and ideas. Only by following a step-by-step process of investigation could theories and principles be verified on the basis of "actualities." [19] If we take Dewey's *Reconstruction in Philosophy* as the standard (without meaning to suggest that it is typical of Dewey's thought), we see that Dewey himself was capable of putting this much emphasis on methodology.[20]

As a promoter of Chinese National Studies, Hu Shih persistently advocated implementation of the genetic attitude and method. "Returning" (*huan*) was one of the catch-words he used to dramatize his point:[21] "Everything must be returned to [that is, understood in] its original condition, and thereafter one can critically determine the truth or falsity" of the ideas and principles of each epoch, school, or individual.[22]

In 1930, Ku Chieh-kang summarized his previously formulated position on the genetic method and National Studies in this grand way:

> We want to have the men of antiquity only be men of antiquity and not be leaders of today. We want to have ancient history only be ancient history and not be the ethical teachings of today. We want ancient books only to be ancient books and not be today's resplendent repositories of the law.

19. Hu Shih, "Tu-wei hsien-sheng yü Chung-kuo" [Dewey and China], *Hu Shih wen-ts'un* [The Collected Writings of Hu Shih]—hereinafter referred to as *HSWT*—12 vols. in 6 (Shanghai: Oriental, 1922–1940), I, 380–382.

20. For example, *Reconstruction in Philosophy,* pp. 149, 193.

21. "*Kuo-hsüeh chi-k'an* fa-kan hsüan-yen" [Introductory Preface to the first issue of the *Journal of National Studies*], *HSWT,* II (Jan. 1923), 7–8.

22. "Cheng-li kuo-ku yü 'ta kuei' " [Reorganizing the Nation's Past and Fighting Ghosts], *HSWT,* III (1927), 123.

This is a great act of destruction, but without it our nation will not find a viable path. Our acts of destruction are not cruel activities; we are only restoring these various things to their historical position. . . . In sum, we are sending them to the museum.

When it comes to the morality, the learning, and institutions of the men of antiquity, what can be preserved for today ought to depend on the needs of today, and whether they can be of any value. This is just as there is no reason why things in a museum cannot be of use to men today. But this is another matter which we will leave for others. Our work is limited to classifying and arranging within the museum.[23]

Ku's demurrer here on the question of making decisions of value is noteworthy and in keeping with his low estimation of 'practical' scholarship. Though he never was able to embrace the 'practical' side of Pragmatism, he did frequently venture outside of the museum to make judgments.

The connection which he makes between geneticism and 'destruction'—iconoclasm, if you will—is also important. To be an iconoclast, of course one need not physically smash the old idols. Ku's imagery of the museum suggests another alternative: Pack the idols off to the nearest gallery. Remove them from an active role in society, and thereby prevent society from becoming a museum. In J. R. Levenson's terminology, Ku would have National Studies render aspects of China's heritage "*historically* significant, that is, a proper subject of study but not a basis for present action." [24]

The National Studies group's efforts to reorganize China's past were not merely iconoclastic, for Hu Shih from the very outset of his reorganization mission made it clear that it had very positive aspects. His Columbia University doctoral thesis, "The Development of the Logical Method in China," was an exemplary response to Dewey's call for *reconstruction,* and it is a lucid example of how American Pragmatic and New Historical

23. *KSP,* IV (1933, Preface dated 1930), 13–14.

24. J. R. Levenson, "Historical Significance," in *Diogenes,* no. 32 (Winter 1960), p. 23. Cf. Ku's image of the museum to Lu Hsün's imagery of China as an antique, cited in *ibid.;* also cf. Levenson's museum imagery for China, in *CCMF,* III, *passim.*

formulations were adapted to the special problems of China. In the introduction to the thesis, Hu Shih posed what became the central problem of National Studies: "How can we best assimilate modern civilization in such a manner as to make it congenial and congruous and continuous with the civilization of our own making?" [25] The solution to this, he argued,

> will depend solely on the foresight and the sense of historical continuity of the intellectual leaders of New China, and on the tact and skill with which they can successfully connect the best in modern civilization with the best in our own civilization.[26]

Hu Shih's plan, which he illustrated in the thesis, was to find

> A congenial [Chinese] stock with which we may organically link the thought-systems of modern Europe and America, so that we may further build up our own science and philosophy on the new foundation of an internal assimilation of the old and the new.[27]

It should be noted that in seeking out those congenial Chinese stocks, the thesis employed some rather facile arguments that find little repetition in Hu Shih's future thought or in other National Studies writings. The arguments in question were devoted to demonstrating that current American philosophical systems had distinct though undeveloped precedents in China's antiquity. For example, Hu Shih found the genetic method in Taoist thought; naturalism in the Confucian philosophies; and the pragmatic method in Mohism and Legalism.[28] Not only was this precedent-hunting minimized in later National Studies writings; but those efforts, particularly those of Ku Chieh-kang, were considerably more China-centered. Their primary goal was not to link European and Chinese cultures, but rather to link China's past and China's present.

Hu Shih passed the baton on to Ku Chieh-kang who, in 1922, published his first apologia for National Studies in the journal which had come to speak for the 'literary revolution' of the

25. *The Development of the Logical Method in China* (Shanghai, 1922), Introduction, pp. 6–7.
26. *Ibid.*, p. 7.
27. *Ibid.*
28. *Ibid.*, pp., 17–18, 40, 65–66, 68, 183.

1920s, the *Fiction Monthly* (*Hsiao-shuo yüeh-pao*).[29] The essay, "The Attitude We Ought to Have Toward Our National Heritage," repeated most of the themes that Hu Shih had raised earlier and added a few extra rhetorical flourishes. Ku found it necessary to criticize the National Essence clique, and in a general reference to the earlier work of Chang T'ai-yen and Chang's associates, he suggested that when the reorganization was first attempted under their leadership, the prevalent attitude toward the past was to select for perpetuation what was traditionally considered to have positive ethical value, and to discard the rest. Scholars like Chang T'ai-yen then formed schools along these lines of selection. In the last analysis, Ku lamented, this perpetuated the kind of "religious attitude" which he was attempting to overturn. But now, Ku claimed, the attitudes of the new youth were free from the biases of schools or cliques, and their goal was "to examine the [historical] positions [of the old thought] and to give credit where it is due." No longer were the criteria of 'good' and 'evil' used to evaluate the past.[30]

Concluding this 1922 argument, Ku felt himself obliged to defend the reorganization effort against those "Chinese to whom the simple distinction of applied and academic interests is perpetually unclear: These people bifurcated the old from the new, [saying] that if you study the National Heritage there is no necessity to have a new literature movement, and vice versa. But a man living now," Ku implored,

> must speak the language of today and therefore he must support [the new literature movement]. He must also know the reasons behind the circumstances of life in the past, and how these compare with those of life today; therefore, he supports [the study of National Heritage].

In later definitions and defenses of National Studies, Ku Chieh-kang laid emphasis more on research techniques and subject matter. He emphasized the broad, virtually limitless scope of National Studies, even though it was basically a his-

29. Ku Chieh-kang, "Wo-men tui-yü kuo-ku ying-ch'u te tai-tu" [The Attitude We Ought to Have Toward Our National Heritage], *Hsiao-shuo yüeh-pao* [Fiction Monthly], CXLI: 3–4 (Jan. 1923).

30. *Ibid.*

torical mode of inquiry. Ancient political institutions and philosophy, folklore and popular culture, non-Chinese cultures within Chinese borders—all of these, he argued, fell within the scope of National Studies; and National Studies, as a branch of the historical sciences, was itself a science. Nor was National Studies decadent because it devoted itself to studies of the past, for a science treats past and present with universal equanimity; science knows no boundaries for its subject matter. "Why should we only study materials from recent times?" he asked. "Science knows no 'old' or 'new'—after all, look at the astronomers. They are scientists, and the heavens are old." [31]

National Studies as Historical Method and Historical Pedagogy

Ku Chieh-kang's concern with the actual application of the genetic attitudes of National Studies was based on his own experiences before meeting Hu Shih, as well as on Hu's guidance, and on a variety of Chinese thought, the most outstanding of which was carried on by Liang Ch'i-ch'ao.[32] This thought ranged from desultory observations on the nature of historical knowledge to the problems of recovering valuable data and the modes of disseminating new historical attitudes and knowledge.

From the point of view of epistemology, National Studies was rooted in a belief that historical knowledge or historical truth was progressive. Members of the New Tide Society had experimented with this idea and it underwent many subtle variations, in the writings of Liang Ch'i-ch'ao and later, primarily in the work of Ku Chieh-kang. For our purposes, the idea of progressive historical truth was best formulated by the Columbia University philosopher F. J. E. Woodbridge, whose popular book, *The Purpose of History,* which was in vogue during Hu Shih's

31. Ku, preface to *Pei-ching ta-hsüeh kuo-hsüeh-men chou-k'an* [Peking University Journal of National Studies]—hereinafter referred to as *Pei-ta chou-k'an*—I:1 (Jan. 1, 1926).

32. See Liang's *Chung-kuo li-shih yen-chiu fa* [Methodology for the Study of Chinese History]—hereinafter referred to as *CKLSYCF*—one-volume ed. (Taipei, 1967; 1st ed., 1937 [Shanghai?]). The title essay is dated 1922.

stay in America, is quite representative of the American Progressives' and Pragmatists' view of history.[33] In the book, Woodbridge wrote that

> the truth of history is a progressive truth to which the ages as they continue contribute. The truth for one time is not the truth for another, so that historical truth is something which lives and grows rather than something fixed to be ascertained once and for all. To remember what has happened, and to understand it, carries us thus to the recognition that the writing of history is itself an historical process. It, too, is something "evolved and acted." . . . The record may be final, but our understanding of what has been recorded can make no such claim.[34]

This attitude reached maturity in China in Ku Chieh-kang's work of the late twenties. In American Progressive historiography, it reached its fullest development (some might say its *reductio ad absurdum*) in the extreme subjectivism of Carl Becker's "Everyman His Own Historian," [35] and the relativism of Charles Beard's "Written History as an Act of Faith." [36] To the Chinese of the early 1920s, the skepticism of Becker or Beard might have been useful as a weapon to overturn old values, but it would have provided little solid ground for the new departures so anxiously sought. The 'progressivism' of Woodbridge and Robinson, however, struck a happy medium between skepticism (about inherited knowledge) and optimism (about the ability to discover new truths).

Hu Shih brought the middle way of Woodbridge and Robinson to a China where Liang Ch'i-ch'ao was already declaring that the old biographies that comprised the bulk of the traditional standard histories of China must be considered as historical data, no longer as historical truth.[37] Indeed, Liang ar-

33. Woodbridge's *The Purpose of History* (n. 17, above) was cited in Hu Shih's *Development of the Logical Method,* and Woodbridge was Fung Yu-lan's teacher at Columbia.

34. *The Purpose of History*, p. 17.

35. In the *American Historical Review,* XXXVII:2 (Jan. 1932), 221–236.

36. *Ibid.,* XXXIX:2 (Jan. 1934), 219–231. Also see Randall, *Nature and Historical Experience* (n. 11, above) for the naturalist formulation; and see Higham *et al., History* (n. 7, above), pp. 121, 122.

37. *CKLSYCF,* part I, pp. 46–47.

gued that all traditional Chinese historical writings should be considered as evidence of how men of the past thought, not necessarily as truthful (that is, accurate) accounts of the periods which they purported to describe. Only by employing the scientific method, Liang wrote, could the data locked up in these old historical writings be released for reassemblage into modern histories. Nor did Liang stop with the histories: all written materials from the past, whether the Classics, philosophy, poetry, or fiction, must be treated in the same fashion—that is, as historical data potentially containing a new understanding of China's heritage.[38] "Each era has its own historical scholarship" (*"ke shih-tai yu ke shih-tai te li-shih"*) was the oft-repeated formula used by Ku Chieh-kang and his associates to summarize the 'progressive' viewpoint of National Studies historiography.

In order to achieve new and better understanding of the past, the first step to be taken, in Hu Shih's words, was that of "closing accounts," or writing "balance sheets." By this, Hu Shih meant that all previous Chinese work in the realms of textual and historical criticism should be evaluated by the criterion of their usefulness to modern Chinese scholarship. It was essential that historical studies be based on a sound and thorough knowledge of reliable sources; therefore, it was of value to collate and publish what earlier textual critics had said about the reliability of specific materials. Once the balance sheet of previous critical scholarship was drawn up, then the account could be closed and the new scholarship could move on. To this end, National Studies sponsored the publication of anthologies of earlier scholarship on troublesome textual problems, in order to illustrate the nature of the problems and to demonstrate what progress had already been made in solving them. From this point of view, certain books in the Classical canon received special attention from Ku Chieh-kang, while Hu Shih gave similar treatment to the texts of some traditional works of fiction.[39]

38. *Ibid.*, pp. 49–52; and Liang's essay, "Chih kuo-hsüeh te liang t'iao ta lu" [Two Great Roads to Putting National Studies in Order], originally a lecture delivered at Southeastern (Tung Ta) University, Jan. 9, 1923, reprinted in *KKTLC*, I, 3.

39. See Hu Shih, "Tsai t'an-t'an cheng-li kuo-ku" [Another Discussion About Reorganizing the Nation's Past], *KKTLC*, I, 21–29; and Hu's

Another task which National Studies deemed basic to the implementation of its genetic point of view was the reclassification of materials potentially useful to its all-encompassing historical research. It was considered necessary to restructure the Chinese scholar's perception of textual materials by abandoning the traditional classifications, which followed a broad four-category division (the *ssu pu:* Classics, histories, philosophies, *belles lettres*). Bibliographies built on a new classification system would be compiled, to give sensitive guidance to 'scientific' historical investigations. Ku Chieh-kang was deeply involved with these kinds of concerns even before he became part of the New Tide Society. As early as 1914, Ku was engrossed in the writings of the eighteenth-century scholar Chang Hsüeh-ch'eng, and thereby became preoccupied with the problems of bibliography.[40] He concentrated his first efforts at criticism on the bibliography of the massive eighteenth-century imperial compilation, the *Four Treasuries* (*Ssu-k'u ch'uan-shu*), and then, intent on organizing the classical scholarship of the Ch'ing dynasty, began to construct chronological tables, in a traditional fashion, which might act as guides to the dense forest of books he was then confronting for the first time.[41] Less than a decade after Ku's rather traditional forays into bibliography and classification, his National Studies associates were advocating the adoption of the Dewey Decimal System and the abandonment of the old Four-Category and collectanea (*ch'uan shu*) devices in these areas.[42]

Hu Shih and Liang Ch'i-ch'ao, while involved in this concern for research-material classification and bibliography, were also concerned about aids for the broader public. They shared the

---

"Cheng-li kuo-hsüeh te san-t'iao hsü-ching" [Third Discussion About Reorganizing the Nation's Past], *ibid.*, I, 122–214.

40. Ku, "Ts'ung wo tzu-chi k'an Hu Shih" [A Personal Look at Hu Shih], *Ta Kung Pao* [The Impartial] (Dec. 24, 1951); and *ACH,* pp. 50–51, 171–172.

41. *ACH,* pp. 51–52, 53; and see Ku's *Chung-kuo hsüeh-shu nien-piao te shuo-ming* [A Chronological Table of Chinese Scholarship] (Peking, 1924).

42. See, for example, Ts'ao Chü-jen, "Ch'un lei chu-ching chih kuo-ku hsüeh [On National Studies], *KKTLC* (Dec. 1925), I, 100 ff.; and Ch'a-hsiu, "Chung-wen shu-chi fen-lei fa shang-ch'üeh" [Revision of the Methods for Classifying Chinese Language Materials], *KKTLC,* III, 1–121.

opinion, in the early twenties, that an intimate part of National Studies was popularization of the national heritage—that is, breaking down the association of high culture with a tiny fraction of the Chinese populace. In fact, what they had in mind was the education of the youth in China's new middle schools—still a very small part of the whole population. In the *Endeavor* and in their own personal publications, Hu and Liang worked closely for a few years to make it possible for everyman to use ancient books, to read in the original sources and thereby obtain an understanding of China's past culture.[43] There was really a dual purpose at stake: when the old books were made accessible to the 'general public,' the people would profit from a knowledge of their own past; and, in addition, the books would lose their sacerdotal qualities and status values that had helped to support the old regime.[44]

Popularization was only possible, of course, if the old books were available in abundance and were comprehensible. To these ends, Hu Shih suggested, the National Studies scholars could lend their talents. They could collate editions of the titles in question, write new commentaries, and punctuate. They could also write detailed prefaces which put the books into historical perspective, telling about the social influences of the book and suggesting to the first-time reader how it might be of value to him. Indexes, Hu Shih said, were also of vital importance to moderns, who lacked the leisure of the old aristocrats and therefore needed efficient guides.[45]

In a fashion quite reminiscent of the pre-1911 National Essence program, Hu Shih and Liang Ch'i-ch'ao devoted a good deal of energy to designing basic reading lists and self-taught instruction programs in National Learning.[46] Though these

43. Hu Shih, "Cheng-li kuo-hsüeh te san t'iao hsü-chin" [Three Introductory Measures to Take for Rectifying National Studies], *KKTLC,* I, 124 ff.

44. Hu Shih, "Tsai t'an-t'an cheng-li kuo-ku."

45. *Ibid.,* pp. 25–26.

46. See, for example, Hu Shih, "Tui-yü kuo-hsüeh shu te t'ao-lün" [Arguments About the Bibliography of National Studies], *KKTLC,* III, 202–256; and Liang Ch'i-ch'ao, *Kuo-hsüeh yen-tu-fa san-chung* [Three Pieces on Readings in National Studies] Taipei, 1968; 1st ed., 1936 [Shanghai?]).

reading guides to China's great books received as much scorn as support and soon floundered, they were not unrelated to the monumental publishing ventures that in fact did make the old books accessible to a growing educated public. In fact, not since the days of the Ch'ien Lung emperor in the eighteenth century had such publishing been carried on in China. But now, with different techniques and contrary intent, companies like the Commercial Press and Kaiming publishers surpassed the earlier output and thereby made some of the basic goals of National Studies at least a physical possibility.

Ironically, although the Commercial Press and others helped Hu Shih to implement many of the goals of his popularization efforts, they often did so by reprinting collections structured by the old classification systems.[47] Form notwithstanding, these collections served very different intellectual functions in the twentieth century than they did when they were first compiled. The *Four Treasuries,* for example, was the ultimate cultural gesture of the Ch'ien Lung emperor to the civilization conquered by his ancestors. The thousands of titles which originally made up this collection were concrete symbols of orthodox high culture, and in printing them, the Ch'ing dynasty thereby reaffirmed its legitimacy, its ability to protect Chinese culture, and its right to rule the Chinese people.

If the eighteenth-century printing of the Classics and the histories and the rest was an affirmation of the place of tradition in Chinese society (and hopefully, the Manchus' place as well), mid-nineteenth-century gestures signified something else. In the 1860s, Tseng Kuo-fan (1811–1872), the Chinese general who led the defense of the monarchy against the Taiping Rebellion, sponsored a small-scale reprinting of the Classics. The Taipings had almost shattered the society; and meanwhile the West had tightened its hold. Reprinting the Classics in the wake of the Taipings was as moving a gesture as the printing of the *Four Treasuries* had been a grandiloquent one; but it symbolized a defense, not an affirmation, of tradition.

47. See, for example, the *Ssu-pu ts'ung-k'an,* (Shanghai: Commercial Press, 1920–1922); the *Ssu-pu pei-yao* (Shanghai, Chung-hua, 1927–1935); and *Ssu-k'u ch'uan-shu* (Ta tung lithograph ed., 1930; Commercial Press Wen-yüan-ko ed., 1934).

Sixty years after the Taiping Rebellion, the efforts of the Commercial Press alone made the Ch'ien Lung emperor look like a piker, as they made it possible for every library in China to have its own set of the *Four Treasuries* (or what was left of it), for every scholar to have a couple of *Ssu-pu*'s, and every student a set of the Classics and histories, if he desired them. The goal now was not affirmation of tradition, nor even defense of it, but rather the assimilation of one aspect of the past into an emerging, broader national identity. Modern presses helped National Studies transform the old books from a basis for present action to a proper subject of study.

Accompanying the National Studies group's attitude toward popularization of the literary heritage was the oft-expressed design to extend the *subject matter* of historical research in a popular direction. By the early twenties, Liang Ch'i-ch'ao had already written derisively about the class-bound nature of the traditional histories in China,[48] and he had stressed the need to have the new history reflect life.[49] The implication was that all aspects of society, no matter how mean, were worthy and necessary subjects for historians. Liang specifically stated that history must no longer be chained, as it had been, to the ruling class or to the intelligentsia, but that it must be for the whole society. Hu Shih and Ku Chieh-kang perpetuated this philosophy in their policy statements for National Studies, and in practice the philosophy was reflected in their passionate concern with Chinese popular culture.[50]

The obverse of this democratization of historical subject matter was the liberalization of the notion of historical data. Breaking down the old Four Categories, and considering all of their contents as potential historical data, was just the beginning. Now it was the historian's obligation to consider every conceivable form of data for his work. It was of basic importance to break away from conventional textual sources, a step made possible by the fabulous archaeological discoveries of the first decades of the twentieth century. Liang Ch'i-ch'ao wrote that

48. *CKLSYCF*, part 1, p. 28
49. *Ibid.*, p. 3.
50. See Part Two, below.

historians would have to become familiar with a whole body of new data in order to write their new history, and by this he said he meant every kind of material, ranging from long-ignored works of fiction and the great encyclopedias to the recently uncovered Tun-huang manuscripts and inscribed bronze vessels.[51] In the early twenties, Liang expressed embarrassment that foreigners were already using the new data more fully and expertly than Chinese scholars.[52]

Liang's attitudes toward new data were carried on through the twenties by Hu Shih and Ku Chieh-kang, especially in their highly publicized treatment of folksong, popular fiction, and folklore of all kinds. As a professional historian, however, Ku regretted that he was never able to take full advantage of the archaeological work being carried on by such outstanding contemporary scholars as Lo Chen-yü (1866–1940) and Wang Kuo-wei (1877–1927). These men pioneered the study of the script inscribed on thousands of slips of bone (Oracle Bones) dating from the second millennium B.C. which were found in northern China. Though he had deep reservations about certain areas of Wang Kuo-wei's competence, Ku recognized that Wang had given new direction and life to the study of ancient Chinese history.[53] The instance of Oracle Bone archaeology illustrates a persistent characteristic of National Studies. Even though Ku and his colleagues called for an expanded awareness and use of new data, and new social-scientific techniques to analyze the data, National Studies remained concerned primarily with textual sources that were by no means new to Chinese scholarship and with techniques that were by no stretch of the imagination an expression of Western social science.

National Studies, Science, and Methodology

From the time of the early New Culture movement, the idea of 'science' in China had implications reaching far beyond that of a research attitude and technique or a mode of acquiring knowledge. As Daniel Kwok has pointed out, Western science

51. *CKLSYCF*, part 1, pp. 49–52.
52. *Ibid.*, pp. 60–63.
53. *ACH*, pp. 93, 95, 106, 153.

easily slipped into "scientism" in China; it became the focus of a heterogeneous, unstable body of values pertaining to all aspects of society. The concept of science or 'scientific' quickly came to be employed as a broad, emotionally-charged metaphor intimately related to all things meriting the designation of 'modernity.' [54]

Hu Shih, in the tradition of American Progressive History, persistently argued the case for the application of the scientific method to Chinese scholarship and for the incorporation of the new social sciences into the historical orientation of National Studies. In part, Hu Shih was echoing the American Progressives' personal need to vindicate their own scientific respectability,[55] but as a Chinese, he felt compelled to bring the Chinese mind into the scientific twentieth century.

While Ku Chieh-kang closely followed Hu Shih's policies on science, Ku's understanding of the problems of science—methodological and epistemological—was even less sophisticated than Hu Shih's. Ku wrote in the *Autobiography* that in spite of his constant call to reorganize the national heritage using the scientific method, his understanding of the method was incommensurate with his zeal for it. His understanding of the scientific method was just this:

> Through my study of logic, I learned that only by the application of the inductive method can one add to one's knowledge. Modern science begins with the building of hypotheses—basing itself on these working postulates, it proceeds to gather more evidence and, on the basis of this evidence, revises the assumptions. By evolving thus from day to day, truth is ultimately disclosed.

"To be perfectly honest," Ku concluded, "these are the only features of the scientific method that have impressed themselves upon me." [56] Among his contemporaries' tedious pretensions about questions of science, Ku's candor is rather refreshing.

Ku's appreciation of the problems of science remained at a

54. Daniel Kwok, *Scientism in Chinese Thought, 1900–1950* (New Haven, 1965).
55. Higham *et al., History* (n. 7, above), p. 108.
56. *ACH*, pp. 175–176.

rudimentary level throughout his career. In this period, his statement on the subject does reveal what is evident throughout his later writings—an empirical bias. For Ku, as for Hu Shih, science "is mainly method. It begins with observation and returns to observation." [57] But they displayed only a glimmer of understanding of the complex relationship between induction and deduction in the scientific method, as it has been developed in the Western natural and physical sciences.[58]

Inherent in Ku's inductive and empirical methodology was an unquenchable, though far from crippling, skepticism, characteristic of his Progressive Historical outlook. More than some of his other colleagues, however, he enjoyed commenting on the impermanence of knowledge and the limitations of man's reason and the fragmentary intellectual coverage man managed to give to the whole of existence.[59] "The more we doubt," he wrote, "the more there is to doubt; the more numerous our encounters, the greater our troubles; the deeper we penetrate into things, the more we fail to see the bottom." [60] This skepticism was due in part to the fact that his 'scientific methodology' was designed to meet the specific needs of discrediting many texts and traditions of Chinese historiography. Ku also said that he eschewed positive conclusions and refused to espouse any formal system of historical analysis (historical materialism, for example) because he wished to give the freest play to his own observations, unencumbered by any framework or sense of finality.[61]

PURE SCIENCE

To a greater degree than his other associates in the New Tide Society and in National Studies (with the possible exception of Fu Ssu-nien), Ku was inclined to consider knowledge and action (scholarship and politics) as mutually exclusive realms, and because of this, 'science' came to mean for him knowledge pro-

57. Kwok, *Scientism,* p. 95.

58. Hu Shih was at least aware that there was a problem here. See his essay "Chih-hsüeh te fang-fa yü ts'ai-liao" [Methods and Materials for Study], *HSWT,* II, 187–205; discussed in Kwok, *Scientism,* p. 95.

59. For example, see *ACH,* pp. 3–4, 61.

60. Preface to *KSP,* IV (1932), 5.

61. Prefaces to *KSP,* II, III.

tectively isolated from action. Traditionally, "knowledge and action" were often considered coordinate and complementary, not antagonistic,[62] and the scholar was only the obverse of the politician. What Ku wanted for contemporary China was an atmosphere, not available in the past, that would foster the development of "pure science"—the only cure for the unfortunate traditional attitude toward learning. (Ku believed that this attitude was epitomized and first completely formulated by the Han Confucianist Tung Chung-shu [179–104 B.C.?], and Ku cited his words as the *locus classicus* of 'practical' scholarship.[63])

In the past, Ku wrote in an eloquent 1929 polemic,[64] strictly speaking, there was no scholarship because

> Books were read to nurture the self, to aid the household, to order the country, and to pacify the world at large. Canonical books were the recorded words of the sages, and sages determined the laws of every kind governing men and society. The men of the past did not distinguish between life and learning, learning and canonical writing.[65]

And Ku concluded that the practical point of view in scholarship had been active and strong enough in the past to cut off all of the most promising new shoots of learning—with disastrous results.[66]

If Ku found the traditional attitude toward learning inimical to pure science, there were contemporary feelings that likewise threatened its existence. The National Studies group was criticized in the mid-twenties for wasting its time on trivia when the nation sorely needed its services. "You will become men without a country," Ku's critics warned. But Ku's rejoinder was that his group might draw near a political party (and then

62. See Benjamin Schwartz, "Some Polarities in Confucian Thought," in A. F. Wright and D. Nivison, eds., *Confucianism in Action* (Stanford, 1959), pp. 50–63; and D. Nivison, "The Problem of Knowledge and Action Since Wang Yang-ming," in A. F. Wright, ed., *Studies in Chinese Thought* (Chicago, 1953), pp. 112–146.

63. Ku's preface to *Pei-ta chou-k'an,* I:1 (Jan. 1, 1926), 172.

64. Ku's preface to *Chung-ta chou-k'an,* VI:62–63–64 (Jan. 16, 1929), 1–16.

65. *Ibid.*, p. 2.

66. *Ibid.*, p. 3.

only for the purposes of facilitating research), but it never would affiliate with one.[67] "We only want to understand the true nature of reality," he said,

> and we certainly have no desire to ameliorate mankind or pacify the people. Therefore, our work transcends the nation. If one's goal is to ameliorate mankind, then one might naturally become mankind's sycophant—or even reach the extreme of misleading mankind like Liu Hsin, or Chang Tao-ling, or in our own day, Liu Shih-p'ei.[68]

And (Ku's non sequitur) in the last analysis political interests must be up to individual tastes. You cannot expect everyone to be interested in politics, any more than in scholarship. Each man's mode of making his way in life must be commensurate with his own nature.[69]

Still other critics of Ku's point of view, he reported, argued that one should look at the example of the West: Here was wealth and power—not due to science, but due to mechanics, artillery, gunpowder. Ku responded that these things were the results of science, if not science itself; they were the results of pure inquiry. It was only when one had the freedom for pure research, completely untrammelled by society's limitations, that one could make new discoveries.[70]

PURE SCIENCE AND INDIVIDUALISM

In Ku's polemics, a discussion of pure science inevitably was transformed into a discussion of individual freedom. The complete autonomy Ku sought for science and learning was the same autonomy he sought for the individual (the scholar in particular). A plea for one was a plea for the other. The knowledge that resulted from pure science was an end in itself, just as individualism was an end in itself. These were values that directly affronted dominant traditional orientations, for Ku refused to see a fundamental social obligation for the scholar, and a social function for learning.

67. Preface to *Pei-ta chou-k'an*, p. 171.
68. *Ibid.*
69. *Ibid.*
70. *Ibid.*

Again, Ku's values here conflicted with those of important early modern thinkers such as Yen Fu (1853–1921)[71] and of his contemporaries Ch'en Tu-hsiu[72] and even Hu Shih. Each of these thinkers, to various degrees, justified individualism on socially motivated grounds—because it ultimately promised to release potential energies that would enhance the power of the polity, or because individual freedom would help revitalize Chinese society, or because it was only through the "whole species and posterity"[73] that individuals could realize themselves. If it could have been shown that the values which Ku associated with pure science were inimical to the welfare of the state, Yen Fu's reactions to them would have been predictable. It is unclear at this stage in the 1920s, however, in spite of Ku's claim of "transcending the nation," whether he would have defended these values if they demonstrably inhibited the progress of the modern Chinese state.

"METHODOLOGIES OF THE SCHOOLS" VERSUS SCIENTIFIC METHODOLOGY

Closely related to the concept of science was that of 'methodology' (*fang-fa*), a word that punctuated the National Studies writings to such a degree that at times it seemed to be a kind of incantation, an *Open Sesame,* to modernity. This concept pointed to the same values associated with the idea of science and it was often juxtaposed with a third idea, the "Methodologies of the Schools" (*chia-fa*), a term which National Studies took to be the traditional antithesis of the methodology of science.

In 1915, when Ku Chieh-kang was deeply involved in an evaluation of the Old Text–New Text controversy, and at the same time was laboring with the bibliographic theories of Chang

71. See Benjamin Schwartz, *In Search of Wealth and Power, Yen Fu and the West* (Cambridge, Mass., 1964).

72. Benjamin Schwartz, *Chinese Communism and the Rise of Mao* (Cambridge, Mass., 1952), p. 36.

73. Hu Shih, Second Preface to *K'o hsüeh yü jen-sheng-kuan* [Science and the Philosophy of Life], 2 vols. (Shanghai, 1923), I, p. 20. Also see Daniel Kwok, "The Individualism of Hu Shih," unpub. ms. (University of Hawaii, March 1963).

Hsüeh-ch'eng, he was led to an explicit denunciation of traditional schools of scholarship (*chia*) in the name of science. In his estimation, schools had been the primary cause of an incorrect perception of reality in the past. Schools had refracted and distorted the truth, and they were procrustean beds for the facts:

> [In the past], each investigator held fast to the particular school in which he was brought up, and was unwilling to penetrate the unity that connects all things, ignoring the fact that learning is common to the whole world, and therefore cannot be restricted to any one country or any particular school.[74]

"If we continue to exalt special schools of thought so as to emphasize . . . [deductive reason] at the expense of [inductive reason]," Ku argued,

> the students of our time will look upon the words of their teachers as law and gospel, with the result that they would rather violate the principles of truth than contradict the words of their teachers. That our scholarship of today is beclouded, and our writings unintelligible, is due to the dominance of these special schools.[75]

The scientific method, Ku concluded, which encourages scholars "to draw their materials directly from ascertainable data," would put an end to the inimical influence of schools. In these passages, Ku almost identified deductive reasoning with prejudice, or tendentiousness; while science, or the scientific method, was a force capable of liberating the scholar from these evils.

Fu Ssu-nien, writing in the *New Youth* in 1918, was in full agreement with Ku as he contrasted science (*k'o-hsüeh*) and the scholarship of schools (*chia hsüeh*). "The former," he said, "takes scholarship as the unit, the latter takes the man as the unit." [76] This was one of the basic problems with traditional scholarship, Fu wrote, and related to it were the contemporary needs in scholarship for individual spirit and for freedom from enslave-

74. From Ku's unpublished *Ch'ing-tai chu-shu k'ao* [A Study of Ch'ing Scholarship], composed ca. 1915, cited by Ku in *ACH*, p. 58.

75. *Ibid.*, pp. 58–59.

76. "Chung-kuo hsüeh-shu ssu-hsiang chia chih chi-pen wu-miu" [Several Basic Errors of Chinese Scholars and Thinkers], *Hsin ch'ing-nien* [New Youth], IV:4 (April 15, 1918); reprinted in *FSNHC*, I, 26.

ment to the past and to the *Tao T'ung*. In addition, the previous dominance of schools, he argued, produced the contemporary need for adaptability to time and place instead of presumptuous claims to universal suitability. And finally, there was the need to do away with the schools' preoccupation with practical learning.[77]

Following the lead of Ku and Fu Ssu-nien, the National Studies scholars contrasted the beneficent force of scientific method with the evils of the Methodologies of the Schools. They hoped to supplant the latter with the former. Methodologies of the Schools, a diffuse concept, referred to the style, the specialty, and the scholarly tradition of a school which had been formed over generations by master and disciples.[78] A school of scholarship thus epitomized itself in its method.

Various contributors to National Studies had their own similar feelings on this matter. Fung Yu-lan reiterated earlier ideas when he wrote the following in regard to his specialty of philosophy:

> [Sung and Ch'ing] philosophy can be said to have developed a methodology when it discussed what it called 'the method of conducting study.' This method, however, was not primarily for the seeking of knowledge but rather for self-cultivation; it was not for the search of truth, but for the search of good.[79]

Similarly, Ch'ien Hsüan-t'ung wrote in the preface to his edition of K'ang Yu-wei's *The False Classics of the New School* that

> From this time forward, when we interpret the Classics, we must make our target the [attitude] of 'seek truth.' And we must absolutely throw out the divisiveness and cliquishness [inherent in the concepts of] The Master's Teachings (*shih-shuo*) and Methodologies of the Schools.[80]

77. *Ibid.*, pp. 28–34.

78. For example, see the definitions in the *Tzu Hai* dictionary, 2 vols. (Shanghai, 1948), I, 420.

79. Fung Yu-lan, *A History of Chinese Philosophy*, 2 vols. (Princeton, 1953), I, 1–2.

80. See Ch'ien's "Chung lün chin Chin Ku Wen-hsüeh wen-t'i" [On the Contemporary New Text–Old Text Question], (Peking, 1956; 1st ed., 1929 [Shanghai?]), p. 462; also see *KSP*, I, (March 23, 1921), 30.

In the influential thought of Chang Hsüeh-ch'eng, whose work was well known to the National Studies scholars, this concept had earlier been developed to an elaborate degree of complexity and significance. According to Chang:

> The work of the bibliographer is the basis of all criticism. His procedure . . . must be to assign correctly each piece of writing to the school (*chia*, 'family') to which it belongs, tracing each school back to its beginnings in the [ancient] Chou political order, and identifying the 'method' or discipline to which each type of writing should adhere.[81]

Chang contended that "the fact that *chia-fa* is not clear is the reason for the continual decline of writing." [82]

For Chang Hsüeh-ch'eng, Methodologies of the Schools attained a metaphysical significance. They embodied the essentials of each school of the Golden Age, and if preserved properly, they would convey to posterity the values of the Golden Age. They became the paradigms after which scholars were to model themselves and through which they could commune with and perpetuate eternal values (the *Tao*). Thus where Methodologies of the Schools perpetuated, scientific method corroded and dissolved. Chang Hsüeh-ch'eng sought to rescue the traditional authority of the Classics and the *Tao* from obscurity. For Ku Chieh-kang, as it was said for Hu Shih, "science demanded two things, correction of authority and release from authority." [83] In addition, Methodologies of the Schools were paradigmatic, but scientific method was concerned with process. Chang Hsüeh-ch'eng primarily sought out basic forms and archetypes, not evolutionary processes and change: Chang searched for the timeless authorities; National Studies invoked the moving authority of 'the times.' National Studies associated the Methodologies of the Schools with deductive thinking and authoritarianism, scientific method with empiricism and the liberation of the intellect. It was because of all these connotations of 'science'

81. David Nivison, *The Life and Thought of Chang Hsüeh-ch'eng* (Stanford, 1966), p. 64.
82. Cited in *ibid.*
83. *CCMF,* III, chap. 2.

and 'methodology' that they came to have such great significance for National Studies. Not only did the terms symbolize the severance of modern intellectuals from traditional values, they were considered to be the chief instruments for completing that separation.

The End of National Studies

National Studies was sensitive about its identity, for its adherents, like those of National Essence, were constantly open to criticism from young intellectuals who felt that their work was inimical to modern tendencies. The kind of criticism leveled at National Studies suggests that it never fully made its case, and indeed never fully came to terms with its own identity. This no doubt accounts in large part for the abandonment of the idea of National Studies by the end of the 1920s.

A typical critique of National Studies contended that it simply was not scientific, and that it was virtually anti-scientific where it relied on the textual-critical techniques of the Ch'ing scholars, a group which was said to be quite irrelevant to the twentieth century.[84] "National Studies," went the criticism, "wants to raise the fire of the good old days out of dead ashes; and wants to recruit followers by playing on blind patriotism." If the National Essence school is called "pure talk" (*ch'ing t'an*), a critic concluded, then National Studies is "pure talk's pure talk." [85] Kuo Mo-jo, a literary radical and sometime historian of antiquity himself, found the National Studies scholars overbearing and inconsiderate of individual needs to follow wherever conscience leads; he too thought that the propaganda for the movement and the recruitment techniques were contrary to the current values of individualism.[86]

The poet Cheng Chen-to, an iconoclast and innovator, found little to appreciate in National Studies, despite the fact that from

84. Ch'eng Fang-wu, "Kuo-hsüeh yün-t'ung te wo chien" [My View of the National Studies Movement], *Ch'uang-tsao chou-pao* [Creation], no. 28 (Nov. 1922).

85. *Ibid.*

86. Kuo Mo-jo, "Cheng-li kuo-ku te p'ing-chia" [A Critique of the Reorganization of the National Heritage], *Ch'uang-tsao chou-pao,* no. 36 (Jan. 13, 1924).

our point of view he certainly does seem to have shared the fundamental values and perspectives of Hu Shih and Ku Chieh-kang. In 1928, Cheng wrote a virulent attack on National Studies in which he differentiated scholars in that school from *real* scientists who studied, through various disciplines, local variations of universal scientific problems (for example, Chinese botany, or the development of astronomy in China). Cheng reminded his readers that National Studies was not a new movement, but rather one that represented the vestiges of a long evolution of the scholar class from earliest times. This class was from the outset a servant of the ruling group, and later, when the literati divided into groups of specialists (on law, pedagogy, etc.), they still remained an adjunct of the gentry (*shih-ta-fu*), the ruling group of more recent times. Cheng attempted to discredit the current National Studies scholars as direct descendents of this gentry class, and he excoriated them for wasting precious energies needed by the nation. Through its "seduction of youth," Cheng charged, National Studies was actually preventing progress and the advance of the nation, for in its involvement with the past it forgot where it was in time and lost sight of contemporary needs and desires. Finally, Cheng wrote that National Studies was a great impediment to the absorption of Western culture and science. "If you are going to compile this *ssu-pu* and that *ssu-pu*," he railed, then why not a *ssu-pu* of Western science; why not set up institutes and libraries for Western learning? [87]

Nor did National Studies escape criticism from its own. Hu Shih's former pupil, Ho Ping-sun, for example, joined the chorus at the end of the twenties.[88] As a disciple of Robinson, Ho did not deny the need to study China's past, but he objected to the confusion and the lack of specialization of National Studies, which he said resulted in its unscientific and even anti-scientific nature. Ho Ping-sun voiced his concern over the ad-

87. Cheng Chen-to "Ch'ieh-man t'an so-wei kuo-hsüeh" [Not So Fast with This Talk About National Studies], *Hsiao-shuo yüeh-pao,* no. 30 (Dec. 1928), pp. 8–13.

88. Ho Ping-sun, "Lün so-wei kuo-hsüeh" [On the So-called National Studies], *ibid.,* no. 20 (1928).

vanced quality of Western studies of China carried on by Pelliot, Anderson, and Cordier, and he feared that Chinese scholars could not match them if scholarship continued to follow the path of National Studies. Ho said that the idea of National Studies raised in him the same unpleasant feeling as the idea of 'Sinology' or 'Egyptology'—that is, the feeling of dealing with a dead civilization. The first step to take was to get Chinese scholarship beyond the provincialism of National Studies and into the mainstream of the scholarly community of the world.

When these themes were picked up and embroidered by Fu Ssu-nien himself, it marked the effective end of National Studies as a movement, and the concept soon dropped out of use by the group that had employed it as their rallying point for almost a decade. In the first issue of the journal of the Academia Sinica's Historical and Philological Research Institute, newly founded in 1928, Fu also expressed his personal offense at the patronizing implications of the Westerners' 'Sinology' (which he too compared to Egyptology), and cited the need for Chinese to study their own culture well enough at least to rival, if not supplant, Western scholarship.[89] National Studies, he said, had become merely a euphemism for a "reformed preserve-the-old clique," and it was too confining and provincial. The study of China must move toward universal methodologies and disciplines and must encompass more than history, philology, and folklore, Fu said; furthermore, mathematics, astronomy, and other sciences must be studied in their Chinese contexts.

Fu Ssu-nien's by-then-familiar call to get beyond National Studies contained programs and guidelines that were, for the most part, virtually identical with those that Hu Shih, Ku Chieh-kang (and Fu Ssu-nien) had proposed all along. There was the same emphasis on the use of new data and auxiliary social-scientific disciplines in historical research; and there was the same encouragement to take up the legacy of eighteenth-century Ch'ing scholarship. The Academia Sinica's Historical and Phil-

89. "Li-shih yü-yen-chiu so kung-tso chih chih-ch'u" [The Meaning of the Work of the Historical and Philological Research Institute], *Li-shih yü-yen yen-chiu so chi-k'an* [Bulletin of History and Philology of the Academia Sinica], I:1 (Oct. 1928); reprinted in *FSNHC,* III, 475–487.

ological Research Institute, under the direction of Fu Ssu-nien, was of course the group that he implied would carry on this legacy, and rescue Chinese scholarship from the shortcomings of National Studies.

Years later, Ku Chieh-kang himself tardily aired a simpler but similar criticism of National Studies. In 1936, when Ku participated in the founding of the *Journal of Historical Studies* (*Shih-hsüeh chi-k'an*), he remarked that "National Studies" was not used in the title as it had been in the journal's predecessor, the *Peking Journal of National Studies* (*Pei-ta kuo-hsüeh chi-k'an*), founded by Hu Shih in 1923. He said that National Studies had become "a term too broad in scope and too inclusive in meaning. It included everything Chinese." [90]

National Studies was in large part formulated in response to the conservative tendencies of the National Essence intellectuals, and this was one of the reasons that National Studies was so sprawling an entity and included "everything Chinese." It had been the primary job of National Studies to find a definition, alternative to that of National Essence, of 'Chinese.' When, from 1928, the Nationalist government began to revive with a vengeance the most conservative aspects of National Essence thought, it surely created a reaction within the intelligentsia against all broad programs devoted to the study of traditional society. Even though the Nationalists openly came into conflict with Hu Shih and Ku Chieh-kang, it seems that the latter and their colleagues found it necessary to abandon the idea of National Studies and thereby avoid any confusion with the Nationalists' neo-traditionalism. In 1934, when the great essayist Lu Hsün wrote about those who were "living among antiques," he no doubt referred to these latter-day advocates of National Essence and he had in mind the same referent as well when he sardonically suggested that "Now is the time, of course, to respect the classical language, quote the Classics, display your culture, and read ancient books." [91] It was this kind of intel-

90. *Kuo-hsüeh chi-k'an,* I:1 (April 1936); and see P. K. Yü's "A Note on Historical Periodicals of Twentieth Century China," *Journal of Asian Studies,* XXIII:4 (Aug. 1964), 585.

91. "Now Is the Time," *Selected Works of Lu Hsün* (Peking, 1957), IV, 56–57.

lectual backlash against the newest phase of National Essence that was largely responsible for driving Ku Chieh-kang and his associates out of their broad program to "reorganize the nation's past" and into the narrower confines of Western-type academic disciplines.

III

Chinese Intellectuals and Chinese Society

[Society] does not really love me, it wants merely to use me.—Ku Chieh-kang

Chieh-kang my brother, your suffering, your melancholy, are the suffering and melancholy of the whole class. —Chou Yü-t'ung

The span of National Studies over nearly a decade marked not only the persistence of a set of attitudes toward scholarship and cultural continuity; additionally, the National Studies movement marked one of the longer-lasting outgrowths of the post-1911 intelligentsia's espousal of cultural reform in lieu of political action. In the vehicle of National Studies, the New Culture movement's apolitical tendencies persisted long after the original mood gave way, from the early twenties, to new and often contradictory orientations. Some of the very same people who criticized National Studies for patriotic zeal and for interfering with their own personal modes of intellectual fulfillment were soon advocating intellectual subservience to 'the revolution' or 'the proletariat.' Kuo Mo-jo, for example, had been a leader of a young clique of hedonistic aesthetes advocating "art for art's sake" when he made his criticism of National Studies. But within a few years, he was an outspoken member of a group of Marxist converts whose passion was now turned outward under the banner of "art for the revolution's sake." [1]

All the while, the scholars of the National Studies movement remained fairly consistently devoted to political nonalignment, gradual cultural reform, and the separation of 'knowledge' and 'action.' Maintaining these latter values into the rapidly changing Chinese society of the 1920s engendered severe strains on the self-identity and peace of mind of professional scholars like Ku Chieh-kang. Indeed, it would appear that many Chinese intellectuals (scholars, teachers, students, professional writers, etc.) experienced persistent difficulty in determining their identity in the new China, and remaining comfortable in it.

Over the course of the 1920s, there is visible within the thought of National Studies a reflection of these tensions, especially where considerations of the Chinese scholar were concerned. In the writings of Ku's associates there was a distinct shift in focus from the scholar as individual to the scholar as 'intellectual' whose identity was involved with the identity of a larger class, 'the intelligentsia.' Earlier in the twenties, before the May Thirtieth Movement, when Ku (or Hu Shih or Fu Ssu-nien) wrote about historians or critics whom they took as their predecessors, the words 'intellectual' or 'intellectual class' were seldom used; they were just scholars, or historians, or critics. Moreover, these earlier scholars often were treated, after a romantic fashion, as unique struggling individuals—moral men in an amoral society. It is true that it was one of the ultimate goals of National Studies to demonstrate that these individual scholars of the past constituted a recessive tradition in the history of Chinese thought, one which could provide a foundation for contemporary thought. Nevertheless, there was virtually no indication that these men might be representatives of a social class; on the contrary, what was emphasized was their personal alienation from conventional institutions and, in some instances, their isolation from society in general.

In the second half of the twenties, the value of individualism

1. See C. T. Hsia, *A History of Modern Chinese Fiction 1917–1957* (New Haven, 1961), chap. 4; and T. A. Hsia, *Enigma of the Five Martyrs* (Berkeley and Los Angeles, 1962).

was certainly still a precious one to Ku Chieh-kang and his circle. Individualism, however, was not the focal concept in the discussion anymore; the emphasis was now put on scholars as members of a class with a collective history and a collective identity in the present. Thus, to the question "Are we scholars, teachers, writers, etc., a class?" the answer given was a qualified "Yes." The qualification was based on the argument that 'we' are (alas) all too recognizable descendants of the traditional scholar-official class, and this accounts for whatever class character 'we' have. But the modern intelligentsia were in a state of transition away from the old class identity, yet still not settled into a new one. Ultimately, to questions about the social obligation of the new intelligentsia and about the final resolution of their modern identity, answers were forthcoming from the same direction—that is, from the direction of the Chinese masses.

Frustrated Scholars Ahead of Their Times

Ku Chieh-kang's first major National Studies project was devoted to what Hu Shih had called "closing accounts." With the latter's guidance and advice, Ku, in 1921, began to gather some select writings of earlier Chinese scholars, in order to determine and publicize their usefulness to modern, scientific knowledge about China's past. The material in question was all devoted to the problem of textual or historical criticism and was broadly concerned with the issues of textual reliability (primarily of the Old Text Classics) basic to research on early Chinese history. The Society for Unadorned Learning published the material in a series of short essays or small anthologies which Ku edited, punctuated, and provided with explanatory prefaces and commentary.

In most cases, the contents of the series were little-known critical studies of some important aspect of classical scholarship, and the authors included in the series usually had been till then as obscure as their work. The introductory essays, written by Ku or one of his colleagues, suggested that the basic purpose of the series was to resuscitate the work of earlier "doubters of antiquity"—that is, scholars who challenged orthodox interpretations of the Classics and even doubted the authenticity of texts in the canon, claiming that they were spurious. (Hence the title of the series: *A Symposium on Critiques of Spurious* [*Classical*] *Literature* [*Pien-wei ts'ung k'an*].) It seems that the unorthodox attitudes of these earlier challengers were to serve as precedents for National Studies, and their methodology was to serve as a prototype. For our present discussion of Chinese intellectuals, the nontechnical evaluations of these early scholars, provided in the prefatory essays, are most pertinent. These essays followed a distinct pattern and were organized around the theme of the frustrated scholar; and in Ku Chieh-kang's case, at least, there was a tendency to identify with the social plight of that scholar.

The model for the frustrated scholars depicted in the *Symposium* was provided by Hu Shih's biographic sketches of the maverick literary critic Chin Sheng-t'an (1627–1662). In Hu Shih's studies of popular Chinese novels, Hu acknowledged the fact that he was drawing heavily on the previous work of this scholar and bringing it to fruition in his own scholarship. Hu's study of the popular novel *Water Margin* (*Shui-hu chuan*) provided him with the occasion to introduce Chin Sheng-t'an as a most unusual man for his era, a man who manifested considerable daring by claiming for *Water Margin* the same literary merit as such ancient greats of historical literature as the *Shih-chi* and *Kuo-tse*.[2] And Chin dared to say, as well, that such writers as Shih Nai-an (one of the creators of *Water Margin*) should have the same rank in literary history as the philosopher Chuang Tzu, the poet Ch'u Yüan, and the historians Ssu-ma Ch'ien and Tu Yu. "How perspicacious," Hu Shih rhapsodized; "how brave!" [3]

Thus the first step in creating this heroic model was to find a scholar who challenged orthodox ideas (in this case he dared to compare novels—traditionally considered a lesser form of literature—to the old masters, and to give them serious scholarly attention). Next it was demonstrated that at best society ignored this creative genius, and in some cases persecuted him. Then it

2. Hu Shih, "*Shui-hu chuan* k'ao-cheng" [Textual Criticism of *Water Margin*], *HSWT*, III (dated July 1920), p. 81.
3. *Ibid.*

was shown how the scholar's thought was relevant for the modern era, how he anticipated contemporary ideas, and to what degree his methodology was scientific. In the work of Chin Sheng-t'an, Hu Shih implied, the twentieth-century Vernacular Literature movement was foreshadowed.

At this point in the celebration of the culture hero, the writer urged his readers to master this scholar's ideas, build on them, and then go beyond them. The standard coda was a caveat: Readers were warned that the hero was, in the last analysis, a "man of his times," and hence of limited use to moderns. "Use him" was the exhortation—"but do not imitate him." [4]

CHENG CH'IAO: TRAGIC EXEMPLAR

Following Hu Shih's model, the first scholar to receive Ku Chieh-kang's attention was the Sung historian Cheng Ch'iao (1104–1162), whose work was probably brought to Ku's attention by Chang Hsüeh-ch'eng's admiration.[5] Before taking Cheng's critical studies of the *Book of Odes* and its commentaries into the *Symposium* series, Ku had lavished considerable attention on a comprehensive bibliography of his writings, as well as a chronological biography. In the latter, Ku introduced the subject by observing that Cheng

> was an outstanding figure in the Chinese world of learning, which is especially true when we consider that he had to overcome the conservatism and deficiencies of the world in his search for truth.[6]

That Cheng Ch'iao did not have great influence, Ku reasoned, was because Cheng and his ideas were so unusual:

> [Cheng's contemporaries] either said of him that he made arbitrary decisions, or fabrications, or that his scholarship was eccentric and distorted, crude and coarse, or that he was pressing for advancement in government service.[7]

4. *Ibid.*, pp. 82–85.
5. "Cheng Ch'iao chuan" [Biography of Cheng Ch'iao], *Kuo-hsüeh chi-k'an* [Journal of National Studies], I:2 (1923).
6. *Ibid.*, p. 309.
7. *Ibid.*

No one, Ku lamented, perceived Cheng's real spirit, and the true nature of his learning, and therefore he was branded with an evil reputation. According to Ku, Chang Hsüeh-ch'eng was the first to be aware of Cheng's accomplishment; and ever since, Cheng's status as a scholar had been rising.[8]

Ku attempted to depict a tragic existence saturated with *sturm und drang,* torn by the conflict between 'progressive,' 'scientific' scholarship and an effete, tradition-bound society:

> Society had not the least understanding of him, and society gave him not the least succor. . . . He endured poverty and he endured sickness, . . . and he had the spirit that [claimed] 'all achievements of literature came from man, not from heaven.' [9]

Cheng suffered politically, Ku reminded the reader, even though "he was only a student of antiquity and a scientist—[and even though] he assuredly had no collisions with contemporary politicians." Yet, Cheng was impeached twice by Imperial Censors, for reasons which are not recorded. Ku speculated that Cheng probably suffered for "arguing with great perversity against the ancient sages." On the other hand, Cheng purposely sought out an insignificant political position in order to be able to devote himself to his studies, "but others merely ridiculed his lack of desire for superior attainments [in status]." [10]

8. In David Nivison's *The Life and Thought of Chang Hsüeh-ch'eng* (Stanford, 1966), Cheng Ch'iao is a prominent concern. For example, Nivison paraphrases and quotes Chang to the effect that "so inverted have standards become that when a true historical genius does appear, such as Cheng Ch'iao in the Sung, a man who 'loves learning, thinks deeply, and is able to make his own approach to the ancients . . . and displays a judgment that is uniquely his own,' he is everywhere reviled" (p. 218).

Nivison's next comment is interesting as a Western scholar's evaluation of Cheng Ch'iao: "This evaluation of Cheng seems strange, for the *T'ung Chih,* aside from its twenty monographs . . . which it has been fashionable to praise, is so far from displaying the original genius Chang saw in it that its chief value today is in the correcting of now corrupt texts in the pre-Sung Standard Histories, of which it is in the main a meticulously faithful copy. But Chang is less interested in the facts than in his opinion that true history is the work of genius—the product of an intelligence that is able to grasp directly the 'significance of historical material' " (p. 218).

9. "Cheng Ch'iao chuan," pp. 330–331.

10. *Ibid.*

What most endeared Cheng Ch'iao to Ku Chieh-kang was that many of Cheng's ideas were directed at "overthrowing the authority of the *sages* and the traditions of the Confucianists." [11] For example, Cheng conflicted with prevailing orthodoxies in not considering the ancient *Spring and Autumn Annals* as a didactic "praise and blame" (*pao p'ien*) document, but rather as a record (*shih-lu*) of the history of political institutions.[12] Most deplorable to Cheng were the Han Confucian commentaries to the *Spring and Autumn Annals* and the *Odes*, which distorted their fundamental substance for doctrinal reasons.

For a candid moment, Ku Chieh-kang admitted that Cheng's "general observations [on the above subjects] were not profound." But after all, Ku was quick to add, Cheng did have the great task of overthrowing and reevaluating the commentaries on the Classics in order to reveal the true visages of the texts which the Confucianists had obscured.[13]

Ku concluded his biography of Cheng Ch'iao eulogistically:

> Society turned an icy visage toward him, but he, by himself, and in the most bitter of circumstances, developed his genius to the full! When we regard him now, we can only see a complete and ample spirit. His spirit will not die! [14]

It is not evident exactly why Ku Chieh-kang felt such a close affinity to Cheng Ch'iao, but that he did is clear in the *Autobiography*:

> Had I been born a few years earlier, in a society in which rational criticism was forbidden, or in which there was no clearly defined historical method, I should have been listed with that class of pioneers whom the public ever regards as fools—men like Liu Chih-chi and Cheng Ch'iao.[15]

11. "Cheng Ch'iao chu-shu k'ao [A Study of the Oeuvre of Cheng Ch'iao], *Kuo-hsüeh chi-k'an,* I:1 (1923), 367.

12. *Ibid.,* and "Cheng Ch'iao chuan," p. 321.

13. "Cheng Ch'iao chuan," p. 321.

14. *Ibid.,* p. 331.

15. *ACH,* p. 153. Liu Chih-chi (661–721) was a historical critic of considerable renown. Ku's reference to him here seems rather less pointed than the reference to Cheng Ch'iao, because Ku gave no special attention to Liu's work, and this is one of the few occasions when Liu's name crops up in Ku's writing.

Some of the scholars included in the *Symposium* were of less personal appeal to Ku, and his apologias for their work sometimes ran into difficulties. The publication devoted to the Ming textual critic Sung Lien (1310–1358) was a case in point.[16] Sung Lien was important to Ku because of his critiques of texts which embodied the thought of the major classical philosophers. Equally important, Sung Lien was a vital link between the Sung textual critics, such as Kao Ssu-sun and Huang Chen, and later critics such as Hu Ying-lin (1551–1618) and Yao Chi-heng (1647–1715?). The latter two were also included in the series. With the work of such scholars, Ku hoped to illustrate, among other things, a continuous tradition of critical scholarship with which to identify modern criticism.

Sung's historical importance notwithstanding, Ku found it necessary to apologize for including Sung in the lineup, and he had to admit that Sung's work was full of faults. In his preface to Sung's *A Critique of the Philosophers* (*Chu tzu pien*), Ku wrote that Sung's prejudices and ineptitudes did make much of his thought worthless, and that many of Sung's attitudes were very much in the spirit of (that bogeyman) Tung Chung-shu. What is more, Ku added,

> [Sung's] attitudes obscure and hobble; his textual-critical technique is superficial in many places; he uses good and evil, merit or demerit [that is, ethical standards] for determining the genuineness or spuriousness of a text.[17]

Anticipating his reader, Ku asked, "If Sung is a guardian of the *Tao*, and superficial in his contributions to contemporary thought, why do we reprint him?" "To shame contemporary scholars," was the answer. Ku said that in spite of his limited training, Sung Lien's contributions were fresh compared to the old-fashioned scholarship still practiced in China.

Ku ended his apologia for Sung Lien by asking his colleagues to compare their work to their predecessors' accomplishments in earlier centuries. Leaning heavily on the Progressive Historical point of view, Ku concluded, generously, that

16. Ming, Sung Lien, *Chu tzu pien* [A Critique of the Philosophers, by Sung Lien of the Ming] (Shanghai, 1928). Ku's preface is dated 1926.

17. *Ibid.*

If we see their errors, we must not think that it is because we are more perspicacious than they. It is just that our circumstances are better.

We must thank our predecessors for sustaining the degree of skepticism that they had—a skepticism which gradually trickled down to us, and upon which we can now build.[18]

TS'UI SHU: PATRON SAINT

Of all the obscure scholars that Ku resuscitated in the *Symposium,* none had been more obscure than Ts'ui Shu, nor did any receive more lavish treatment and studied reverence. Ts'ui was a perfect subject for the scholar's hall of fame because of the range and brilliance of his critical thought, his charming style of writing, and, of course, his mistreatment by the Chinese scholar-official world.

The pattern of the Ts'ui Shu revival was strikingly similar to that of Cheng Ch'iao. Hu Shih had apparently learned of Ts'ui, and seen his potential use, in the writings of Chang Hsüeh-ch'eng.[19] While Ku Chieh-kang was immersed in his project of collating and punctuating Ts'ui's collected works, Hu introduced the new patron saint of the modern antiquity-doubters in his 1923 article, suggestively entitled "Ts'ui Shu, Scientific Ancient Historian."

While Hu Shih's eulogy of Ts'ui followed the usual pattern, there was one notable issue which he pressed. In the process of making a general evaluation of Ts'ui, Hu Shih tried to 'place' him in relationship to two dominant scholarly traditions—the Han Hsüeh, or school of Han Learning, in the Ch'ing, and the Sung school in the Sung dynasty. Hu Shih tried to demonstrate here that, essentially, there was little difference between the two traditions. What bound the two was their common source in the textual research tools and concepts first developed by Chu Hsi. "Han Learning," Hu argued, is just a meaningless, invidious label invented by the Confucianists of Ch'ing to differentiate themselves from the Sung Confucianists.[20] This underlying sim-

18. *Ibid.*

19. See Hu's article, "K'o-hsüeh te ku-shih chia Ts'ui Shu" [Ts'ui Shu, Scientific Ancient Historian], *Kuo-hsüeh chi-k'an,* I:2 (April 1923), 302.

20. *Ibid.,* p. 288.

ilarity of the two traditions explained the resemblance of the scholarship of Ts'ui Shu, who venerated Chu Hsi, to that of Tai Chen and Mao Chi-ling, who abhorred Chu Hsi. Actually "they all draw near Chu Hsi," Hu insisted, "and draw away from Mao Kung and Cheng Hsuan." [21] But what made Ts'ui Shu superior to many of the Han Learning scholars, and what made him a 'scientist,' according to Hu, was the fact that in his textual studies of the Confucian Classics, Ts'ui's methodology called for a direct investigation of the sources, by-passing the Han commentaries and the opinions of the "Hundred Schools" as well.[22]

What Hu Shih was trying to do here was similar to what underlay Ku's study of Sung Lien: they were artfully discovering in Chinese scholarship a convention of 'scientific' protest, as it were. Using a ploy which I shall call legitimacy-by-association, Hu Shih was attempting in the above argument to get around Ts'ui Shu's ineffectualness in his own day by associating him with Chu Hsi and the chief schools that followed him.

Ku Chieh-kang spent much of his formal working time between 1921 and 1925 assembling the work of Ts'ui Shu and preparing it for a 'popular' audience through such devices as punctuation and indexes.[23] After numerous delays, the seven-volume work was finally published in 1936 under Ku's editorship.[24] It is by far the most important accomplishment of the *Symposium* series, and the single body of thought most influential on Ku Chieh-kang's studies of antiquity.[25]

In the *Autobiography*, Ku's cautious identification with Ts'ui Shu is evident: "It never occurred to me that Ts'ui Shu and I," he wrote, "were both guilty of the same shortcomings—that is to say, carrying our questions to extremes of detail." [26] Ku said that his pride was slightly deflated when he discovered that Ts'ui Shu had anticipated his studies of spurious literature. He was

21. *Ibid.*
22. *Ibid.*
23. *Ts'ui Tung-pi i-shu* [The Collected Works of Ts'ui Shu]—hereinafter referred to as *TTPIS*—7 vols. (Peking, 1936), I, 1–2; also see *ACH*, pp. 82, 104.
24. See n. 23, above.
25. See Part Three, below, for details.
26. *ACH*, p. 83.

then left in the ambiguous position of appreciating Ts'ui's greatness while recognizing the severe limitations of his work ("excessive faith in the Classics and the doctrines of Confucius and Mencius"). Yet he felt it unfair to reproach Ts'ui Shu for this, since he had been raised in a home imbued with the prevailing modes of thought and belief. The duty of modern Chinese, Ku said, was to go a step beyond Ts'ui Shu, overthrow his prejudices, and reconstruct classical studies on a new foundation.[27] Ku felt obliged to write in the *Autobiography* that, in spite of his praise of scholars like Ts'ui Shu and Cheng Ch'iao, he was certainly not their disciple, nor did he bear them any special reverence.[28] Be that as it may, Ku was nevertheless their most diligent and outspoken exponent; and he did bear them a special debt for their usefulness to the causes of National Studies.

J. R. Levenson has said of the thought of Tai Chen (1724–1777), a scholar who was also highly celebrated during the 1920s, that the "historical importance of [his ideas] really consists in their historical unimportance." [29] The same applies to the other scholars who received the attention of Ku Chieh-kang and Hu Shih in the *Symposium* series. It was partially because of their unimportance in their own day that these scholars served the needs of National Studies so well. They provided the first means for Ku Chieh-kang and his colleagues to be modern and remain Chinese. Cheng Ch'iao, Ts'ui Shu, and all the rest were doubtless part of China's past; but, it was repeatedly emphasized, they were not part of that intellectual tradition that shaped China's moribund Confucian tradition. Because they were isolated, these scholars were safe from the taint of the *main* tradition—the tradition of Tung Chung-shu, and of the 'schools.'

The *Symposium* series set out to create an alternative intellectual tradition, outside of and in conflict with the tradition that was to be rejected. The heritage of proto-scientists was meant to provide *Chinese* precedents for National Studies innovations in order that Ku and his colleagues might avoid the need

27. *Ibid.*

28. *Ibid.*, p. 157.

29. J. R. Levenson, "Historical Significance," *Diogenes*, no. 32 (Winter 1960), p. 22.

to imitate the West. Here was one early response to Hu Shih's call for some indigenous intellectual stock on which contemporary thought could be grafted. Here National Studies saw a manipulable heritage, a filiation, and a source of continuity between old China and new. "It dawned on me," Ku wrote,

> that long before my time, there had existed an unbroken line of critical scholars, who had attacked spurious elements in Chinese literature. But the credulity of former scholars toward ancient writings was so strong, that they not only ignored the critics but often employed forcible methods to suppress them, with the result that their labors were almost nullified.[30]

A Modern Scholar's Frustration

Ku Chieh-kang identified with the earlier scholars not only because of the subjects they studied or the methodology they employed; the personal discontent he himself experienced in the 1920s was a source of closer emotional ties with the perennial suffering (in his telling) of Chinese intellectuals who dared to be independent and to seek truth regardless of political or social considerations. The plight of the Chinese academic community during the twenties was indeed troubled. Financial disability, bloody political clashes, censorship, and attempts at outright control by the government all made the so-called ivory tower one of the last places to seek escape from the tumult and anxiety of the surrounding world.

During the years when Ku was initiating the *Symposium*, the Peking University academic community was in a constant state of tension with the central government. In 1920 and again the next year, Hu Shih and a number of other professors formally expressed their frustration and displeasure with the Peking government's failure to move in the direction of "true republicanism," and with the tyrannous behavior of the various political parties.[31]

Added to this was the first of a long series of educational strikes directed against the financial abuse of teachers by the

30. *ACH*, p. 75.
31. *MFM*, pp. 239, 240.

central government: from December 4, 1919, to June 1920, Peking teachers struck because the central bank refused to redeem paper money given to them for salaries; eighty percent of their salaries had been paid to them in highly unstable currency. In March of the next year, professors in higher education struck because the government had not financed the schools for over three months.[32] Ku Chieh-kang recalled that classes at Peking University were at first discontinued "because of financial embarrassment," and then indefinitely postponed because of the strikes.[33] This all culminated in the June Third Movement of 1921—a massive demonstration in which thousands of students, supported and led by venerable scholars like Ma Hsü-lun, marched on the residence of the President of the Republic, Hsü Shih-ch'ang, to demand back pay and "independence of educational financing from direct government control." [34] The financial difficulties of which Ku Chieh-kang constantly complained in the *Autobiography* were thus endemic throughout the entire academic community.[35]

Ku Chieh-kang was meanwhile trying to support himself with the income from various research and writing assignments found for him by Hu Shih, but he was displeased with all of them. He worked for a time in the Peking University library and then joined the university's newly organized Research Institute for National Studies. In 1921 he accepted a lectureship in Chinese literature in the Preparatory Department of the university, but soon resigned the post.[36]

There were again clashes between the academic community and the Peking government in 1922. In the fall, tensions mounted to such a pitch that the Peking University faculty voted to disassociate itself from the Ministry of Education because of the latter's recent policies on university reorganization. In August, demonstrating students demolished the Peking resi-

32. *Ibid.,* p. 261.

33. *ACH,* pp. 84–85.

34. *BSCS,* pp. 50–51; *MFM,* p. 261.

35. *ACH,* pp. 139, 177, 178–179, 183; and see Ku's preface to *TTPIS,* I, 1.

36. *ACH,* pp. 92–93.

dence of the Minister of Education and caused his resignation —though it is not evident what, if any, policy changes resulted.[37]

Now, again thanks to Hu Shih, Ku financed his research activities with advances from the Commercial Press for a history textbook project (the *Elementary National History* [*Pen kuo shih*]).[38] Ku admittedly found it difficult to cooperate with the press because of his own stubbornness, and after a flareup of temperament, ill health, and family problems, he took a four-month leave of absence from the project, only to quit it altogether after his return in January 1924, on the grounds that he was sacrificing precious time for the company's profit.[39] Just how he managed financially at this time is not clear. His salary from the Institute was apparently small to begin with, but he had accepted his post at the university, he said, willing to make the economic sacrifice out of love for his work. The government still continued to hold back salaries for months at a time and paid, when it did, in fractions. By 1925, Ku said, there was "hardly enough for bare subsistence, to say nothing of a decent living." [40]

By the middle of 1925, the general political chaos in China was escalated to new heights by the eruption of the May Thirtieth Movement. The academic community, students and faculty, took advantage of the general atmosphere of manifest discontent (primarily with the foreign economic hold on China) to express their own frustration and rancor over the academic policies of the central government. Chiang Monlin, a professor and administrator at Peking University at the time, wrote that the teachers in Peking had by this time come to rely on the instrument of the strike to squeeze a fraction of their back salaries from the Ministry of Education.[41] But now the government, rocked by the massive disruption of the whole society, was short of patience and treated demonstrations for salary arrears as if

37. *BSCS,* p. 9.
38. *ACH,* p. 102.
39. *Ibid.,* p. 103.
40. *Ibid.,* p. 177.
41. Chiang Monlin, *Tides from the West; A Chinese Autobiography* (New Haven, 1947), p. 133.

they were attempted *coups d'etat.*[42] In September 1925 the *North China Herald* reported that a group of "radical" Peking University professors, under the leadership of Li Shih-tseng, had just won out over the Hu Shih "moderates" and declared for independence from the government.[43] There was no follow-up story on this event, and it is not evident just how it affected the university. Within a few months, however, such resolutions were to mean little: Peking was a battleground, and the Peking University community was in a state of dissolution.

As he completed editing the first volume of the *Critiques,* in the midst of this remarkable scene, Ku Chieh-kang's mood was somber and self-pitying. To work out his confused feelings, he wrote and then published an introspective, lyrical essay called "Insomnia." With great candor, he attempted to express his attitudes toward the repulsive demands that society seemed to be making of him, and his disillusionment with the society itself. Ku felt that the basis of his malaise was his lack of concern for the problems of 'life' and his narrow preoccupation with personal satisfaction through his work. He said that selfless service to society was not his cup of tea, and that he would not be harnessed on any account. Though he did not have an aristocratic background, and therefore had to earn his living, it did not follow, he said, that he must yield to social pressures and do something contrary to his desire to be a scholar. At one point in the essay, Ku wrote that scholarship was his means of self-realization; at another, that it was "a chloroform used to escape melancholy, . . . a by-product of depression." In any case, "a life of pure scholarship is an illusory desire in contemporary China," he lamented; "but then, in contemporary China, it is only in illusion that one can find any personal satisfaction." [44]

The *Autobiography* was written from January to April of 1926, and in it the mood of "Insomnia" did not improve. Though the *Autobiography* was primarily a catalogue of Ku's

42. *Ibid.,* pp. 133–134.

43. *North China Herald* (Sept. 5, 1925), p. 291.

44. "Pu mei" [Insomnia] in *Wo-men te liu yüeh* [Our Sixth Month] (Shanghai, 1925).

scholarly accomplishments to date, and a sketch of the social background of those accomplishments, it was more importantly a *cri de coeur* that wanted to say publicly that China was doing itself ill by making life difficult for its promising young intellectuals. "[Society] does not really love me," he wrote, "it wants merely to use me." [45]

Before Ku finished the *Autobiography*, there exploded in Peking yet another 'incident,' more ferocious than the previous ones involving the academic community and more serious in its repercussions. On March 18, 1926, a large group of students demonstrated before the residence of Tuan Ch'i-jui (who was then Chief Executive of the Provisional Government), protesting his pusillanimity in the handling of an international dispute about a reputed Chinese violation of the Boxer Protocol.[46] The police opened fire on the crowd, claiming hundreds of victims and killing many.[47] The Peking intellectual world was shocked and disgusted. Their feelings were perhaps best expressed by Lu Hsün in his essay "More Roses Without Bloom," [48] and by Chou Tso-jen in his sardonic article "The Ways of Dying," [49] both written in memory of the dead students and in protest against the intolerable relations between the political and academic communities. These emotions underlay the breakup and diaspora of the Peking University faculty in 1926.

Up to this date, Peking University had been at the center of scholarship and revolution. This distinction, which it had main-

45. *ACH,* p. 174.

46. Dwight Edwards' account in his *Yenching University* (New York, 1959): "In the course of a struggle between rival military groups, there had been a violation of the Protocol of 1901, signed after the Boxer uprising, and stipulating that hereafter, access to Peking from the sea must always be kept open to avoid a repetition of the 1900 siege. The eight foreign nations which were parties to this treaty delivered an ultimatum insisting that this interference must cease. The Chinese Provisional Government made a reply which the students thought was too weak; so they protested in the hope of inducing the government to take a stronger stand" (p. 148).

47. *Ibid.*

48. Lu Hsün, *Selected Works of Lu Hsün* (Peking), II (1957), 248. Also see his "In Memory of Wei Su-yuan," *ibid.,* IV (1960), 65–70.

49. Chou Tso-jen, "Szu fa" [The Ways of Dying], mimeo reprint (Berkeley, 1960).

tained since the days of the May Fourth Movement, in 1919, now passed from it to other universities and to other sections of the country. In the migration of professors that followed, leaders of important intellectual cliques found new areas of the country to work in. Hu Shih, for example, left for Shanghai, and then spent some time in the United States. Ku Chieh-kang, no longer having any means of subsistence, had to accept a position at Amoy University, though he managed to complete the *Autobiography* and to see the first volume of the *Critiques* through the press before leaving. Anticipating the necessity to leave the capital and regretting his situation for the past half-decade he wrote, at lowest ebb,

> In this land of impoverished people, oppressed by military lawlessness, there are multitudes of promising men who are forced to accept aimless and temporary employment simply to obtain a living —an atmosphere in which it is impossible to foster genuine research. . . . Under such conditions there is nothing left but to restrict my research to the minimum, [though] my life may end in vexation and despair [for doing so].[50]

PERIPATETICS: 1926–1929

As Ku Chieh-kang brought his work in Peking to a close, the entire city was in chaos, thanks to the in-fighting between Warlord Feng Yü-hsiang and his latest adversaries, Wu P'ei-fu and Chang Tso-lin.[51] Ku took up his responsibilities at Amoy in October 1926, shortly after Chiang Kai-shek's Northern Expedition, fighting its way to Nanking from Canton, captured Hankow. Amoy provided little more than an income for Ku; he found it quite an uncomfortable place for a number of reasons. First, Lu Hsün had also accepted a position there, and the two headstrong gentlemen clashed intensely on what seemed some rather petty administrative issues.[52] Lu Hsün complained, for example, that Ku Chieh-kang and other newly-arrived members

50. *ACH,* p. 113.
51. *Ibid.,* pp. 182–183.
52. See Ch'en Meng-chao, *Lu Hsün tsai A-men* [Lu Hsün in Amoy] (Peking, 1955). Also personal letter from Wang Yi-t'ung to author, dated Feb. 7. 1964.

of the "Hu Shih clique" attempted to inundate the university with their influence, to the detriment of Lu Hsün.[53] Lu Hsün left Amoy for Canton and Sun Yat-sen University in January 1927, after teaching at Amoy for only one semester. He said that he quit the position because of financial considerations, not because of his friction with Ku, nor because of any involvement in the student strikes which occurred at Amoy during the winter.[54]

In addition to his clashes with Lu Hsün, Ku found the atmosphere at Amoy uncongenial to his serious efforts to build an interest in folklore studies throughout China. Though folklore research had become an important element in National Studies, the Amoy faculty ridiculed his efforts.[55] In the summer of 1927, Ku also received an invitation to accept a position at Sun Yat-sen University. His decision to accept the offer was accelerated by a new wave of student strikes at Amoy.[56] Going south to Canton, Ku said, was merely being swept along "by the tides of academe"—that is, thanks to the chaos in the north, Sun Yat-sen University was fast becoming an important new center of scholarship.

By the time Ku arrived in Canton, in the fall of 1927, the Kuomintang had already begun to illustrate how it intended to deal with the Communists, its erstwhile ally. On April 12 and 15 of that year, as part of Chiang Kai-shek's general anti-Communist coup, the Canton Kuomintang massacred a considerable number of young Communists and Communist sympathizers. Lu Hsün reported that a number of his students were arrested or killed. "The cruelty of the purges and their aftermath," writes one of Lu Hsün's more reliable biographers, "made 'his hair stand on end' and shattered his faith in the Kuomintang."[57]

53. Ch'en, *Lu Hsün tsai A-men*, p. 39.

54. Lu Hsün, "A Letter Written at Sea" (dated Jan. 16, 1927), *Selected Works*, II, 315.

55. Ku's preface to *Min-ke chia-chi* [Anthology of Folksongs] (Canton, 1928), reprinted in *Min-su* [Folklore]—hereinafter referred to as *MS*—no. 13–14 (1928), pp. 12–13.

56. Hsieh Yün-sheng, preface to *Min-ke chia-chi*, p. 1.

57. Harriet Mills, "Lu Hsün and the Communist Party," *China Quarterly*, no. 4 (Oct.–Dec. 1960), p. 19.

He left Canton for Shanghai even before Ku arrived; however, one of his zealous young camp followers revived the Amoy clash with an intentionally provocative article in a Hankow newspaper.

In this article, Lu Hsün's student (who had followed him from the north to Amoy and Canton) accused Ku Chieh-kang of being the "strategist-advisor" of the Amoy administrators who tried to suppress the student demonstrations there. Accompanying the article was a letter from Lu Hsün to the student, in which Lu Hsün likewise suggested that Ku was responsible for the expulsion of rebellious Amoy students.[58] Weeks later, the newspaper pieces were brought to Ku's attention when they were reprinted in yet another newspaper. Appalled, Ku wrote to Lu Hsün and warned him that he was going to seek redress by way of a libel suit (which, by the way, never materialized). Ku denied the accusations of the article and said that "If I truly have engaged in anti-revolutionary activities, I would willingly accept the death penalty were it given to me!" [59] Further, Ku expressed his interpretation of his clash with Lu Hsün: he thought that Lu Hsün had considered him, in some fashion, unsympathetic to the "principles of the Kuomintang." [60] This was incomprehensible and wrong, Ku said; and he implied that he was every bit as patriotic and revolutionary as Lu Hsün and his student.

The Kuomintang, then, seems to have symbolized for many Chinese intellectuals all hopes for the proper continuation of the revolution. But as the Northern Expedition moved toward Nanking and then Shanghai, its coups and purges began to raise serious doubts. The clash between Lu Hsün and Ku Chieh-

58. Hsieh Yü-sheng, "Lu Hsün hsien-sheng t'o-li Kuang-tung Chung-ta" [Professor Lu Hsün Leaves Canton's Sun Yat-sen University], *Chung-yang jih-pao* [Central Daily News], no. 48 (May 11, 1927); cited in *Lu Hsün ch'uan-chi* [Selected Works of Lu Hsün] (Peking, 1957), IV, 500.

59. *Ibid.*, IV, 50–51.

60. *Ibid.* The *BDRC* (II, 246) says that "Lu Hsün commemorated these incidents by caricaturing Ku as a stammering, red-nosed pedant in his story 'Li-shui' [Controlling the Waters], in which Ku, identified as Niao-t'ou hsien-sheng (Mr. Birdhead, an obscure structural pun on the character for Ku's surname), is represented as arguing against the historicity of Yü the Great."

kang is a vivid illustration of sudden shifts in sentiment away from the Kuomintang. While Ku was swearing loyalty to the revolutionary principles of the Kuomintang, thinking that this was what Lu Hsün was after, Lu Hsün himself, having experienced the recent events in Canton, was well on his way to complete disaffection with the Kuomintang.[61] This disaffection became a generalized phenomenon among many Chinese writers and academics within a few years.

Ku remained at Sun Yat-sen University for two years. In addition to his studies on ancient China, he now found a wide and willing audience for his interests in folklore studies, and his considerable efforts of recent years bore fruit. Under his influence the scattered interest in folk culture, begun years earlier in the north, was revitalized and given a sophisticated intellectual structure in which to grow. Ku successfully encouraged young folklorists to make a specialty of their work, and through his efforts, Sun Yat-sen University sponsored a prolific journal, *Folklore* (*Min-su*), which acted as a polished forum for this new field of research.

Though his involvement in the academic community seems to have been complete and quite successful, Ku was happy to accept a new post, back in Peking, when the opportunity presented itself. He was invited by Fu Ssu-nien to become a charter member of the historical section of the Academia Sinica in 1928, but he refused this offer in order to join the faculty of the recently organized Harvard-Yenching Institute in Peking. About the same time that he began teaching there, in the autumn of 1929, he also assumed a dominant position on the board of the National Academy of Peking (Kuo-li Pei-ching yen-chiu yuan), a research institute which, along with the Academia Sinica, was responsible for the most sophisticated and influential publications on Chinese history.

61. See Mills, "Lu Hsün and the Communist Party," for Lu Hsün's feelings toward the Kuomintang up to mid-1927.

INTELLECTUALS AND THE KUOMINTANG DURING THE LATE TWENTIES

The scholar's life at Yenching was a realization of most of what Ku Chieh-kang had earlier clamored for. There was freedom (because of the administration's policies, as well as the extraterritorial exemption of the university from political interference), and a very respectable salary paid at regular intervals.[62] Ku had ample time to fulfill his teaching obligations and to carry on diverse publishing enterprises. In addition to teaching courses on the intellectual history of the Han dynasty and on the geographical materials in *The Book of Documents* (*Shu-ching*), he was chairman of Yenching's historical research department and, as of December 1930, editor-in-chief of the *Yenching Journal* (*Yen-ching hsüeh-pao*).[63]

However, while Ku enjoyed the independence afforded him by the Harvard-Yenching Institute, the general relations between the academic community and the new Nationalist government deteriorated. At the outset, the problem was the arbitrary and often deadly treatment the Kuomintang dealt out to young students, writers, and artists whom they suspected of Communist activities. Very soon, the clash was direct, as the government began to restructure the educational system according to its own lights. 'Liberal' educational thought and administration (a la Ts'ai Yüan-p'ai) were blamed for "lagging academic standards" and for the student strikes.[64] Education was frankly declared an integral part of party functions, and a standard curriculum for middle schools was introduced. Party Doctrine was allotted its own place in Social Studies, and great emphasis was placed on science and engineering in higher education. In order

62. Professor Kenneth (K'uan-sheng) Ch'en, who was a Yenching student of Ku's in the early 1930s, describes the salary for a full professor like Ku Chieh-kang as very adequate to support a family and to stock a personal research library. (Interview with author, Berkeley, Aug. 1965). Dwight Edwards concurs (*Yenching University* (n. 46, above), p. 154).

63. Ku was on the editorial board of the journal from issue no. 6 (Dec. 1927) to issue no. 20 (Dec. 1936).

64. T'ang Leang-li, *Reconstruction in China* (Shanghai, 1935), pp. 73 ff.; cited in Y. C. Wang, "Intellectuals and Society in China, 1860–1949," *Comparative Studies in Society and History*, III:4 (July 1961), 413.

to increase enrollment in the latter fields, faculties of arts and social sciences were not permitted to have more students than faculties of science and engineering.[65]

Ts'ai Yüan-p'ei's policy of educational independence from the political structure, promulgated in 1917, seemed to have been repudiated, once and for all. In April 1929, the Third Party Congress of the Kuomintang formally declared its educational aims (through its propaganda department, on which no professional educators sat).[66] The educational community was severely criticized by party leaders for removing education so far from the people's daily lives, for failing to develop physically and morally healthy students, and for neglecting "to promote the development of production through the application of practical sciences." [67]

The fear that was now abroad among the former New Culturalists was summarized by Chou Tso-jen: "For the last six years," he wrote in 1927,

> I have daily feared the advent of the reactionary movement, and now it has come at last. . . . What is this reaction? It need not be 'conserve the old and restore the ancient'; it applies to all bullying for conformity of thought. The extermination of the Reds in the north goes without saying; the purge in the south is also one of the kinds of reaction that I fear, because it condemns not only crimes of action, but also crimes of thought; to execute a person for his ideas is I feel the most terrible thing.[68]

Shortly thereafter, Hu Shih was doing his best to confront the Kuomintang through his bitter criticism of its politics and its intellectual tendencies. In 1929, he published an iconoclastic article in which he criticized the political elitism of Sun Yat-sen's thought and its frightful ambiguity.[69] As a result, a branch

65. Wang, "Intellectuals," pp. 413–414.

66. A. B. Linden, "Politics and Education in Nationalist China," *Journal of Asian Studies,* XXVII:4 (Aug. 1968), 775.

67. *Ibid.*

68. Translated in D. E. Pollard, "Chou Tso-jen and Cultivating One's Garden," *Asia Major,* XI, part 2 (Dec. 1965), 197.

69. Jerome Grieder, "Hu Shih and Liberalism: A Chapter in the Intellectual Modernization of China, 1917–1930," doctoral thesis (Harvard University, 1963), pp. 329–334.

of the Kuomintang censured Hu Shih and recommended him for punishment for insulting Sun Yat-sen and his ideology. Hu Shih had "violated the limits of scholarly discussion." [70] Ignoring the party's threats, Hu Shih went on to write the devastating article in which he traced the conservative tendencies of the Kuomintang over the past years and then branded the party "reactionary," pure and simple.[71] The overall result of the literary revolution of the twenties, Hu Shih wrote, should have been liberation of the intellect; but due to the struggle of the Kuomintang against the Chinese Communist party, literature and thought had lost all of its spontaneity—"an absolutely despotic situation." [72]

Not only were newspapers repressed when they disagreed with Kuomintang party-line, Hu Shih said, but honest, competent works of scholarship were also subject to the whim of the party.[73] He cited as an example the case of Ku Chieh-kang's high school textbook, *Elementary National History*. In the course of reviewing the materials used in the secondary schools, someone in the Kuomintang administration took offense at Ku's historical treatment of the Golden Age in the textbook. Ku had written it up as a series of myths and legends, to which the Kuomintang responded:

> Academic argument is permitted, but such theories as these are not permitted in a textbook; otherwise, the self-confidence of the people will be shaken, which is, of course, harmful for the nation.[74]

Hu Shih reported that Tai Chi-t'ao, a high Kuomintang official in academic policy, insisted on fining the Commercial Press a million *yüan* for publishing the textbook. Although the fine was ultimately forgotten, "this excellent history textbook (which even Warlords Wu P'ei-fu and Ts'ao K'un did not interdict)

70. *Ibid.*, pp. 334–339.
71. Hu Shih, "Hsin wen-hua yün-tung yü Kuo-min-tang" [The New Culture Movement and the Kuomintang], *Hsin-yüeh* [The Crescent Moon], II:6–7 (Sept. 10, 1929), 1–15.
72. *Ibid.*, p. 4.
73. *Ibid.*
74. Ku's preface to *SHK*, p. 25.

still did not receive authorization for distribution" in the schools.[75]

The 'Liberal' Intelligentsia: Identity and Anxiety

It was in this environment of instability, conflict, and oppression that Chinese academics and professional writers attempted to reach some understanding of their role and status in modern China. Men like Ku Chieh-kang were satisfied neither with the way modern Chinese society was treating its intellectuals nor with the self-images and general social orientations of many of their colleagues.

Illustrative of the general problem as well as of Ku Chieh-kang's special situation is a short essay written by Chou Yü-t'ung in 1926, on reading Ku's *Autobiography*.[76] Chou, a specialist in the literature of the Old Text–New Text controversy, was full of admiration for Ku's accomplishments, and he was in complete sympathy with his self-portrait: "Chieh-kang my brother, your suffering, your melancholy, are the suffering of the whole class," [77] Chou wrote, as though there were a common understanding that there was indeed a Chinese 'intellectual class.' That society did not understand Ku Chieh-kang, and made him do things he did not want to do; that his life lacked peace; that he felt desiccated—all of these problems, Chou Yü-t'ung wrote, "were relevant to the whole of the contemporary intelligentsia (*chih-shih chieh-chi*)." [78]

As far as Chou was concerned, there were only two social classes then in China, the ruling class and the oppressed class. The intelligentsia belonged to the latter.[79] This simple estimation of the nature of Chinese society and the intellectual's role in it was not so clear to others as it was to Chou Yü-t'ung. A number of troublesome questions which were contemplated

75. Hu Shih, "Hsin wen-hua yün-tung yü Kuo-min-tang," p. 4.

76. Chou Yü-t'ung, "Ku chu *Ku-shih pien* te hou kan" [On Reading the Critiques], *KSP,* II, 319–331.

77. *Ibid.,* p. 327.

78. *Ibid.*

79. *Ibid.,* p. 88.

and debated over the decade of the twenties bore directly on Ku Chieh-kang's personal self-image and his scholarship.

The most persistent question regarding the Chinese intelligentsia was: Is it really a class? If so, what was the historical relationship of this new intellectual class to the old scholar-official class? A related issue, and one that preoccupied Ku Chieh-kang and the New Tide Society, was the problem of the individual intellectual's responsibility to self and to society. Ultimately, all of these questions funneled into one final problem: What was the new intelligentsia's relation to the Chinese masses?

The greatest concern of those who wrote about the Chinese intellectual was that he was perpetuating the class character and affiliation of the old scholar-officials—that is, he was merely an outgrowth of the old gentry and a servant to their class interests (as Cheng Chen-to had said of the National Studies scholars). In 1919, Fu Ssu-nien had demanded of China's new university students that they examine themselves and their teachers carefully:[80] If you were born in the imperial era, Fu wrote, did you actually make a firm decision not to enter officialdom? If you were students during the epoch of the examination system, did you firmly decide not to support it? He doubted that many of his contemporaries, or many of the Peking University faculty, had had the "animal courage" to do these things.

The frame of reference for the new intellectuals' behavior, the group to which they should compare themselves, Fu wrote, should no longer be the traditional Confucian man of virtue and accomplishment (the *hao jen*). Instead, Fu thought that comparison should be made with such men as Yuan Chi (A.D. 210–263), one of the escapist, antinomian "Seven Sages of the Bamboo Grove"; or Li Chih (d. A.D. 610), an official who threw away his official post for a life devoted to Buddhism; or Yüan Mei (1715–1797), a literary eccentric and colorful social nonconformist. Unless the new intellectuals were like these men,

80. Fu Ssu-nien, "Chung-kuo kou yü Chung-kuo jen" [Chinese Dogs and Chinese Men], *Hsin ch'ing-nien* [New Youth], VI:6 (Jan. 1, 1919); reprinted in *FSNHC,* III, 355–358.

future generations would compare the New Culture generation to those who supported the examination system and to the useless degree-holders whose feelings were never "suited to the times." [81]

Again, during the days of the New Tide Society, Fu Ssu-nien was an early and articulate spokesman for another side of the issue: Just what should the new intellectual do once he had severed himself from the social nexus of the old scholar-official? Should he devote himself to social service or to self-fulfillment (assuming that self-fulfillment did not take the form of social service)? He once wrote to Ku Chieh-kang and Yü P'ing-po that there was a serious conflict between intelligence guiding one to an interest in the life of man and a personal, spontaneous life of self-indulgence.[82] "In the end then," he wrote, "should I love spontaneity? Or should I love mankind?" [83]

THE PROBLEM OF SPONTANEITY

The imagery, the syntax, and the examples that Fu Ssu-nien used in these early statements about the new intellectuals all seem to echo the traditional knowledge–action dichotomy and the Confucian–Taoist nexus. Superficial similarities notwithstanding, Fu is truly a modern, and not merely an updated Chinese literatus. Fu did not employ the idea of 'spontaneity' in the same way that philosophic Taoists (like the Seven Sages of the Bamboo Grove) did when they protested against the corruptions and decadence of conventional society. Granted that for the Taoists as for Fu Ssu-nien, 'spontaneity' meant permitting the individual to be in harmony with nature or natural tendencies. But for the Taoists, 'natural tendencies' did not include the changes wrought by civilization (such as political institutions, or education). Any change toward social complexity was a change for the worse. The philosophic Taoist ideal was Arcadian: the simple agricultural society, uncluttered by complex institutions and complicating ideas. The body of ideas

81. *Ibid.*, p. 358.

82. Fu Ssu-nien, "Tzu-jan" [Spontaneity], *HC*, II:3 (Jan. 1920); reprinted in *FSNHC*, III, 387–391.

83. *Ibid.*

and institutions which we in the West call Confucianism were periodically for the philosophic Taoists the major symbols of the corruption of their ideals; indeed, philosophic Taoism is best understood as a conventional form of protest against Confucian conventions.

Though Fu Ssu-nien may have rejected the same conventions as the Seven Sages or Yüan Mei, he certainly was rejecting them for different reasons, in spite of his appeal to spontaneity. Spontaneity, for a New Tide spokesman like Fu Ssu-nien, was a kind of freedom which permitted an individual to realize his own capabilities and pursue his own interests, in accord with the nature of his times. For a member of the New Tide Society, it was as wrong to advocate a return to the idyllic days before the examination system, the monarchy, and the rest, as it was to have continued to support them. In brief, then, the use of the concept of 'spontaneity' by Fu Ssu-nien and his circle shared the philosophic Taoist's emphasis on a liberation from convention, but it pointed toward a continual readjustment to new and updated conventions. The examples that Fu cited were meant to be understood in the very broadest sense: he was not asking his colleagues to behave like the Seven Sages, inebriated in their sylvan retreats, or to carry on like Yüan Mei. Rather, he was asking modern Chinese to be brave, to reject, to be themselves—in the abstract. To imitate the Taoists, to repeat their performances in substance—this would have been anachronism and folly.

Finally, the New Culturalists' understanding of spontaneity was new because spontaneity was understood (as in the example of Fu Ssu-nien) in juxtaposition to a kind of social service that was quite distinct from Confucian social service. The latter was defined rather closely (at least from the twelfth century) as a life beginning with study of a circumscribed orthodoxy, proceeding through the examination system, and culminating in an official position in the bureaucracy—wherein the official, sage-like, would implement the knowledge of the *Tao* he had acquired in his earlier training. All this was precisely what was to be rejected by the New Culturalists; though it is not clear what 'social service' meant to them at the outset, it seems to have had something to do with joining the politically active side of the Chinese revolution. Social service in this sense was objected to, not because it led to a corruption of the natural purity of agricultural society, but merely because it might require an individual to compromise his predilections for other forms of personal satisfaction.[84] Fu Ssu-nien or Ku Chieh-kang's conflicts with the values of spontaneity and social obligation are thus substantially different from the traditional intellectuals' conflicts with the polarities of knowledge and action, or self-cultivation and social responsibility, or Taoism and Confucianism.

FROM INDIVIDUAL SPONTANEITY TO CLASS RESPONSIBILITY

By the end of the twenties, intellectuals like Fu Ssu-nien had begun to see the problem through the medium of more recent and less ambiguous terminology, informed with the notion of class and status. At this time, in an attempt to account for the "decadence" of Chinese education, Fu wrote that the basis of the problem was that gentry (*shih-ta-fu*) attitudes toward education still prevailed in China.[85] Originally, he said, learning was the sphere of the group called *Shih*, a group which in due time acquired political power and eventually allied with the dominant ruling class, but only as tools of that class. Finally (from the twelfth century), the ruling class was virtually all *Shih*, in the sense that all learning was used by them for acquiring degrees from the examination system; and degrees were used to acquire political office.

Fu continued his critique by comparing the European intelligentsia to the Chinese. The former were a much more united group, and could be designated as "clerics" (Fu used the English word) whose function it was to help their allies, the aristocracy, to oppress the common people. However, in the West, while the intelligentsia remained merely the servants of the ruling class, a

84. See Martin Bernal's "The Triumph of Anarchism Over Marxism, 1906–1907," in Mary Wright, ed., *China in Revolution; The First Phase, 1900–1913* (New Haven, 1968), pp. 97–143; and Michael Gasster, *Chinese Intellectuals and the Revolution of 1911* (Seattle, 1969), p. 169.

85. Fu Ssu-nien, "Chiao-yü p'eng-i chih yuan-yin" [The Source of Educational Problems], *Tu-li p'ing-lün* [The Independent Critic], no. 9 (July 17, 1932); reprinted in *FSNHC,* V, 715–722.

new class (the middle class) developed power and independence. In the fields of knowledge and education, Fu said, this middle class was responsible for Europe's scientific advances. But in China, the virtual identity of intelligentsia and ruling class, and the lack of a middle class, left no room for intellectual or educational innovation. It was Fu's opinion that during the late Ch'ing, when there was an opportunity for change, the "new education" was merely wed to the old examination system, and thereby stunted;[86] and official position persisted as the postgraduate professional goal right up to Fu's own time.[87]

These themes, dealing with class background and contemporary class identity, characterized the discussion of the intelligentsia in Ku Chieh-kang's circles in the late twenties. 'Individualism' and 'spontaneity' were no longer the main issues, it seems. In 1927–28, the journal *I-pan* (In General) featured a series of discussions which explored all aspects of the problem of intellectuals, and which serve as a lucid illustration of contemporary concerns. The first question was always: Do the intelligentsia comprise a real class? One writer equated the old *Shih* not with the entire intelligentsia in the past, but only with the bad elements—the kind who, in the definition of the Confucianists, worked with their minds and were served by others.[88] Their descendants, according to this argument, were the parasites who had lacked their own special ideology and instead merely served to provide legitimacy for political usurpers and such. In the 1920s, these intellectuals, still parasites of the ruling class, could be seen in league with warlords, imperialists, and the bourgeoisie.[89] Thus, the *I-pan* article cautioned its readers, one should not speak of the intelligentsia as if they were one class; they rather are divided into the bad elements (today's *Shih*), which must be overthrown, and the good elements. Who are the 'good' intellectuals? They are those who help laborers "liberate themselves"; those who "join the ranks of labor and no longer

86. *Ibid.*, p. 717.
87. *Ibid.*, p. 718.
88. Hsin Ju, "Tsung 'Ta-tao chih-shih chieh-chi' k'ou-hao chung so jen-shih te" [What I Understand by the Slogan 'Overthrow the Intelligentsia'], *I-pan* [In General], No. 3 (Shanghai, 1927).
89. *Ibid.*, p. 37.

avoid it personally."[90] The essayist concluded with the admonition that Chinese intellectuals must

> acknowledge the true strength of labor, and must be willing to devote themselves to aiding the laborers. . . . [For] if the intelligentsia persists in thinking in terms of the life of parasitic slaves, or in terms of parasitic emperors, they must end up by being overthrown. Those intellectuals who from now on will be saved from destruction must certainly be 'laborized' and 'popularized' (*lao-tung-hua, min-chung-hua*).[91]

Another *I-pan* essayist (Hsia Mien-tsun, a member of Ku Chieh-kang's inner circle of friends),[92] took issue with any attempts to equate the new intelligentsia with the old *Shih*.[93] The latter were a much more homogeneous group, he said, and therefore it was useful to see them as a class. But the present-day intellectuals were fragmented by their disparate employment and incomes: the upper intelligentsia, who were close to the bourgeoisie, had the most economic security and were found in some of the best universities; the lower were found teaching in elementary schools, and earned salaries so low that they were quite near, if not part of, the proletariat.[94] Hsia argued that a category like 'the intelligentsia,' which included students, professors, artists, doctors, and newspapermen, could not be usefully considered a class.

On the other hand, Hsia felt that this heterogeneous group could be characterized as generally suffering from 'overproduction,' on one hand, and their own narrow social aims on the other. Toward the end of the nineteenth century, he said, there was a lucrative market for the services of highly educated men;

90. *Ibid.,* p. 41.

91. *Ibid.*

92. Hsia Mien-tsun, according to C. T. Hsia, collaborated with Yeh Shao-chün and Chu Tzu-ch'ing in compiling "several textbooks of Chinese literature and [writing] a number of introductory studies in Chinese literature and rhetoric which were quite popular with high school students" (C. T. Hsia, *A History of Modern Chinese Fiction* [New Haven, 1961], p. 58). Also see *MFM,* pp. 306, 349.

93. Hsia Mien-tsun, "Chih-shih chieh-chi te yün-ming" [The Fate of the Intelligentsia], *I-pan,* no.. 5 (1928).

94. *Ibid.,* p. 101.

but thereafter, the new schools in China and overseas training produced far too many men for the two most popular fields of employment, government and teaching.[95] If these men and the educated youth today would deign to go into agriculture, business, or industry, Hsia said, there would be no problem. The source of the problem was a confused class-consciousness. Even though a member of the intelligentsia might be penniless, Hsia suggested, he would not "enter into the ranks of the propertyless physical laborers" for fear of losing his "footing" as a member of a special and higher class, and a chance at upward mobility.[96] Hsia had gloomy doubts about what would become of the many educated men who held menial positions as paper-shufflers rather than break into new employment sectors of suspect status.[97]

Conclusion: Who Killed Wang Kuo-wei?

All of these issues regarding the troubled identity and obligations of intellectuals were woven together by Ku Chieh-kang in one of his most brazen and audacious pieces of rhetoric. When the great scholar Wang Kuo-wei committed suicide in June 1927, Ku Chieh-kang seized the shocking incident as an opportunity to rail against the wretched situation of the Chinese intellectual in modern China. In the form of an obituary,[98] Ku evaluated the scholarship and social attitude of Wang Kuo-wei from a personal point of view, and used Wang and his tragic fate as an example of a gross social malady. The tone of the piece is repeatedly evocative of Ku's earlier evaluations of scholars like Cheng Ch'iao, and echoes of the *Autobiography* are unmistakable.

Wang Kuo-wei died by drowning in the lake of the Imperial

95. *Ibid.*, pp. 102–103.

96. *Ibid.*, pp. 105–106.

97. *Ibid.* Also see similar sentiments in essay by the prominent essayist Chu Tzu-ch'ing (1898–1948), "Na-li tsou" [Where Are We Going?], *I-pan*, no. 4 (March 1928). And compare similar views of a leading 'historical materialist,' T'ao Hsi-sheng, in his *Chung-kuo she-hui chih shih te fen-che* [The Periodization of Chinese History], (Taipei, 1954; 1st ed., Shanghai, 1929), pp. 9–10, 125–133.

98. Ku Chieh-kang, "Tao Wang Ching-an hsien-sheng" [Obituary for Wang Kuo-wei], *Wen-hsüeh chou-pao* [Literary Journal], V (1928), 1–11.

Summer Palace, a short distance from Tsinghua University where he had currently held a professorship. His motivation, the sources of his despair, were debated then and are still being discussed: Was it because he was distraught by the news that the Nationalist troops were advancing northward, and that Peking was due to fall any day? Or was it because of "unpleasant financial quarrels" with his associate and father-in-law, the scholar Lo Chen-yü? [99] Ku Chieh-kang, of course, had his own explanations.

Pointing to the political sources of Wang's suicide, the obituary suggested that Wang had overreacted to the severe treatment meted out to venerable scholars by local potentates and the Chinese Communist party. The latter had executed Yeh Te-hui[100] when they took Changsha in 1927, and the authorities of Chekiang had earlier confiscated the property of Chang T'ai-yen. According to Ku, Wang Kuo-wei could not bear to see scholars treated in such a way. But Ku, himself, had to condemn Wang's "too hasty sympathy" for these men and the Royalists (*Fu-p'i p'ai*): Yeh Te-hui was merely an "evil tyrant" and co-leader of the Society to Plan for Stability (*Ch'ou an hui*) with Liu Shih-p'ei; Chang T'ai-yen had become a "henchman of the Warlords" and repeatedly published anti-revolutionary polemics in the press. The obituary insisted that in spite of appearances (Wang wore the pigtail, and was Imperial Tutor for a while), Wang himself was not one of the latter-day restorationists; he was, rather, a scholar who "transcended" politics.

Searching for other political sources of Wang's despair, Ku dismissed the advent of the Warlords in Peking as a factor, because Wang had witnessed only the most minor of public disturbances (like the public ritual of cutting off the queues of those who still wore them). More important, perhaps, was the conflict which Wang had had with Peking University in the

99. See *BSCS*, pp. 79–82; and Chester C. Wang, "Wang Kuo-wei, His Life and His Scholarship," doctoral thesis (University of Chicago, 1967).

100. Yeh Te-hui (1864–1927) was an obstreperous Hunanese bibliophile and conservative politician who opposed the One Hundred Day reformers of 1898, and later opposed Huang Hsing's anti-Manchu revolutionaries. (See *BSCS*, pp. 83–85; and Li Chien-nung, *The Political History of China* (New York, 1956), pp. 163, 165.)

early twenties. His position as Imperial Tutor was out of keeping with the newly-implemented administrative policy that university faculty should not hold government positions. Nevertheless, Wang's scholarship was held in the highest esteem by the academic community.

From this summary of Wang's political life, Ku Chieh-kang's obituary concluded that Wang really had no reason to kill himself; his "sacrifice" was empty and absurd, and he simply had not suffered any "humiliation" (as he had claimed to have done in his will, written shortly before his suicide).[101] Ku wanted to find the ultimate causes of Wang Kuo-wei's despair and suicide in the unfortunate general condition of the scholar in modern China. He felt that if China had earlier made a place for a man of Wang's scholarly interests to find intellectual satisfaction and economic security, then Wang would not have had to turn to a destructive dependence on Lo Chen-yü and a job as Imperial Tutor. "The government gave him no sympathy or comfort; society did not understand him," Ku lamented in a syntax that echoed his encomium to Cheng Ch'iao, and his own self-portraits as well.

Ku could not resist the opportunity to make an example of Wang Kuo-wei, and to extract from his tragedy a lesson for his contemporaries. The obituary suggested that the first measures to take in avoiding further repetitions of Wang Kuo-wei's situation should be taken by the universities: they should make no demands of teachers outside of normal teaching and research duties; each scholar should only be asked to carry on his own special work, without any responsibility for the running of the school; and above all, there should be no pressures (within or outside of the university) to join any political parties or cliques.[102] The case of Wang Kuo-wei was that of a man who simply wished to do his own work and not become a merchant or a politician, and it seemed a general thing to Ku Chieh-kang that a man fully interested in learning had little taste for politics. Surely, Ku said, when a man does not wish to dilute his personal

101. *BSCS,* p. 81.
102. "Tao Wang Ching-an hsien-sheng," p. 7.

interests with politics, he has not shirked his responsibility to society.[103]

The most crucial measure to take was a more substantial one. The obituary asserted that China must create an atmosphere wherein the scholar could be separated, once and for all, from the gentry, and "returned to the working class (*kung-jen chieh-chi*)." Pure science had been impossible in the past, in China, because the object of scholarship had been either to serve the ethical demands of society or to obtain degrees and become an official. The gentry's inflated image of the scholar was likewise an inhibition to pure learning. The gentry had made the scholars feel like transcendent beings, superior to the common people and "capable of judging what was noble and valuable in life"; and in the end, scholars were merely training to become gentry themselves. The scholar, according to Ku's corrected picture of him, was basically not at all as the old gentry saw him; he was no more mysterious or special than the farmer or the craftsman. Yet when things had gone wrong, it had been the scholars who received the blame; they had been destroyed by social impositions that prevented them from being creative. In brief, the scholars simply were not the 'high and mighty' group that they had always been made out to be; they required money to feed and clothe themselves, just like everyone else.

Ku concluded that it was these gentry-derived attitudes of transcendence and aloofness that were largely responsible for Wang Kuo-wei's death. However, he did not explain precisely how this occurred, and the reader is left to infer that Wang's fatal flaw was his "separation from" and "refusal to draw near" the common people.[104] Be that as it may, Ku explicitly closed his obituary with the note that over the 1920s, for all his brilliance, Wang Kuo-wei became haughty and gave support through his behavior to the gentry idea that the scholar was an exalted being and worthy of reverence.[105] The effusive obituary ended with an resounding indictment and rather surprising call to arms:

103. *Ibid.*, pp. 8–9.
104. *Ibid.*, p. 9.
105. *Ibid.*, p. 10.

A nation which did not have the means for specialized scholarship killed Wang Kuo-wei!
We must establish means for specialized scholarship.

The gentry class frame of reference killed Wang Kuo-wei!
We must knock down the gentry class!

We are not gentry!
We are all common people!

Ku Chieh-kang's 1928 "Obituary for Wang Kuo-wei" was a dramatic summary of Ku's troubled estimation of the place of scholars like himself in contemporary China; it obviously served in part to explore the sources of his own malaise, as well as the causes of Wang Kuo-wei's suicide. In addition, the obituary brought together major themes that were current in the writings of Ku's associates as they too attempted to find a place for the intellectual in the shifting sands of twentieth-century China. Though Ku Chieh-kang's arguments, and those of Fu Ssu-nien and the writers in the *I-pan,* continued the somber mood of earlier discussions on scholars and society, like those found in the *Symposium on Critiques of Spurious Literature,* an evident development had occurred.

The *Symposium* did not evaluate scholars on the basis of their social class nor their proximity to the masses. However, there was a decided shift to just these kinds of considerations by the end of the twenties, even in Ku Chieh-kang's un-Marxist circles. In his obituary for Wang Kuo-wei, Ku added a new factor to his earlier discussions about the scholar's tensions with society —the triangle of gentry, scholar, and common people. It was the class identity of the scholar which he hammered at when he assessed Wang's tragedy. Wang's suicide was brought about only in part by an institutional problem; it was only partially a result of China's failure to create a functionally specific professional role for the scholar after the old educational system was scrapped. Of greater importance to Ku Chieh-kang in his mood of the late twenties was the failure of the modern scholar to divest himself of former class affiliations and attitudes and to "draw near the people."

Ku's admonition to "draw near the people" is a rather ambiguous one, for it was never made clear just what one should do there, nor to what extent this drawing-near would interfere with that intellectual autonomy Ku persistently advocated. By this time in the late twenties, Ku had demonstrated just how close *he* would approach the masses and to what end. As the leader and nationwide promoter of the Folkstudies Movement, he began to operationalize his admonitions; but he discovered that, in drawing near the common folk, the chasm between intellectuals and the people grew more apparent. Ku's call to disengage from gentry values and associations was certainly consistent with his desire to disengage the scholar from traditional political commitments. But disengaging from the gentry did not mean automatic identity with the common people. At best Ku and his circle found themselves in, but not of, the masses. In the varied realm of the Folkstudies Movement, Ku, his followers, and his antagonists all concentrated their efforts on the problem of the relationship of the intellectuals to the people, and of both of these groups to the Chinese nation.

Part Two: The People

IV

The Folkstudies Movement and Its Populist Milieu

> *Then I rationalized the matter to myself, saying: Home was always like this, and although it has not improved, still it is not so depressing as I imagine; it is only my mood that has changed, because I am coming back to the country this time with no illusions.*—Lu Hsün, "My Old Home," 1921

> *"Why are you going into the country?" I asked a friend. "We speak so much of the people," he answered, "but we do not know them. I want to live the life of the people, and suffer for them."*—from a Russian novel of the 1870's

In 1921, Lu Hsün wrote of his momentary return from the metropolis to the village of his childhood, after an absence of twenty years. More poignantly perhaps than in any other statement of the period, there was captured in his essay "My Old Home" a feeling of the disjunction between the new intellectual and the roots of the old life.

While Lu Hsün explored the "lamentably thick wall" that had grown up between himself and the country friends of his youth, other young, educated revolutionaries were razing similar barriers. That same year, for example, in the south of China, P'eng P'ai's peasant movement got under way.[1] Years

1. See Shinkichi Eto, "Hai-lu-feng—The First Chinese Soviet Government," *China Quarterly*, no. 8 (Oct.–Dec. 1961), part 1, and no. 9 (Jan.–March 1962), part 2.

earlier, during the first phases of the New Culture movement, Li Ta-chao (1889–1927), co-founder of the Chinese Communist party, had already formulated a "Youth to the Villages" movement modeled on the late nineteenth-century Russian populist examples. Li's efforts bore little fruit, but they were perhaps the earliest examples of the perennial concern of modern Chinese intellectuals about their separation from 'the people,' and the role of 'the people' in the formation of the new China.[2] And from 1919, the year of the May Fourth Movement, a variety of populist student organizations sprang up, each in its own way devoted to removing the intellectual from his traditional position "aloof from the masses" and ignorant of physical labor. Short-lived "work-study" and "work-and-learning" societies were established in the Peking area to implement these goals, and equally short-lived campaigns were launched to bring literacy and the new culture to the masses of the countryside.[3]

"To the People"

One of the central themes of Ku Chieh-kang's writings was the miscasting of the intellectual in China's past, and the need to change his role in the present. For him, the intellectual had been, from Han times forward, and with little variation, "a parasite of the aristocracy." [4] As such, it was of course impossible for the intellectual to "draw near" the people, to sympathize with them, and significantly alter the circumstances of the common man. Out of this situation, there grew not merely a permanent cleavage between the common people and the scholar, but the scholar developed an attitude of superiority and, at

2. Maurice Meisner, *Li Ta-chao and the Origins of Chinese Marxism* (Cambridge, Mass., 1967), pp. 80 ff.

3. *MFM,* pp. 98, 193. Also see Benjamin Schwartz regarding the Chinese intelligentsia and populism in (1) his article "The Intelligentsia in Communist China—A Tentative Comparison," in Richard Pipes, ed., *The Russian Intelligentsia* (New York, 1961), p. 164; and (2) his *Chinese Communism and the Rise of Mao* (Cambridge, Mass., 1952), pp. 21–22.

4. For example, see Ku's "Sheng-hsien wen-hua yü min-chung wen-hua" [Culture of the Sages and Culture of the Masses], *MS,* no. 5 (April 17, 1928), p. 3; Ku's 1933 preface to *KSP,* IV, 10; and *CHFSJS,* p. 53.

best, aloof paternalism toward the masses. The traditional idea of the sage received considerable attention from Ku, because in it he saw a mythological representation of this inimical relationship between intelligentsia and masses.[5]

Ku Chieh-kang's attitude toward the Chinese masses, past and present, was very much in the tradition of Yen Fu. They both pummeled the traditional idea of the Sage—not only because it depicted the Sage as a superman, but because it pictured the masses as totally ignorant and perennially incapable of cultural creativity,[6] and therefore completely reliant on the creative genius and good will of the Sage. As we shall see, the *raison d'etre* of the Folkstudies Movement was the belief that it was *only* the masses that were capable of innovation in certain areas of the total culture (such as literature). However, if Ku Chieh-kang and his fellow folklorists came to consider all that was good in literature to be 'of the people,' they were far from considering all that was 'of the people' to be good. Ku saw the people, as a social and political entity, again as Yen Fu had seen them—that is, "having an infinite capacity for enlightenment, but . . . [their] enlightenment must be brought in from outside." [7] Ku Chieh-kang, like Yen Fu, had great faith in the future of the Chinese masses; but when he personally 'drew near' them, he could only remark on their pitiful lack of development. If the great potential of the Chinese people was to be actualized, it could only be done from without the masses, through a long, gradual process of education, guided by an educated elite. On this point Ku, Yen Fu, and influential political moderates like Liang Ch'i-ch'ao were in strong agree-

5. See *KSP,* II, 130–139, for Ku's study of the development of the idea of the sage. Of primary importance in his study of the subject were his essays on the *I-ching* [The Book of Changes], for which see *KSP,* III (1931), 1–44, 45–70.

6. See Benjamin Schwartz, *In Search of Wealth and Power, Yen Fu and the West* (Cambridge, Mass., 1964), p. 65; cf. Y. C. Wang, *Chinese Intellectuals and the West* (Chapel Hill, 1966), who sees the intellectual generation of the 1920s in China as an "amoral" group which had abandoned the traditional literati's position of responsibility for, and intimacy with, the masses.

7. Schwartz, *Wealth and Power,* p. 146.

ment.[8] It was obvious to Ku that the next step was to draw the educated elite down from its traditional heights and send them "to the people."

That was apparently not an easy task, if we may judge from the recurrent calls to action which Ku felt he had to make throughout the 1920s. In 1925 he made his first major statement on the subject, in a typically oratorical preface to one of his first studies of folk customs.[9] According to the tenets of the Socialist movement, he wrote, we ought to know the circumstances of the life of the masses (*min-chung*). However, "we educated ones are too far from the people; we consider ourselves cultured gentlemen and them as vulgar; we consider ourselves as aristocrats (*kuei-tsu*) and revile them as mean people (*ch'ien-min*)." Ku castigated his fellow intellectuals for their failure to know more of the people of the nation other than the officials and teachers (with the added exception, perhaps, of sing-song girls and actors). It was no wonder, he said, that the common people had continued to be self-effacing and still did not aspire to "our level."

Getting down to politics, a rarity for him, Ku pointed out that "ever since the establishment of the Republic, the constitution had clearly stated: 'The people united in equality under law.' " But this was merely a statement in the constitution and still not a reality, he observed. Even though generations had passed since a few members of the gentry monopolized the government, "the government's duties still really do not derive from the collective responsibility of the people of the entire nation." The intelligentsia, Ku concluded, were not yet in a position to undertake the responsibility of government; therefore "we not only should not break off intercourse with the masses, we ought indeed to join ourselves with them." It was perhaps for this latter purpose, Ku speculated, that in recent years the slogan "to the people" had been so loudly cried throughout China. Nevertheless, because the intelligentsia had

8. See Chang P'eng-yuan, "The Constitutionalists," in Mary Wright, ed., *China in Revolution; The First Phase, 1900–1913* (New Haven, 1968), pp. 153–154.

9. Ku Chieh-kang, *Miao Feng Shan* [Mount Miao Feng] (Canton, 1928).

found it so hard to throw off their evil self-image as 'worthies' and 'nobles,' "to the people" remained only a slogan and not a reality.

The suggestion here of an alliance between the masses and the educated elite was no more than an enticing peek into Ku Chieh-kang's political thought. Though he did not elaborate this idea, he probably had in mind the Sun Yat-sen brand of populism, which saw a general will embodied in a knowledgeable party elite. The Communist version of this alliance between people and elite was certainly unacceptable to Ku, the patient gradualist. But in spite of the mutual need of the scholar and the masses suggested by this 1925 statement, Ku ended on a patronizing note: If we truly want to grow closer to the people, he said, we must first know the people, and permit the people to know us. By using various techniques (such as gathering folklore), Ku assured his readers, the intellectuals could know the people better; this knowledge would permit closer ties, and these in turn "would dispel [the people's] doubts of us as they come to know our sincerity; then they will accept our teaching and will not doubt our knowledge."

The use of the slogan "to the people" (*tao min-chien ch'ü*), which the Chinese borrowed from the Russian 'generation of 1870,' is thus highly misleading, because neither the populism of the non-Marxists such as Ku Chieh-kang, nor that of the Communists such as P'eng P'ai and, later, Mao Tse-tung (in Yenan), carried with it the peculiar qualities of Russian populism of the seventies. Chinese populism, gradualist or revolutionary, could hardly be described, a la Venturi's characterization of the Russians who went to the people, as "a collective act of Rousseauism," and a "passionate longing for liberation which took as its banner the repudiation of learning in order to find a true, healthy and simple life." [10]

Nor will the Chinese intellectuals of the 1920s, in spite of occasional poses, fit Malia's description of those "alienated" Russian *intelligenty* who went to the people

10. Franco Venturi, *Roots of Revolution: A History of the Populist and Socialist Movements in Nineteenth Century Russia* (New York, 1960), p. 503.

to learn the great human truth of a humiliation far deeper than theirs, a truth beside which their own 'rationality' paled into insignificance. Their final ambition was to become the authentic spokesmen of this truth. The quest of the intelligentsia for its own 'humanity' ended in the ultimate democratic pathos of 'merging with the people.' [11]

In short, were we to have asked a young Chinese populist why he was going into the country, we could not have expected him to reply meaningfully (as did his Russian counterpart in a novel from the seventies): "We speak so much of the people, but do not know them. I want to live the life of the people, and suffer for them." [12] Mao, in his speeches at Yenan in 1942, warned his cadres that their involvement with the people would cost them "suffering and conflict" [13]—but this is suffering because of the people, not suffering *for* them. When the young Russian aristocrats went to the people it was, in part, a religious act of contrition: a means of redeeming the sins of their fathers who had caused suffering to the peasantry. Living the life of the people was as much an act of contrition as it was an effort not to burden the peasants among whom they lived. Chinese history provided no precedents for such an interpretation of its twentieth-century populism.

As early as 1923, we find an exchange of short essays in the *Endeavor,* then edited by Hu Shih, on the Russian idea of "to the people." Despite the rhetorical trappings from Russian populism, the educationalist mentality prevailed: "I believe that if Good Men (*hao jen*) wish to do their best," one writer argued,

then they ought to leave the filthy, 'righteous' world of Peking, and *go to the people,* organizing education. If this basic reform of society is not undertaken, then it is foolish to consider reforming the gov-

11. Martin Malia, "What is the Intelligentsia?" in Pipes, *The Russian Intelligentsia,* p. 16.

12. From a novel by Klements, quoted in Venturi, *Roots of Revolution,* p. 476.

13. Mao Tse-tung, *Talks at the Yenan Forum on Literature* (Peking, 1959), p. 50.

ernment; it [will be a wasted effort]. Society has no hope of being reformed unless Good Men concentrate their efforts, and everyone desires to go into each and every village to wear [the villagers'] simple clothing, eat their coarse food, and make special efforts to educate the people. Therefore, I look to the slogan of the Russian Populists of the past—"To the People." [14]

Two replies to these remarks in the same journal expressed doubts that Russia's experience was at all applicable to China.[15] Such a movement must be very weak in China, they argued, because even though the Chinese government was not very good, "Chinese society is still a classless one." Thus, the interest in the masses which was possible in Russia would not stir up the same kind of interest in China. And equally important, the replies continued, China is too pragmatic and lacks that rich mysticism which was prevalent in Russia. Would it not be better, then, to avoid the use of a mystique of the people and, more simply, to educate the youth?

Later, those evaluating the populist activities of the twenties typically spoke of them with derision and sarcasm. One writer observed that of the many who clamored to go to the people, very few went. Unfortunately, those few themselves sought only to have the peasants imitate urban life: "This approach takes the rural people and carries them to the city, and is not really going to the villages." [16] Still another critic likened the scholars who mouth the slogan "to the people" to the freeloading Buddhist priest who cries the name of Buddha and then wanders about the countryside in search of the village with the best accommodations and food.[17]

14. Unsigned essay, "Tao min-chien ch'ü" [To the People], *Nu-li chou-pao* [The Endeavor], no. 40 (Feb. 4, 1923).

15. Ching Sung, "Tao nei-ti ch'ü" [To the Hinterland], *Nu-li chou-pao,* no. 66 (Aug. 19, 1923); and unsigned essay, "Tu-le Ching Sung hsien-sheng te 'Tao nei-ti ch'ü' chih kan-hsiang" [On Reading Ching Sung's Essay], *ibid.,* no. 68 (Sept. 2, 1923).

16. Hsü Chu-cheng, "Ting-hsien p'ing-chiao ts'un-chih ts'an-kuan-chi" [Investigation of Education and Government in Ting Hsien], *Kuo-wen chou-pao* [Journal of National News], III:4 (Feb. 28, 1930), 9.

17. Chang Ts'ui-yu, preface to *Min-chien* [The People], I:6 (Nov. 1931).

Throughout the 1920s and early 1930s, the experiences of the Russian populists did not cease to fascinate the Chinese. Ch'ü Ch'iu-pai, for example, was a most sensitive and thorough chronicler of their activities.[18] When he examined the Chinese groups advocating a movement to the people, he denounced them as 'small-time' reactionaries who sat and waited for the people to come to them, that is, the intellectuals.[19] And T'ien Han wrote penetratingly of the disillusionment which the young Russians of the seventies had been destined to suffer because of their over-romantic conception of the masses. He spoke of the disillusionment they bequeathed to those in other nations who took them as an example.[20]

Soochow, Without Illusions

Ku Chieh-kang anticipated the tone which much of Chinese populism was to take when he returned to his old home and meticulously recorded the nature of marriage and burial customs practiced there.[21] Ku's pioneering 1924 study on marriage was based on marriage documents and interviews with elders of his own family. (He became interested in the project when he was married for the second time.) Ku's purpose was not merely to play the part of the detached empirical observer, any more than he intended to 'merge' with the rural environment and lose his identity as a sophisticated, urbane scholar. Quite the contrary, the ultimate purpose of the study patently was to

18. Ch'ü Ch'iu-pai, "Shih-yüeh ke-ming te ch'ien te O-lu-ssu wen-hsüeh" [Russian Literature Before the October Revolution], esp. part 11 on "The Generation of the Seventies" and part 12 on "The Literature of the Populist Movement and the Generations of the Sixties and Seventies," in *Ch'ü Ch'iu-pai wen-chi* [Collected Writings of Ch'ü Ch'iu-pai], 4 vols. (Peking, 1953–1954), II.

19. Ch'ü, "Hsüeh fa wan-sui" [Long Live the Literary Revolution] (dated June 10, 1931), in his *Luan Tan* [Vulgar Music] (Shanghai, 1939), p. 133.

20. T'ien Han, "Tao min-chien ch'ü," *T'ien Han wen-chi* [Collected Writings of T'ien Han] (Shanghai, 1936), pp. 112–115.

21. See Ku Chieh-kang and Liu Wang-chang, *Su-Yüeh te hun sang* [Marriage and Mourning Customs in Soochow and Canton], a monograph of the Chinese Folklore Society of National Sun Yat-sen University (Canton, 1928).

use the 'genetic method' to demonstrate the survival and perpetuation of harmful and stupid customs and to recommend their abolition. In these surroundings, he apparently found it difficult to maintain that distinction between 'knowledge' and 'action' which he advocated during the 1920s.

Reviewing the expensive items on a long traditional dowry list, Ku was appalled by the useless, perfunctory nature of most of them. Why, when the original ceremonial meaning of these gifts had long been forgotten, should such customs survive? It was not the fault of the common people, Ku warned, but the corrupting example of the capitalists, whose prodigality and need for display (we would say "conspicuous consumption") kept such customs alive. And further, Ku added, it was probably the fault as well of the merchants who profited from the sale of the ceremonial items.[22] After deftly applying his genetic methodology and illustrating the historical origins and development of the ceremonies in question, Ku appealed for understanding on the part of his citified readers:

> Toward these meaningless ceremonies we naturally have a great deal of contempt, but if we are aware that they were originated bit by bit we can commiserate and be sympathetic toward the foolish men [who still practice them]. We can understand their ways and not merely hate and curse them.[23]

Ku's discussion of Soochow funeral customs followed the same course. After describing the nature of the customs, he roundly condemned them as financially ruinous to the poor villagers and a source of invidious display for the upper classes. Again the capitalist class was condemned for perpetuating and strengthening evil customs, and Ku lamented the fact that just when the old gentry 'high culture' had begun to break down, portions of it were taken over by the *arriviste* capitalists who

22. Cf. Mao Tse-tung, "Report of an Investigation of the Peasant Movement in Hunan," where he suggests that bans on harmful customs are in part a "form of self-defense against exploitation by city merchants" (p. 42).

23. Ku and Líu, *Su-Yüeh te hun sang,* p. 29.

had no basic conventions (*t'i-chih*) of their own, but only took money as their guide.[24]

The use of class concepts in Ku's appraisal is rather striking, but we would be misled to think of them as part of any systematic, Marxist-like critique of society. It would be best to attribute Ku's vocabulary here to a jargon common to Marxist and non-Marxist alike in China during the 1920s. However, one could attribute some of Ku's anti-capitalist rancor to the fact (as he recorded it) that he himself, poor as he was, had to spend exorbitant amounts of money when he married for the second time and when he took the responsibility for his grandmother's funeral.[25]

What followed from Ku's brief venture into the study of folk customs? Certainly no call for class warfare, or even a design for reform, but rather an ambivalent attitude toward the folk and a rather narrow plan of action. Ku's contact with the artistic aspects of people's culture led him to characterize it as "approaching natural innocence," but his experience with the realities of their lives led him to a qualified appreciation of peoples' culture: "It also has a good deal that is crude and much that is unsuitable for modern times."[26] How was the plight of the masses to be alleviated? By a painfully slow process of data-gathering and study, on the order of the prototypical studies Ku himself had made. And only after the scholar had 'drawn near' the masses, studied them up close, and compiled his data, could plans be made, in Ku's words, "for their enrichment"[27]—that is, for their education.

24. Cf. Mao, "Report of an Investigation of the Peasant Movement in Hunan," p. 39, on the subject of banning "harmful feasts." Also cf. Hu Shih's "Wo tui-yü sang-li te kai-ke" [My Position on Reform of Burial Customs], *HSWT*, I, 709–723. This essay, dated 1918 and published in 1923, presents sentiments identical to Ku's and was also drawn from personal experience—the death and burial of Hu Shih's mother in 1918.

25. Ku and Líu, *Su-Yüeh te hun sang*, p. 41.

26. Ku, "Sheng-hsien wen-hua yü min-chung wen-hua (n. 4, above)," p. 4.

27. For example, Ku's *"Ch'üan-chou min-chien ch'üan-shuo, hsü"* [Preface to The Folktales of Ch'üan-chou], *MS*, no. 67 (July 1929), pp. 1–2.

Educating the Masses

Traditional savants like Chang Hsüeh-ch'eng and modern ones like Mao Tse-tung both advised future sages and cadres, respectively, to be good pupils in the school of common man, to be good people-watchers, before they attempted to realize their calling. Said Chang:

> The worthy man is one who learns from a sage; and the gentleman is one who learns from the worthy man. But the sage himself is one who learns from the common people.[28]

Said Mao:

> The duty of learning from the workers, peasants and scholars precedes the task of educating them. . . . Only by becoming their pupil can [one] become their teacher.[29]

But neither Chang nor Mao was hereby advocating any democratic humility. Chang Hsüeh-ch'eng's sage was looking for the eternal *Tao* and was to find traces of it "in the ebb and flow of man's life." "Seeing this," (according to Nivison's explanation),

> [the sage] sees the needs, the anxiety, the evil that must be alleviated; seeing what *is* the case, he sees what he *must* do, and so performs his history-making acts of fashioning institutions and legislating.[30]

The *tao* that Mao sought was, need we say it, the namable *tao* of flux and revolution. Mao wanted his cadres too to make history, and quickly. He wanted them to learn how to work with the peasants; how not to alienate the masses, so that they might most rapidly be organized, politicized, and marshaled for a "militarized mass insurrection." [31]

Over the course of the later 1920s and early 1930s in China, there appeared a small group of young intellectuals who, in

28. David Nivison, *The Life and Thought of Chang Hsüeh-ch'eng* (Stanford, 1966), p. 138.

29. Mao, *Talks at the Yenan Forum* (n. 13, above), section 2, pp. 21, 29.

30. Nivison, *Life and Thought*, pp. 144–145.

31. Chalmers Johnson's euphonious phrase; see his *Revolution and the Social System* (Stanford, 1964).

their relationship to the masses, stood somewhere between the rejected idea of the paternalistic sage and the resisted notion of an educated elite guiding a mass social revolution. These men, mostly trained in England or America (if they were educated abroad), were wedded to a singularly unspectacular and gradual process of mass education and rural reconstruction based on 'scientific' study of the realities of contemporary peasant life. Politically, their goal was to help the people, after sufficient education, to organize themselves along democratic lines.

The undramatic role as intellectuals that these populists chose for themselves permitted no transplantation of Kropotkin's plan "to be fused with the people . . . to adopt the life of the peasant and the workmen, and merge with it." [32] If the Chinese rural reconstructionists and folklorists resembled any of the Russian 'generation of 1870,' it would seem to have been those, such as Nikitenko and Aksakov, whom A. P. Pollard has characterized as the liberal intelligentsia, those who saw their duty to be the spread of education and enlightenment and "assimilating the people into itself." [33]

With increasing frequency over the course of the late twenties, greater numbers of young populists chose the less precipitous, more prosaic role of educationalists[34] (reformers through

32. Venturi's description, *Roots of Revolution* (n. 10, above), p. 484.

33. A. P. Pollard, "The Russian Intelligentsia: The Mind of Russia," *California Slavic Studies,* III (Berkeley, 1964), pp. 23–24. Pollard says that Nikitenko saw the intelligentsia as having no class character, providing a third force between the government and the people, and performing this function inadequately.

In their relationship with the people, according to Pollard, Nikitenko "believed that the intelligentsia had nothing whatever to learn from the people, who were on the whole savages. The intelligentsia were the only representatives of civilization in the country; their sole duty, therefore, was to enlighten the masses and thus bring Russia into the company of civilized European nations" (*ibid.,* p. 17).

Also see comments by Mary B. Rankin on the revolutionary Chinese intellectuals (ca. 1905–1911) and their relationship to Russian models, especially in regard to attitudes toward the masses. ("The Revolutionary Movement in Chekiang: A Study in the Tenacity of Tradition," in Wright, *China in Revolution* [n. 8, above], pp. 320, 340.)

34. See the semi-autobiographical novel *Ni Huan-chih* by Ku's friend Yeh Shao-chün. It was translated into English as *Schoolmaster Ni Huan-chih* (Peking, 1958). The novel is the most poignant in a series which

education)—a group which had already earned Mao's contempt in his 1927 report on the Hunan peasant movement.[35] As the Folkstudies Movement grew apace, Y. P. James Yen in 1925 launched his Chinese Mass Education Movement in Ting Hsien.[36] And in 1931 Liang Sou-ming established the Shantung Rural Reconstruction Institute at Tsou Chou-ping, an outgrowth of his earlier work at Han Fu-chu, in Honan. Liang was much influenced by the Russian populists. According to Lymon van Slyke, he stressed the

> reintegration of the urbanized intellectuals and youth with the peasant masses: He compared the reconstruction movement to a giant whose trunk and limbs categorically denied that the intellectual could help China apart from the masses. . . . This was an attempt to give the intelligentsia a position of leadership increasingly denied them by the KMT.[37]

By 1933, the Sociology Department of Yenching University had co-opted most of the major educationalist and rural reconstruction projects in North China as part of its policy of "back to the people," [38] including the projects of Liang Sou-ming, the

---

dramatized the conflicts and bitter frustrations inherent in the role of rural educationalist. It was originally published in 1930.

35. Mao, "Report of an Investigation of the Peasant Movement in Hunan" (n. 24, above). He writes: "Before long tens of thousands of schools will have sprung up throughout the province; this is quite different from the empty talk about 'universal education' which the intelligentsia and the so-called 'educationalists' have been bandying back and forth, and which after all this time remains an empty phrase" (p. 45).

36. See Sidney D. Gamble, *Ting Hsien, a North China Rural Community* (New York, 1954); Hsü Chu-cheng, "Ting-hsien p'ing-chiao ts'un-chih ts'an-kuan-chi" (n. 16, above); and Li Ching-han, *Ting Hsien she-hui kai-k'uang tiao-ch'a* [A General Investigation of Ting Hsien Society] (n.p., Society for Mass Education, 1933).

37. Lymon van Slyke, "Liang Sou-ming and the Rural Reconstruction Movement," *Journal of Asian Studies,* XVIII:4 (Aug. 1959), 466. Also see Sun Pen-wen, *Hsien-tai Chung-kuo she-hui wen-t'i* [The Contemporary 'Chinese Society' Question] (n.p., Shangwu, 1944), vol. III, *Nung-ts'un wen-t'i* [The Peasant Question], esp. chap. 20.

38. According to Dwight Edwards (*Yenching University* [New York, 1959], pp. 286, 289–290), the school's projects included the Yenta Relief Federation, from 1929; and from 1933, a number of organizations under the North China Council for Rural Reconstruction, whose projects included Ting Hsien and Tsinging Hsien, model village projects in the

Mass Education Movement, and the much publicized Ting Hsien model village. And in the same year, the Nationalist government itself entered actively into the area of rural reconstruction, prodded no doubt by the Yangtze flood of 1931 and by the notoriety of the Kiangsi Soviet.[39]

A decade had passed since Lu Hsün had returned briefly to his old home and had left, speculating on the hopes he had for China. And it was ten years also since the Communists had first actively experimented with the idea of coming back to the old home. It was during this period that Ku Chieh-kang and his fellow folklorists, in a labor of love, developed their ideas of popular culture in the Chinese Folklore Movement.

The Collector

In his *Autobiography,* Ku Chieh-kang's account of the development of his interest in folk culture was written with a histrionic touch and was told like the story of a religious conversion. Recalling his pre-populist attitude, he wrote:

> Although I had developed a hatred of the literati, I could not help being contaminated with their characteristic spirit. It is natural, therefore, that I should have developed contempt for the vulgar tales which story-tellers rehearsed on the streets, and considered it a waste of time to listen to them. Scorning, similarly, the coarseness and sensuousness of the novels, I had no time for them either.[40]

As a child of fifteen, he recalled, he had refused to accompany schoolmates to witness Soochow festivals because they were "superstitious," and he also had a deep aversion then to the "vulgarity" of dancing girls' songs: "It is not surprising that I was quite cut off from ordinary social life. . . . I had entirely

---

south of Shantung province. Agricultural extension, village industries, irrigation, rural co-ops, local self-government, and tax reform were instituted.

39. Chiu Kaiming also adds the factor of the Japanese invasion of Manchuria to these two as "the chief events responsible for the participation of the central government in rural rehabilitation" at this time. See his essay, "Agriculture," in H. M. MacNair's *China* (1st ed., New York, 1947), p. 479.

40. *ACH,* p. 31.

forgotten the traditions that circulated among the common people."[41]

It was through the medium of Peking Opera that Ku was set on the road that led back to the people. According to his own reports, he became an avid theatergoer after he entered the university preparatory school. So taken was he with the theater that one wonders when he found time to attend classes. It was only after becoming a buff that he was able "to repress the scholar's pride and get into more direct touch with the thoughts of ordinary people."[42]

In 1918, Liu Pan-nung, among other Peking University faculty, began publishing folksongs, gathered from various parts of contemporary China, in the university student daily. These songs, added to his enthusiasm for Peking theater, were yet further incentives to Ku's growing populist tendencies. "It never occurred to me," Ku wrote, "that such verses were meritorious enough to put into print."[43] Within a short time, however, Ku himself was a folksong collector and among the first Chinese to devote serious scholarly efforts to the classification and analysis of the genre.

Shortly after Ku Chieh-kang was first introduced to the art of collecting folksongs, a small group of Peking University professors decided to coordinate their private studies of Chinese folksong. In February 1918, the Department of Folksong Collection was instituted under the guidance of professors Liu Pan-nung, Ch'en Chun-tien, and Chou Tso-jen, who also functioned as editors of the department's new and short-lived journal, the *Bulletin for Nationwide Contemporary Folksong Collection.* "Regional dialect" editors were Ch'ien Hsüan-t'ung and Shen Chien-shih.[44] In the platform of this group we find the follow-

41. *Ibid.,* p. 32.

42. *Ibid.*

43. *Ibid.,* p. 67.

44. See Ku Chieh-kang, "*Wu ke chia-chi* tzu-hsü" [Preface to The Folksongs of Wu], reprinted in *Ke-yao chou-k'an* [Folksong]—hereinafter referred to as *Ke-yao*—I:97 (June 28, 1925). Also see Jung Chao-tsu, "Pei-ta ke-yao yen-chiu hui chi feng-su tiao-ch'a hui te ching-kuo" [The Vicissitudes of the Peking Folksong Study Society and the Folklore Research Society], part 1, *MS,* no. 15–16 (July 1928), pp. 1–10, and part 2, no. 17–18 (July 1928), pp. 14–30. Also see Lou Tze-k'uang, "Chung-kuo min-su-hsüeh yün-

ing goals enunciated in May 1918: to gather folksong materials from the period of the Sung dynasty to the present; to give attention to folksongs "dealing with soldiers away from home, . . . grieving concubines . . . but not those dealing with the lewd and obscene. All songs must be those which are spontaneously wrought." And finally, the outline stressed the gathering of songs which spontaneously became popular throughout China, for whatever period of time, as well as folksongs which had become common throughout a particular region.[45] These principles became profusely elaborated and warmly debated over the coming two decades.

Although the Department of Folksong Collection had a hiatus of activity[46] during 1919, the year of the May Fourth Movement, Ku Chieh-kang reported that his most active period of folksong gathering was from February to September of 1919.[47] By January of the next year, Ku had published his first article on the folksong, following the advice of his friend Kuo Shao-yü.[48] At the end of 1920, Ku entered more formally into the field of folkstudies when he became a founding member of the Peking University Folksong Study Society (*Pei-ta ke-yao yen-chiu hui*), the broader organization to which the Department of Folksong Collection had given way. Chou Tso-jen and Yu Ch'en-chien were instrumental in putting the organization together, and Chou along with Ch'ang Hui and Ku Chieh-kang was largely responsible for launching the society's journal, *Folksong* (*Ke-yao chou-k'an*), which saw the light of day in December 1922.[49]

The purpose of the organization, which flourished until the

---

tung te tso-yeh ho chin-ch'en" [The Past Night and Present Dawn of the Chinese Folklore Movement], *Min-chien*, II:5 (1933), 1–17.

45. Jung Chao-tsu, "Pei-ta ke-yao yen-chiu hui," part 1, p. 3.

46. *Ibid.*

47. Ku, "*Wu ke chia-chi* tzu-hsü."

48. Ku, *ibid.* The article was "*Wu yu chi-lu* hsü" [A Preface to a Collection of Songs from Wu], *Nung pao* [The Peasant], Jan. 20, 1920.

49. Lou Tze-k'uang, "Cung-kuo min-su-hsüeh yün-tung," p. 3; and Jung Chao-tsu, "Pei-ta ke-yao yen-chiu hui," part 2, p. 3. Also see *Kuo-hsüeh chi-k'an* [Journal of National Studies], I:1 (Jan. 1923), 398–399.

The first issue of *Ke-yao chou-k'an* is dated Dec. 1922; it suspended publication with no. 97 (June 1925). It resumed publication with no. 98 (April 1936) which was the equivalent of (n.s.), II:1, and ran for 29 more issues.

middle of 1925, was to gather folk materials, songs in particular, for purposes of "pure study," as well as for the "nourishment of contemporary art." [50] The preface to the first issue of *Folksong* heavily emphasized the need to gather folk materials, no matter how crude their appearance, with an open mind, for the purpose of pure research. However, it anticipated the compilation, in the near future, of a selection of all the folksongs gathered, to reveal "the heartsound of the nation's people." And it hinted that out of the folksongs, and the popular feelings which they represented, a new, national poetry would be born.[51]

The diaspora of the Peking University faculty cut short the life of *Folksong*. Before its demise in June 1925, it had greatly expanded its membership and activities; it published ninety-seven issues and several monographs, and sponsored the collection, from all parts of China, of thousands of folksongs and "folk sayings." [52] Ku Chieh-kang had begun to dominate the journal from late 1924, and continued to do so until its demise in 1925, with his impressively thorough studies of the legend of Lady Meng-chiang and his pioneering collection of folksongs from the Soochow area.[53]

The Maturation and Decline of the Folkstudies Movement, 1927–1937

Ku Chieh-kang acted as the Johnny Appleseed of the movement when he traveled and taught in the south of China from 1926 to 1929. It was Ku who personally influenced a number of students at Amoy University to establish an active folklore research society. And Ku was responsible for stimulating the interest of his friend, Chung Ching-wen, in folkstudies.[54] By

50. Lou Tze-k'uang, "Chung-kuo min-su hsüeh-hui yün-tung."

51. Jung Chao-tsu, "Pei-ta ke-yao yen-chiu hui," part 1, p. 9. Also see Richard M. Dorson's foreword to Wolfram Eberhard's *Folktales of China,* 2nd ed., rev. (Chicago, 1965), p. xxv. Dorson gives some further details on the development of the Chinese Folklore Movement from 1918 to 1937. He bases his account on Chao Wei-pang, "Modern Chinese Folklore Investigation," *Folklore Studies,* I (Peking, 1942), 55–76.

52. Lou Tze-k'uang, "Chung-kuo min-su hsüeh yün-tung."

53. See *Ke-yao,* I:69 through 96.

54. Lou Tze-k'uang, "Chung-kuo min-su hsüeh yün-tung," p. 4. Chung Ching-wen, as of 1932, was a professor of literature at National Chekiang

1933, the Folklore Movement had centered itself at Sun Yat-sen University, and Chung Ching-wen was its leader. Thus, Ku Chieh-kang represents the link between the roots of the movement in the north and its further development in the south. By this time, there were active folklore groups all along the coast; however, the most significant developments were in Canton, where Ku began teaching in late 1927.

Shortly after Ku's arrival at Sun Yat-sen University, the university's Historical and Philological Research Institute published the first issue of what was to become the folk movement's most prolific and versatile journal, *Folklore* (*Min-su*). For the first year of its life the journal was known as *People's Literature and Art* (*Min-chien wen-i*),[55] and it introduced itself to its small circle of readers through the exhortations of Tung Tso-pin, better known in his role as an outstanding archaeologist.

CHINA'S TWO CULTURES

Tung, who contributed heavily to *People's Literature and Art,* wrote the lead article for its first issue. The initial subject Tung drummed into his audience was that of China's 'two cultures,' a concept which had been in the process of formulation since the early May Fourth period and which now, though still inchoate, became a standard part of folklorists' credo. Tung wrote:

> In the historical development of Chinese society, society became divided into two classes, the aristocracy (*kuei-tsu*) and the common people (*p'ing-min*). Not only in life were they different, but their cultures were separated as well. Doubtless, China's culture for more than a thousand years has only been that of the aristocracy: the twenty-four histories are the genealogies of their clan and their family records. All literature was the instrument of their play and

University and editor of the journal of the National Folklore Society. A professional folklorist, he has an extensive bibliography on all aspects of the field.

55. The first issue of *Min-chien wen-i* is dated Nov. 1, 1927. Issue no. 1–12 is dated Jan. 10, 1928. With no. 13, the title was changed to *Min-su chou-k'an.* Chung Ching-wen was editor of *Min-chien,* and he thus became the first editor of *Min-su.*

pleasure. The obligations of morality and the laws of government were used as screens to hide their wrongs and as weapons to slaughter the common people.

The slogan Tung formulated for the new journal, and the Folklore Movement, was a response to this baleful situation:

Overthrow the traditional old outlook of corrupted aristocratic literature and art!
Use the spirit of research scholarship to become informed about the people's literature and art!
Employ the critical outlook on art and literature to appreciate people's art and literature!
Use the methods of social reform to innovate within people's art and literature!
Comrades who are zealous about people's art and literature—unite!
Promote a fresh and living art and literature! [56]

We should note that in addition to making the two cultures a standard point of departure for folklore ideologists of the future, Tung, in item four above, introduced another large consideration. Here, he made it clear that 'people's culture' was not a sacerdotal entity, off-limits to the contrived innovations of the literary reformers. Just how this idea reconciled itself with the emphasis on spontaneity, which we saw in the platform of the Folksong Society, remains to be seen.

Earlier in the same year that Tung Tso-pin called his comrades together, Ku Chieh-kang had written an equally enthusiastic essay as the introduction to his 1928 book on Soochow customs. Ku spoke there of the "unconscious cultural creations" of the common people which had failed to develop and gone unnoticed by scholars of the past. "Never was it dreamed by men of the past," Ku exulted, "that folkstudies could be considered a type of scholarship." Today, he continued, the libraries are full of books commissioned by the emperors; but, when all is said and done, they are extensive but superficial records, telling little of the practical realm of life. Thus, scholars of the past

56. "Wei *Min-chien wen-i* chin-k'ao tu-chi" [A Respectful Admonition to the Reader], *Min-chien wen-i*, no. 1 (Nov. 1, 1927), pp. 2, 4–5.

were blind to popular customs even when the customs were not hidden from their view.[57]

Ku introduced into the standard patter some interesting metaphors which further enriched the emerging conception of "people's art and literature." He was pleased that his generation was aware of the people's life and culture. Because of this,

> we can make these fertile fields and rich lands into our farms; and we can make these excellent plants and rare fruits into our agricultural produce. Knowing that we can take hold of such a great possession in our own times, how can we be unhappy, how can we keep from crying out: "We want to develop this new, rich territory! We want to gather in the abundant harvest!"

If Ku wanted to feed modern Chinese culture on the vegetable genius of popular culture, he confused the issue with his concluding metaphor:

> But if you want to gather in the harvest, how is it possible to go about it at will? We have no hoes or plows or other tools and we are unable to sow the fields and plant the orchards. Without the proper tools we can neither harvest nor store away the grain and fruit. We must therefore develop the tools first.

Ku's general intent was plain enough here: he was once again encouraging his colleagues to acquire the scientific tools, the *methodology,* necessary to develop the field of folklore properly, especially the methods required to gather folkloric data (interview, transcription, etc.). But if the 'produce' here represented popular culture, and was attractive for its "natural innocence," as Ku suggested elsewhere, or if its value was at all related to its spontaneity or naturalness—why should it be necessary for the *folklorist* "to sow the fields and plant the orchards"? The Chinese folklorist mentality here again seemed to find it difficult to remain outside of the natural process of organic cultural growth, as it were. The folklorist wanted to help his garden grow.

In March 1928, *People's Literature and Art* changed its name

57. *Su-Yüeh te hun sang* (n. 21, above), Introduction, pp. 1–2. The discussion in text below is based on these same two pages.

to *Folklore*[58] under the editorship of Chung Ching-wen, and Ku Chieh-kang was given the honor of writing the introductory statement. Ku was now the chief spokesman and publicist for the Folklore Movement, and so he was called upon to write a spate of hortatory prefaces to the folklore monographs which began to pour out of Sun Yat-sen University.[59] Over and over again, without any lapse of eloquence, he reminded his readers that they too were essentially "of the people"; that the masses should become known *in situ*—not through the distorted, laconic record left by the aristocracy. Go into the field, he chided, and personally become familiar with every variety of people's life, so that all of China's society can be known. Only in this way could the researcher "overthrow his own gentry frame of mind," and ultimately "destroy that history which takes the culture of the sages as a fixed life pattern, and finally promote a history of the masses." [60]

It had become Ku's job to legitimize the study of folklore, to argue the case for the value of folklore data, and to urge his colleagues to gather data while circumstances still permitted it. In 1928, for example, he compared the collecting of folk data to Lo Chen-yü's efforts to collect Oracle Bones, and he pleaded with his readers "You must consider folklore materials to have the same status that you attribute to Oracle Bone literature." [61]

In 1929 Ku's prefatory essays fought battles on two fronts. On one hand, they argued against impatient folklorists who demanded some kind of system to follow. "A system without data,"

58. *Min-su chou-k'an* appeared on March 21, 1928. It ran continuously to No. 110 (April 30, 1930). At this point, it stopped publication until it was revived with No. 111 (March 21, 1933). It folded with the combined issue No. 116–117–118 (May 1933). A new series of the journal appeared sometime in 1936—vol. I:7 of the new series is dated Jan. 1937.

59. For example: "Hsü, *Ming ke chia-chi*" [Preface to Fukien Folksong Anthology], reprinted in *MS,* no. 13–14 (1928), pp. 11–14; "Kuan-yü *Mi-shih*" [History of Riddles], reprinted in *ibid.,* pp. 19–23; *"T'ai-shan ke-yao chi,* hsü" [Preface to Folksongs of Mt. T'ai], reprinted in *ibid.,* no. 49–50 (March 6, 1929), pp. 1–2; "Ch'uan-shuo chuan-hao, hsü" (Preface to Special Issue on Legends), *ibid.,* no. 47 (Feb. 13, 1929), pp. 1–2.

60. Ku, "Sheng-hsien wen-hua yü min-chung wen-hua" (n. 4, above), p. 4.

61. "Hsü, *Ming ke chia-chi,*" pp. 12–13.

Ku retorted, "is a false system." [62] Others, Ku wrote, wanted to take the folksongs and organize them into a representative anthology arranged from the literary point of view. But Ku's feeling was that these demands were impossible at that stage of development because, among other reasons, there were areas of China from which sufficient amounts of data had not yet been collected. In another statement, Ku expressed a fear that folksong in China was dying out, and that the folklorists' job would never have an opportunity to reach completion: As more children go to school, he pointed out, their songs are learned from a fixed repertory. And, again, as life in China continually becomes more oppressive, mature men "will lose the desire to sing." If the songs were not gathered soon, they would be lost forever.[63]

After Ku Chieh-kang left Sun Yat-sen University in 1929, the folklore interests there began to wane, and by the following spring *Folklore* stopped publication. Funds were lacking, and previously active participants were also leaving the university.[64] In 1930 Chung Ching-wen, now a specialist in folklore, organized a National Folklore Society with its home office in Canton.[65] By 1933, Chung Ching-wen's Folklore Society had absorbed or replaced most of the other folklore groups and claimed its own branches in almost every province,[66] but the fervor of the late twenties was not recaptured.

For a brief moment in the mid-thirties, there was an attempt to revive the old Folksong Study Society at Peking University. In 1935 one of the university's institutes invited some of the earlier folksong fanciers (among them were Ku Chieh-kang, Hu Shih, Chou Tso-jen, Ch'ang Hui, and Lo Ch'ang-pei) to resus-

62. "*Foochow ke-yao chia-chi,* hsü" [Preface to Foochow Folksong Anthology], reprinted in *MS,* no. 49–50 (March 6, 1929), pp. 6–9.

63. Ku's preface to "Ch'uan-shuo chuan-hao."

64. Chu Hsi-tsu, preface to *MS,* no. 111 (March 21, 1933); and Jung Chao-tsu "Wo ts'ui-chin yü 'min-su hsüeh' yao shuo te hua" [Some Things I Must Say About Folklore Studies of Late], *ibid.,* pp. 6–19.

65. Along with Chung Ching-wen were Chiang Shao-yuan and Hsi Tzu-hu. The society published the *Min-su-hsüeh chi-chien* [Folklore Symposium] beginning in the early 1930s. This journal was edited by Chung Ching-wen and Lou Tze-k'uang.

66. Lou Tze-k'uang, "Chung-kuo min-su hsüeh-hui yün-tung."

citate *Folksong*. Their goal was to systematize the study of folksongs, to organize the data gathered in the previous ninety-seven issues of the journal, and to edit a new monograph series which would deal with folksongs of various regions of China.[67] Hu Shih became chairman of the new Folksong Study Society during its brief second life. Probably under his influence, the new *Folksong* showed somewhat more versatility than its predecessor. In addition to mere folksong transcription, characteristic of the latter, the new journal published folktales, translations of fairy tales, and folksongs from other languages, as well as analytical articles. Thirty-one issues of the journal were published before it stopped, for the last time, in January 1937.

FOLKLORE AND EDUCATION

In 1928, Ku Chieh-kang wrote a short piece in *Folklore* which expressed his great concern over current inimical attitudes toward popular culture. His own personal goals, like those of the Folksong Study Society, he said, were simply to gather folk materials, to understand them, and to clarify them. However, there were two other schools of thought which had more grandiose designs, and folk culture was beginning to suffer because of them. The Education school sought to "reform customs," but Ku felt that it was blind to the realities of folk society and merely acted in accord with its own conceptions of the masses. What this school sought to reform, or to glorify and preserve, was only a response to its own narrow vision of reality. The Political school, on the other hand, sought only to "glorify the spirit of the nation," and this was its sole criterion for judging and altering folk society.[68] Ku Chieh-kang was not the only one with reservations about the two schools. The reaction of other folklorists to them enlivened the tone of folkstudies in the late twenties and throughout the 1930s.[69]

When the Ting Hsien experimental village project published

67. Hu Shih, preface to *Ke-yao,* II:1 (March 4, 1936), 1.

68. "Kuan yü *Mi-shih*" (n. 59, above), p. 20.

69. For a similar classification, and a rather sardonic evaluation of the Folklore Movement, see Lu Yung-heng, *Kuang-chou erh-ke yen-chiu* [A Study of Children's Songs from Kwangtung] (Canton, 1928?), chap. 1.

its first set of data in 1933, the prefatory statement to the compilation contained a barb obviously directed at Ku Chieh-kang's idea of folkstudies. The object of the Ting Hsien studies, it said, was indeed to understand realities, but this understanding was only the beginning, not the end, of their work. To study for study's sake was not their goal. It was social reform.[70] Thus, although the non-Communist populists shared a belief in a gradualist, educationalist approach to the problems of rural China, it was evident by 1928, at the latest, that the most conservative of these conservatives were the participants in the Folklore Movement. Inaction spoke louder than exhortation, and Ku Chieh-kang's suggestions that folkstudies were the basis of reform came to take on the cast of a scholastic's apologia for his failure to balance knowledge with action. The folklorist visualized reform in some dim, distant future. However, there was a strain within the movement which quite early began to take a 'functional' approach to folklore and to see everything from proverbs to songs as potential educational media and natural channels for reform of the masses.[71] By the late 1920s, with the growth of rural reconstruction, the folklore journals were brimming with these ideas.

One folklorist, for example, introduced his 1929 study on Hunan province ballads (*ch'ang-pen*) with a statement advocating folklore studies for the immediate aim of reforming the social evils of folk society.[72] China is a particularly corrupt society, the author suggested, and ballads were excellent devices for revealing all sorts of social evils and discontents. They should be studied because they were one of the few expressions of what

70. Yen Yang-ch'u, preface to *Ting Hsien she-hui kai-k'uang tiao-ch'a* (n. 36, above), p. 2.

71. In the early 1920s, one sees isolated examples, such as Yu Tzu-i's 1921 essay, prefixed to Wu Shou-chen's *Wu chin yao-yen chi* [Collection of Rumors About the Coming of War] (Shanghai, 1929). Yu Tzu-i was a professor of elementary school education who felt that proverbs, if properly employed, could be turned to good use in formal education.

72. Yao I-chih, *Hunan ch'ang-pen t'i-yao* [Introduction to Hunan Ballads] (Canton, 1929), preface by Ku Chieh-kang. Also see Ch'en Yuan-chu, "T'ai-shan ke-yao chi" [Anthology of Folksongs from Mt. T'ai], *MS,* no. 49–50 (March 1929), pp. 4–5, which contains similar ideas regarding folksongs.

the people themselves felt was wrong with contemporary society. In this book, the ballads were classified according to plot, and the introductory remarks discussed what kind of social evil each category revealed: Plots concerned with love, for example, help reformers "perceive that China's marriage system has need of reform, in order to rescue and relieve future youth." Other categories tell their own story: "Hating poverty, desiring riches"; "family questions: inheritances, sister-in-laws, concubines . . . ," and so on.

This singularly unromantic approach to folk culture was similarly manifested by the Ting Hsien sociologists. In their 1933 report, they recommended that folk amusements such as folksong singing and *yang-ko* (the dramas performed to celebrate the rice harvest) be utilized "to raise the level of the peasant's life, to reform the peasant's habits, to advance the peasant's knowledge." [73] "Although there are some unsatisfactory spots in the *yang-ko*," the sociologists wrote in the introduction to a collection of the dramas compiled in the Ting Hsien area, "still they should not be completely discarded." [74] The Ting Hsien sociologists were concerned that suppression of the *yang-ko* would rob an already drab peasant life of one of its few forms of entertainment:

> Thus, we do not advocate overthrowing the *yang-ko*—which in fact would not be easy to overthrow—but we want to take the *yang-ko* that already exist and correct and improve them, preserving their good points. Going one step further, we can write new *yang-ko*, introducing new ideas, gradually replacing the old *yang-ko*. In this way, we will not cause the farming village with its lack of activity to lose this popular recreation, and we can also establish it as a suitable form for social education.[75]

In the early 1930s, this trend had reached such a considerable force that Chiang Shao-yüan, a co-founder of the National Folk-

73. Li Ching-han, *Ting Hsien she-hui kai-k'uang*, p. 325.

74. Li Ching-han and Chang Shih-wen, Preface to their *Ting Hsien yang-ko* [The Rice Sprout Dramas of Ting Hsien] (Shanghai, 1933), p. 3. Translated in C. Moy, "Communist China's Use of the Yang-ko," *Papers on China from Seminars at Harvard University*, VI (Cambridge, Mass., 1952), 117.

75. *Ibid.*

lore Society, felt it incumbent upon himself to speak out on the use and abuse of folklore. "Folklore ought to be able to aid the masses to be conscious of themselves," he wrote, "and to liberate their own instruments of labor." Folklore, he continued,

> is not merely something which can prepare the upper classes to drive away the masses in order to protect themselves, nor is it merely [something to study] the growth of mankind's thought, nor something in which to find exotic interests, nor something to provide a relief from one's studies.[76]

Chiang offered no alternative to the prevailing folk-reform and folk-education attitudes.

The folklorists opened themselves to such criticism due to their sometimes careless rhetoric and because of their conspicuous aloofness from the masses they studied. In the thirties, there was more than a reverberation in folklore circles of Charlotte S. Burne's *Handbook of Folklore,* which the folklorists translated from English and cited repeatedly in their writings.[77] Burne's handbook was primarily used because it provided a detailed outline for gathering folk materials through interview and observation, and for classifying the materials. Her supercilious attitude is evident from the outset of the book, where she explained that the book was not for professionals, but for all of those who might happen to come into contact with "uncivilized, semi-civilized, uneducated" peoples who might yield some interesting materials. Burne suggested that folkloric knowledge would promote better understanding between the "governing and the governed" and make the latter more amenable to the inclinations of the former. In all fairness, the handbook seems to give rather sound, practical advice to aspiring folklorists. However, its attitude of condescension is inescapable.[78]

76. Quoted by Jung Chao-tsu, "Pei-ta ke-yao yen-chiu hui (n. 44, above)," p. 7.

77. Charlotte Sophia Burne was vice president and sometime president of the Folklore Society of England. The Chinese used the 1914 edition of the book, published in London. Lou Tze-k'uang reports that the book was used a great deal by Cheng Chen-to, Ch'en Hsi-hsiang, and Lo Sih-ping in their research.

78. After forming this opinion of Burne's handbook, I was interested to read the Chinese Communist opinion. In 1957, Chung Ching-wen, still a

The Education school, which Ku Chieh-kang had acknowledged with foreboding (though in principle, its viewpoint seems only to be an extension of his pronouncements throughout the 1920s), found its final expression before the war in the journal *Mass Education* (*Min-chung chiao-yü*). From time to time in the 1930s it published large special issues devoted to folk arts, customs, literature, and educational reform.[79] Burne's point of view prevailed in the rather insipid, unimaginative, rehash apologias for folkstudies which appeared in all the issues. The folklorists here, for the most part, tried to divorce themselves completely from their subjects. There was no suggestion that folksongs might be of value because of their potential use for modern Chinese literature. Indeed, the folklorists here prided themselves on their 'functional' approach, a point of view which aimed only to discover the sociological role of a custom or art form in order that reformers might better know how to implement their programs.

There is one particularly arresting feature about *Mass Education*. Scattered throughout its folkstudies issues are numerous banal articles similarly entitled "New Year's Customs in My Old Home," "Painting in My Old Home," "Medical Customs in My Old Home," etc. There is a *froideur* about these mechanical set-pieces, which only sought faithfully to make records in the most detached, unemotional fashion for some unstated reformist goal. We are nevertheless left with the distinct feeling that the writers wanted us to find a measure of quaintness in the folk institutions they described, and thus the burden they convey is not scientific folklore, but nostalgia and sentimentalism. Next to Lu Hsün's short stories—"My Old Home," or "Medicine," for example—the little folklore exercises of the journal begin

---

prominent folklorist on the mainland, was impeached for being a "salesman of capitalist folklore." His use of Burne's book was cited as evidence, because the book averred "that knowledge of folklore would make possible improved treatment by governing nations of 'subject races under their sway.' " (Cited in Dorson's Foreword to Eberhard's *Folktales* (n. 51, above), p. xiv.)

79. *Min-chung chiao-yü* (*chi-k'an*) [Mass Education] was published by the Chekiang Institute of Adult Education. The special numbers are III:1 (Feb. 1933), V:4–5 (Feb. 1937), and V:9–10 (July 1937).

to look like pseudo-scientific poses. Such poses apparently obviated the need to acknowledge the cruel aspects of an old society which ultimately had to be acknowledged as one's own source of origin. When Lu Hsün returned to the old home, he found tragedy and pathos in which he himself was deeply involved. But these self-styled folklorists of the thirties found only data.

FOLKLORE AND SUPERSTITION

If Ku Chieh-kang became irritated with the attitudes of the Education school toward folk culture, it was alarm he expressed at the potential destructiveness of the "anti-superstition" campaign which the Nationalist Government launched soon after Chiang Kai-shek's Nanking regime was established. Ku felt that a cultural crisis was being precipitated, and as a result we see him come to associate popular culture with the past and to identify it with China's *true* cultural heritage.

Very early in the development of the Folklore Movement, Chou Tso-jen had taken a rather firm stand on the question of "popular superstition." Quoting Sir James G. Frazer, Chou wrote that "If we were to study these superstitions which submerge our nation's people into darkness, superstitions which the people adamantly perpetuate, we would be greatly shocked. It would become apparent that the most enduring parts of life are exactly these oldest and most exaggerated of superstitions." [80] Chou Tso-jen, not unlike his brother Lu Hsün, was unsentimental about life in the old home. He felt that rural life gave to China its most pervasive and characteristic culture—and that was not the culture of Confucianism and the orthodox institutions, but "shamanism." [81] He was uncompromising in his prescription: "All vestiges of animal temperament," he warned in

80. This is my paraphrase of Chou's translation from Frazer's *Psyche's Task*. See Chou's "Hsiang-ts'un yü tao-chiao ssu-hsiang" [The Countryside and Taoist Thought], in his *T'an Hu Chi* [Speaking to the Tiger], 2 vols. (n.p., 1929).

81. *Ibid.*; see also his "San-man te li-chiao ssu-hsiang" [The Orthodox Thought of Shamanism], dated 1925, in *T'an Hu Chi,* pp. 339–342.

1918, "can, with ancient practices, obstruct the higher development of man, and all ought to be abolished or changed." [82]

Ku Chieh-kang's reports on Soochow customs, though phrased with more circumspection, further built up the leading folklorists' critical outlook on peasant culture. Despite this, the Nationalist regime by 1929 had come to regard folklore, in Wolfram Eberhard's words, "as a dangerous field." Eberhard, who was pioneering German studies of Chinese folklore at the time, observed the sources of tension between the government and the Folklore Movement in China.[83] In retrospect, he writes,

> Whereas Chinese society, it was believed, was quickly developing and was well on the way to becoming more and more rational and scientific, folklorists were accused of keeping alive the superstitious beliefs and attitudes of an era which should not be cherished but, instead, should be allowed to die.[84]

In addition, the folklorists were accused of "violating the official dogma of a unified Chinese culture," because in the course of their field work in various parts of the country they "tended to emphasize local differences, even to isolate local subcultures." [85]

The particular issue that brought out the conflict most strongly was that of popular icons and idol worship amongst the peasantry. Sidney Gamble, in his study of North China villages in the late 1920s, reported that in the north many temples were secularized as the icons were taken down and religious services were discontinued. He recorded that in Honan, "Feng Yü-hsiang, a Christian, tried to suppress the old religious activities. The images were taken out of many of the temples, and the land and buildings were turned over to the schools and

82. Chou, "Jen te wen-hsüeh" [Humane Literature] dated Dec. 1918, in his *I-shu yü sheng-huo* [Art and Life] (Peking, 1931).

83. During the early 1930s, Professor Eberhard was in close communication with such leading folklorists as Chung Ching-wen and Lou Tze-k'uang. *Min-chien yüeh-k'an,* journal of the Chinese National Folklore Society, published some of the Chung-Eberhard correspondence. It also reviewed some of Eberhard's books on Chinese folklore and local culture.

84. From Eberhard's Introduction to his *Folktales of China,* p. xxiv.

85. *Ibid.*

the village administrations." [86] And in 1928, the Nationalist government adopted a law "which called for the closing of temples in which purely legendary persons and spirits were worshipped." [87]

We should note that this type of activity was also being sponsored by Communist organizations. Mao, in his 1927 report on Hunan peasant associations, was very pleased to observe the successful destruction of superstitions as a result of closing up temples and converting them into schools. But Mao warned the associations and the party against precipitous action in this area of peasant reform. "It is the peasants who made the idols," he wrote, "and when the time comes they will cast the idols aside with their own hands; there is no need for anyone else to do it for them prematurely." Mao wanted the Communist party's propaganda policy in such matters, at this time, to be

> 'Draw the bow without shooting, just indicate the motions.' It is for the peasants themselves to cast aside the idols, pull down the temples to the martyred virgins and the arches to the chaste and faithful widow; it is wrong for anybody else to do it for them.[88]

Ku Chieh-kang and his student, Jung Chao-tsu,[89] were the most outspoken of the folklorists generally to condemn idol-smashing and the disruption of peasant customs. However, they did agree with Mao on one point of procedure. Ku explicitly deplored the Nationalist government's interdiction of certain

86. Sidney Gamble, *North China Villages: Social, Political and Economic Activities Before 1933* (Berkeley and Los Angeles, 1963), p. 125.

87. *Ibid.*

88. Mao, "Report of an Investigation of the Peasant Movement in Hunan" (n. 24, above), p. 34.

89. Jung Chao-tsu was a student at Peking University in the early 1920s. He studied at Amoy University, where he came under the influence of Ku Chieh-kang, particularly Ku's ideas on the *I-ching* [Book of Changes]. In 1928, he went with Ku to Sun Yat-sen University. Jung contributed heavily to the various folklore journals and was largely responsible for keeping the movement alive at Sun Yat-sen University until Chung Ching-wen took responsibility in the early 1930s. Jung is the author of many scholarly works on Chinese legends, particularly those transmitted in classical texts. Samples of these can be found throughout the *KSP*.

festivals and customs, because he felt this would alienate the people from the intellectuals and would make it difficult, if not impossible, to pass their knowledge on to the masses.[90] Similarly, Mao seemed to be cautioning the cadres that if they moved too quickly and too clumsily, the reform of peasant institutions would merely be an illusory superimposition and would no doubt render the peasant hostile to the Communist party.

But Ku Chieh-kang and Jung Chao-tsu were less interested in reform strategy in these matters than in the wanton destruction of China's cultural heritage, a fact that can be seen in Ku's long campaign to preserve the Buddhist iconographic sculpture attributed to the sixth-century artist Yang Hui-chih. In 1918, Ku became interested in this ill-preserved statuary in Soochow's Pao-sheng Temple. Soon thereafter, he began publishing articles on the history of the icons and calling for some kind of plan to guarantee their preservation.[91] After a few years' respite, Ku renewed his campaign in 1929, when he used the Yang Hui-chih issue as grounds for condemning the destructive activities of the new government. "What has been preserved for thousands of years," he wrote, "comes down to our generation and suffers catastrophic annihilation. How can we not consider this our shame?" Ku then continued,

I hear it said that ever since last year, when the Nationalist Government prohibited 'excessive religious rituals,' generally wherever the Northwest Army happened to be, Buddhist and Taoist temples were greatly damaged, and Buddhist icons were destroyed. Military men have come to prepare cultural programs. I strongly feel that this is to be feared. In this one year, who knows how many ancient works of art have been destroyed? The nation has not established a national museum, and therefore cannot take these works out of the temples themselves! As a result, superstitions are not necessarily

90. See Ku's "Lün Chung-kuo te chiu li-hsin-nien" [Former Chinese New Year's Customs], *Min-chien,* II:2 (Sept. 1932), 1–4.

91. See his letter, dated October 13, 1922, in the *Pei-ta kuo-hsüeh chi-k'an* [Peking Journal of National Studies], I:1 (Jan. 1923), 201. Also see his "Yang Hui-chih te su-hsiang" [The Iconography of Yang Hui-chih], dated Dec. 1923, *Hsiao-shuo yüeh-pao* [Fiction Monthly], XV:1 (Jan. 10, 1924).

overthrown, while the artistic legacy of earlier men is indeed overthrown.[92]

This crusading spirit to preserve elements of the past, "to preserve certain data which the reformers wish to destroy," in Jung Chao-tsu's words, did not confine itself to popular culture. In a 1933 article, Jung recalled how the Folklore Society of China (the one founded in 1930) rescued a group of idols from the countryside where an anti-superstition campaign fostered rampant iconoclasm. He juxtaposed this event to the lone efforts of the History Department of National Sun Yat-sen University to preserve the state papers of Yüan Shih-k'ai. "To destroy idols is not to overthrow superstition," Jung protested, "and the historians and folklorists collecting idols cannot be said to be contrary to the goal of overthrowing superstition." Uneasily, he concluded that preserving Yüan's state papers was not contrary to the work of Kuomintang party members.[93]

Inexorably then, the folkloric interests of Ku Chieh-kang and his close associates took on a deep concern for China's past and were given a historical orientation. Read by themselves, the syntax and fervor of Ku's calls to arms for the folklore societies gave the appearance that they were written by just another, perhaps somewhat more zealous, rural reformer. But if it is at all permissible to place him within the varied realm of such reformers, he must be considered the most conservative and lethargic of them. It would seem more instructive, however, to see him in another context altogether; for if the masses were ever his concern at all, they were a remote one. It was not the common people who received the attention of his considerable energies, but rather it was the common people's culture—quite a different thing.

92. "Ssu chi, Yang Hui-chih su-hsiang" [Fourth Comment on the Iconography of Yang Hui-chih], *Chung-ta chou-k'an,* X:117 (Feb. 5, 1930), 11.

93. Jung Chao-tsu, "Wo ts'ui-chin yü 'min-su hsüeh" (n. 64, above), pp. 18–19. Also see a fuller development of this argument in Jung's preface to his book, *Mi-hsin yü ch'uan-shuo* [Superstitions and Legend] (Canton, 1929).

V

Popular Culture as a Modern Alternative

In all the three thousand or more years of China's literary history, which new forms of literature did not come from the people?—Hu Shih, *History of Vernacular Literature,* 1925

'Literature of the masses' is self-contradictory. The masses have no literature. There is no room for the application of the democratic spirit in literature.—Liang Shih-ch'iu, "Literature and Revolution," 1928

The discovery of the People and their culture was of the greatest significance to Ku Chieh-kang. Under the guidance of Hu Shih, and then independently, Ku experimented with the usefulness of cultural populism, and he found it appealing to his vital concern for the continuity of tradition which could be identified as Chinese. Throughout the 1920s Ku contemplated with horror what he thought to be the extinction of Chinese civilization. At times he toyed with the idea of eugenics to improve the survival chances of the Chinese; and he cast a hopeful glance at the (as yet) untapped and undeveloped potentials of China's minority ethnic groups (such as the Mongols, Mohammedans, Miao, and Yao).[1] But it was from the culture of China's own common *Han* masses that he most sought at least a partial solution. "When one

1. See *ACH,* pp. 166–169; and Part Four, below.

views Chinese culture in terms of the educated classes," he wrote in 1926, "one cannot avoid the conclusion that it is old and decrepit, but looked at from the standpoint of the population as a whole, it is still immature." [2] In this immaturity he saw potential vitality and cultural creativity.

The Uses of Popular Culture

In the course of his involvement with it, popular culture served Ku Chieh-kang (and his associates in the Folklore Movement) in a number of ways. It served as an instrument to destroy the effete upper-class (aristocratic) cultural tradition. At the same time, popular culture was meant to supplant that tradition—to take its place in the past and to replace it altogether in the future. In this, its second role, popular culture would fulfill a third function. It obviated the danger that Western culture would be the sole alternative to a rejected aristocratic (Confucian) past.

The alternative of "total Westernization" was entertained by some participants of the May Fourth literary movements. And the realm of literature, particularly poetry, often came to be the microcosm where more extensive issues relating to cultural change were tested. In a 1919 issue of *New Tide*, for example, we find this statement promoting an unceremonious Westernization of Chinese literature on these grounds:

> Western literature clings to man's life; Chinese literature flees it. Western literature promotes the common spirit of mankind; Chinese literature is written for a discrete group of individuals. Western literature seeks out reality; Chinese literature is fabrication. Western literature is popular (*p'ing-min te*) and spontaneous (*t'ien-jan te*); Chinese literature is aristocratic (*kuei-tsu te*) and contrived. Western literature produces originality; Chinese literature wants us to be just like the men of antiquity.[3]

The characteristics of Western literature enumerated here came quickly to be desiderata which New Culturalists sought for their new literature. However, Hu Shih, Ku Chieh-kang,

2. *ACH,* pp. 166–169.

3. Lo Chia-lun, "Shen-mo shih wen-hsüeh" [What is Literature?], *HC,* I:2 (Feb. 1, 1919).

and the folklorists argued strenuously that these very desiderata could be fulfilled without depending on the West. Hu Shih's Vernacular Literature and, even more so, the folklorists' folk literature were the answers. In the polemics advocating these two native genres, Hu Shih and Ku Chieh-kang were not attempting to convince their contemporaries to accept this literature, as such, as the core or even the point of departure for modern Chinese literature. Their design was to argue and demonstrate that in these indigenous materials, radical inspirations for the new literature—which some intellectuals believed were forthcoming only from the West—could readily be found.

Hu Shih and Vernacular Literature

In Hu Shih's writings there is not any systematic, much less precise, definition of the category of literature which he called Vernacular Literature (*pai-hua wen-hsüeh*). He tended to cite examples from this category more readily than he delimited the specific literary characteristics which these examples share. A few common characteristics can be inferred from his famous 1917 essay, "Tentative Suggestions for Literary Reform":[4] use of common language and ideographs; a simple, familiar written style; unity of the written and spoken languages; a literature in the "living language of the people."

Was there, however, a *specific* body of literature which could be pointed to and identified as Vernacular Literature? Hu Shih submitted that throughout Chinese literary history (at least up to the Ming dynasty) there had been a general tendency toward the unity of spoken and written languages: thus, even works accepted into the orthodox canon fulfilled a basic requisite for membership in this classification. But though the twelfth-century master philosopher Chu Hsi, for example, may have written in an idiom similar to Sung or Yüan dynasty prose fiction, did Chu Hsi's writings represent what Hu Shih meant by Vernacular Literature? Probably not. What primarily interested Hu Shih

4. Hu Shih, "Wen-hsüeh kai-liang ch'u-i" [Tentative Suggestions for Literary Reform], in W. C. Liu *et al.*, eds., *Readings in Contemporary Chinese Literature* (in Chinese) (New Haven, 1953), III, 77–91. Original in *Hsin ch'ing-nien* [New Youth], II:5 (Jan. 1917), 1–11.

was not a set of stylistic and linguistic peculiarities, but rather Vernacular Literature in its incarnation as a specific genre of Chinese literature, namely fiction (*hsiao-shuo*)—the tale, the romance, and particularly, the novel.

If Hu Shih's Vernacular Literature primarily, if not solely, meant fiction, why did he state his arguments in terms of a broader category? If it was primarily in fiction that he saw an answer to the problem of cultural alternatives, why did he bother to bring other genres into his polemics? After all, neither the great T'ang poet Po Chu-i nor Chu Hsi needed help from Hu Shih, even though they wrote in a vernacular idiom. The problem was this: Fiction as a genre in itself had never been accepted into orthodox literary circles, nor was it about to be easily accepted by the vestiges of those circles (e.g., the Southern Society or Liu Shih-p'ei's Kiang-Che faction) in Hu Shih's time. It was necessary then to argue around the issue, and gradually. It had to be demonstrated that fiction shared (separate, though) equal membership in a class of literature whose roster listed prominent members of orthodoxy, even canon (Chu Hsi). The hoped-for result, it seems, was legitimacy by association. (In the literary reform essay, for example, the names of prominent novelists are grouped repeatedly with those of historians Ssu-ma Ch'ien and Pan Ku, or with model essayists "Han, Liu, Ou, and Su," almost as if an effort were being made to condition the reader into accepting the unorthodox associations.)

THE VALUE OF VERNACULAR LITERATURE

Hu Shih's argument, in outline, was this: (By definition) all Vernacular Literature is aesthetically good literature. All such literature has been natural and relevant for the age in which it was composed. Fiction is a class of Vernacular Literature, therefore good, natural, etc. The aesthetic superiority of Vernacular Literature was really a premise and was demonstrated by examples, not logic. Thus: Who can deny the literary and artistic superiority of Po Chu-i or a novelist like Ts'ao Hsüeh-chin? And their work is typical of Vernacular Literature.

The historical argument was more systematic, and its *locus classicus* in Hu Shih's writings is the 1928 introduction to his

History of Vernacular Literature.[5] In this widely-read polemic, he concluded that the overall history of the dominant literary tradition had been a history of literary imitations in which originality and appropriateness were sacrificed to the gods of orthodoxy. Vernacular Literature, tracing a pattern parallel to Classical tradition, had a history of literary creativity. This was a living literature which had constantly evolved in response to the changing needs and tastes of each age; it maintained its historical relevancy throughout the ages by ignoring the fixed, artificial, and arbitrary standards of Classical aesthetics. ("If you do not imitate the ancients, you can represent your age.") Hu Shih, now talking to his more conservative colleagues, also argued that the so-called modern literary revolution was no revolution at all, and the aesthetic which it promoted was no intrusion into Chinese history. These were merely the latest products of centuries of natural evolution in China, somewhat speeded up in recent decades because of a coincidence of events and the self-consciousness of the modern participants. One of his prime goals, Hu Shih said, was to reveal and explicate the true course and content of Chinese literary history, so long obscured.

Largely by a process of redefinition, Hu Shih created a possible cultural alternative: We have mistaken Classical Orthodoxy, he implied, for the *only* Chinese literary tradition. However, not only was there another tradition, but it was *the* tradition. Thus, he concluded,

> looking at the situation from the point of view of historical evolution, it can definitely be said that Vernacular Literature is the True Heritage of China's literature and will be the instrument of the literature of the future.

In this process of redefinition there was a tendency to narrow the intent of the Vernacular Literature concept. It became identified solely with non-orthodox *oeuvres* and secular genres such as Yüan drama, and especially with fiction (thus excluding philosophic tracts):

5: Hu Shih, *Pai-hua wen-hsüeh shih* [History of Vernacular Literature] (Shanghai, 1929).

Most men of today despise fiction as the lesser tradition, not knowing that Shih Nai-an, Ts'ao Hsüeh-chin, Wu Chien-jen [all novelists] all comprise the True Heritage of literature, while Parallel Prose and formalized poetry (Lü Shih) are truly the Lesser Tradition.[6]

Hu Shih did not complete his work on the general history of Vernacular Literature. Instead, he devoted more attention to the study of novels. The particular novels that Hu Shih chose to study are important here: For example, the *Dream of the Red Chamber* (*Hung lou meng*), of major interest to him, was widely read by the scholar-official keepers of Orthodoxy; generations before his own time, it was universally accepted on aesthetic grounds as superior artistry—but because it was fiction, it could not become the legitimate subject of serious and devoted literary criticism and exegesis. Hu Shih's most serious and personal intellectual commitment was to the study of the *Dream of the Red Chamber* and a few other novels of similar stature. But he was committed to these books not merely as things in themselves, but as representatives of a class of literature.

The popularity and acclaim of these novels as independent works of art perhaps helped to mitigate the strength of conservative criticism of Hu Shih's new scholarship. Throughout the twenties, Hu Shih and his fellow scholars deepened the commitment as they turned to the study of *Water Margin* (*Shui Hu Chuan*), *Journey to the West* (*Hsi Yu Chi*), and *Romance of the Three Kingdoms* (*San Kuo Yen-i*). They worked first on these widely accepted novels because (aside from their artistic attraction per se) they hoped to build prestige into the class of literature which these books represented. Later study was to have been extended to less prominent works which, nonetheless, were worthy because of their membership in the fiction category, as well as their artistic merit.

CRITIQUES OF VERNACULAR LITERATURE

Even as Hu Shih made his claims for Vernacular Literature, there was serious criticism awaiting him. The most notable of

6. "We-hsüeh kai-liang ch'u-i," p. 87.

the early critics was Liang Ch'i-ch'ao. He argued cogently that Vernacular Literature, rather than forming a distinct and valuable literary development quite apart from the Classical tradition, was its handmaiden, reinforcing its values:

Our novels were the principal cause of the perversion from which our society died. It was our novels which inoculated our students during the centuries with the rage of desire to finish first in the supreme literary examinations; to become ministers of state without any other baggage than the art of composing eight-legged essays. [Novels] gave adventurers the idea to gain a throne by practicing brigandage. They have filled heads with all kinds of phantasmagoria propagating the belief in geomancy, astrology, divination.[7]

Liang did not want social reformers to abandon fiction because of its role in the past, but rather to use it to their own ends, lest that form of literature continue to poison society in the future as it had in the past.[8]

The Critical Review (Hsüeh Heng)

Writers in the *Critical Review* also were not long in registering their deep apprehension of new literature derived from popular sources.[9] *Critical Review* objections centered around a number of concepts which they felt were the weakest elements in popular culturalists' arguments. First, they deplored the distinction which the latter made between 'old' and 'new' literature, and argued that an evolutionary point of view was useless

7. From the French translation of Leon Weiger, ed. and trans., *Chine moderne* (Hien-hsien, 1931), Vol. I, *Prodromes,* pp. 101–102.

8. Henri van Boven, in his *Histoire de la litterature chinoise moderne* (Peking, 1946), p. 14, lists the titles of some experimental novels that Liang himself wrote for purposes of social reform. Van Boven suggests (p. 13) that Hu Shih, around 1910, had advocated the use of choice, expurgated Classical novels for literary and moral education.

9. This discussion is based primarily on three exemplary articles from the *Hsüeh Heng* [the Critical Review]: (1) Wu Fang-chi, "San lün yu-jen yen chung chih hsin-chiu wen-hsüeh kuan" [Third Discussion Regarding the Viewpoints on Old and New Literature], *Hsüeh Heng,* no. 31 (1924); (2) Liu P'u, "Pi wen-hsüeh fen kuei-tsu p'ing-min chih-wei" [Criticism of the Division of Literature into Aristocratic and Popular], *ibid.,* no. 32 (Aug. 1924); (3) Ts'ao Mu-kuan, "Lün wen-hsüeh wu hsin-chiu chih i" [Literature Does Not Have an Old and New], *ibid.*

in establishing what was advanced or decadent in literature. Some contributors to the *Critical Review* condemned Hu Shih and his associates for their historical relativism in the realm of aesthetic values; for they, like their predecessors in the Southern Society, defended a timeless, universal aesthetic which claimed, for example, that certain poetry of the T'ang dynasty was aesthetically of the highest value—in modern times as well as in the T'ang. Literature, claimed the *Critical Review*, has no 'old' and 'new'—only what is true and what is false. And because the New Culturalists failed to realize this, they were becoming as destructive as the book-burning under the first Ch'in emperor in the third century B.C. The new literature was weak, according to this criticism, precisely because it failed to rely upon its literary predecessors and to recognize the "unity of literary history."

The second, and more substantive, area of *Critical Review* reactions dealt with the popular claims and interests of the new literature. Primarily, this criticism rejected the distinction between popular and aristocratic literature. Those novels which Hu Shih had claimed to be part of the popular tradition (for example, the *Dream of the Red Chamber*) were in fact, said the *Critical Review*, written by members of the intelligentsia who in turn came from the aristocracy. Even when specific literature did originate with the common people (such as folksongs or popular dramas), it was written down only by the intelligentsia —a group which the *Critical Review* associated only with the upper classes.

The *Critical Review* refused to acknowledge that the folk could produce 'literature,' for their definition of that concept revolved about the ideas of refinement and discipline. Crudeness, naïveté, or vulgarity (which it associated with popular culture) simply had no place in true literature. In sum, the *Critical Review* considered literary and artistic creation in general to be an elite phenomenon; there was no mass literature, just as there was no mass science. If there is no learning, there is no art. Leisure, according to this theory, is central to artistic creation. Thus, when the peasant, merchant, or laborer are without the leisure for art, they are represented by the literary man. Even among the literate, it was argued, few write; and even in a period of great literary production, only a few men produce the literature. The idea of mass literature, then, was an absurdity and an impossibility from every standpoint, to the *Critical Review.*

Ch'ü Ch'iu-pai and the Marxist Response

The most sustained and severe criticism of Hu Shih was delivered in the early 1930s by Ch'ü Ch'iu-pai, erstwhile leader of the Communist party and self-appointed *bete noire* of Vernacular Literature.[10] While he agreed with Liang Ch'i-ch'ao's basic criticism of traditional fiction, Ch'ü Ch'iu-pai violently objected to the use of popular literature for the purposes of reforming the masses. (And here I am sure he was thinking of the rural educationalists as well as those of Liang Ch'i-ch'ao's ilk.) Those who were involved in such schemes he accused of aiding the arch-reactionaries by "insinuating themselves into the good graces of the people and anxiously planning to alter whatever strong national feelings they might have." When national feelings are drained off, the class feelings of the reformers are substituted, he said, to the detriment of the masses and China.[11]

Ch'ü Ch'iu-pai then turned his critical barrage on *pai-hua,* the reputedly popular vernacular language which Hu Shih had been promoting for over a decade. That Hu Shih's vernacular movement had made significant advances over the literary reforms of Lin Shu and Liang Ch'i-ch'ao, Ch'ü was willing to acknowledge. However, he charged that from the outset Ts'ai Yüan-p'ei, Hu Shih, and Ch'en Tu-hsiu only sought reform, not revolution, in Chinese literature.[12] They sought only to find a base in tradi-

10. For another example of the Marxist critique of Hu Shih's Vernacular Literature, see Wang Li-hsi, "Huo wen-hsüeh shih chih szu" [The Death of the History of Living Literature], *Tu-shu tsa-chih* [Readers' Miscellany], I:3 (June 1931).

11. "Hsüeh-fa wan-sui" [Long Live the Literary War], dated June 1931, in Ch'ü's *Luan T'an* [Vulgar Music] (Shanghai, 1933), p. 132. This essay, and the other Ch'ü Ch'iu-pai essays cited in this chapter, with the exception of the letter to Lu Hsün, may also be found in the small collection published under Ch'ü's name as *Lün Chung-kuo wen-hsüeh ke-ming* [Discussions of the Chinese Literary Revolution] (Hong Kong, 1949).

12. "Hsüeh-fa wan-sui," p. 114.

tional literary forms (*ku-wen*) for the vernacular, and never dreamed of using vernacular exclusively. The chief failure of the May Fourth literary movements, according to Ch'ü, was the failure to produce a literature that was really written in the language of the masses (*p'u-t'ung hua*) as it was spoken in *contemporary* China. With effective redundance, Ch'ü's essays argued that the vernacular promoted by Hu Shih was a dead language of the common people of the Ming dynasty, or the Ch'ing—that is, the periods in which Hu Shih's favorite novels were written. Ch'ü conceded that Hu Shih had made a significant cultural advance when he initiated the broad acceptance of fiction, but the language of that literature was no longer to be heard on the streets.[13]

In 1916, the banner of the literary revolution read "Overthrow the literature of the aristocracy." "Has it been overthrown?" Ch'ü Ch'iu-pai asked. If so, he answered, it has been converted into the literature of the gentry-merchant, an advance only to the degree that this class was contemporary in its interests and that it was nationalistic.[14] This literature, like the vernacular literature of the past, still remained for the most part upper-class; it was merely neo-Classical (*hsin wen-yen*).[15] The neo-Classical was an amalgam of foreign languages, Classical Chinese remnants, and the vernacular; neither living nor dead, old nor new, fish nor fowl. In a word, a "mule." [16]

It was not the technical aspects of language and literature that most troubled Ch'ü Ch'iu-pai in his critiques of Vernacular Literature. It was the political implications, and the implications for class conflict. He called the contemporary literature, which based itself on Vernacular Literature, "bourgeois." It deserved this anathema because it was the product of mixing European culture with the vestiges of China's aristocratic literary tradition. Therefore, not only was this literature not pop-

13. See Ch'ü's "Kuei-men kuan i-wai te chan-cheng" [The Great Wall Outside of the Kweimen Gate], dated May 1931, in *Luan T'an,* pp. 141–155.

14. "Hsüeh-fa wan-sui," p. 116.

15. "Ta-chung wen-i te wen-t'i" [The Question of Mass Literature], dated March 1932, in *Luan T'an,* pp. 243–244.

16. "Hsüeh-fa wan-sui," pp. 112–113.

ular, it was being used, just as Classical literature had been used, to oppress the masses.[17]

In a manner reminiscent of Liang Ch'i-ch'ao, Ch'ü Ch'iu-pai denounced the fiction which Hu Shih sought to glorify: "Fiction was but the means whereby the ruling class deployed their nets and snares to catch and control the masses . . . the tools with which to implement the slave education of the working masses." [18] The next step of the literary revolution could only be the complete acceptance of the language of the streets, especially the language of the proletariat, for a truly popular and revolutionary literature. Ch'ü called for a war against the "Lin Shu's in the midst of the masses" (the advocates of traditional fiction) and "all such reactionaries." [19]

Hu Shih's most significant answer to Ch'ü Ch'iu-pai's challenge was only a bolder restatement of his 1928 thesis. The *History of Vernacular Literature* had cautiously dissociated vernacular literature from the concepts of class and revolution; in 1933, Hu Shih's book *The Chinese Renaissance* brought them together, perhaps in an effort to show the Communist critics that he was not the Lin Shu they made him out to be.[20] But the trump card belonged to Ch'ü Ch'iu-pai. In a letter to Lu Hsün, who was also an early promoter of traditional fiction, Ch'ü summarized the basic weaknesses of Hu Shih's arguments for a tradition of popular culture. Now agreeing with the *Critical Review,* Ch'ü pointed out that the people never wrote down their 'literature.' Folksongs, legends, tales, all belonged to an oral tradition. It was the members of the aristocracy who recorded this tradition, and while some very few did plagiarize the people's literature, they tended to do a very poor job of it. Inevitably, the people's literature suffered alteration as the aristocrats tried to put it into whatever was considered to be

17. "O-hua wen-i ho ta-chung-hua" [Europeanized Literature and Popularization], dated May 1932, in *Luan T'an,* p. 278.

18. "Ts'ai lün ta-chung wen-i ta Chih-ching" [Another Discussion of Mass Literature in Answer to Chih-ching], dated July 1932, in *ibid.,* pp. 254–255.

19. "Wo-men shih shui?" [Who Are We?], dated May 1932, in *ibid.,* p. 274.

20. See Hu Shih, *The Chinese Renaissance* (Chicago, 1933), pp. 52–53, for key passage.

proper literary form. Further, poor recording occurred when class position prevented the aristocrat from truly presenting the people's ideas. Finally, the aristocrats' awkward, abstract kind of writing, being very confused and muddy, prevented accurate transcription. Therefore, virtually no true literature of the people survived from the past. It was either lost, unnoticed, or obscured and transformed through written transmissions. All of the vernacular literature which Hu Shih called "of the common people" was really proto-bourgeois literature, deeply influenced by the culture of the aristocracy.[21]

Ch'ü Ch'iu-pai did not object to the New Culture's being a popular culture, properly understood. It was rather that he saw a link between the nonrevolutionary politics of Hu Shih and his efforts to find roots for popular culture deep in the past. Hu Shih's emphases on evolution and historical precedents were very much a reflection of his political conservatism (relative to the Communists). Although the logic of the popular-culture arguments resolved itself into an argument based on the concept of class, Hu Shih studiously avoided its political implications. Ch'ü Ch'iu-pai might have summarized his case against the Hu Shih school with Herzen's evaluation of the Slavophiles:

> They have no roots in the people . . . They remember what the people have forgotten, and even about the present they hold opinions which in no way correspond to those of the people.[22]

The Folklorists and Folk Culture

When the folklorists exhorted one another to go to the people, their most fundamental and persistent motivation was the belief that out there was to be found a fresh source of inspiration for a new, true poetry. The folklorists' credo repeated Hu Shih's dictum that all innovations in literature derived from the common people; however, where Hu Shih focused his studies on traditional fiction, often an undeniably sophisticated and urbane

21. "Kuan-yü cheng-li Chung-kuo wen-hsüeh shih te wen-t'i" [The Question of Reorganizing China's Literary History], *Ch'ü Ch'iu-pai wen-chi* [Collected Writings of Ch'ü Ch'iu-pai], 4 vols. (Peking, 1953–1954), II (dated Oct. 1932), pp. 968–977.

22. Quoted in Martin Malia, *Alexander Herzen and the Birth of Russian Socialism, 1812–1855* (Cambridge, Mass., 1961), p. 304.

art form, the folklorists "drew near" the illiterate masses to learn what they might from their crude but inspired folksongs.

What were the characteristics of this folk culture (*min-su wen-hsüeh*) which was to become the source of a new literature and the identity of the old literary tradition? There is no *locus classicus* to which we can turn here;[23] the concept was built up over two decades by the casual remarks of a score of folklorists, literary critics, literary historians, and omnicompetents ranging from Liang Shih-ch'iu to Lu Hsün. An interesting collage resulted.

The concept of "two cultures" was the point of departure for formulating folk culture. Folk (or popular) culture was conceived as the antithesis of aristocratic culture.[24] The essence of the former was originality, of the latter—imitation.[25] Not only

23. See the essay by Wu Yen-yin containing a concise statement of most of the ideas which are discussed below in text—including a critique of the *Book of Odes* which is very close to Ku Chieh-kang's critique: Preface (dated Nov. 1922) to Chou T'ien-min's *Ke sheng tung-yao chi* [Anthology of Tales from the Provinces] (Shanghai, 1923).

In 1938, Cheng Chen-to originally published a book which can be considered a summation of the thought and schoolarship of the folk culture school: *Chung-kuo su wen-hsüeh shih* [A History of China's Common Literature], 2 vols. (Peking, 1954).

24. In the following items the development of the idea of 'two cultures' can be traced: Ch'en Tu-hsiu, "Wen-hsüeh ko-ming lün" [Critique of the Literary Revolution], *Hsin-ch'ing-nien* [New Youth], II:6 (Feb. 1917), pp. 1–14; Chou Tso-jen, "P'ing-min te wen-hsüeh" [Common People's Literature], dated 1918, in his *I-shu yü sheng-hua* [Art and Life] (Peking, 1931), pp. 1–10; Ku Chieh-kang, "Ch'ien-lo te ke" [Songs of Ch'ien-lo], *Hsiao-shuo yüeh-pao* [Fiction Monthly], XIV:3 (1923), and *KSP,* I (dated Jan. 1925), p. 54; and also Ku's "Sheng-chien wen-hua yü p'ing-min wen-hua" [Culture of the Sages and Culture of the Masses], *MS,* no. 5 (1928).

The theme of 'people's culture' versus 'anti-people's culture' is also employed or debated in the following items: Chou Chih-hsin's preface to Ch'iu Yu-lin, *Ch'ih-jen yü chiao-jen ku-shih* [Tales of Fools and Cunning Men] (n.p., 1939); Li Sung-chia, "Min-chien wen-hsüeh te li-lün chi chia-chih" [The Principles and Structure of Mass Literature], *Min-chien* [The People], I:7 (Dec. 1931), 4; Ch'ü Ch'iu-pai, "Kuan-yü cheng-li Chung-kuo wen-hsüeh shih te wen-t'i" (n. 21, above), p. 973.

25. The intent of the folklorists was to employ the two concepts as, for example, Edward Young had done in eighteenth-century England: "Imitations are of two kinds; one of nature, one of authors: The first we call originals and confine the term imitation to the second." *Conjectures on Original Composition, 1759* (Leeds: The Scholar Press, 1966), p. 9.

was the aristocratic literary tradition built up through a series of literate authors imitating their aristocratic predecessors, but it was able to survive only by plagiarizing the culture of folk tradition. The latter 'imitated' only nature; it was a spontaneous reflection of the realities of the people's lives. Folksong was considered, rather arbitrarily, to be the purest distillation of folk culture, and hence the richest embodiment of its truths.

The "originality" of folk literature was a generic quality under which a number of other characteristics were subsumed. Sometimes these qualities were couched in florid metaphors: If art can be compared to wild flowers, wrote Liu Pan-nung in 1928,

> then the art of folksong can be compared to the fragrance of the wild flower. Now there may be times when we are cloyed by the aromatic fragrance of the delicate iris, or worse, we get a headache from the fragrance of "Spring Forest" face powder or from the Coty company's perfume. [When this happens] let us go out to the wilds, and let us breathe in the all-pervading fresh fragrance of the wild flowers in order to arouse our spirits.[26]

Ku Chieh-kang wrote of the "natural genius" of folklore and song,[27] and others wrote of folksongs "flowing forth from the mouths of the common people," telling simply of their lives in a manner untainted by the artificiality of the aristocracy—"it is all natural melody, and has not undergone cutting and polishing." [28] The most frequently listed attribute of folk culture was its spontaneous (*tzu-jan*) nature, which was contrasted to the contrived literature of the aristocracy.[29]

26. Quoted in Chu Tzu-ch'ing, *"Yüeh-tung chih feng,* hsü" [Preface to Airs of East Canton], *MS,* no. 36 (1928), p. 1.

27. *"Ch'üan-chou min-chien ch'üan-shuo,* hsü" [Preface to The Folktales of Ch'üan-chou], *MS,* no. 67 (1929), p. 1; and "Su-chou te ke-yao" [Folksongs of Soochow], *MS,* no. 11–12 (1928), p. 11.

28. Hu Hua-shen, *Chung-kuo min-ke yen-chiu* [A Study of Chinese Folksongs] (Shanghai, 1925), p. 2.

29. For example, see Wang Pi-ting, "Tsen-yang ch'u yen-chiu ho cheng-li ke-yao" [How to Study and Organize Folksongs], in Chung Ching-wen, ed., *Ke-yao lün-chi* [Symposium on Folksongs] (Shanghai and Peking, 1928), pp. 291–296.

Cheng Chen-to summarized the prevalent ideas of the folklorist when his rather systematic study of popular culture listed these additional characteristics: The authors of folk literature are anonymous; the literature is transmitted orally, and has undergone considerable change by the time it happens to be written down by the educated classes; it is always fresh, but crude; the imagination it displays is quite free and wide-ranging; and folk literature bravely incorporates new things and foreign influences.[30]

An issue which vexed the folklorists as long as the Folklore Movement lasted was whether folksongs were a collective or individual phenomenon. A folklorist, raised on the individualist ethos of the May Fourth period, grew uneasy with the idea of an anonymous and collective authorship for the new national heritage.[31] Answers to this problem and many others were offered by Arnold van Gennep's *Le folklore*, which was translated into Chinese and used extensively.[32] Van Gennep provided the Chinese with sophisticated Durkheimian arguments about the delicate rapport between the individual and the mass, and he

30. *Chung-kuo su wen-hsüeh shih* (n. 23, above), I, 1–6.

31. The following articles argue that folksongs, like all folk art, are first created by a 'man of genius' and then transmitted through the collectivity, which alters the original creation; and that the difference between folk and aristocratic art is not the means of creation, but the means of transmission and circulation: Li Ch'ang-chih, "Ke-yao shih shen-mo" [What Is Folksong?], *Ke-yao* [Folksong] (n.s.) II:6 (May 9, 1936); "Lün ke-yao nai shih ko-jen-te ch'uang-tso" [Which Folksongs Are Created by Individuals?], *ibid.*, II:20 (June 20, 1936); and Lin Keng "Wei 'ke-yao' tso wen yu k'an" [Another Look at the Issue of Making Folksongs into Literature], *ibid.*

That folk art is a collective phenomenon is argued by Cho-sun in "Hsieh kei 'Ke-yao shih shen-mo' te tso-che" [In Response to the Writer of 'What Is Folksong?'], *ibid.*, II:10 (June 6, 1936), 2–4.

32. *Le folklore* (Paris, 1924) was translated by Yang Yüeh into Chinese. Professor Wolfram Eberhard informed me that the book had a great influence in the Folklore Movement in China.

Arnold van Gennep is best known for his formulation of the concept of "rites of passage." The major source of his inspiration came from the tradition of positivism, and he was influenced by his contemporaries Henri Hubert, Marcel Mauss, and Emile Durkheim—all representing the tradition of functional anthropology. See S. T. Kimball's Biographical Introduction to the English translation of van Gennep's classic, *Rites of Passage* (New York, 1960).

suggested that while folksongs were a collective phenomenon, they were not created collectively.[33] In van Gennep's book, cultural populists also found lucidly formulated discussions on the anonymous, undatable nature of folklore, and the mode of its growth and transmission. Van Gennep's writing radiated a love of "the people" and encouraged his readers to grow more intimate with, not scientifically aloof from, the masses. And when he extolled the intimate relationship in French civilization between cultivated intellect and the countryside, he provided encouragement for those folklorists who sought a new literary tradition amongst the peasants.[34]

DOUBTS ABOUT THE FOLKLORISTS, DOUBTS ABOUT THE FOLK

The claims the folklorists made for folksong and folk culture, and their version of China's literary history, did not go unchallenged. They escaped much of the criticism of Ch'ü Ch'iu-pai because they largely devoted themselves to contemporary manifestations of folk (if not proletarian) language and literature. It was from non-Marxist sources, within and outside the Folklore Movement, that the most telling blows were scored. However, no matter what the nature of the disagreement, seldom did a critic deny the possibility that Chinese folksongs might provide the new literature with a reservoir of fresh inspiration.[35]

For example, Hu Shih himself had reservations about the direction in which the folklorists set off under Ku Chieh-kang's leadership. On reading Ku's pioneering collection of folksongs, Hu raised some doubts, in a manner reminiscent of his own critics, of the truly popular nature of these songs. Too many of the songs in this particular collection came from "the women's apartments" (that is, they were formal compositions) and not enough from the people. But this was no wonder, Hu said, since

33. *Le folklore,* pp. 24–25.

34. *Ibid.,* pp. 15, 120–121.

35. It was no surprise to find but one participant in the folksong study group who followed out the logic of its ideologues: Wang Tu-ch'ing wrote that if it were true that folksongs were natural, spontaneous, and heaven-sent—in a word, original—then their spirit could not be preserved if they were imitated. Preface to Chung Ching-wen, *Lang Chuang hsing-ke* [Lyrics of the Lang and Chuang Tribes] (Canton, 1928), p. 1.

Ku Chieh-kang was born in the urban section of Soochow and those many friends who helped Ku to gather the songs were likewise city-dwellers. None of them had to any great degree drawn near the people of the villages, or the migrant laborers, and therefore they had missed the true productions of the folk. And there were too many songs in the collection, Hu concluded, that were "handed down or inherited" (and hence polished and routinized) at the expense of fresh creations.[36] Yet Hu Shih had no doubts that, through greater efforts, truly popular culture could be explored and extended to the greater good of Chinese literature.

More severely and persistently critical, Chou Tso-jen would not submit to the view that all good literature, and all poetic innovations, came from the people; nor to the equation "all that is of the people's culture is good." "The spirit of the common people can be said to be what Schopenhauer called the 'will to live,'" Chou wrote in 1923, "and the aristocratic spirit would then be what Nietzsche called 'the will to victory'":

> The former needs to have a limited, commonplace existence; the latter needs to have unlimited transcendent development. The former is completely this-worldly, the latter is almost a bit other-worldly.[37]

He argued that the common people were largely preoccupied with the petty details of day-to-day life. How then could they provide society at large with new forms of beauty? How could they be the source of literary innovation when they could not transcend the present? The literature of the common people is limited by the nature of their basic outlook—admiration for the achievements of the aristocrat's life, and the desire to have that kind of life for themselves.

Chou Tso-jen believed that a period of real literary development must more or less embody the aristocratic spirit. "The will to live," he said,

36. Hu Shih, '*Wu ke chia-chi,* hsü" [Preface to A Collection of Songs from Soochow], *HSWT,* III (dated 1925), 659–663.

37. "Kuei-tsu te yü p'ing-min te" [Aristocratic and Common], in Chou's *Tzu-chi te yüan-ti* [Our Own Garden], (n.p., 1923), pp. 13–16.

certainly is the basis of life, but if there is no will to victory which calls man to strive energetically to seek the life that is completely good and beautiful, then the survival of the fittest easily will retrogress.[38]

He prescribed a new literature based on the spirit of the common people and highly seasoned with aristocratic spice. In Chou's prophetic, Germanized formulation:

From the literary point of view, the best thing would be an aristocratized common-people—the superman-ization of the common man. For if the common man does not think of becoming the superman, then he will become the last man.[39]

More directly put, Chou Tso-jen plumped for what we now call the "seepage theory" of cultural innovation. The aristocracy has the wealth and the leisure to experiment and invent. The results seep down to the common man for further modification.[40]

Added to Chou Tso-jen's reservations about the primacy of popular culture were his more straightforward comments on the common people's folkways, religious beliefs, and sundry institutions. Unequivocally, he found them superstitious, backward, ugly, stagnant. And although he did cautiously agree with the most devout folklorists that folksong's genuineness, sincerity, freshness, and honesty profited the high culture and the new literature of new China,[41] he could not see any evidence of a benevolent evolution working through the masses for the advance of Chinese civilization.

From another corner of the literary world, Liang Shih-ch'iu, even as a colleague of Hu Shih in the rather conservative Crescent Moon Society, leveled his eloquent objections to the ideas of the cultural populists.[42] In 1928 he wrote, as we might expect of a student of Irving Babbitt, that

38. *Ibid.*

39. *Ibid.*

40. Van Gennep employed the seepage theory, but the folklorists ignored him on this point (*Le folklore,* p. 106).

41. For example, see his "Ke-yao" [Folksong] in Chung Ching-wen, ed., *Ke-yao lün-chi* (n. 29, above), p. 33.

42. See C. T. Hsia, *A History of Modern Chinese Fiction* (New Haven, 1961), pp. 1–18, 121, 317, for discussions of Liang's training and activities.

Present-day sentimental revolutionaries and superficial humanitarians have an unrestrained sympathy for the teeming masses . . . [which] often gets the upper hand over the considerations due to civilization. A number of writers are also infected by the same unrestrained sympathy and therefore shout loudly about 'literature of the masses.' . . . If there are people who hum praises to the breezes and the moon, who write love poems or love stories, or who discourse upon ancient art, then charges such as 'aristocratic,' 'petty bourgeois,' and so on will be heaped upon their heads. What is the reason for this? It is because such literature is individualistic, . . . of the few and not . . . of the many! . . . 'Literature of the masses' is self-contradictory—the masses have no literature. . . . There is no room for the application of the democratic spirit in literature.[43]

The growing appreciation of folksongs Liang interpreted to be the first symptom of that most onerous disease, romanticism.[44] Still, Liang Shih-ch'iu ended up by giving his qualified support to the Folklore Movement. In 1936 he wrote that the more aesthetically defensible of the folk poems should be publicized, because they could provide a model for the new poetry. Primitive as the folk poetry might be, still its tonal structures alone made it considerably more useful than the most modern of Western poetry: Of what use to the structure of a Chinese poem, he asked, is the work of even a Mallarmé?[45]

Over time, the fear of relying too much on Western culture brought doubters into the populist fold, and even made them outspoken defenders of the folklorists' cause. In 1936, Liang Shih-ch'iu defended Ku Chieh-kang against the charge of advocating a return to the past, because of Ku's involvement in the publication and publicizing of a Ch'ing dynasty folksong anthology.[46] This collection and other similar ones are vivid evidence that Ku saw a special role for himself in the Folklore

43. "Wen-hsüeh yü ke-ming" [Literature and Revolution] translated in Huang Sung-k'ang, *Lu Hsün and the New Culture Movement of Modern China* (Amsterdam, 1957), pp. 111–112.

44. See Chu Tzu-ch'ing, *"Yüeh-tung chih feng,* hsü" (n. 26, above); and Liang Shih-ch'iu, "Ke-yao yü hsin shih" [Folksong and the New Poetry], *Ke-yao* [Folksong], (n.s.) II:9 (May 30, 1936), 1–3.

45. Liang Shih-ch'iu, *ibid.*

46. *Ibid.*

Movement. Reluctant supporters of the movement, like Chou Tso-jen and Liang Shih-ch'iu, were primarily interested in what folklore could contribute to the future development of Chinese literature. Ku Chieh-kang did not speculate on the future technical usefulness of folksong. He was most interested in reordering the past so that the new culture of China would appear to have grown out of an undeniably Chinese tradition, and from a (hopefully) viable popular heritage.

FINDING PREDECESSORS FOR FOLKSTUDIES

In sponsoring the publication of folksong collections compiled by enthusiasts of the Ming and Ch'ing dynasties, Ku Chieh-kang was guided by the same motives that prompted Hu Shih to resuscitate the work of Chin Sheng-t'an. However clumsily, Hu Shih and Ku both sought out predecessors for their own studies of obscured and ignored literary traditions. They hoped that in this fashion more solid ground might be found for their claims that Vernacular Literature and Folk Culture were traditions deserving attention and respect, and that they were the means to make the new culture continuous with the past.

In 1927, Ku Chieh-kang wrote the preface to a new edition of Li Tiao-yuan's *Airs of Kuangtung*, originally printed in the eighteenth century.[47] He rhapsodized about Li as the predecessor of the modern Folklore Movement, "a man who would not be bound by traditional thought." Men of the past in China, Ku wrote, had only cynically used folksong, of doubtful authenticity, to sound out the political discontents of the masses, or to stage phony plebiscites and political prophecies (like Wang Mang). Li Tiao-yuan was willing "alone, to search out clear streams in the desert, and fragrant grasses in the wilderness." In the study of poetry and literature, Ku wrote, only Chin Sheng-t'an and Yuan Tsu-tsai are comparable in spirit to Li Tiao-yuan, the ancestor of the modern folksong specialist.[48] When Ku Chieh-kang learned that Li Tiao-yuan had been schooled by an

47. *Yüeh feng* [Airs of Kwangtung] was edited by Chung ching-wen (Peking, 1927), and Ku's Preface is dated April 1927.

48. *Ibid.*, Preface, p. 5.

even earlier collector of folksongs, he did not lose the opportunity to push the heritage back another century or so.[49]

Even more useful for establishing precedents of the Folklore Movement was the opportunity that presented itself in the mid-1930s to publish a modern edition of *Hill Songs*, originally compiled by the late Ming scholar Feng Meng-lung.[50] To Ku Chieh-kang's delight, Feng had denounced contemporary Ming poetry as "artificial" and had extolled the folksongs as "genuine" and expressive of the true feelings of the masses.[51] But what of Ch'ü Ch'iu-pai's claim that such collections as these could not be considered people's literature? Ku really had no defense here. He admitted that many of the songs in the collection were written either by literary men or by "professional poets of the people." Nevertheless, he protested that whatever the authorship might be, the songs truly reflected the emotions and thoughts of the masses.[52]

More generally, Ku answered the criticisms of Ch'ü Ch'iu-pai by agreeing with them, and then lamenting that so pitifully little of the folk tradition had survived, that so great a tradition had been manipulated by the imitative aristocracy and corrupted by the parasitic intelligentsia. He refused to admit what would follow from Ch'ü Ch'iu-pai's arguments—that whatever the nature of the tradition of popular culture, it could not be known in the present. Rather than abandoning the past and focusing on popular culture of the present and the future, Ku Chieh-kang urged his readers to cling to its frayed remnants and cherish them all the more for their rarity. It was not the limitations of Feng Meng-lung's book he dwelt on, but the rich if tiny sample the *Hill Songs* provided the cultural populist:

How fortunate that a sympathetic man like Feng Meng-lung happened along, a man who did not consider [these folksongs] as crude or libertine [in their frankness]; who scattered the pestilential

49. See Ku's "*Yüeh feng* te ch'ien shen" [The Former Spirit of Airs of Kwangtung], *Min-chien,* II:8 (dated July 1936), 131.

50. *Feng Meng-lung, Shan ke* [Hill Songs by Feng Meng-lung] (Shanghai, 1935) was edited by Cheng Chen-to.

51. *Ibid.,* Preface, p. 2a.

52. *Ibid.,* pp. 3b–4a.

miasma of the orthodox teachings; who took the daydreams and sighs of the numberless oppressed and passed them down to us.[53]

CENTRALITY OF THE "BOOK OF ODES"

If Ku Chieh-kang and the folklorists considered collections of folk poems from the Ming or Ch'ing to be valuable contributions to the establishment of popular culture, it seems reasonable that an older vestige of folk culture would be all the more valuable. The *Book of Odes* (*Shih-ching*), the most venerable member of the Classical canon, was cautiously transformed into such a vestige, as a group of textual critics, Ku Chieh-kang prominent among them, rescued this ancient anthology from the aristocratic cultural tradition. The *Odes* not only was to go to the popular cultural tradition, it was to become its point of departure. A degree of coherence and continuity was thus given to an otherwise amorphous and haphazard Folklore Movement by the concern for the 'true nature' and contemporary value of the *Book of Odes*.

The *Book of Odes* was as central to China's literary tradition as the Homeric epics have been to that of the West. And the *Odes*, like the Homeric classics, was problematic from the points of view of origin and interpretation. For those who were formulating a popular cultural heritage, this anthology of ancient poetry became an indispensable resource. It also became the nucleus of Ku Chieh-kang's scholarship, and the hub of his diverse and seemingly unrelated early work in textual criticism, history, and folklore.

The study of folklore was for Ku Chieh-kang, and perhaps for other early members of the folklore societies, a virtual epiphenomenon of the study of the *Odes*. In the *Autobiography*, for example, Ku admitted that

> I take very little interest in the investigation of folksongs as such; the sole purpose of my studies has been . . . to determine whether or not any portion of the verses recorded in the *Odes* were really vernacular songs of antiquity.[54]

53. *Ibid.*, p. 6b.
54. *ACH*, p. 145.

Whatever progress I have made [in the study of folksongs] was motivated by a desire to make a comparative study of similar phenomena in the *Odes*.[55]

Ku Chieh-kang and those folklorists who were concerned with the *Odes* developed three broad themes in their dialogues and monographs on the subject: First was the relationship of the *Odes* poetry to folksong. Were there any actual folksongs in the corpus? Was its poetry derived in some way from folksong? Secondly, this anthology was considered to be the classic example of how the Confucianists corrupted precious ancient texts with their commentaries, how the aristocracy corrupted the purity of folk art, and how the initial (popular) direction of China's cultural development was artificially rechannelled. The final theme was the urgent need for contemporaries to restore China's cultural stream to its proper channel, and to set it off again in its proper, folkish direction.

Historical Origins of the Odes

In 1923 Ku set about examining the historical context of the *Odes*.[56] He reasoned that one must understand the changes in the social function of poetry, and the methods of creating it, over the span of time during which the *Odes* was compiled. In this fashion, one could determine whether or not it was true (as some earlier scholars had claimed, and as it might appear to a casual observer) that the anthology contained *bona fide* folksongs, gathered directly from the people of antiquity. One could also more authoritatively refute and overthrow the orthodox interpretations of the poems.

Ku Chieh-kang brought to his readers' attention first the relationship of poetry, music, and ritual in antiquity. He demonstrated that the three were closely connected, even fused, from

55. *Ibid.*, p. 149.

56. "*Shih-ching* tsai Ch'un-ch'iu Chan-kuo chien te ti-wei" [The Place of the Book of Odes in the Spring and Autumn and Warring States Periods] was first published serially in the *Hsiao-shuo yüeh-pao* from XIV:3 (1923) through XIV:5 (1923); it was reprinted in modified form in *KSP,* III, 309–367.

the time of the eleventh century B.C. down to the age of Confucius. After this point, the three began to break apart. Ku cautiously speculated that during this first period there occurred on a significant scale a continuous process of transforming folksong (literally *t'u-ke,* or spontaneous songs) into "crafted songs" (*yueh-ke*). This took place when professional musicians transcribed and arranged the songs which they heard amongst the people. These crafted songs were often used side by side with original professional compositions at the courts of the nobles for various ritual occasions, and less often, for remonstrance. It was from such crafted songs as these that the poetry of the *Odes* was compiled.

In the second period, there was an accelerating tendency to secularize music and song, and to separate music from poetry. Confucius desired to use music for purposes of ethical cultivation. For the same purpose he wanted to interpret the poetry of the *Odes* anagogically, instead of merely employing it without interpretation as the text of liturgical music. By the fifth century B.C. secularization was complete, and the music to which the *Odes* poetry was sung, even in the time of Confucius, no longer accompanied them. The *Odes* was merely read now, and now scholars began to take an interest in the historical content of its text.

In Ku Chieh-kang's judgment, during the first period minstrels and court nobility used the poetry casually and paid no attention to its historical content, or to what it might say about the common people. However, they preserved it without distorting its initial meaning. In the second period, although scholars did begin to pay attention to the actual content of the poetry, a precedent which earned them Ku's approval, unfortunately "not everyone had historical knowledge to help him with the study." [57] Hence there began the distorting glosses and forced interpretations which came to obscure the true meaning of the *Odes*. This was especially true from the time of Mencius (whom Ku Chieh-kang accused of being the initial corrupter of its true meaning).

57. *KSP*, III, 367.

Folksongs in the Odes

There still remained a question which was of great interest to the folksong enthusiasts of the 1920s. Were any real folksongs preserved in the *Odes*? After years of exploration, Ku's major statement was made in a 1925 essay which demonstrated the technical lessons he had learned from studying contemporary folksongs.[58] It also displayed a brilliant and balanced application of these lessons to antiquity. In his study of this problem, we can see how Ku's own scholarship was influenced by the thought of Cheng Ch'iao, who had argued that the *Odes* could only be fully appreciated and understood if one first considered its sound structure and remembered that its poetry was a product of popular song melded with gentry poetry.[59]

There was a considerable body of scholarship which claimed that, to one degree or another, the *Odes* contained authentic folksongs—especially the "Airs of the States" (*kuo-feng*) section. What a boon it would have been to the Folklore Movement to have had this position defended and developed by Ku Chieh-kang. If he had, the folklorists would have been able to make immediate claims to the hoary heritage of the *Odes*.[60] His thesis stubbornly stated, however, that much, perhaps all, of the poetry was originally crafted song, and that only a small number of these crafted songs (especially in the "Airs of the States") were demonstrably taken from folksongs. He found it technically much easier to demonstrate that the *Odes* contained no folksongs than to show that the crafted songs were folksong derivatives.[61] Subsequent research by Chinese scholars, and more im-

58. "Lün *Shih-ching* so lu chuan wei yüeh-ke" [On the Possibility that the Contents of the Book of Odes Are All Derivations from Crafted Songs], *KSP,* II, 608–658. And see Ku's letter to Ch'ien Hsüan-t'ung, "Lün *Shih-ching* ching li chi Lao-tzu yü tao-chia shu" [Relationship of Book of Odes to Taoists], *KSP,* I (dated Jan. 1923), 53–57.

59. Cheng Ch'iao had hypothesized that "the roots of the *Odes* are in sound," but apparently he did not study the problem as extensively as Ku did. See Ku's "Cheng Ch'iao chuan" [Biography of Cheng Ch'iao], *Kuo-hsüeh chi-k'an* [Journal of National Studies], I:1 (1923), 322.

60. See Ku's Preface to *Yüeh feng* (n. 47, above), p. 4.

61. To demonstrate that there were no folksongs in the anthology, he drew on two sources of information: (1) His study of the structure of

portantly, by Western scholars who were not involved in the ideological ramifications of the problem, have borne out and elaborated Ku Chieh-kang's thesis.[62]

Freeing the Odes *from Classical Commentaries*

Although Ku Chieh-kang's proximate motivation for studying the *Odes* was not directly related to the Folklore Movement, ultimately his research did redound to the benefit of cultural populism. His first goal was to help his colleagues find a reliable means of discounting, once and for all, the traditional interpretations which Confucian orthodoxies had affixed to the *Odes*. The initial stage of his research was devoted to demonstrating that what made the *Odes* a classic was only the commentary. By showing that virtually all of the poems were originally songs which were sung on various ritual occasions, and that some poems still showed traces of their folk origins, an anagogical interpretation of the poetry would no longer be justified; it could no longer be held that the poems were originally written solely to convey ethical or political lessons.[63]

Kiangsi folksongs, and similar studies by his contemporaries, suggested that the poetry in the *Odes* was much too complex and ordered to be pure folk; (2) historically, there was no evidence to suggest that in antiquity folksongs were ever collected and preserved intact; Ming and Ch'ing collections seemed to be the first of their kind.

62. Hu Hua-shen's *Chung-kuo min-ke yen-chiu* (n. 28, above), pp. 3–9, follows Ku's thesis closely but with little technical detail. The extensive work of Wen I-to and Chu Tzu-ch'ing complements Ku's work.

Marcel Granet's *Festivals and Songs of Ancient China* (translated from the French by E. Edwards, London, 1932) is perhaps closest to Ku's work of all major non-Chinese studies of the *Odes*. It emphasizes the original ritual function of the poetry in the *Odes;* but, where Granet speaks of popular, mass seasonal rituals, Ku focuses on the ritual of the nobles' courts. Granet is far from Ku's conclusions, however, when he writes that the "songs of the [*Kuo-feng* chapter] give the impression of being products of rural improvisation" (p. 89). That is, they "reveal none of those literary processes which mark the art of the author. Their art is entirely spontaneous" (pp. 86–87).

Bernard Karlgren's work most fully complements and substantiates Ku's thesis that there are no actual folksongs in the *Odes*. ("Glosses on the Kuo-feng Odes," *Bulletin of the Museum of Far Eastern Antiquities*—hereinafter referred to as *BMFEA*—no. 14 [Stockholm, 1942], pp. 71–245.)

63. For the development of Ku's concern with these problems and

Within this problem of interpretation, the key issue to which Ku Chieh-kang addressed himself was the "licentious" or "obscene" nature (according to the terminology of traditional criticism) of some of the poems.[64] Traditional criticism was vexed with the need to explain the presence of earthy love songs and amorous trysts in the texts of some poems. How could one explain the incorporation of this kind of subject matter into sacred canon, the reputed work of sages? From antiquity down to the twelfth century, these "licentious" poems were not taken literally; they were considered to be esoteric codes. Chu Hsi, whose opinion became canon, was troubled by these poems in the twelfth century, but he felt that they should be understood literally, and then taken to be negative examples, caveats for lax morals. Some critics followed Chu Hsi and chose to understand the poems in question on a literal level, but then they went beyond him by arguing that these poems were not part of the original anthology, reputedly compiled by Confucius. The obscene poems were considered to be interpolations into the original, and it was suggested (to no avail) that they be thrown out. Ch'ing scholarship returned to the position of antiquity which held that there were not really any licentious poems in the *Odes,* just ethical teachings couched in misleading allegory and metaphor.

---

others related to the *Odes,* see his "Tu-shu tsa-chi" [Miscellaneous Notes], *Hsiao-shuo yüeh-pao,* XIV:1 (Jan. 1923) through XVI:5 (May 1925).

64. For this summary see Ku Chieh-kang, ed., *Wang Po, Shih i* [Doubts On the Odes, by Wang Po] (Shanghai, 1928), Preface, pp. 1–10.

Also see Karlgren, "Glosses on the Kuo-feng Odes," pp. 73–74, for a similar history of the fate of the *Odes.* He adds that Yao Chi-heng and Ts'ui Shu (whom Ku studied in the 1920s) were notable exceptions to the Ch'ing return to Han interpretations of the *Odes.* Karlgren concludes that "it is only in the last decades that modern Chinese scholars have had the courage entirely to reject the trammels of the [*Odes'*] Preface [the *locus classicus* of the anagogical interpretations], and the whole moralizing conception of the *Odes.*" He cites *KSP,* III, in which Ku's studies are published, as the chief example of this courageous rejection, and adds that, as of the early 1950s, no new comprehensive interpretation of the whole *Odes,* in the spirit of the *KSP,* has been produced.

Cf. Cheng Chen-to, "Tu Mao Shih hsü" [On the Mao Preface to the Odes], *Hsiao-shuo yüeh-pao,* XIV:1 (Jan. 10, 1923).

It was Ku Chieh-kang's goal to supplant all of these traditional approaches to the *Odes* with a contemporary one. Scholars would now consider the content of the poems as "historical data" to be examined from the point of view of the men of high antiquity whose lives it reflected. To the traditional charges that many of the poems were obscene, Ku responded, in essence, *honi soit qui mal y pense*. He felt that the realities of the common people's lives could not be considered impure, and that even if such a judgment were permitted, the data which recorded such realities were neutral, and transcended moral judgments. Ku employed much the same kind of argument to defend the earthy candor of contemporary folksongs, frequently at the same time that he discussed the *Odes*.[65]

In order to illustrate how the anagogical tradition could best be destroyed, Ku chose to analyze a poem from the *Odes* which was assuredly one that retained evidences of its folksong origins in form and content.[66] He did not, of course, expect to destroy the anagogical tradition with his commentary on one poem. This was merely a prototypical study whose lessons he expected his colleagues and students to apply to the entire corpus in the future. Nevertheless, if we look at the confident discussions of the *Odes* that crop up in his essays on folklore, it is evident that he felt the critical steps in separating the *Odes* from its commentary had been taken by the late 1920s. What remained was the job of actually using the *Odes* for historical and folkloric research.

The purpose of discrediting the orthodox body of commentary on the *Odes* had been to disassociate a potentially valuable document from the taint of the aristocratic, Confucian tradition.

65. The best example of this is Ku's 1927 Introduction to Li Tiao-yüan's *Yüeh feng* (n. 47, above).

66. See Ku's "Hsieh ke tsa-chi: 'Yeh yu szu chün' " [Song Miscellany: 'A Dead Doe in the Field'], *Ke-yao,* I:97 (May 17, 1925); also see dialogue on this poem which took place among Ku, Hu Shih, Yü Ping-po, *et al.,* in *Yü ssu* [Threads of Conversation], no. 31 (1925).

For further examples of Ku's refutations of traditional interpretations of the *Odes,* see: *Ke-yao,* I:94 (June 7, 1925); "Hsia-tzu tuan-pien te i-lieh —'ching nu' " [Example of a Blind Man's Judgment—'The Lovely Maid'] *KSP,* III, 510–518; "Mao *Shih hsü chih* pei-ching yü chih-ch'u" [Background and Purport of the Mao Preface to the Odes], *KSP,* III, 402–404.

Still, to promote this study was to open oneself to the criticism of more radical moderns who were disconcerted by such a concern for antiquity and would have had the *Odes* forgotten. Thus it was necessary to demonstrate its value in terms of the historical insight it could give into the lives of the common people of antiquity. Added to this was its aesthetic value: Freed from the crushing commentary, which in the past had usurped the first consideration of the reader, the *Odes* could now be appreciated as art of universal beauty, closely associated with the folk tradition.

In spite of Ku Chieh-kang's cautious first essays, in the second half of the 1920s the folksong origins of the *Odes* were increasingly emphasized. The *Odes* came to serve very much the same function for folk culture that the *Dream of the Red Chamber* served for Vernacular Literature. Once the *Odes* came to be intimately associated with it, folk tradition gained in legitimacy and propriety in the scholarly world. Or again, the legitimacy which the novel gained by being associated with the writings of "Han, Liu, Ou, and Su" is like the legitimacy which the folksong gained by being associated with the poetry of the *Odes*. When the aristocratic excrescences on the *Odes* were being "swept away" by Ku Chieh-kang and his colleagues, the *Odes* was not being devalued; it was being transvalued into people's literature. Its awesome antiquity and its ubiquitous role in all aspects of Chinese thought made it an unsurpassable symbol of China's proper (folk) cultural tradition, gone astray, and an unshakable foundation for a new people's culture.

Concluding Remarks on Popular Culture

During the period under consideration, the idea of popular culture remained inchoate. The desultory speculations of the folklorists, in spite of the confident rhetoric of such spokesmen as Ku Chieh-kang, resolved themselves, at best, into a series of ambiguities:

Individualism and the Collectivity

The first ambiguity that strikes us is Ku Chieh-kang's dual concern with the individual, in the spirit of the early New Culture movement, and with the masses. How are we to reconcile his preoccupation with scholar-heroes—outstanding individuals of unique intellect—with his promotion of popular culture?

Ku Chieh-kang's writings in the *Symposium on Critiques of Spurious Literature* extolled scientific imagination controlled by personal judgment and working in strict subordination to the facts. In the balance, this was a world view that wanted to be voluntaristic ("Ts'ui Shu was a man *ahead* of his times"), though it often wavered ("Ts'ui Shu was a man *of* his time"). In contrast, the Folklore Movement dwelt on the features of spontaneity, free imagination, and a collective, anonymous, unconscious genius. Particularly due to Hu Shih's evolutionary characterization of Chinese literary history, the folkloric world-view tended to be deterministic. History, working through the masses, had inexorably moved Chinese literature from one stage of development to another.

Chou Tso-jen's critique of the Folklore Movement added a further complexity. He opted for voluntarism, and spoke of the active wills of aristocratic individuals and individual commoners. And if his thinking was less deterministic than Hu Shih's, it was also less optimistic; he could find no reason to believe that beauty and creative innovation had ever been, or in the near future could be, forthcoming from the common masses.

What united the individualist and collectivist interests of Ku Chieh-kang was the concept of the aristocracy, or aristocratic culture (to which Chou Tso-jen had strongly demurred). Both interests were devoted to 'emancipating' new China from the stranglehold of the aristocratic past. The body of thought which we have characterized as individualistic was intended to correct, and ultimately to destroy, the cultural authority of the aristocracy. The collectivistic concerns were devoted to creating an alternative to aristocratic culture, and ultimately to supplanting it.

POPULAR CULTURE AND SUPERSTITION

When Ku Chieh-kang discussed folk culture, he subscribed to Hu Shih's evolutionary scheme of literary history, and to the logic of Hu Shih's 'Vernacular Literature' argument. When he studied the customs of the common people, the indelicate realities of their everyday lives, he could not help but agree with Chou Tso-jen that the common people were superstitious, backward, crude, and so on. (One thinks of Heine's chiding mimicry of his contemporary *Volk*-worshipers:

> We would willingly sacrifice ourselves for the people, for self-sacrifice is among our most refined pleasures, but the pure and sensitive part of the poet shrinks from any close personal association with the people and even more are we horrified at the thought of its caresses, from which God may preserve us.)[67]

Ku Chieh-kang did not publicize his revulsion with the masses, *in situ,* lest these feelings of his interfere with the success of the folk culture campaign. While he did suggest that the common people were in need of considerable reform, he tempered his writings on the subject with the usual plea for gradualism, caution, and careful study.

The ambiguity here is evident. On one hand, evolution had made the common people the fount of all good literature. The New Culture movement, therefore, should study the people in order to build on their heritage. On the other hand, the common people was the brackish backwater of China's contemporary culture; the reservoir of ignorance and ugliness. The New Culture movement should therefore be responsible for studying the people in order to reform them according to the lights of the intelligentsia.

The solution is familiar. Once again, the aristocracy. Because the aristocracy imitated the literature of the common people, that literature had at least an indirect survival and was permitted to evolve to higher forms. However, in order to secure their aristocratic class position, the evolution of other aspects of the life of the common people had to be suppressed. And eventually, the growth of these more mundane aspects of common existence was stunted.

67. Quoted in Hans Kohn, *The Mind of Germany* (New York, 1960), p. 112.

PRIMITIVISM AND PROGRESSIVISM, IMITATION AND ORIGINALITY

Another set of tensions grew out of the studied appreciation of the 'naturalness' and 'purity' of folk literature. Hu Shih (accidentally, it would seem) had managed to avoid the pitfalls of combining aesthetic primitivism with an evolutionary progressive historical outlook: His Vernacular Literature simply was not the literature of primitives. However, the folklorists, though definitely not Rousseauists (primitive life was not attractive to them), nevertheless were developing two mutually exclusive points of view. This resulted from their belief that folksong could be used as the basis for a new poetry. If the need for a new poetry came about because of the imitative aristocratic tradition, and the usefulness of folksong was based on its originality, then how could the new poetry use folksong without itself being imitative? And again, how could moderns create a poetry suitable for their age if primitive poetry was the model?

Perhaps more than anyone else at the time, Ch'ü Ch'iu-pai sensed the confusion and weakness of folklorist thought due to these unanswered questions. He even had answers—a progressivist philosophy wedded to an aesthetic modernism. The latter would feature a literature "that could be understood, could be spoken" by the twentieth-century Chinese common man; it would be a literature which especially reflected the life of *the* twentieth-century man, the proletarian.

PAST AND PRESENT

Ku Chieh-kang's influence in the Folklore Movement produced a strain between those who saw the folklorist as a student of the immediate present and those who were most concerned about linking present and past through the idea of folk culture.

Van Gennep's influential book had decried the overemphasis on history in European scholarship during the nineteenth century. He saw folklore as a corrective, because it was devoted to the "direct and living fact." He had hoped to have folklore known in its essential function as a "psychic pivot." In *Le folklore* he wrote:

> The present which one observes must not only be considered as a present, but it is necessary to consider it as the germ of a future. . . . Thus, the folkloric sensation is that the observed fact contains possibilities in germ, while the historical fact gives the sensation that all the possibilities of this fact have already been expressed.[68]

It was a useful point of view for the generation of the New Culture movement, but rather out of step with Ku Chieh-kang's concern for the historical roots of popular culture and with his study of the *Odes* in its historical context.

Chung Ching-wen took it upon himself to mediate (and he was the only folklorist to do so). He explained that folksong was a repository of the nation's history and the people's beliefs. Folksong and lore also were tools for educating the common people in the immediate future. Folksong, lore, customs—all of these, according to Chung, were embodiments of the old and new. There were popular cultural survivals in modern China; but the people were nevertheless always creating anew for themselves. The old folksongs were still sung; but new ones were always being created. In the instance of folklore, Chung Ching-wen sought to have the old and the new seem not to be opposites, but to be complementary.[69]

PURE AND PRACTICAL RESEARCH, REFORM AND REVOLUTION

Intimately related to the tension between past and present within the Folkstudies Movement were the disparate attitudes displayed by the scholars involved toward the immediate goal of their research efforts. Ku Chieh-kang was exemplary of one extreme when he emphasized pure, historical research, with only a token nod toward possible future application of his findings to some popular social or cultural phenomenon. He wrote in the *Autobiography* that his sole purpose in assembling folkloric materials "was to use them to corroborate [his] historical investigations." "I had no intention," he said, "of becom-

68. Van Gennep, *Le folklore,* p. 35.

69. "*Chiang-su ke-yao chi,* hsü" [Preface to A Collection of Kiangsu Folksongs], dated 1923, reprinted in *Min-chung chiao-yü* [Mass Education], III:1 (1935).

ing a specialist in [folklore].[70] . . . I am utilizing the materials derived from folksongs merely as a help to my study of history." [71] However, in his early studies of folk customs, Ku was closer to a practical, pragmatic goal: Through a genetic study of folk institutions, their appropriateness for contemporary society could be determined.

But even here, Ku and his close associates were on the periphery of those growing numbers of folklorists who had a markedly social-scientific bent and whose explicit major goal was not literary renaissance but social reform. One observer of the prototypical folklore journal of the twenties, *Folksong,* notes that although the programmatic statements in the journal stressed literary goals, "by far the greater number of articles approached the folksongs collected from the viewpoint of social science rather than for the sake of promoting a renaissance of national poetry." [72]

Antipathetic to most of Ku Chieh-kang's folkloric enterprises, but still within his universe, were the likes of the Ting Hsien rural reconstructionists. Their goals did not encompass the problem of aesthetics; nor were they apparently concerned with the relationship of the popular culture of the past with the New Culture of the modern age. The villages were not seen by them primarily as the source of a new aesthetic for China, but rather as "a living social laboratory" wherein it could be learned how to improve the economic and social well-being of the entire rural community (without, it must be emphasized, revolutionizing its class structure).[73]

In sum, the populist excursions of Ku Chieh-kang and his circle during the twenties, in spite of the confusion and instability of the ideas involved, provided at least partial satisfaction to two nagging needs: They demonstrated (to the folklorists, at least) that popular culture was a viable cultural alternative

70. *ACH,* p. 124.

71. *Ibid.,* p. 149.

72. Chao Wei-pang, "Modern Chinese Folklore Investigation," *Folklore Studies,* I (Peking, 1942), 63.

73. See comments of Paul Linebarger, *The China of Chiang K'ai-shek* (Boston, 1941), pp. 218–221.

to the unacceptable traditions of the aristocracy. And the exploration and promulgation of popular culture also provided a means for the Chinese intellectual to shape his new identity in modern China, and to dissociate himself from his culpable role in the definition and defense of the aristocratic tradition.

Part Three: The Counterfeiters

VI

From Textual Criticism to Social Criticism

And because they were practical, they perennially obstructed the differentiation of present and past, and the illumination of truth and spuriousness. . . . Thus, what we *are left with is merely tortuous literary sleight-of-hand, together with the knowledge of only apparent reality.*—Ku Chieh-kang

The central role of the intellectual in Chinese history, and the centrality of history to the Chinese intellectuals—this is the most persistent theme in Ku Chieh-kang's iconoclastic and revisionist historiography.* His interests in China's past and China's present met in his concern with the place of intellectuals and scholarship in the larger society. Ku's repeated calls for pure scholarship were elicited by his belief that China's progress in the twentieth century depended largely on her ability to foster a scientific intellectual community unencumbered by political involvements and constraints.[1] The passion with which he espoused this belief was at once cause and symptom of his interpretation of China's failure to realize its potential for progress in the past. This failure he ultimately attributed to "the parasites of the aristocracy," the intelligentsia, who, in order to

* A variant of this chapter appeared in the *Journal of Asian Studies,* XXVIII:4 (August 1969), pp. 771–788, and is published here by permission of the journal.

1. For example, see Ku's preface to the *Pei-ta chou-k'an,* I:1 (Jan. 1, 1926); his "Tao Wang Ching-an hsien-sheng" [Obituary for Wang Kuo-wei], *Wen-hsüeh chou-pao* [Literary Journal], V (Feb. 1928); and his Preface to *Chung-ta chou-k'an,* VI:62–63–64 (Jan. 16, 1929), 1–6.

profit from an alliance with the ruling class, betrayed their obligation to pursue truth. Repairing their damages and returning scholarship to its proper place in society are goals which inform all of his thought. Ku approached his goals by way of an unrelenting subversion of traditional Chinese historiography.

He systematically sought to challenge and disprove the historicity of China's age of Sage Kings, a 'Golden Age' which periodically had been questioned in its details from the earliest times,[2] but remained substantially intact and played a role in history and philosophy right up to Ku Chieh-kang's own generation.[3] However, Ku's 'antiquity doubting' was not merely a challenge to the generally accepted chronology of antiquity, nor to the historical details of that particular epoch. Beyond these, it undermined a philosophy of history which revolved around the Golden Age concept.

This philosophy of history had become a primary medium for the transmission and rationalization of political authority, intellectual orthodoxy, and social propriety. Consequently, China's resilient traditionalism was structured by a complex historical consciousness which buttressed its conservative world-outlook with two groups of ideas: The first centered around a series of charismatic heroes (the Sages of the Golden Age) whose acts

2. For example, see Burton Watson, *Ssu-ma Ch'ien, Grand Historian of China* (New York, 1958), Appendix A, translations from the *Shih Chi,* "Basic Annals of the Five Emperors," and "Preface to the Chronological Table of the Three Dynasties," pp. 183–184. And for a broad sampling of "antiquity doubters" since the time of Ssu-ma Ch'ien (145–90? B.C.), see Ku Chieh-kang, ed., *Pien-wei tsung-k'an* [Symposium on the Critiques of Spurious Literature], 8 vols. (Peking: 1928–1935).

3. For examples of his contemporaries' refusal to call the Golden Age a myth, see *KSP,* I and II, esp. the writings of Liu Yen-ta, Hu Chin-jen, and Chang Ying-lin (who is not to be confused with Chang Ping-lin). Chang T'ai-yen's resistance to the demolition of ancient history by K'ang Yu-wei, and by Ku Chieh-kang and his associates, is epitomized in Chang's *Kuo-hsüeh kai-lün* [An Outline of National Studies] (Taipei reprint, 1965).

Also see Mary Wright, *The Last Stand of Chinese Conservatism* (Stanford, 1957), chap. 12. Golden Age events and characters continued to find their way into Sun Yat-sen's *San Min Chu-i* lectures (translated into a number of editions under the title of *The Three Principles of the People*); Chiang Kai-shek's *China's Destiny and Chinese Economic Theory* (New York, 1947); and Ch'en Li-fu's *Philosophy of Life* (New York, 1948), esp. chap. 6.

of cultural creativity (e.g., the invention of writing) or political innovation (e.g., government by virtuous men) were treated as trans-historical archetypes. The unprecedented acts of the Sages were sometimes loosely fitted into a chronological framework, it is true, but they were essentially viewed out of time, as sacred or epic entities. In the canon, it was the *Book of Changes* (*I-ching*) that most fully attempted to explain these sacred creative acts in a systematic fashion, contending that fundamental aspects of civilization were 'invented' by the Sages when they contemplated a set of magic symbols (the hexagrams) which contained seminal suggestions for each invention. Ku took great relish in demolishing the naïve essentialism of the *Changes,* for this aspect of China's 'great tradition,' emphasizing timeless being and sacred origin, was quite prominent in conceptualizing the continuous existence of Chinese society.

However, the idea that the truth concerning the primal acts of the Sages "could only be inferred by presuming their continuity with the traditional character of the *li* [or governing rituals] as inherited by the present" was of at least equal prominence in antiquity.[4] Thus, the second group of ideas that structured China's traditionalism focused on the ideas of transmission and inheritance, not creation. Confucius (in the Old Text characterization of him) is the central figure here.

J. G. A. Pocock is quite right to suggest that Confucius was not simply being modest about his own role when he characterized himself as 'a transmitter, not a creator.' "He meant," Pocock argues, "that what he was teaching possessed the character of a tradition, whose authority was derived from the continuity of its transmission" (as opposed to its sacred origin).[5] Here, the historiographical implications for Ku Chieh-kang were profound, and much more a challenge to his attack than the simplistic *Book of Changes.* Pocock observes that

4. J. G. A. Pocock, "Time, Institutions and Action: An Essay on Traditions and Their Understanding," in *Politics and Experience: Essays Presented to Professor Michael Oakeshott on the Occasion of His Retirement* (Cambridge, England, 1968), p. 216.

5. *Ibid.,* p. 218.

There are several recorded sayings in which Confucius makes it plain that we know what form the *li* possessed under the Hsia and [Shang], the earliest of the three dynasties which he thought historical, only by inference from our better documented knowledge of the usages of Chou, the most recent dynasty; and if we know Hsia and [Shang] only by presumption, the same may be true of the [earliest sages]. His confidence and presumption was very high: he held that he could reconstruct what institutions had been like in the past by simple extrapolation from their form in the present, and regretted only that independent evidence did not survive to corroborate him.[6]

The authority of tradition thus stood on two legs—sacred origins and continuity of transmission. And these in turn were grounded on knowledge of or assumptions about the Golden Age of high antiquity.

The philosophy of history, and the view of tradition and the transmission of authority which Ku considered inimical to China, he found most systematically formulated by the scholar Chang Hsüeh-ch'eng (1738–1801).[7] In addition, he found that Chang's formulations, particularly about the meaning and relationship of the Classics and written history, had strong parallels throughout the writing of Ts'ui Shu, and they echoed as well in the Old Text scholarship of Chang T'ai-yen.[8] Although Ku admired and emulated much of the scholarship of these men and the eighteenth- and nineteenth-century schools which they exemplified, ultimately he was outraged by the perennial

6. *Ibid.*

7. Ku began reading Chang's *Wen-shih t'ung-i* in 1914. (See Ku's article, "Ts'ung wo tzu-chi k'an Hu Shih" [A Personal Look at Hu Shih], *Ta Kung Pao* [Impartial] (Dec. 24, 1951); and *ACH,* pp. 170–171). His interest in Chang continued strongly into the early twenties, and it seems that he would have devoted himself to a major study of Chang were it not for Hu Shih's rival interest in the subject, and Hu's suggestion that Ku's efforts be devoted to a study of Ts'ui Shu (See *KSP,* I, 7–19; *TTPIS,* I, 1.).

8. On Ts'ui Shu's thought and Ku's reaction to it, see below in text. For an example of such an echo, see Chang T'ai-yen, *Kuo-hsüeh kai-lün,* esp. chap. 2. Also see *CCMF,* I, chap. 6; and Liang Ch'i-ch'ao, *Intellectual Trends in the Ch'ing period,* trans. by I. C. Y. Hsü (Cambridge, Mass., 1959), pp. 111–112.

Confucian values which he believed he saw in their thought.

Before illustrating how Ku Chieh-kang attacked their outlooks and interpretations, I would like to sketch a paradigm, an ideal type, of the assumptions which informed their understanding of the Confucian Classics, written history, and the Golden Age. Then we shall see how Ku supplanted the paradigm with one of his own.[9]

A Paradigm of Ancient Historiography

The first tenet of the paradigm is the existence of a Golden Age in China's high antiquity—that is, the period dating from the epoch of the Three Emperors and Five Kings (traditionally, the third millennium B.C.) through the Hsia, Shang, and West-

9. Although this paradigm is modeled closely after the thought of Chang Hsüeh-ch'eng, I believe it reflects the intellectual attitudes of a larger body of thinkers. Thus, Ku's challenge to the paradigm had subversive implications for some deep-rooted tendencies in traditional thought about the past. For example:

(1) See Paul Demiéville, "Chang Hsüeh-ch'eng and His Historiography," in W. G. Beasley and E. Pulleyblank, eds., *Historians of China and Japan* (London, 1961), pp. 179–181, for discussion of the typicality of Chang's attitudes on the role of the Golden Age in history; the relationship of the Tao, history, and the Classics; and the immanentist tendencies of this thought.

(2) On the typicality of the polarity of knowledge and action which structures this paradigm, see Benjamin Schwartz, "Some Polarities in Confucian Thought," in A. F. Wright, ed., *Confucianism in Action* (Stanford, 1959), pp. 50–63, and his Foreword to Liang Ch'i-ch'ao, *Intellectual Trends,* pp. xi-xxii. See also David Nivison, "The Problem of Knowledge and Action Since Wang Yang-ming," in A. F. Wright, ed., *Studies in Chinese Thought* (Chicago, 1953), pp. 112–146, and his *Life and Thought of Chang Hsüeh-ch'eng* (Stanford, 1966), esp. chaps. 6 and 8. Also see Ku Chieh-kang, "Wang Shou-jen wu-ching chieh shih shuo" [On Wang Yang-ming's Thesis that the Five Classics Are All History], *Tse-shan pan-yüeh k'an* [Exhortations to Virtuous Action Journal], I:11 (Sept. 16, 1940), pp. 20–21; Watson, *Ssu-ma Ch'ien,* pp. 134–154, for "Ssu-ma Ch'ien's Theory of History"; and James T. C. Liu, *Ou-yang Hsiu* (Stanford, 1967), pp. 18, 100.

(3) The first chapters of Liu Hsieh's (ca. A.D. 465–522) *Wen-hsin tiao-lung* are an early formulation of the essentials of our paradigm, even though they are speaking of literature in general and not historical literature specifically. See Vincent Shih's translation, *The Literary Mind and the Carving of Dragons* (New York, 1959), pp. 8–21. Also see Demiéville, "Chang Hsüeh-ch'eng and His Historiography," pp. 178–179, for Chang's relationship to the thought of Liu Hsieh.

ern Chou dynasties, ending with the reign of the Duke of Chou (twelfth century B.C.). The quintessential feature of this Golden Age, what made it golden, was the unity of knowledge and action. Knowledge of the Tao was coupled with the ability to act out the Tao's requirements for the good life.

There was in this age no distinction between scholars (those who knew the good) and officials (those who could act). The Sages who ruled during this age saw "study, doctrine, and government [as] part of one whole." [10] As a result, all-under-heaven was ordered, and the people prospered. However, when knowledge and action were separated, when those who had virtue and knew of the Tao, like Confucius, could not govern, the Golden Age ended, and society underwent a general decline. When man's ethical knowledge was no longer a working part of the daily business of society and government, the people suffered. In sum, during the Golden Age, the Tao was evident in the workings of society; after the Golden Age, the Tao was eclipsed.

The fundamental role this Golden Age played can be seen in the 'problem of knowledge and action' as the problem is expressed in the relationship of the Tao, the Confucian Classics, and historical writings: In Chang Hsüeh-ch'eng's formulation, "The Six Classics are all history." This primarily means that the Classics are the "documents of the government of ancient kings" who ruled the Golden Age.[11] Thus, the Classics illustrate the Tao by documenting the history of this age. The Tao, itself unknowable and beyond ken, relies on the factual stuff of history to communicate itself to the times.

In the critical view of a modern Chinese historian like Ku Chieh-kang, this scheme had one predominant characteristic. Benjamin Schwartz summarizes it this way:

[The Confucian] concept of a good society was not like Plato's *Republic*—an ideal structure constructed by a step-by-step process of deductive reasoning and contrasted with all "conventional" societies which had actually existed. [Their] good society [they be-

10. Nivison, "The Problem of Knowledge and Action," p. 132, citing Yen Yüan (1635–1704).

11. Nivison, *Life and Thought,* pp. 201–202.

lieved] had actually existed in the past. To know the essential facts about the culture and social order of the early Chou was, in effect, to know the [Tao]. . . . To know history was to know the norms which had in the past actually been realized in history.[12]

Ku Chieh-kang's point of attack on this view of history was not on the premise that there is a Tao, an unchanging, supra-historical body of ultimate values or truths. On this issue he simply offered: "*My* 'Tao' is historical: I acknowledge the evidence for the changes in circumstances and things." [13] His historical research and his polemics were devoted to the destruction of the historiographical foundations of the Tao. Ku's historical writings demonstrate that, in effect, there was no Golden Age, and thereby obviate the need to dispute an irrefutable Tao.

His first problem was the historicity of the Classics. Ku, like Liang Ch'i-ch'ao before him, took the formula "The Six Classics are all history" and parodied it "The Six Classics are basically ancient historical materials." [14] Originally, Ku explained,

The learning of antiquity was solely the province of the aristocracy; and the intelligentsia was only the parasite of the aristocracy. The aristocracy had an office of music, and the intelligentsia gathered up many songs, and thus came about the *Book of Odes*. The aristocracy had an office of divination, and the intelligentsia recorded many events; hence, there came about the *Book of Documents* and the *Spring and Autumn Annals*. . . .

To speak the truth, the various books comprising the Classics were all things of daily use for the lords of the [ancient] states and the great officials and personages. The ideas of these books were simple, and there was nothing mysterious about them.[15]

In addition to Ku's observations on class relations, of which more later, the Classics are treated here in a fashion radically different from that of a Chang Hsüeh-ch'eng or a Ts'ui Shu.

12. Schwartz, Foreword to Liang Ch'i-chao, p. xvii.

13. Ku, "Lün K'ang Yu-wei pien-wei chih ch'eng-tse" [On K'ang Yu-wei's Accomplishments in Critiques of Spurious Literature], *Chung-ta chou-k'an,* XI:123–124 (March 26, 1930), 13.

14. Ku's preface to *SLTC,* p. 1. On the Classics-and-history question, see also *CCMF,* I, chap. 6, and Liang Ch'i-ch'ao, *CKLSYCF,* pp. 47, 49.

15. Ku's preface to *KSP,* IV (1933), 10.

Ku's intent here was to limit the value of the Classics to mere data which pertain solely to the periods in which they were produced. So far, however, it was only his word against Chang T'ai-yen's Old Text school, for example, that the Classics were not written in the Golden Age.

But when *were* the Classics written? This is the jarring question which Ku posed, like many a textual critic before him—yet not in quite the same way. It was his special interest to demonstrate that much of the canon was spurious, and that all written material from antiquity purporting to document the Golden Age was also spurious. In his *pien-wei*—his critiques of the spurious—it was his object to authenticate the date and authorship of the books in the canon. Doing so, he could show that none of the canonical writings could validly be called *ching,* Classics, if that term was supposed to mean 'records of the Golden Age kings.' He specifically appointed himself the task of approaching texts from the point of view of "spurious history" (*wei shih*)—that is, a process of investigation based on a systematic appraisal of the events described in a text, and informed by a knowledge of the rules that governed the creation of spurious literature.[16]

The simple yet fundamental quality that Ku Chieh-kang initially found to be most essential to the concept of 'spurious' was intentional distortion. A text (spurious or not in authorship) might contain the record of many questionable events, yet these could have come about for many reasons: faulty transmission of text; stupidity of the historian; repetition of error in another source: etc. Only wilful distortion warranted the epithet 'spurious.'

Contributions of Ts'ui Shu's Criticism

The writings of Ts'ui Shu (1740–1816) supplied Ku Chieh-kang's first detective kit with a set of tools-of-the-trade and an illustrated instruction book. While the Ch'ing textual critics are primarily known for their use of philological methods of detecting spurious literature, Ts'ui Shu relied on historical means. In a lean, direct, and often folksy prose, he explained

16. *KSP,* I, pp. 7, 17, 23, 24–25.

that an understanding of fashions-of-the-times (suggestive of our *Zeitgeists*) can be of crucial importance to the perceptive antiquity-doubter. A creator of spurious literature inevitably tips his hand in his counterfeit product because the "fashion" (*feng-ch'i*) of his own epoch will inadvertently show up in whatever he does. The dynasties of the Golden Age had their own forms of literary expression (*wen*), as did the Warring States, the Ch'in-Han, and all other eras. "This was not only true of literary expression," he wrote,

> but the conduct of men [during these periods] was also of a different quality. Because of this, men of the Warring States period elaborated the details of the circumstances of the Three Dynasties; this was the fashion of the Warring States period.
>
> The men of the Ch'in-Han elaborated the details of the Spring and Autumn period; such was an expression of the Ch'in and Han.
>
> The *Historical Records* (*Shih-chi*) straightforwardly recorded the literature of the commentaries on the *Book of Documents* and the *Spring and Autumn Annals*; however, it could not avoid intermixing the vocabulary of the Ch'in and the Han. The *Spurious Book of Documents* made an extreme effort to copy the literary forms of the T'ang [dynasty of Yao], the Yü [dynasty of Shun], and the Three Dynasties; however, in the end it could not escape from the mannerisms of the Tsin era.
>
> In all cases, what [these men] commonly heard and saw around themselves was taken for granted, and they were not self-conscious of [their milieu]. This being the case, these things disclosed themselves at an unguarded moment.[17]

In order to profit from those unguarded moments, Ts'ui Shu's *Examination of Beliefs* (*K'ao hsin lu*) took a series of important steps toward systematizing the "fashions" of key periods of antiquity, and the motivation and the *modus operandi* of textual counterfeiters. Broadly, Ts'ui Shu made Ku Chieh-kang acutely aware of the preeminence of political legitimacy (*T'ien-ming,* or the mandate of heaven) as a motivation

17. Ts'ui Shu, "K'ao hsin lu, t'i-yao" [Summary of the Examination of Beliefs], chap. 1, p. 1, in *TTPIS,* II. For Chang Hsüeh-ch'eng's concept of fashions or *feng-ch'i,* see Nivison, *Life and Thought* (n. 9 [2], above), p. 160.

for creating spurious literature, and he demonstrated that there were a number of patterns which the culprits tended to follow.[18] Most attractive to Ku Chieh-kang was the suggestion that the very conception of history, or the historical systems which textual forgers employed, was a major device for distorting texts for political purposes, and was therefore the source of the best clues. The genealogies of the Sage Kings of the Golden Age, for example, varied from period to period in the texts of middle antiquity, and provided Ts'ui with a means of judging the authenticity of a text. He also recognized that the historical system structured by the Five Virtues had been developed at datable times in antiquity; and therefore, when the Five Virtues system was employed in an ancient text, one could say something about its time of origin and authorship.[19]

Ku Chieh-kang's lessons from Ts'ui Shu were reinforced by the work of K'ang Yu-wei and K'ang's pupil Ts'ui Shih (1851–1924). Even more forcefully than Ts'ui Shu, they emphasized the issue of political legitimacy as crucial to the creation of spurious literature, and developed similar devices for detecting forgeries. Ts'ui Shih himself had independently produced a more highly refined technique for employing the Five Virtues historical system to ferret out interpolations and otherwise expose untrustworthy literature.[20]

For Ku Chieh-kang's education, Ts'ui Shu was superior to K'ang and his pupil when he emphasized the cumulative nature of spurious literature. K'ang had a mania for attributing virtually all of the spurious canonical literature of antiquity to one man, Liu Hsin (d. A.D. 23), but Ts'ui Shu gave to Ku the fundaments of his "stratification" theory, which the *Examination of Beliefs* adumbrated in this way:

Earlier men greatly valued the essentials; later men greatly esteemed quantity. The earlier the time, the more circumspect [are historians]

18. Ts'ui Shu, "Pu shang ku k'ao hsin lu" [Adding on to Antiquity], *TTPIS*, II, chap. 2, p. 31.

19. *Ibid.*, pp. 31–35.

20. *KSP*, V (1935), pp. 255, 259. Also Ts'ui Shih, *Shih Chi, t'an yüan* [Deep Inquiries into the Shih Chi], 2 vols. (Taipei: Kuang-wen reprint, n.d.).

about what is selected; the later the time, the more they seek complexity.[21]

Thus, Confucius talked about antiquity only as far back as Yao and Shun in 'his' preface to the *Book of Documents.* Three centuries after Confucius, Ssu-ma Ch'ien began his chronicle of antiquity with the earlier Yellow Emperor; and still more recent historians begin their story with the Yellow Emperor's predecessor, Fu Hsi.[22] In a long section of the *Examination of Beliefs* entitled "Adding on to Antiquity," Ts'ui Shu repeatedly demonstrated how the details of an event or the attributes of a personage had been expanded and piled up over time without any justification other than the personal whim of the culpable historian.

TS'UI SHU AS CONFUCIAN FUNDAMENTALIST

For all its usefulness to him, Ku claimed that Ts'ui's work was decidedly limited by Ts'ui's fundamentalist attitude. Ku said that Ts'ui was ultimately "a Confucianist criticizing ancient history; not a historian criticizing ancient history." [23]

At the outset of the *Examination of Beliefs* Ts'ui Shu stated his credo, and did so in the tone of vigorous affirmation that pervades his writings: "The Tao of the Sages resides in the Six Classics—and that is that. . . . Outside of the Six Classics, there is nothing that can be called the Tao." [24] The central theme of his critical evaluation of China's textual tradition is a familiar one in the late Ch'ing. The original Classics, not the profusion of commentaries on them, must be the point of departure for historical (and hence moral) knowledge; the greater proximity of the Ch'in-Han scholars to antiquity makes them no more knowledgeable of the Golden Age than a good scholar in the eighteenth century. Indeed, Ts'ui held little more than contempt for the Ch'in-Han scholars, because they so permitted their uncontrollable prejudices to blind them to the nature of the Classics and of high antiquity.

21. *TTPIS,* II, chap. 2, p. 31.
22. *Ibid.,* p. 32.
23. *KSP,* I (dated May 1923), 59.
24. *TTPIS,* II, chap. 1, p. 1.

The perennial fault of past scholars, according to Ts'ui, was that they "failed to turn back and study the roots" of Han Confucianism, that is, the Classics. Because of this the people of China stopped reading the Six Classics and instead began to sully their minds with such things as the *Hill and Sea Classic* (*Shan Hai ching*), the *Annals of Lü* (*Lü-shih ch'un-ch'iu*), or the philosophers of the Hundred Schools. This trend developed most rapidly during the Ming dynasty, and was very much accelerated by the examination system, until at last

the Six Classics came to be considered but brambles and beans, while these other books came to be considered bears' paws and pheasant fat [that is, delicacies].[25]

Despite all of his skepticism and rigorous, systematic criticism of the history recorded in commentaries to the canon and in extra-canonical literature, Ts'ui Shu had no doubts about the history within the Six Classics proper. Interpolations into the body of the *Analects,* which seemed so obvious to Ts'ui (and have since been confirmed), did not shake his belief in the ultimate authority of the Classics.[26] On the contrary, with each new discovery of a layer of counterfeit history over the authentic Classical stratum, Ts'ui became more assured that he was performing his calling to "protect the Tao, protect the Sages, and protect the canon." [27]

Those technical aspects of Ts'ui Shu's textual criticism which Ku Chieh-kang extolled as "scientific" were time and again compromised by Ts'ui when he permitted his notions of the Sages to become the criteria of last resort for judging the authenticity of historical accounts. When Ts'ui read of one of the Golden Age Sages, or of Confucius, and found behavior described by the account to be "unsagely" (according to Ts'ui's unformulated criteria), he judged the account spurious. (For

25. *Ibid.,* pp. 14–15.

26. Ts'ui Shu, "Chu ssu k'ao hsin lu," "Examination of Beliefs" *TTPIS,* III, chap. 2, p. 17.

27. This is evident throughout the "T'i-yao" and is discussed with insight by Chao Chin-shen in his continuation of Hu Shih's essay, "K'o-hsüeh te ku-shih chia Ts'ui Shu" [Ts'ui Shu, Scientific Ancient Historian], part 2, *TTPIS,* I, 108.

example, in some texts the Sage Emperors Yao and Shun are said to have made grand inspection tours of the realm. Though he argued partially from internal textual evidence against the historicity of such tours, his ultimate argument was that they are spurious history because "a Sage would not have to make such a tour.")[28]

Ts'ui Shu's goal as an historian was to perceive the ultimate truths, the Tao, in the stuff of history. And since it was the behavior of the Sages that most clearly illustrated the Tao, it was essential to recover the true record of their activities: "I humbly say," he wrote,

> that the Way of the Sages is great and difficult to observe, but when the activities of the Sages are made manifest, *it* is easy to see. . . . I want to distinguish between the true and the false, the actual and spurious concerning the activities of the ancient God Kings and Sages.[29]

A SKEPTICAL PROBE OF THE CLASSICS

With the purpose of destroying the kind of values which motivated Ts'ui Shu's historiography, Ku Chieh-kang set about to test and develop Ts'ui's critical apparatus. Having the desire neither to affirm nor defend Confucian values, Ku placed the burden of historicity on the Classical texts themselves, and he demanded of them that they show him why all their accounts of high antiquity should not be considered mere legend.

Ku now began experimentally to trace the development of accounts of some selected Golden Age protagonists. In addition, the writings of Cheng Ch'iao suggested to him that Ts'ui Shu's stratification theory of spurious history might also be elaborated and polished by applying it to popular legends which seemed to be derived from canonical literature.[30] These studies demonstrated that Ts'ui Shu's theory of fashions was a practicable one.

28. Ts'ui Shu, "T'ang, Yü k'ao hsin lu" [Examination of Beliefs About the T'ang and Yü Dynasties], *TTPIS*, II, chap. 2, pp. 8–10.

29. Ts'ui-Shu, "K'ao hsin lu, t'i-yao" (n. 17, above), part 2, p. 4.

30. See Ku's "Cheng Ch'iao tui-yü ke-tz'u yü ku-shih te chien-chieh" [Cheng Ch'iao's Views on Folksong and Legend], *Hsiao-shuo yüeh-pao* [Fiction Monthly], XIV:11 (Nov. 1923).

Subsequent variations on the earliest traceable form of the legends could, in most cases, be attributed to and associated with datable changes in the society and polity.[31]

Ts'ui Shu's laconic and sketchy formulations were restated by Ku Chieh-kang with an assurance based on the early successes of his first experiments:

> The nearer a period in time to us, the older the claim of the legends;
>
> The nearer the period to us, the greater embellishments of the prestige and greatness will they give the central heroes of their major legends;
>
> The nearer in time to us, the farther back the pretended knowledge of ancient history. The less detailed the early documents, the greater the later knowledge of the ancient history.[32]

Something more than this feeling for mechanics came out of Ku's earliest experiments, and this was a firsthand awareness of the peculiarities of traditional Chinese historiography. As he wrote later in his career, "Antiquity [for Confucius] only had exemplary personages, but it had no history." [33] Ku's experiments taught him directly that the Confucian 'historical' tradition was from its inception primarily concerned with making prototypical moral judgments and with constructing archetypes of proper and improper social and (more often) political behavior. So preoccupied did the historian become with static paradigms that process, change, and development—"evolution," in Ku's usage—found little place in the Confucian historical outlook.

In a discussion of the legend of the 'bad last emperor' of the Shang dynasty, Ku suggested that the biographies written about

31. In particular, see Ku's studies of the legend of Meng-chiang nü (Lady Meng-chiang), part of which is published as "Meng-chiang ku-shih chih li-shih te hsi-t'ung" [A Historical Filiation of the Lady Meng-chiang Legend], serialized in *Hsien-tai p'ing-lün* [The Contemporary Critic], III, Nos. 75, 76, 77 (1926).

32. *KSP,* I, 60.

33. Ku, "Chan-kuo Ch'in-Han chien jen te ts'ao wei yü pien-wei" [The Criticism and Creation of Spurious Literature by the Men of the Warring States, Ch'in-Han Era] *KSP,* VII, part 1, p. 9.

the men of high antiquity were merely exercises in categorization. Such biographies did not consider men as individuals, but merely looked at their "positions, images, and tags." [34] The need to stereotype and categorize, according to Ku's findings, originated in and was perpetuated by the demands of political legitimacy and social status, from the time that the Chou people conquered Shang and invented the legend of the evil last ruler to explain their right to establish a new regime.

In further studies of King Wen, the first emperor of Chou, and of the Duke of Chou, Ku arrayed disparate accounts of their lives found within the Classics. "Which account will you take for the truth?" he teased his readers; and why have only certain accounts of these exemplary political figures been adopted by the historians of middle antiquity at the expense of accounts and details which depict them in an unflattering light? [35] And again he suggested that these accounts are due primarily to intentional designs, suited to the fluid political situation of the Warring States period: the arrivistes' needs for political legitimacy and precedent guided the historians' brush. Ku Chieh-kang's earliest writings suggested the irony that out of a fluid political situation and a society which even the Classics characterize as rapidly changing, there emerged a historical outlook that emphasized the persistence of values and social forms, and discouraged the recognition of novelty and change.

Indirect History

Ku Chieh-kang next made a crucial shift of emphasis from a direct concern with the events of high antiquity to an "indirect" concern with the historical outlooks of the men of middle

34. Ku, "Chou o ch'i-shih shih te fa-sheng tzu-ti" [The Sequence of the Creation of the 'Seven Evil Deeds of Emperor Chou'], *KSP,* II, 82–92.

Cf. also D. C. Twitchett, "Chinese Biographical Writing," in Beasley and Pulleyblank, *Historians,* pp. 95–115; Arthur Wright, "Sui Yang-ti: Personality and Stereotype," in A. F. Wright, ed., *The Confucian Persuasion* (Stanford, 1960), pp. 47–76; and also Wright's "Values, Roles, and Personalities," in A. F. Wright and D. Twitchett, eds., *Confucian Personalities* (Stanford, 1962), pp. 3–23.

35. *KSP,* I, pp. 149–150; and also Ku's "Chin T'eng, p'ien chin tu" [A Commentary and Translation of the Chin T'eng Chapter of the Book of Documents], *KSP,* II, pp 63–75.

antiquity. By the mid-1920s, he had decided to study a set of constructs ("historical systems") which informed the historiography of middle antiquity. First were the historical and cosmological systems that structured the movement of human events and their relationship to the natural order (Yin Yang, Five Elements, Five Virtues, and Three Stages). Second was the system which ordered the hierarchy of the pantheon and detailed the filiation and succession order of the Sage Kings. And last, there was the system of imperial institutions which dealt with such activities as imperial tours of inspection, special sacrifices and rituals, and the geopolitical division of the empire.[36] Each of these systems—Ku was convinced of it before he began his detailed research—had evolved in patterns similar to legends he had studied, and for the same reasons.

He now made it clear to his readers that he was not a specialist on the reconstruction of high antiquity; rather, he was strictly a historian of the Warring States period, and the Ch'in and Han. Still, he was not even concerned with all of the latter —only the thought and scholarship of the period which would reveal the period's theories about high antiquity. As for the spurious literature, it provided the data for this study.[37] "Properly speaking," he once explained, "there is no history [of the time] before the Eastern Chou. [What evidence we have for that period] is only the product of spurious history." [38] As for the *true* nature of high antiquity, it was surely fathomable; however, Ku left that job for the archaeologist.

In this area of antiquity-doubting there is an important contrast to be made between Ku's historiography and that of K'ang Yu-wei, whose studies of spurious canonical literature deeply influenced Ku's early intellectual development.[39] K'ang attempted to show that the Old Text canon was completely forged by Liu Hsin during the Wang Mang era (ca. A.D. 1–23); but he

36. Ku's Preface to *KSP*, IV (1933), 4.

37. Ku's Preface to *KSP*, II (1930).

38. *KSP*, I (dated June 1921), 35.

39. This is repeatedly expressed by Ku throughout his *ACH*. Also see Ku's "wu te chung-shih shou hsia te cheng-chih ho li-shih" [Politics, History and the Theory of the Five Virtues Cycle]—hereinafter referred to as *WTCSS—KSP*, V, 538–554.

also claimed that his own 'legitimate' New Text canon was the product of the imagination of Confucius. The logical implications of this are that the Golden Age was either the substance of an esoteric prophecy from the mind of a Sage, or a cynical fabrication from the mind of an ideologue. Take your choice. In either case, the nature of high antiquity was unknowable.[40]

When K'ang determined that a text was spurious, he threw it on the rubbish heap. His purpose was to establish a true canon; false Classics were dross. On the other hand, Ku said his own purpose was to establish what was historically true about middle antiquity by exposing what was historically spurious for high antiquity.[41]

Thus, while Ku Chieh-kang often closely emulated K'ang Yu-wei's destruction of Old Text historiography, he avoided K'ang's anti-historical outlook. In order to salvage what K'ang Yu-wei would throw out, Ku proposed that "the appearance of spurious history is actually the reflection of true history." [42] For example, he said,

> The society of the Han dynasty was one that took for the core of its thought Yin and Yang, and the Five Elements; and thus this kind of juggling act really was a true product of this society. Can we ignore this juggling act if we want to study the thought of the Han dynasty and its influence on the history of high antiquity? This is just like the case of the diviners and astrologers: Their preachings are of course false, but their own lives are nevertheless real lives; their false words are a reflection of their true lives.[43]

K'ang Yu-wei had left China's antiquity an empty shell; he was primarily interested in what the Classics (*his* Classics) prophesied for the future. Ku Chieh-kang 'reorganized' antiquity and gave it new substance by employing a new epistemology ("If we cannot know the history of the Eastern Chou from Eastern Chou

40. Also see discussion of Liao P'ing (1852–1932) and the New Text revival in *CCMF,* III, chap. 1; and Fung Yu-lan, *History of Chinese Philosophy* (Princeton, 1952), II, 705–722.

41. Ku's preface to *KSP,* II (dated 1930), 4–6.

42. Ku's preface to *KSP,* III, 6–7.

43. Ku, "Chung-kuo shang-ku-shih yen-chiu kuo ti-erh hsüeh-chi chiang-i hsü-mu" [Preface to First Collection of Lectures on Chinese High Antiquity], *KSP,* V (1935), p. 362.

times, we can at least know the history of the Eastern Chou according to Warring States times)." [44]

Perspectivism

The significant reality for Ku was now no longer high antiquity, but the concept of the past in the minds of the scholars of middle antiquity. This was, of course, a most dramatic way of dismissing high antiquity (in the traditional telling) as no more than a construct. Here, he was beginning to occupy a position which Hu Shih's mentor, John Dewey, has called "perspectivism"—that is, a view which sees historical inquiry "as [a process] controlled by the dominant problems and conceptions of the culture of the period in which it is written." [45] This might seem reminiscent of Ts'ui Shu's "fashions," but it has far-reaching implications that ultimately contradict the metaphysical assumptions of Ts'ui's historiography.

Ts'ui Shu had seen corrupting "fashions" and the historical writings which they informed as *peculiar* to one epoch or another. He could not, as would Ku Chieh-kang or American "instrumentalists" like Dewey, see them as potentially *appropriate* for a given time and situation. Ts'ui Shu could never have agreed with Ku Chieh-kang that spurious history was ever appropriate; he could never have judged the creation of spurious history according to whether or not it served the needs of social evolution of the times. Ts'ui Shu was only interested in revealing what was true for all times by "scraping clean" the Classics; spurious history and the act of counterfeiting were always antithetical, never appropriate, to this purpose, which should be the purpose of all ages.

Thus, when Ku Chieh-kang said that Ts'ui employed the viewpoint of historical evolution, he was greatly distorting

44. *KSP,* I (dated Feb. 1923), 60.

45. John Dewey, "Historical Judgements," reprinted in Hans Meyerhoff, *The Philosophy of History in Our Times* (New York, 1959), p. 169. Dewey's statement continues: "It is certainly legitimate to say that a certain thing happened in a certain way at a certain time in the past, in case adequate data have been procured and critically handled. But the statement 'It actually happened in this way' has its status and significance *within* the scope and perspective of historical writing."

Ts'ui's intent. Ku, in an effort to praise Ts'ui Shu for his modernity, attributed this viewpoint to him; however, Ts'ui's stratification theory, quite consistent with his Confucian fundamentalism, did not make him an evolutionist, a position contradictory to all he professed as a Confucianist.[46]

Ku Chieh-kang continued to pursue perspectivism into some interesting terrain. Over the course of the 1920s, his writing increasingly committed itself to the question of the *source* of middle antiquity's historical perspectives, and it was seldom that he would analyze one of the systems on his list without clearly indicating that there was an organic, functional relationship between the perspectives and social conditions. Though we shall see him take yet another orientation, in this position Ku Chieh-kang was suggesting that historical outlooks (or any ideas, for that matter) were the reflections of some combination of social, economic, and political conditions. Because of this, the outlooks could be considered appropriate for the particular kind of society which produced them. However, it was understood that since society was constantly subject to evolution, the ideas and perspectives must also change in order to remain appropriate.

Using this scheme, Ku described and analyzed with neutral or approving sentiments the spurious history concocted during middle antiquity. When speaking of Mohists' philosophy and the legends which they created to support it, he wrote

> There first had to be the conditions of the Warring States period, then there could be the possibility of the Mohist ideology (*chu-i*); and once there was the Mohist ideology, then there could be [the legends about antiquity which they contrived].[47]

Or, after describing political fragmentation and pressures for social mobility during the Warring States period, he wrote

46. See Ku's "Juan Yüan Ming tang lün" [Juan Yüan's Arguments on the Hall of Light], *Chung-ta chou-k'an,* XI: 121 (March 1930), 13.

47. Ku Chieh-kang, "Shang-jang ch'uan-shuo ch'i yü Mo-chia k'ao" [A Study of How the Abdication Legend Arose from the Mohist School]—hereinafter referred to as *SJCMC—KSP,* VII, part 3, p. 50.

> Because there was a desire for unification, there was the lore of Yü's Ninefold Division of the whole of China, and the lore of Yao's harmonizing the ten thousand kingdoms. Because they desired equal rank, there was the lore of the abdication of Yao and Shun.[48]

The thought of specific individuals (those with whom he was sympathetic) was likewise a reflection of conditions or times. Hsün Tzu (ca. 298–238 B.C.) was praised by Ku for his critical attitude toward accounts of antiquity; however, Ku noted that Hsün Tzu failed to follow his doubts to their logical conclusions and succumbed to spurious history. "But after all," Ku concluded,

> he was a man of the Warring States period, so how could he escape the conditions (*feng-ch'i*) of the Warring States epoch? [49]

In analyzing intellectual content in this manner, Ku Chieh-kang was tacitly applying to that content what Karl Mannheim calls the "*particular* conception of ideology," [50] and in doing so he thus implemented the Pragmatic view of history.[51] Herein,

48. Ku, "Ch'un-ch'iu shih te K'ung-tzu ho Han tai te K'ung-tzu" [The Confucius of the Spring and Autumn Era and the Confucius of the Han "Ch'un-ch-iu shih Era], *KSP,* II (dated 1926), 135.

49. *SJCMC,* p. 82. Also see similar examples regarding Chang Heng (*CHFSJS,* p. 143), and Liu Hsin (Ku's preface to *KSP,* V, 6–7).

50. According to Mannheim, this conception "signifies a phenomenon intermediate between a simple lie at one pole, and an error, which is the result of a distorted and faulty conceptual apparatus, at the other. [And the conception is being employed] when we no longer make individuals personally responsible for the deceptions which we detect in their utterances, and when we no longer attribute the evil to their malicious cunning . . . [and] when we more or less consciously seek to discover the sources of their untruthfulness in a social factor." *Ideology and Utopia* (New York: Harvest paperback ed., n.d.), p. 61.

51. Dewey epitomized this view in this way: "History . . . has discovered itself in the idea of process. The genetic standpoint makes us aware that the systems of the past are neither fraudulent impostures nor absolute revelations; but are the products of political, economic, and scientific conditions whose change carries with it change of theoretical formulations. The recognition that intelligence is properly an organ of adjustment in difficult situations makes us aware that past theories were of value so far as they helped to carry to an issue the social perplexities from which they

there is no argument that thought systems are consciously or unconsciously distortions of realities in the interest of some group within the society. Nor does one properly speak of motivation here, but, rather, of causality. And an ethical relativism prevails: not true or false, good or evil, but appropriate or inappropriate. Thus, though the disciples of the philosopher Mo Tzu may have been instrumental in counterfeiting the history of the Golden Age (Ku claimed they invented an important political myth)[52] he exonerated them on the grounds of the appropriateness of their thought to their times. This was primarily due to the fact that Ku and others of his generation saw the Mohists as heralds of an egalitarian society that had broad appeal for moderns seeking a palatable alternative to the rejected Confucian heritage.[53]

In a recent survey of the development of the concept of ideology, George Lichtheim has suggested that two images capture the dominant usages of the concept in the West.[54] The first, ideology as reflection, we have already characterized in the preceding discussion, and have illustrated with the example of Ku Chieh-kang's 'pragmatic' treatment of the historical perspectives of middle antiquity. The second image is ideology as mask. Here, thought systems (perhaps, thought per se) are not instruments whose function is to aid society in adjusting to some evolutionary scheme, but tools to protect and further the interests of specific groups within the society. To perform this function, ideology must distort, cover over, or disguise the realities of society and the conditions of the times.

It was this second image of ideology which dominated Ku Chieh-kang's thought during his last attempt to design an ap-

---

emerged." From the speech "Intelligence and Morals," delivered at Columbia University, March 1908, and reprinted in Dewey's *The Influence of Darwin on Philosophy* (New York, 1910), p. 68.

52. This is the burden of Ku's *SJCMC.*

53. See for example, Ku Chieh-kang *et al.,* "Mo Tzu hsing-shih pien" [Discussions on the Name Mo Tzu], *Shih-hsüeh chi-k'an* [Journal of Historical Studies], I:2 (1936), 151–175; and also Hu Shih, *The Development of the Logical Method in Ancient China* (Shanghai, 1922), part 3, for a reevaluation of the role of Mohist thought in antiquity.

54. George Lichtheim, "The Concept of Ideology," *History and Theory,* IV:2 (1965), 164–195.

proach to spurious history. From 1929 to 1933 he developed a research paradigm which he called the "Four Idols" (*Ssu O-hsiang*); and in this paradigm, we can see him reverse his previous position regarding historical perspectives.[55]

A brief look at the Four Idols scheme will reveal that it is a synthesis of methodology, subject matter, and normative judgments. It lucidly illustrates Ku's understanding of the relationship of historical consciousness to the establishment of a continuous cultural tradition and the transmission of political authority. He labeled them respectively the Idols of the Clan, Politics, Moral Principles, and Scholarship.

The Four Idols of Traditional Historiography

The Idol of the Clan was the factitious genealogy of Sage Kings. Because of the inimical influence of this Idol, it was the contemporary historian's job to demonstrate that the many *reputedly* genuine ancient genealogies were produced over a considerable period of time to suit the needs of competing families and states during the Warring States period. The function of the genealogies must be demonstrated to have been the legitimization of parvenu families and political factions.

The Idol of Politics was the factitious history and cosmology of the Three Stages (*San T'ung*) and Five Virtues (*Wu Te*) systems. It required the historian to demonstrate that these systems were designed to serve the political needs of the monarchy. The systems must be revealed in their primordial functions: rationalizing the change of ruling houses; demonstrating the receipt of the mandate of heaven; and trumping up signs and portents of legitimacy for new regimes.

The third Idol, Moral Principles, was the concept of the Orthodox Confucian Tradition (*Tao T'ung*)—that is, the monistic doctrine of social ethics, handed down inviolate from Sage to Sage and valid for all times. The historian must destroy the thesis of the Idol and its claim to divine origin and transmission. He could do so by determining that the whole scheme

55. This discussion of the Four Idols is based on Ku's preface to *KSP*, IV (1933), 4–12.

was devised piecemeal, and created in strata, at the whim of mortal factions seeking political and economic gain.

Fourth is the Idol of Scholarship, the tradition of Classical Studies (*ching hsüeh*). By exposing the arbitrary manipulation of the Classical canon, the historian could demonstrate that the Classics are not the embodiments of ultimate values but, rather, mere products of the intelligentsia who themselves were the parasites of the aristocracy.

Ku Chieh-kang argued that these Four Idols lay at the heart of spurious history, and that they must be understood as a point of departure in the study of that subject. If we compare these Four Idols to their Baconian prototype, we can see that, herein, Ku is taking a position quite different from his first one as a perspectivist. Similar to Bacon's Idols, each of Ku's four is responsible for creating a barrier to the investigation and apprehension of truth: They are responsible for distorting middle antiquity's perception of the realities of high antiquity. In this sense, Ku Chieh-kang's Idols might be a species of Bacon's "Idols of the Theatre." However, he was making a distinct departure from Bacon, and from his own earlier position regarding the sources of perspectives. Ku now emphasized the specific political and social class derivation of perceptual error.

In this new orientation, Ku Chieh-kang was no longer in a relativistic humor. Each of the Idols, unlike the historical perspectives in the first orientation, was not a reflex (and hence a potentially clear revelation) of the conditions of the times. It was rather the product of specific social groups that acted out of conscious self-interest. The historical and ethical systems which were involved served as masks for the self-interest. Here we can rightly speak of *motivation* instead of *cause*.

Ku Chieh-kang could no longer entertain the appropriateness of the perspectives, or ideology, which related to each of the Idols. This was so because he perceived a tendency over middle antiquity for orthodoxy, that is, inflexibility, to accompany and fossilize them. He acknowledged that during part of the Warring States period, freedom and flexibility of thought were a reflection of the high degree of social mobility, economic development, and political experimentation. During this epoch, he wrote in a characteristic description,

> because communications are more convenient, trade expands, and the commoners (*shu-jen*) gain an independent position. All of the feudal lords are consolidating; geographical power is expanded; the great states increase in wealth and power. The declining, degenerate great hereditary clans were not in a position to handle the new demands of the new kinds of states, and therefore, talented individuals from the common people could rise in status and overthrow the hereditary officials. If a great family wanted to have political power, it had to have education. Accordingly, all of these social changes had considerable influence on scholarship, [the idea of] ancient history, and legend.[56]

However, as the empire became centralized, and as Confucianism emerged as the dominant intellectual faction, perspectives became rigidified. The ensuing orthodoxy was the medium in which each of the Four Idols fused into an unshakable intellectual edifice. Times and conditions would change, but each epoch from the Latter Han dynasty on could no longer really enjoy its own appropriate historical perspectives.

In such writings as his *Alchemists and Confucianists of the Ch'in and Han,* Ku placed the onus of the Four Idols roundly on the Confucian intelligentsia of middle antiquity. As parasites of the ruling class, they were motivated in their scholarship by political and economic factors, not the quest for truth. "The purpose of the Confucianists," he charged,

> was concentrated on upholding the old classes. They held that if a lord was not completely evil—evil as Chou or Hsieh—then he ought not to be overthrown. And after he was overthrown, and a new lord was put in his place, the class system went on as usual.
>
> . . . [While] the Mohists wanted to question the source from which Emperors and the feudal nobles were derived, the Confucianists would not discuss this [issue]. The Confucianists were only interested in the ceremonies for establishing a dynasty; the rules for an aristocrat's inheritance [and so on].[57]

56. "Chan-kuo Ch'in-Han chien" (n. 33, above).
57. *CHFSJS,* pp. 43–44.

In sum, it was the 'sell-out,' the betrayal of the Confucian intellectuals, which made it possible for the Four Idols to be fashioned. Nor could the Idols—the false perspectives, and the factitious systems of history which they embodied—have been perpetuated without the literary skills which only the intellectual class possessed.

The Role of the Intelligentsia in Antiquity

This brings us to Ku's final area of attack on the paradigm we sketched earlier. He turned the model on its head, and implied that in middle antiquity, when knowledge and action were *separated,* China experienced, if not a golden age, surely an age of great progress, unmatched in promise before the twentieth century. On the other hand, the *combination* of knowledge and action was responsible for a decline of Chinese culture and for internal discouragement of progress from which Chinese society suffered thereafter.[58]

In 1929 he wrote that

> Sun Yat-sen did not say 'Knowledge and action are one,' but rather, he said 'Knowledge is difficult, action is easy.' And it is precisely because the scope of learning far exceeds that of life that we say life is easy, learning is difficult; life is shallow, learning is profound.[59]

But because the men of Han and after did confuse the realms of knowledge and action, promising new shoots of progressive learning were cut off forever. "Look here," he lamented,

> China's astronomy quite early was far-reaching, but [those who insisted on confusing knowledge and action] caused astronomy and man's life to become of one piece so that the heavenly bodies might reveal the good or evil of men's affairs. And the theories of the Yin Yang and Five Elements schools were shaped to the beliefs of the multitude: Thus, calendar studies were likewise carried off and made suitable to geomancy.
>
> The armillary sphere, . . . the compass—oh, what things the Chinese knew about natural science. But a group of The Orthodox Ones considered the Sagely Way to be important, while making

58. This theme is best seen in *ibid.*
59. Ku's preface to *Chung-ta chou-k'an,* p. 2.

light of ingenuity. Thus: lost traditions! decadence! (For example, the use of the compass by geomancy to determine *feng-shui!*)[60]

Ku Chieh-kang characterized the late Spring and Autumn period and the Warring States epoch as a golden age of promise because during this age the evils of aristocratic society were being combatted; the rigid, highly stratified social system was being broken down, and there was a great increase in social mobility. A universalistic ethic, favorable to the welfare of the common people, was replacing the oppressive particularism of state, class, and family. The philosopher Mo Tzu and his followers were the major proponents of this universalistic ethic. Also to the benefit of the common people were the limitations being placed on arbitrary government by the political theories of Tsou Yen[61] and, again, Mo Tzu.[62]

Both symptom and cause of this golden age of promise was the liberation of thought and learning from the rigid strictures of religion and politics. The 'Hundred Schools' of philosophy, which were major symbols of post-Golden Age decline for traditional thinkers like Ts'ui Shu, are the hallmarks of progress and promise for Ku Chieh-kang.[63]

Ku depicted the men-who-knew, the intelligentsia, *before* the time of the Hundred Schools of philosophy, as men-of-action only by virtue of their parasitical relationship with the ruling class, the aristocracy. As such, the intelligentsia were a tool of the ruling class. Thus, the ruling class used knowledge, as it were, for the actions required to maintain their position of supremacy over the suffering masses. The Hundred Schools symbolize a separation of knowledge from action, for Ku Chieh-kang, because they indicate a separation of the intelligentsia from the aristocracy.

Ku Chieh-kang's golden age was short-lived, and its promise never realized. He tells us that the first emperor of the Ch'in

60. *Ibid.*, p. 3.
61. See Ku's *WTCSS.*
62. *SJCMC,* esp. part 3, pp. 30–119.
63. Cf. Chinese Communist evaluations in Donald J. Munro, "Chinese Communist Treatment of the Thinkers of the Hundred Schools Period," *China Quarterly,* No. 24 (Oct.–Dec. 1965), pp. 119–141.

overcompensated for the political decentralization of the preceding era and set the trend for the reunification of scholarship and politics, and for the general submission of thought to the state.[64]

Ku's studies of the intellectual currents of the Ch'in-Han period took the position that the monarchy did not bring the intelligentsia back into the service of the ruling classes by force. It was rather that the ruling classes made it too profitable for the intelligentsia to refuse to serve. And so the Hundred Schools, in Ku's historical narratives, degenerated into a hundred cliques and factions, competing for the patronage of the monarchy and aristocracy.

In his estimation, it was no accident that the Confucian clique triumphed, for it primarily drew on two intellectual resources, both of which served the interests of the new state. First of these were the reactionary elements in the social philosophy of Confucius, which rationalized the return to particularism, class distinction, and aristocratic rule:

> The Confucianists advocated a return to the past; they agreed to the preservation of classes. And ever since [Han] Wu Ti established [Confucianism] as a national religion, this idol has been upheld for two thousand years. Thus, although at the end of the Warring States period old institutions were completely overthrown, still the old ideas were perpetuated by the Confucianists, who created numberless clans and the most oppressive family system. This caused the people on one hand to forget the nation, and on the other, to forget the self.[65]

Second and more important, because it underlay the Confucian world-view, was the 'practical' attitude toward scholarship fostered by Tung Chung-shu (179?–104 B.C.), a major formulator of Han Confucianism. Learning and scholarship for Tung were wasteful and unjustified unless they had a direct social and political application for their goal.[66]

64. See *CHFSJS,* esp. chaps. 2–4; and also Ku's *Ch'in Shih Huang Ti* [The First Emperor of Ch'in] (Chungking, 1944).

65. *CHFSJS,* p. 50.

66. See Ku's "Tung Chung-shu ssu-hsiang chung te Mo-chia ch'eng-fen" [Mohist Elements in the Thought of Tung Chung-shu], *Wen-lan hsüeh-pao* [The Literary Wave], III:1 (March 1937).

Ku Chieh-kang brings us back to the question of the Classics, because, he tells us, it was through so-called "Classical Studies" (*ching hsüeh*) that the scholars served the ruling class. During middle antiquity, scholars manipulated the history about high antiquity in order to provide precedents for institutional changes, and to provide legitimacy for new political regimes. This manipulative predilection was responsible, among other things, for the legends of the Golden Age, and for spurious Classics:

> Ever since the men of Han took the Five Classics and saw them as 'Heavenly Classics and Earthly Ideals,' they also took their own personal notions plus their own transitory desires and smeared them on top of the [so-called] Classics. This caused the present not to be the present and the past not to be the past. And because they were practical, they perennially obstructed the differentiation of present and past, and the illumination of truth and spuriousness. . . . Thus, what we are left with is merely tortuous literary sleight-of-hand, together with the knowledge of only apparent reality.[67]

We must not be misled, Ku cautions us, "by the efflorescence of Classical Studies [during the Western Han, because] it relied on the seduction of profit; the spirit of Classical Studies of that time basically did not differ from the Eight Legs of the Ming and Ch'ing." [68]

And finally, what of Liu Hsin and the institutionalization of the Old Text cannon? K'ang Yu-wei conveniently had seen Liu Hsin's work as a *sui generis* crime of forgery. Ku Chieh-kang saw it as the culmination of a disastrous historical process: the completed fusion of the historian's craft and statecraft. Liu Hsin's Old Text Academy "was [yet another instance] of using the [same] ploy which Emperor Wu Ti of Han used when he established the Academy of the Five Classics." [69] In the last analysis, Ku argued, the *raison d'être* of an orthodox cannon was the cannon's practical use for the rationalization of political acts. "Thus," he concluded, "we must come to understand the

67. *CHFSJS,* p. 81.
68. *Ibid.,* p. 65.
69. *Ibid.,* pp. 104–105.

evolution of the Old and New Text factions within the context of the needs of the Han dynasty ruling class." [70]

The course of Ku Chieh-kang's historical thought began with a Pragmatic point of view, evolutionary in its configuration and relativistic in its judgments of institutions and ideas. But his history gradually shifted to a more caustic, and sometimes cynical, evaluation of the past, based on arguments from class and politics. When he began to see the aristocratic tradition of Classical Studies as an ideological mask for class interests, the focal point of his studies became the opprobrious role which the intelligentsia had played in that tradition. By demonstrating their culpability, he sought to expose myth posing as historical fact and ideology masquerading as scholarship. But it was at this point that his own political and social biases became most evident and began to inhibit the growth of his considerable contributions to the development of modern Chinese historiography.

His awareness of the formation of Chinese historical consciousness was second to none in China, and his analysis of the relationship of political institutions and social situations to historiography is of universal value. His work was weakened, however, by a rather oversimple division of antiquity into popular and anti-popular camps and by judgments too casually derived from twentieth-century 'New Culture' values. He might have argued that he, like all historians, was tendentious in his dealing with the past, and that he naturally brought certain sets of values to bear on his analyses of the past. But in saying so, I am sure he would have considered his historiography ideological only in the sense of 'reflection,' and not 'mask.' Thus, no apologies were needed, for that was the proper character of historical thought, according to his Pragmatic stance. The question remains, however, to what degree Ku's abridgment and criticism of traditional history did obscure the nature of ancient society.

The major instance of the limitations imposed on his historical understanding by his biases is his treatment of Con-

70. Ku's 1955 Introduction to *CHFSJS,* p. 8.

fucianism. Ku evaluated Confucianism (particularly in its systematic Han dynasty formulation) as a mask for interests imposing stasis, out of a conservative bias. He did not even entertain the possibility that the Han Confucian 'mask' might itself be a reflection of social institutions. It is quite clear that during the Han the intellectual mood was syncretic, and Confucian orthodoxy's highest good was 'harmony.' This was a distinct departure from the atomistic contention that characterized the Warring States period and its 'Hundred Schools' of philosophy. It seems a most useful point of view to consider Han intellectual orthodoxy as a reflection of the high degree of post-feudal stasis and stability (relative to the Warring States period). But Ku did not explore the possibility that Confucianism was a world-view appropriate to a stable social system with remarkable regenerative powers.

If Ku's major goal was to understand the relationship of certain thought systems with social situations, he was least successful here. It was not necessary for him to approve of the values borne by Confucianism in order for him to understand its social origins and functions; however, just Ts'ui Shu could not deem historically 'appropriate' those rivals of Confucianism which he abhorred, so Ku Chieh-kang could not deem Confucianism historically appropriate under any conditions.

VII

The Past Reorganized

The burden of Ku Chieh-kang's historiography in the 1920s and 1930s was the destruction of traditional conceptions of the past and the values conveyed in those conceptions. While setting the historical record straight he sought out and magnified men, ideas, and events consonant with modern values and contemporary needs as he saw them. And so for a counterfeit Golden Age of Sage Kings, Ku substituted a real, if abortive, golden age of Mo Tzu, Tsou Yen, and the Hundred Schools of philosophy—indigenous traditions alternative to what he disposed of as the aristocratic tradition.

As we examine more closely here some of the major subjects of his studies, his persistent attempt to reduce the role of Confucianism in certain areas and to accentuate it in others becomes more evident: Where antiquity seemed to offer things of value, in his judgment, Confucianism was denied any credit; where there was social or political oppression, Confucianism was culpable. And another pattern of his historiography also emerges. In his quest to find the sources of historical consciousness in antiquity, two figures are central: the philosopher Mo Tzu and the would-be emperor Wang Mang. Each in his own fashion was a radical, and after the fashion of rebels in traditional societies, each was a reactionary advocating political reform on the grounds of ancient (Golden Age) authority. In his quest after the sources of the legends about high antiquity, Ku focused on these radicals who argued from precedent, for he was aware (as Pocock expresses it) that "the strategy of return does not depend on the tradition's conserving any image of its sacred or other origins; if [the sages] do not exist, the radical is often capable of inventing them." [1]

Mo Tzu and the Abdication Myth

This discussion demonstrates the importance of Mohist thought for Chinese history—the Mohist blood in the Confucian skin.[2]

For Confucian political philosophy, one of the most treasured moments of the Golden Age occurred when the Sage Emperor Yao abdicated his throne—not to a blood relative, but to Shun, a stranger, and a commoner at that. Ku Chieh-kang's study of the Yao–Shun story was designed to do three things: (1) To show that the political values that informed the act of abdication were nowhere evident in the society which, according to the study of Oracle Bones and bronzes, did exist near that age in which Yao purportedly lived. Drawing primarily on Wang Kuo-wei's study of high antiquity, Ku Chieh-kang argued that, during this early epoch, political institutions and their attendant values were one with the values and structures of the primitive clan. And these in turn evolved directly into an aristocratic-feudal order. (2) To demonstrate that the portions of the text (the *Book of Documents*) in which the abdication legend first appeared were forgeries of the Warring States period —when the ideas dramatized by the account (social mobility, political succession based on rule by men of virtue and ability) were tenable. (3) To attribute the forgery, not to the Confucian school, but to the school of Mo Tzu, one of the important rival schools of Confucianism during the Hundred Schools epoch.

It is the third point that gives this study its special quality; for on one hand, Ku (like many of his contemporaries) approved of the normative implications of the abdication legend, but on the other, he was not willing to credit any value to the

1. J. G. A. Pocock, "Time, Institutions and Action: An Essay on Traditions and Their Understanding," in *Politics and Experience: Essays Presented to Michael Oakeshott on the Occasion of His Retirement* (Cambridge, England, 1968), p. 222.

2. Ku, *SJCMC*, p. 107.

account of the Confucian school. Ku Chieh-kang was willing to give credit to the Mohists for the legend and for their social philosophy in general, which appealed to his own social values and to his sense of historical appropriateness.

Outside of the *Book of Documents,* a notoriously corrupt text—and demonstrably so[3]—the account of the abdication appears earliest in texts which are safely datable within the Warring States period (the *Mencius* and the *Hsün Tzu*).[4] Demonstrating that the historical account of the abdication was a legend concocted in the Warring States period was a relatively routine first step for Ku Chieh-kang; the real goal of his research was to show that the 'Confucian' philosophers Mencius and Hsün Tzu were inspired by the legends created by the Mohists and that, with important alterations, these two incorporated the legends into their own writings.

The Mohists, not the Confucianists, 'reflected' the dominant social conditions of the early Warring States period, and their philosophy, expressed in the form of the Yao-Shun legend, served the function of providing historical precedents in the Golden Age for contemporary revolutionary changes.[5] Ku Chieh-kang described Confucius as one who dreaded the forthcoming age, which the Mohists heralded: a scion of Lu, the model state of the old feudal-aristocratic order, Confucius deplored the destruction of the class system and the social order that it imposed; the Mohists were exponents and perpetuators of the great social leveling that began to take place after Confucius died.[6]

3. See Ku's contributions in Ku Chieh-kang, ed., *Shang-shu yen-chiu chiang-i* [Commentaries on the Study of the Book of Documents]—hereinafter referred to as *SSYCCI*—5 vols. (Peking: Harvard-Yenching, 1933), I, III, V.

4. The "Yao yüeh chang" chapter of the *Lun Yü* also contains a discussion of this event and further discussion of the Yao–Shun–Yü succession. This is an interpolated chapter, and recognized as such by Ts'ui Shu and critics after him. See *TTPIS,* II, chap. 2; and Arthur Waley's introduction to his translation of the *Lun Yü, The Analects of Confucius* (New York: Random House paperback ed., n.d.).

5. *SJCMC,* pp. 49–50.

6. Cf. Hsu Cho-yun, *Ancient China in Transition: An Analysis of Social Mobility, 722–222 B.C.* (Stanford, 1965), p. 143.

The Mohist first principle, "Honor the Worthy" (with political office), emanated from the early Warring States period, when the decadence of the old aristocracy's officialdom and the expanded needs of the newly consolidated states required new blood to govern a more complex political structure. Thus there was a gradual breakdown of class rigidity, and commoners were raised in function and status. Ku Chieh-kang was careful to note that while the Confucianists might well have advocated a similar honoring of the worthy, they compromised this principle by also valuing specificity in all social relationships. (Hence, the ruling group might reward talent with office, but it would only look to its own closest affiliations and familial relations for that talent.) It was the peculiar Mohist virtue to emphasize universalism in selecting talented officials, just as it advocated "Universal Love." The second Mohist political principle was "Honor Equally," which Ku interpreted to mean that the talented and virtuous of all social classes should be eligible for rewards, and thus make possible a balanced political system that fostered class mobility.

In the last analysis, Ku argued, the Abdication Legend could not have originated with the Confucianists—it permitted a commoner to become emperor, while the *sine qua non* of early Confucianism was a rigid hierarchy of social relationships and functions which discouraged such presumptuous leaps. The Confucianists (Mencius, Hsün Tzu, and Tung Chung-shu) borrowed heavily from the philosophy of Mo Tzu, and thus their most attractive (to Ku Chieh-kang) values were only theirs secondhand.[7] Moreover, the Confucianists took the edge off of the Mohist philosophy's implications for class structure: The leveling tendencies of Mohism were more far-reaching (Universal Love, for example) than those of the Confucianists, which retained the norms of a hierarchy of personal relationships and an emphasis on aristocratic values.[8] Again, while

7. See *CHFSJS,* p. 35, on the eclecticism of Mencius; and p. 49 on Tung Chung-shu. Also see Ku's "Tung Chung-shu ssu-hsiang chung te Mo-chiao ch'eng-fen" [The Mohist Elements in Tung Chung-shu's Thought], *Wen-lan hsüeh-pao* [Literary Wave], III:1 (March 1937).

8. *SJCMC,* p. 78.

the Mohists were voluntarists, philosophically speaking, the Confucianists were determinists (because of their emphasis on "fate"). Ku argued (with weak evidence) that the idea of fate encouraged the bottom rungs of the social hierarchy to be satisfied with their lot, while the Mohists refused to justify permanent class divisions in any way.[9] And finally, for the Mohists the abdication legend was taken literally; for them, its principles and example were supposed to have been regularly emulated. However, for the Confucianists, the events of the legend had no immediacy; they were abstractions, and a similar act of abdication was not expected to repeat itself within a conceivable future.[10]

In his study of the Mohists, Ku Chieh-kang could not deny that the Confucianists, after the time of Confucius, did advocate some social and political values which were not contradictory to his own. In spite (perhaps because) of this, he wanted to steal the thunder of the Confucianists for the Mohists, who had been pushed into the historical background after the Hundred Schools period. Further, it was the Confucianists whom he belittled for plagiarizing the abdication legend, and (especially in the case of Menicus) for corrupting history by incorporating the legend into their historical accounts of high antiquity.[11] The Mohists, fabricators of the legend, merely reflected the times by doing so.

However, Ku's stated purpose was not only to demonstrate that "Chinese history does not depend only on Confucian thought."[12] Just as important, he sought to prove that "if it were not for Mohist thought, the class system of antiquity would not have been overthrown as quickly or as completely, and Chinese history would not have had the aspect that it did thereafter."[13] Thus, he argued heatedly that if the Mohist ideology

9. *Ibid.*
10. *Ibid.*, p. 79.
11. Ku, "Chan-kuo Ch'in-Han chien jen te ts'ao wei yü pien-wei" [The Criticism and Creation of Spurious Literature by the Men of the Warring States, Ch'in and Han], *KSP,* VII, part 1, pp. 25 ff.
12. *SJCMC,* p. 107.
13. *Ibid.*

was a reflection of a salutary social revolution, the elements of Mohism which found their way into Confucianism were corrupted by the ultimate Confucian aim to inhibit the revolution. In *Alchemists and Confucianists,* he attempted to show that when Confucianism co-opted Mohist ideas, they too became masks for a despicable social situation.

Ts'ui Shu had first directed Ku Chieh-kang's attention to the problem of the abdication legend—though we find none of the tendentious class analysis nor favoritism toward the Mohists in Tsui's work. He was primarily concerned with the integrity of the Yao–Shun–Yü imperial sequence, and while he did not question the historicity of the abdication of Yao to Shun, he was convinced that the abdication of Shun to Yü was spurious history. According to Ku, Ts'ui Shu was virtually the only scholar in the past to have cast any doubt on the legend.[14] Ku himself was thus the first to explore the implications of Ts'ui's doubts. This is further evidenced in Ku's study of the Great Yü, queller of the primeval flood and first emperor of the Hsia dynasty.

Emperor Yü: Barbarian Blood in the Hua Skin

Over a period of thirteen years, Ku Chieh-kang published his investigations of the Sage King Yü in an effort to piece together the stages of his metamorphosis and to determine the time and place of his origin. The legend of Yü was of special importance to Ku Chieh-kang, because it was a keystone in the edifice of the Golden Age and because Yü was the most profoundly charismatic figure of high antiquity. The doubtful lore of Yü cast doubt on the whole of the abdication legend, and the formation of the lore provided an exemplary illustration of the stratification thesis. It was Ku Chieh-kang's special delight to use this legend to demonstrate the contribution of 'barbarians' to the formation of Chinese culture.

Years before he attributed to the Mohists the legend of the

14. *SJCMC,* pp. 55–58, 101; and see Ts'ui Shu, "T'ang Yü k'ao-hsin lu" [Examination of Beliefs About the T'ang and Yü Dynasties], *TTPIS,* II, chap. 2.

abdication of Yao to Shun, Ku Chieh-kang was able to show that Shun's abdication to Yü was a later accretion to the original legend. Building on the groundwork of Ts'ui Shu, he demonstrated in 1923 that it was the abdication lore itself that had been the medium for the first association of the great triumvirate of the Golden Age. Using the same techniques that he applied to the Lady Meng-chiang legend, Ku meticulously arrayed every mention of the three Sage Kings, whether alone or together, in pre-Han texts.[15] He discovered, for example, that Yü appeared in the *Book of Odes,* but not Yao and Shun. In the *Book of Documents,* Yü appeared in the chapters written last and occasionally in other chapters. However, Yao and Shun, who appeared with Yü in these former chapters, do not accompany him in the chronologically earlier ones. Similar evidence led Ku to conclude that Yü was not originally part of a triumvirate, and further, that Yü "rose to prominence" in the lore of Chinese culture before Yao and Shun. Thus, although in the final version of the Golden Age history Yü appeared chronologically last, this was only because Yao and Shun were arbitrarily placed anterior to him in the process of fabricating the history of high antiquity.[16]

When was the triumvirate forged, and why? Ku Chieh-kang's chart of textual appearances showed that Yü 'arose' in the middle of the Western Chou; Yao and Shun in the latter part of the Spring and Autumn era. Originally independent figures serving various cults in various regions, they were reshaped and fitted together because they were handy, seasoned timber for structuring the 'abdication' political philosophy. And this philosophy itself arose out of the problems of the Warring States period.[17]

15. Of course, Ku had a considerable basis on which to build when it came to determining which texts were safely datable before the Han dynasty—the work of the Ch'ing textual critics, for example. On the use of pre-Han texts, see Bernard Karlgren, "Legends and Cults in Ancient China," *BMFEA,* no. 18 (1946), pp. 199–367; and see Henri Maspero, "Legendes mythologiques de le *Chou Ching,*" *Journal Asiatique,* CCIV:1 (1924), 1–100.

16. See *KSP,* I (dated 1923), 125–133.

17. *Ibid.,* pp. 130–133.

The swift current of Ku Chieh-kang's research always carried him down to the social base of the spurious history. Already, in his earliest publications, he moved within a single essay from a dry and punctilious exploration of texts to a personal and effusive evaluation of 'the times.' The Warring States times, according to Ku's earliest description of them, were ugly and bitter: the people suffered because of the perennial wars brought on by ambitious states that planned to unite the fragmented political world. Moreover, the aristocracy

> was wasteful and extravagant; they maimed the lives of the people; they cruelly snatched up the wealth of the people. The people suffered under a tyrannical government, and it was indeed lacerating and painful for them.[18]

Although some scholars sought to remedy the situation by way of their political philosophy of 'Loss of Mandate,' they did little for the growing misery of the masses.

Ku Chieh-kang directly equated his own day with antiquity:

> In that time, the relationship of the people with the King of the State was just like the relationship of our present-day people to the Warlords. Although the people suffer intensely, and want, themselves, to rise up and cast them out, they have not the strength to do so. In this situation, the spirit is willing, but the flesh is weak: So [the people of antiquity] took their desires and made an idea which contained a basic solution to the problem, and they used it for propaganda. The idea was the moralization of the government.[19]

It is not clear just how far the simile was meant to be carried, but Ku went on to argue that the abdication legend, along with others, was fashioned at this time to serve the purpose of buttressing the "moralization of the goverment"—ultimately, a device to make the rulers more responsive to the needs of the people. Ku attributed this abdication legend in its earliest form (Yao and Shun) specifically to the Mohists. The Confucianists added the finishing touch (Yao, Shun, and Yü).

18. *Ibid.*, p. 129.
19. *Ibid.*, p. 130.

THE ORIGINS AND METAMORPHOSIS OF YÜ

Even those colleagues of Ku Chieh-kang who accepted his theory about the origin of the Sage King triumvirate had doubts about his related work, that is, the origins and metamorphosis of Yü. Although Ku had been able to show that the historical relationship of Yü with Yao and Shun was not at all what it appeared to be, he still felt obliged to go on and demolish the historicity of the Yü lore itself. Again using the relatively simple technique of collation, Ku let the texts reveal a steady metamorphosis of Yü; but surprisingly, the process which informed Yü's attenuated transformation was not apotheosis. In the earliest texts, Yü was first depicted as a god or heavenly spirit, and then he became a man (albeit a superman). This fact perfectly suited Ku's design, for if the earliest texts had shown Yü to have been mortal, then it would not have been so easy to write the Sage off as purely the by-product of religious imagination. Fung Yu-lan, for example, was reluctant to agree that Yü was pure legend. However, his argument that Yü might *originally* have been a historical figure was based on the example of Siddhartha, who became the supernatural Buddha.[20] One of Ku Chieh-kang's first triumphs, and it remained one of his most provocative accomplishments, was his demonstration that the more recent the text in which Yü appeared, the fewer were his purely supernatural characteristics and the more numerous his features as a mortal man-king.[21] Though vestiges of his godly past remained, Yü's transformation (his "descension," as Ku put it) was completed in the Warring States period, when he came to serve as a Golden Age archetype for contemporary radical political action.

Still, Ku Chieh-kang was not satisfied to disprove only the historicity of the most prolific of the Sage Kings. Just as he seemed compelled to show that the abdication story was a myth and then to give credit for the myth to non-Confucianists, so

20. *ACH,* pp. 119–120.

21. For summary of Ku's earliest work on the subject, see *ACH,* pp. 96–98, 120–121, 133; and *KSP,* I, 114, 118.

he probed until he found a non-*Han* Chinese source of origin for the legend of Yü. In his first encounter with the problem of Yü's origins, Ku made a fumbling attempt to use linguistic techniques: Relying on the ancient *Shuo wen* dictionary, he devised a callow etymological argument to prove that Yü was a god related to the reptilian motifs on the ancient bronze sacrificial vessels.[22] Even his patrons Hu Shih and Ch'ien Hsüan-t'ung criticized him severely for his inept use of philology.[23] Ku never again relied solely, or even primarily, on linguistic arguments, and he bridled his enthusiasm for tarnishing the Golden Age with such aspersions ("Yü was a reptile") on its heroes.

Nevertheless, Ku did learn from this incident that in antiquity, the proto-Chinese people of the Central Region (*Chung-yuan*)[24] did characterize various outer regions with a terminology derived from the animal or insect world.[25] The reptilian element was usually part of the ideographs which named peoples in the Southern regions. Ku argued that the hydraulic labors of Yü made a perfect legend for a people who occupied the then-marshy lands (today's Szechwan and Hupei provinces) between the Yellow and Yangtze rivers, which required draining and reclamation before they could be inhabited and cultivated. These hydraulic problems were not preponderant in the early Central Region.[26] Ku concluded his case by adducing textual evidence substantiating his belief that, as the Central Region increased contact with the South, the lore of Yü (as a flood-controlling deity) gravitated North, through the auspices of the State of Ch'u. The lore was then adopted by the culture of the Central Region, where Yü ultimately got "mixed up with the ancestors of Chou." [27] So important did the legend of Yü be-

22. *KSP,* I, 63–64.

23. *Ibid.,* p. 38.

24. Geographically speaking, the *Chung yüan,* or Central Region, would in its earliest form pertain to the area around the southeastern bend of the Yellow River.

25. *KSP,* I, 118–127. And see Edward Schafer, *The Vermillion Bird* (Berkeley and Los Angles, 1967), p. 13.

26. *KSP,* I, 122–124.

27. *Ibid.* And cf. Maspero, "Legendes mythologiques," p. 71.

come for the Central Region that its growing boundaries and influence became symbolized in the mythic exploits of Yü. His 'footprints' came to represent the geographical scope of the Central Region, and the name of his dynasty became identical with the culture (*Hsia* or *chu-hsia*) of the proto-Chinese.[28]

THE POLITICAL GEOGRAPHY OF THE GOLDEN AGE

Intimately associated with Emperor Yü of Hsia, and that chapter of the *Book of Documents* which bears his name (the "Tribute of Yü" or "Yü Kung"), is a cryptic account of the extent of 'China' in his day and a description of how the realm was sectioned for purposes of rule. The "Tribute of Yü" (and it is just the most prestigious of the perpetrators) gives the impression that China, in the Golden Age, already encompassed the considerable scope of the Warring States' realm and even that of the immense Ch'in-Han empire. Moreover, it describes a unified empire, centralized but segmented into divisions called the Nine Realms (Chiu Chou).

Ku Chieh-kang was able to isolate at least four disparate accounts of the Nine Realms (regarding scope and boundaries, for example) in the Classics. All four claimed that the concept of the Nine Realms originated with Emperor Yü. It was Ku Chieh-kang's thesis that the political geography of the Golden Age described in the "Tribute of Yü" chapter, and other related textual sources, was actually the political geography (real or theoretical) of the Warring States and the Ch'in and Han eras—projected back into the past. The existential base which reflected the legendary boundaries of the Hsia dynasty and its subdivisions was the formidable pressure (from the time of the Warring States forward) for a single unified and centralized state. Emperor Yü's Nine Realms in the *Book of Documents* was only a hypothetical system of Warring States thinkers, designed to bolster their own efforts to produce a unified and centralized state in their own day.[29] From Ku's point of view,

28. *KSP,* I, 117–118.

29. See Ku's "Ch'in-Han t'ung-i yu-lai te ho Chan-kuo jen tui-yü shih-chieh te hsiang-hsiang" [The Sources of Ch'in-Han Unification and the Conception of the World During the Warring States Period], *KSP,* II, 4.

'China' did not exist before Ch'in and Han in the third century B.C. *If* there were a Hsia dynasty, its realm could only have been a tiny area couched in the bend of the Yellow River. The proto-Chinese Central Region was real, but it too was minuscule; it varied in size according to the fate of the tribal group which inhabited it and struggled with surrounding rival tribes. Hence, the 'China' of early Chou times only comprised Shensi, Honan, Shantung, and the southern parts of Shansi and Hopei.[30]

In an effort to make his reading audience clearly aware of the primitiveness of the reputed Golden Age, Ku further emphasized that if the size of China was small and varying in high antiquity, so was the world outlook of the people. It was a narrow and fragmenting clan or tribal point of view, not the universalistic view which came later. The "nation was more like a village of today"; and its culture "was a high one only relative to the surrounding aborigines." [31] Because of the relative superiority of the proto-Chinese, they were able to expand gradually, to open new lands and fuse with many different ethnic groups.

There is an interesting twist in Ku Chieh-kang's evaluations of middle antiquity's distortions of the geopolitics of high antiquity. On one hand, he permitted a certain degree of exoneration to the distorters on the grounds that they were motivated by a worthy desire to see the imperium united; on the other, he was critical of Ch'in-Han writers (especially the Latter-Han historians) for being so gullible and sloppy. Beyond this, however, there was at issue a reality more crucial than just the dimensions of pre-unification China. This was the role of 'non-Chinese' peoples in the formation of *that* China's culture. When the Golden Age was depicted as a unified, centralized, and extensive empire, it was also depicted as a culturally homogeneous, distinctly 'Chinese' entity. The population of the Three Dynasties of the Golden Age consisted of Chinese (*Hua,* or *Hua-Hsia*) and barbarians. Ethnic groups within the Central Region, and those that continued to contribute to its culture, lost their identities when Warring States historians, in their passion for unity, pasted over the differences and either ignored these

30. *Ibid.,* p. 3.
31. *Ibid.*

groups or claimed that they, just like the Chinese, descended from the Yellow Emperor, Yao, Shun, and Yü.

In his observations on contemporary society, Ku Chieh-kang himself was given to pasting over the cracks between Chinese (*Han*) and non-Chinese peoples living within the empire. In his historical studies, however, he was consistent in his desire to demonstrate that the culture of the "Men of *Han*" was the product of an evolutionary development to which many distinctly non-Chinese cultures made crucial contributions. The lore of Yü's Ninefold Division of China was a case in point, for it was the object of a series of his most fascinating studies to show that the materials for this lore came from the Jung and Chiang peoples who lived in western Honan and central Shensi during the formative centuries of the Central Region's culture. It was jarring enough to claim that Yü and his empire were legendary; it was giving the knife an extra turn to attribute the legend to barbarians.

When we last saw Yü, he had migrated from south of the Central Region; thereafter, the Jung tribes appropriated the Yü lore, developed it, and added to it the nation of the Nine Realms. The Four Sacred Mountains which were symbols of the Chiang people's culture were added later. Ku Chieh-kang was able to trace the development of the Chinese concept of the imperium (*T'ien-hsia*) out of the Jung's Nine Realms. Out of the Chiang's Four Mountains evolved China's Five Sacred Mountains. And Yü, Ancestral God of the Jung, became the foremost Sage King of China's Golden Age.[32] Thus, these cul-

32. I have greatly simplified Ku's findings which demonstrate the cultural role of non-Han peoples and which make it possible to decipher much more of the obscure geographical terminology which is pertinent to an understanding of ancient history. His most important studies on these subjects are the following: (1) "Lün Chin-wen Shang-shu chu-tso shih-tai shu" [On the Date of Composition of the New Text Book of Documents], *KSP,* I, esp. p. 202; (2) "Chiu chou chih shuo shih tsen-yang lai te?" [Whence the Theory of the Nine Realms?], in *SSYCCI,* III; (3) Ku Chieh-kang and Tung Shu-yeh, "Han-tai i-ch'ien Chung-kuo-jen te shih-chieh kuan-nien yü yu-wai chiao-t'ung te ku-shih" [Legends of the Chinese of the Han and Earlier Regarding Geographical Outlook and Foreign Intercourse], *Yü Kung* [the Tribute of Yü]—hereinafter referred to as *YK*—V:3–4

tural factors which seemed to derive from the very heart of primordial Chinese (*Hua*) culture were really from the Jung. The reason for this confusion "was the firmly guarded prejudice of the men of the [late Chou] who despised outsiders as stupid and ignorant." [33] Ultimately, Ku Chieh-kang claimed, the Jung and the Chinese were of the same ethnic stock, but when the latter gained political preeminence in the Central Regions. they considered themselves superior to the Jung. When the Jung were finally amalgamated into the new Chinese realm, their earlier identity was obliterated, "and the true aspect of antiquity was covered over in a dust storm." [34]

The Five Virtues Cycle

Ku Chieh-kang was among the first scholars to delineate the growth of the cyclical historical theory known as the Five Virtues (*Wu Te*), which was used in ancient texts to explain the interrelated behavior of the cosmos and the history of man.[35] He pioneered the study of the social and intellectual motivations for creating this theory, and he has provided the most seminal suggestions for the political implications of its use during middle antiquity. Though his favoritism toward chosen historical

(April 1936), 97–120; (4) "Chiu chou chih Jung yü Jung Yü" [The Nine Realms of the Jung, and the Yü of the Jung], *YK,* VI:6–7 (April 1937); (5) "Kung chou" [The Nobles' Realm], *SLTC,* pp. 46–53; (6) Ku's introduction to his "Yü Kung: ch'uan wen chu-tse" [A Commentary on the Complete Text of the Tribute of Yü], in Hou Jen-chih, ed., *Chung-kuo ku-tai ti-li ming-chu hsüan tu* [A Symposium of Famous Writers on Chinese Ancient Geography] (Hong Kong, 1963), pp. 1–6.

33. Ku, "Chiu chou chih Jung," p. 138.

34. *Ibid.*

35. An important predecessor to the study of this subject was Hu Wei (1663–1714); see Liang Ch'i-ch'ao, *Intellectual Trends in the Ch'ing Period,* trans. by I. C. Y. Hsü (Cambridge, Mass., 1959), p. 35. And see Liang Ch'i-ch'ao's study, "Yin-Yang Wu hsing shuo chih lai-li" [The Origins of the Yin-yang and Five Elements Theories], *Tung-fang tsa-chih* [Far Eastern Miscellany], XX:10 (May 25, 1923).

The Five Elements or Virtues in question were Earth, Fire, Wood, Metal, and Water. As the cosmological system developed, each of the five was associated with points of the compass, colors, tastes, totems, etc., much as was done in Western astrology.

actors and his political biases are nowhere stronger than in his studies of this subject, still these studies lucidly reveal the intimacy in early Chinese history of political philosophy and institutions with forms of historical consciousness.

It was directly from Ts'ui Shu, again, that Ku took up his study of the subject.[36] Ts'ui had found the Five Virtues Cycle an intolerable corruption and confusion of Golden Age history. Ku interpreted it solely from the view of political developments during middle antiquity, and he found the theory to be both symptom and device of political wisdom during the Warring States period. Tsou Yen, the reputed originator of the theory, was a villain to Ts'ui Shu. But for Ku Chieh-kang, he had the stature of Mo Tzu.

TSOU YEN AND THE FIVE VIRTUES CYCLE

According to Ku Chieh-kang, Tsou Yen's school co-opted the primitive Yin Yang and Five Elements (*Wu Hsing*) cosmological theories of their day and transformed them into one coordinated system, cyclical in its historical pattern and far-reaching in its specific political implications. The crucial departure Tsou Yen took was to identify each element in the recurring cycle with a successive political epoch in China's history. Tsou wanted to use his completed system as a check on the whims of his contemporaries who sought to become emperor. If you wish to become emperor, his theory seemed to be saying, you must find corroborative evidence in the Five Virtues system to support your claim and thereby demonstrate your receipt of the Mandate of Heaven.[37] Tsou Yen's purpose was to condemn and inhibit the political extravagances of the feudal states and the pretensions of their kings to the position of emperor of the ecumene (*T'ien-hsia*);[38] he tacitly admonished the political leaders of the Warring States not to hope for something outside of their own fate—for without the rotation of the Five Virtues,

36. See Ts'ui's "Pu shang k'ao-hsin lu" [Adding on to Antiquity], chap. 2, in *TTPIS,* II, 31–35.

37. *WTCSS,* p. 419.

38. *Ibid.,* p. 418.

one could not of his own will become emperor.[39] Tsou Yen's mechanistic theory was meant to do more than discourage wilful political climbing. It further served as a warning that the Heavenly Mandate was not a perpetual one: One Virtue declines while another rises, endlessly. His hope, according to Ku Chieh-kang, was that if men would not fight over the throne, the emperor, whoever he might be, would in turn not bring misery to the empire.[40]

From the time that Tsou Yen first devised his scheme, in the third century B.C., to the time of Tung Chung-shu in the second century B.C., the Five Virtues theory underwent many alterations and variations. The most important change, completed by the philosophy of Tung Chung-shu, was concerned with the character of the succession of the Virtues. While the cyclical theory was still in its most primitive form, Tsou Yen had said that each of the Five Virtues supplanted its preceding Virtue in the cycle by 'overcoming' it. (Thus, the Water Virtue vanquishes the Fire Virtue; just so, the Ch'in dynasty, whose Virtue was Water, vanquished the Chou dynasty, whose Virtue was Fire.) The tone of this theory is one of conflict; and its implications are political revolution (*ke-ming*). Tsou Yen's theory thus reflected the *realpolitik* of his day, when political legitimacy was still very much a direct function of military conquest.

With the transition from Ch'in to Han, legitimate dynastic succession became a major concern; however, 'might' no longer sufficed for political 'right,' and smooth, peaceful political development became the preoccupation of ideologues as the Han stabilized its regime. Thus it was that Tung Chung-shu met the ideological needs of the Han by revising Tsou Yen's theory to the end that it would show that each successive Virtue (and its corresponding political-historical epoch) spontaneously and peacefully grew or evolved out of its predecessor.

According to Ku Chieh-kang's account, Tung Chung-shu's 'Mutually Producing Cycle' was just one example of the thought

39. *Ibid.,* p. 465.
40. *Ibid.*

of the period, which dramatized smooth transition and continuity. Other examples were to be found in the prominent political legends of this period, which were altered or rationalized to show that, in the past, political successors (to a kingship or emperorship) were the aristocratic ministers of their predecessors, blood relatives, or 'worthies' who received their position by way of abdication. In the political literature of Emperor Wu Ti's reign, there was no 'legitimacy-by-conquest'—with the exception of Shang's defeat of Hsia, and Chou of Shang.

If the implication of the earliest Five Virtues theory was revolution (*ke-ming*), its implication by the time of Emperor Wu Ti of Han was 'abdication' (*shan-jang*), in the broad sense of yielding to one's 'natural' political successor without conflict. The juxtaposition of these two concepts, in Ku's discussion of the Five Virtues, brings us to the relationship of the philosophy of his two heroes of middle antiquity, Mo Tzu and Tsou Yen. Tsou Yen had used the Five Virtues to discourage the ambitions of political parvenus; Mo Tzu's philosophy had thrown the door open to 'the virtuous,' no matter what their station, and seemed thereby an encouragement to the (virtuous) parvenu. Still, Tsou Yen's system did permit *anyone* who could justify his position with the appropriate arguments based on Five Virtue logic to become the king or emperor. Even though the logical extreme of Tsou Yen's thought is revolution, while that of Mo Tzu's is peaceful continuity or transition, both, according to Ku Chieh-kang's evaluation, deserve the respect of moderns. They both obliged the ruler to be responsible to forces outside of his control, or to values independent of his manipulation, and they thereby circumscribed despotic caprice. Both emphasized the transiency of political power and the necessity of responding to 'the people.'

Consistent with his other efforts to reveal the Mohist elements in Confucian thought, Ku emphasized the central role of Mohist political philosophy in the great philosophical synthesis of Tung Chung-shu. The Mohists' 'abdication' ideal was subsumed under this broader and more complex cyclical system of political history. In its mythopoetic form as the Golden Age succession of Yao, Shun, and Yü, it became the archetype of the natural cycle of peaceful political change. Ku insisted that Tung Chung-shu's great philosophical edifice was constructed in the spirit of the Mohists, and that all of Tung Chung-shu's political philosophy was merely commentary on the idea of 'abdication.' [41] As for Tsou Yen and his followers, they seem only, in Ku's presentation of them, to have restructured the Mohists' political values, given them a historical logic, and transformed them into a universal process.

Although Ku's research supported Ts'ui Shu's suggestion that Tsou Yen was a figure of prime importance in the shaping of middle antiquity's view of high antiquity, Ku's evaluation of Tsou Yen's role was antithetical. Again, Ku Chieh-kang, like Ts'ui, gave great emphasis to the development of the 'mutually producing' cycle; however, Ku placed the development in Emperor Wu Ti's reign (140–86 B.C.), not in that of Wang Mang, half a century later. Finally, both Ts'ui and Ku agreed that as imperial doctrine, the first implementation of the political philosophy of the Five Virtues occurred during the reign of the first Emperor of Ch'in.

THE FATE OF THE FIVE VIRTUES CYCLE

The political philosophy of Mo Tzu and Tsou Yen for a short time enjoyed great success. In Ku's telling, it was the impetus for, and actually informed, the elaborate imperial institutions whose primary function was to prevent an emperor from losing sight of his obligations to 'the people,' and to prevent an emperor from taking his legitimacy for granted. Ku Chieh-kang interpreted such imperial rituals as the Wind and Hill (*feng-shan*) sacrifices on Mount T'ai (*T'ai Shan*) as one of the fruits of Tsou Yen's philosophy. In this ritual, the emperor who had just received the mandate humbly acknowledged this fact and did obeisance to heaven by way of the sacrifices. This was a critical development of Tsou's cyclical theory, according to Ku, because it was a public ceremony which indicated that generations of emperors had made these sacrifices. Hence, the new emperor was reminded that many others before him had been degraded from their high office. There was also herein a

41. *Ibid.*, p. 484.

reminder that if the emperor was responsible for causing the cosmos (*Shang T'ien*) to stop nourishing the masses, he would lose his mandate.[42]

The reign of the first Ch'in emperor was crucial for the development of the Five Virtues Cycle which, for the first time, was welded to a series of other instruments of political legitimacy (such as portents and signs, ritual sacrifices, and ritual acts at court).[43] Yet at the same time that the Ch'in dynasty was experimenting with such devices it was corrupting and perverting them. It was the Ch'in which taught later emperors and would-be emperors (especially Wu Ti of Han, and Wang Mang) how to twist institutions and ideas, originally designed to hobble their power, into devices manipulable at their whim.

Ku Chieh-kang did not address himself to the legitimacy of the Ch'in (an important issue traditionally), nor was he overly concerned with the suppressions that took the form of 'burning of books' and 'burying of scholars.' He actually minimized the latter events, which were made so heinous a crime by the Confucian historians, because he felt they had been greatly exaggerated. In *Alchemists and Confucianists of the Ch'in-Han Era,* he argued that there was actually a marked continuity in thought and political personnel from the late Warring States through the Ch'in. What was new to the Ch'in, and what most attracted Ku Chieh-kang's criticism, was the Ch'in's unprecedented designs to politicize all thought and scholarship. However limited its success at this, it provided a model followed with great success in the Han.

Ku Chieh-kang did not permit his readers to overlook what his research revealed to be the central role of Confucianists in this politicization. In one summary of the issue he wrote:

When the first Ch'in emperor unified thought, he did not allow people to read books; his method was a system of punishments. When Han Wu Ti unified thought, he permitted men to read only one kind of book; his method was the seduction of profit. As a result, the Ch'in emperor lost, and Wu Ti won. The Li Ssu who exhorted the Ch'in emperor to unify thought was a disciple of the great Con-

42. *Ibid.,* pp. 465–466.
43. *CHFSJS,* pp. 3, 6, 13.

fucianist teacher Hsün Tzu. The Tung Chung-shu who exhorted Wu Ti to unify thought was a specialist in the *Spring and Autumn Annals.*[44]

Still, it was not solely the politicians, the officials, nor even the ideologues, Confucian or Legalist, who were blamed by Ku Chieh-kang for the corruptions of Tsou Yen's system and its ramifications. Instead, he brought onto the stage a group of intellectuals that he had been keeping in the wings for just the dramatic moment. It was a faction which he called the Alchemists (*fang-shih*) that acted as the corrupting agent of the best fruit of the One Hundred Schools.[45] The typical alchemist was an amalgam of Merlin and Machiavelli; he summoned ghosts and spirits, smelted cinnabar to produce potions of immortality, and gave political advice at the emperor's court through occult, esoteric media. Originally consulted by the emperor for their knowledge of immortality, the Alchemists soon appropriated the philosophy of the Five Virtues system and even the Wind and Hill sacrifices as devices for their all-encompassing "sycophancy and illicit activities." [46] (For example, the Confucianists had understood the Wind and Hill sacrifice purely in its role in the receipt of the imperial mandate; for the Alchemists, it was an act performed in an effort to achieve immortality.)[47]

Ku Chieh-kang believed that the threat of the Alchemists to the Confucianists was so great that, in order to triumph, the Confucianists had to beat them at their own game. With time, the Confucianists devoted themselves, like the Alchemists, to enhancing the position of the emperor, until in the end, "the emperor utilized the Confucianists to the profit of his personal religion; and likewise the Confucianists utilized the emperor to gain profit for their own personal religion. Whenever the emperor had any needs, the Confucianists, assuredly, had some-

44. *Ibid.,* p. 50.

45. I have translated *fang-shih* as "alchemist" primarily because "fang" in its usage here denotes a "recipe" or "formula" (to produce a substance for prolonging life or to achieve immortality). Also, the aura of the fang-shih in Ku's narrative in the *CHFSJS* is quite reminiscent of the alchemist in Western lore.

46. *SJCMC,* p. 418; *CHFSJS,* p. 20.

47. *CHFSJS,* p. 20.

thing to furnish him." [48] In order to provide this service to the emperor, the Confucianists studied and employed the methods of their rivals and, eventually, became "Alchemist-ized." Although the Alchemists seemed to have disappeared, in reality they joined the ranks of the triumphant Confucianists for their own survival.[49] Thus, it was Ku's tacit implication that even before the full incorporation of Mo Tzu's and Tsou Yen's values into Tung Chung-shu's political philosophy, Confucianism was irremediably tainted by a mentality that could only corrupt the legacies of Mo Tzu and Tsou Yen.

The Three Emperors

Clearly, the picture of the Golden Age, gradually assembled over middle antiquity, was structured and given a dynamic quality by different adaptations of the Five Virtues cycle. And the latter period of the Golden Age was finally characterized as the Three Dynasties, ruled respectively by Yao, Shun, and Yü. But who came before the triumvirate? According to a version of the Golden Age prominent in Western discussions, for example, three man-gods prevailed: Fu Hsi, Shen Nung, and the Yellow Emperor. Ku Chieh-kang's last great undertaking in his quest to reveal the historical thinking of middle antiquity was a ponderous study of the Three Emperors (*San Huang*)—a generic term, actually, for the protean pantheon of god-emperors which was placed anterior to the Three Dynasties.

In the book *A Study of the Three Emperors* (*San Huang K'ao*), which he published in 1936 with Yang Hsiang-k'uei, Ku Chieh-kang employed familiar techniques to demonstrate the relationship of disparate accounts of the early Golden Age to intellectual and political factions in middle antiquity.[50] In this bulky, unwieldy stuly one learns more than he cares to know about the perennial purges of the pantheon by ideologues from the Warring States through the Wang Mang epoch. The

48. 1955 introduction to *CHFSJS,* p. 8.
49. *Ibid.,* p. 9, and in detail throughout the book.
50. *San Huang K'ao* [A Study of The Three Emperors]—hereinafter referred to as *SHK*— (Peking: Harvard-Yenching Institute, 1936), reprinted in *KSP,* VII, part 2.

reader early surrenders to the primary thesis of the book: that K'ang Yu-wei and his pupil Ts'ui Shih were wrong in attributing the fabrication of the Three Emperors to Wang Mang's brain trust, the Old Text scholars.

K'ang Yu-wei had much oversimplified the issue, Ku Chieh-kang argued, by attributing every appearance of the Three Emperors in texts important during Wang Mang's "New Dynasty" (A.D. 9–27) to original fabrications and interpolations by Liu Hsin.[51] K'ang and Ts'ui Shih concluded that the Three Emperors only appeared after the *Rites of Chou* (*Chou-li*) and the apocrypha (*wei-shu*) were written. The *Study of Three Emperors* abundantly demonstrates that these legendary figures were already present at the end of the Warring States, over two centuries before K'ang and Ts'ui's attribution.[52] Ku's study agreed with the New Text scholars' assertions only insofar as it concluded that the Three Emperors became firmly secured in their position as the most venerable protagonists of the Golden Age when Wang Mang had them interpolated into prestigious Confucian texts such as the *Tso Commentary* and the *Rites of Chou,* and also into the apocrypha.[53]

The detailed examples and analyses permitted Ku Chieh-kang to illustrate some crucial historical factors which he had earlier emphasized in *Alchemists and Confucianists.* Both books give considerable attention to a school of intellectuals, the "Astronomers," and to a series of texts (apocryphal and prophetic) which had been little explored by anyone before the 1920s.[54] The thought of the Astronomers, particularly during the height of their political influence under Wu Ti of Han, was shown to have been a crucible in which an important stage of historical thought was pounded into shape. They were responsible for a comprehensive shakeup of the pantheon and for a systematic

51. *Ibid.,* pp. 96–97.
52. *Ibid.,* pp. 100–101.
53. *Ibid.,* pp. 51, 101.
54. Paul Pelliot wrote in 1920 that no Sinologist had yet undertaken to study the apocrypha, which are so important to an understanding of the traditions current in the Han dynasty. (*T'oung Pao,* XIX, 356; cited in Tjan Tjoe Som, *Po Hu T'ung, The Comprehensive Discussions in the White Tiger Hall,* 2 vols. [Leyden: Brill, 1949], I, 106–107.)

cosmology, related to a cyclical historiography. These prophetic texts and the apocrypha further expanded modern knowledge of the intricate development of Han intellectual history and its relationship to the politics of the court. Ku's presentation of this material laid the foundation for further studies of the evolution of controls on monarchical despotism, particularly through the use of astronomy.

Ku's discussions of the apocryphal texts, in particular, are extremely valuable insights into the growth of a strong intellectual tradition outside of, yet intimate with, the mainstream of what we in the West now call Confucianism. This esoteric tradition absorbed many of the historical innovations and whims which drew on the Five Virtues and related cyclical systems. As satellites of the Classical canon, the apocrypha bore tell-tale scars from interminable intellectual feuds. These feuds would have left even more mark on the Classics without the intervention of this esoteric tradition.[55] Surely this is one of Ku Chieh-kang's most significant and unique contributions to the study of the historical outlook of middle antiquity and its evolving image of the Golden Age. Though these traditions, aberrant to the Confucian mainstream, were further corruptions of Mo Tzu and Tsou Yen, Ku nevertheless treated them with obvious restraint and equanimity as precious historical documents. They further demonstrated his view that the history of antiquity was not only the history of Confucianism.

Wang Mang

In Ku Chieh-kang's scholarship, all roads in textual criticism and historiography lead to the New Dynasty of Wang Mang. Ku's *Alchemists and Confucianists,* the synthesis of his major ideas on the intellectual history and historical outlooks of middle antiquity, culminates in its analyses of the Wang Mang epoch. For this reason, and because of its general search for the counterfeiters of China's ancient history, the book should be at least partially viewed as a descendent of K'ang Yu-wei's *False*

55. *CHFSJS,* chaps. 19, 20, 21; and *SHK,* pp. 135 ff. Also see discussion of these subjects in Tjan Tjoe Som, *Po Hu T'ung,* where the insights of Ku Chieh-kang are repeatedly acknowledged (I, pp. 108, 120).

Classics of the New School. The two books overlap in methodology and in their stress on the pivotal role of the New Dynasty to all future understanding (or misunderstanding) of ancient Chinese history. But they differ fundamentally where Ku argued that Wang Mang's regime brought to culmination the political manipulation of the form and content of ancient historiography.

It was the political crisis represented by the New Dynasty that provided the necessary impetus to rigorous systemization of the many extant *ad hoc* versions of Golden Age history. Ku Chieh-kang ascribed to the aristocracy and the people a loss of confidence in the Han ruling house from the latter years of Emperor Wu Ti's reign; however, with no revolution forthcoming from 'the people,' the Han ruling house was left to be toppled by more subtle means. Ku's descriptions and analyses of the economic and social conditions of the first century B.C. are even sketchier than his accounts of the Warring States; however, his narratives of the Han dynasty's fear of losing the mandate, and the intellectual results of this, are minutely and dramatically detailed.[56] In contrast to the tendency of the modern New Text school's analysis, Ku Chieh-kang emphasized Wang Mang's continuity with and debt to earlier Han political thought. Long before Wang Mang's elaborate campaign to legitimize his *coup d'état,* the Han ruling house had argued its own legitimacy in terms of the Five Virtue system (the Han as 'Fire,' and the Ch'in as 'Metal') and legendary ancestry (the founding Emperor of Han as the descendent of Emperor Yao).[57] Wang Mang then carried the cyclical view of history to its extreme, and he utilized the notion of the Golden Age to a greater degree than it had ever been used before.

There is a curious kind of sympathy and patience exhibited by Ku Chieh-kang for Wang Mang's historical outlook that we do not find in his evaluation of the Alchemists or the Confucianists. Throughout traditional Chinese historiography, for the most part, the Wang Mang epoch had been grossly distorted by Confucian historians who were preoccupied with its illegitimate 'usurpation' and its presumptuous social economic reforms.

56. *WTCSS,* pp. 465–483.
57. *Ibid.,* chaps. 12, 13.

More immediate to Ku Chieh-kang was the New Text obscurantism which heaped staggering intellectual crimes on Wang Mang's ideologues. For Ku Chieh-kang, the legitimacy and the reforms of the dynasty were not an issue. New Text criticism he found, quantitatively, a gross exaggeration. In Ku's estimation, it needed tempering because of the fact that Wang Mang and company were not unique in their counterfeiting activities, but, at worst, the most systematic of a long line. Ku Chieh-kang's restraint in analyzing Wang Mang's literary products is especially noteworthy because, if we extrapolate from Ku's discussions of the Alchemists and Tung Chung-shu, it would seem that it was Wang who most fully exploited and corrupted the principles of Mo Tzu and Tsou Yen. It is not untenable, however, to argue as Hu Shih did, in effect, that Wang Mang's regime represents an implementation of their principles: Wang after all did employ legends and historical systems for political remonstrance; and the 'Mutually Producing' historical concept seems to have provided an ideological key to a bloodless revolution.[58] Ku's silence on this issue prevents us from attributing his restraint to this kind of interpretation.

In the balance, his analyses of Wang Mang do not depict Wang as a cynical manipulator of historiography, though he did at times refer to Wang's "dark schemes" [59] or to his "trumping up" omens.[60] Ku Chieh-kang's prevailing attitude was that of the Pragmatist teaching his pupils to appreciate the fact that men at different times understand their relationship to the past in radically different ways. In *Alchemists and Confucianists,* he carefully explained to his readers that "*We* know that society grows over time and through various changes; history certainly cannot repeat itself." But in Wang Mang's day,

They took just the opposite [point of view]; they considered that if it cannot repeat itself, then it cannot be considered history. They saw history as a merry-go-round lantern (*ts'ou ma teng*)—what comes

58. Hu Shih, "Wang Mang, the Socialist Emperor of Nineteen Centuries Ago" (in English), *Journal of the North China Branch of the Royal Asiatic Society,* LIX (1928), 218–230.

59. *CHFSJS,* p. 118.

60. See *KSP,* II, 130–139.

will go, and what goes will come again. The theory of the Five Virtues . . . and the Three Stages . . . are practical examples of this outlook. When Wang Mang everywhere imitated the Duke of Chou, it was as if the Duke of Chou were born again.[61]

It was not merely that Wang tried to emulate the Duke; he *became* the Duke of Chou.[62] And, in the process of convincing himself and the rest of China that this was the case, Wang polished and restructured the cyclical historical theories, promoted texts, and reproduced events (signs and prodigies) and symbols traditionally associated with the great Duke. Further, Ku attributed to Wang's need for legitimacy the considerable attention given to Emperor Yao's abdication to Emperor Shun in the apocrypha.[63] In the end, the Golden Age took on a new aspect due to the methods Wang Mang employed to become emperor. First, he appropriated the old god-emperors as his personal ancestors and fixed a well-ordered ancient genealogy. Then he appropriated the example of the abdication of the dynasty of Emperor Yao to the dynasty of Emperor Shun and applied it, by way of a cyclical interpretation, to the Han dynasty and his own New Dynasty: Wang designated himself the lineal descendent of Shun. And finally, Wang Mang appropriated the 'Mutually-Producing Five Elements' theory and used it to designate himself the embodiment of the Earth Virtue, in order to be able to say that his dynasty was the appropriate one to follow the Han (imbued with the Fire Virtue).[64]

Now the systems of ancient history became more intimate with the realities of middle antiquity's politics than they had ever been before; and now, miscellaneous gods and unrelated legends were forged into a tight, chronologically specific, common tradition.[65] So comprehensive and effective was Wang Mang's ideological success, Ku wrote, that in spite of Wang

61. *CHFSJS*, p. 96.

62. *SHK*, p. 524.

63. *CHFSJS*, p. 132. Ku considered Wang Mang to be one of the major influences on the apocrypha (*wei-shu*); the other was the thought of the Astronomers' school (*SHK*, p. 135). Also see Tjan Tjoe Som, *Po Hu T'ung*, I, 118–119, 141–142, on the nature and origins of the wei-shu.

64. *WTCSS*, chaps. 13, 16, 24.

65. *CHFSJS*, pp. 101, 118.

Mang's political failure, its effect was felt on China's "academics and religion" down to the twentieth century.[66]

Liu Hsin

Chang T'ai-yen has said that after Confucius the greatest personage is Liu Hsin, and this is not false. But [Liu's] scholarly excellence is one thing. His manipulation of authentic and spurious texts is another thing; and just because we are grateful to him does not mean that we exonerate him.—Ku Chieh-kang[67]

Wang Mang used counterfeit actions to usurp the Han state. Liu Hsin used counterfeit classics to usurp Confucian studies; the two of them like counterfeiters, the two of them like usurpers. Counterfeit lord, counterfeit scholar; usurping lord, usurping scholar.—K'ang Yu-wei[68]

It was a scholar, a textual critic at that, Liu Hsin, who was made by K'ang Yu-wei and the New Text school the chief culprit of the New Dynasty. It was Liu who had the intellectual facilities necessary to counterfeit the Old Text classics to Wang Mang's political specifications. Partially, Ku Chieh-kang agreed: "Whenever Wang Mang wanted something, Liu Hsin had it."[69]

However, Liu Hsin, his complicity notwithstanding, was awarded great stature by Ku Chieh-kang. Liu's discovery of new historical materials (the *ku-wen* texts) he compared to the modern discoveries of the Tun Huang literary treasures and those of the Imperial Library.[70] If this were the case, Ku asked, why were Liu's contemporaries not elated at his great find? Because, Ku answered, they feared for their rice bowls; their reliance on both the oral tradition and very fragmentary extant materials would have been overthrown by the highly detailed, older materials. And why was Liu's work attacked in modern China?

66. *SHK,* p. 110.

67. Ku's Preface to *KSP,* V, 13.

68. K'ang Yu-Wei, *Hsin hsüeh wei-ching k'ao* [The False Classics of the New School] (Peking: Chung-hua reprint, 1959), chap. 6, p. 143.

69. *CHFSJS,* p. 11.

70. The finds in the Imperial Library refers to the discovery of the Ch'ing administrative (Nei Ko) archives (*CHFSJS,* p. 71). Also see praise of Liu Hsin by Ku in *CHFSJS,* p. 66; in his introduction to *KSP,* V, 11–13; and in *SLTC,* p. 25.

Because he was not an objective reorganizer of ancient materials, but a subjective changer of these materials; because he caused many spurious and real materials to become confused. Liu mixed up the old and the new, and was arbitrary to the extent that modern critics have had to expend great energies to repair his damage.[71]

In some of his accounts of Liu Hsin, Ku Chieh-kang depicted him much as he did the scholars of the *Symposium on Critiques of Spurious Literature.* The preface to the fifth volume of the *Critiques* called Liu a brilliant, revolutionary scholar of vast and lasting influence; a pioneer in studying ancient texts. However, Liu was

> unfortunately born in that age, and he was unable to systematize literary remains objectively so that later men might be able to see the true aspect of old texts; he only wanted to change old documents in order to make them suit the circumstances of his contemporary world. His outlook was 'construct a unified canon for practical purposes' (*t'ung-ching chih-yung*).[72]

It was this latter, 'practical' attitude toward the canon that was Liu's greatest sin, in Ku Chieh-kang's eyes. There was only one purpose for a canon—to provide an intellectual foundation and a mystique for political activities having nothing to do with an honest search for truth. Canon, Old *and* New Text, was the poisonous product of the Wang-Liu regime, and its real onus on future generations.[73] For it was the regime's attempt to establish an exclusive orthodoxy to bolster itself that created the Old Text–New Text controversy in the first place. This put a price on scholars' allegiance to an orthodoxy and not to an independent search for truth.[74]

Thus Ku Chieh-kang, like modern New Text scholars, had to chasten Liu Hsin, but he did so for different reasons. In fact, it is often difficult to distinguish his evaluations of Liu Hsin from his evaluations of K'ang Yu-wei: they are both praised and

71. *CHFSJS,* p. 71.
72. Ku's preface to *KSP,* V, 17.
73. *CHFSJS,* p. 81.
74. *Ibid.,* pp. 104–105.

blamed for the same things (using the past for political reform, establishing a canon for practical ends), and with similar rhetoric.[75] One also feels that Ku Chieh-kang has failed to keep K'ang Yu-wei and Liu Hsin firmly rooted in their respective historical contexts; he seems to have seen Liu Hsin and K'ang as part of one ambiance. His essays seldom juxtapose the thought of K'ang to a contemporary representative of the Old Text school (like Chang T'ai-yen); usually, one finds him making K'ang speak across the millennia directly to Liu Hsin. But K'ang was not debating with ghosts; he was speaking as much to his own time as Ku Chieh-kang spoke to his.

Though Liu Hsin was not exonerated by Ku Chieh-kang, his culpability was greatly lessened in the area where the New Text school attacked him most directly—that is, where he was said to have been the forger of all of the Old Text literature, including that pivotal document, the *Tso Commentary*. In both instances, Liu was cleared of the charge: Many of the forgeries and interpolations attributed to the New Dynasty were made earlier—which is not to say that Liu was not in charge of whatever texts were put together in the Old Text canon. The *Tso Commentary,* while it may first have been associated with the *Spring and Autumn Annals* by Liu Hsin, was not forged by him, but originated centuries before.[76]

For Ku Chieh-kang, the most characteristic feature of Liu Hsin's scholarship, and at the same time its most distressing feature, was its paradoxical relationship with spurious history. Never had any scholar before Liu Hsin displayed such an awareness and grasp of the problem of forged texts and spurious history; never had any previous intellectual been in such a commanding position to set the record of the past straight. No one

75. On one occasion, Ku actually defended K'ang Yu-wei against Bernard Karlgren's charge that K'ang was merely a politician of no scholarly value (*WTCSS,* pp. 538–554).

76. *CHFSJS,* pp. 106–107. Ku's characterization of Liu Hsin and his role in Han–Hsin scholarship is supported by other students of the problem: (1) Fung Yu-lan, *A History of Chinese Philosophy* (Princeton, 1953), II, 135, 574; (2) Tjan Tjoe Som, *Po Hu T'ung,* I, 145; (3) Bernard Karlgren, "The Early History of the *Chou-li* and the *Tso-chuan* Texts," *BMFEA,* III (1931), 44.

before Liu Hsin had exposed more spurious history, treated the problem more systematically, nor created an atmosphere more conducive to doubting antiquity. Yet Liu Hsin, Wang Mang, and their aides were responsible for systematically counterfeiting more history and forging more texts than any group or individual before (and perhaps, after) them.[77]

Ku Chieh-kang seems to be saying about the counterfeiters: "It takes one to know one." Though he drew no specific conclusions from this observation, perhaps we are being asked to see that those most capable of knowing truth are also those most capable of obscuring it. This is no doubt why Ku permitted Liu Hsin and K'ang Yu-wei to fuse and to lose their historical moorings: They were both past-masters in the art of revealing their enemies' sins—and substituting their own instead.

Tacitly, Liu Hsin became for Ku Chieh-kang the culminating symbol of his studies of antiquity. Liu Hsin was at once the epitome and *sine qua non* of the intellectuals' betrayal, and his career was the final act in the destruction of the progressive potentials of middle antiquity. It was not only that Liu Hsin juggled the books and absconded with the past. He and the intellectuals he represented also ran off with the future as well —that is, with a chance for China to progress in the future toward a social and intellectual order which the late Warring States seemed to be heralding.[78] Thus, the New Dynasty intellectuals made it possible for 'the people' once again to be exploited without recourse, and for aristocratic culture to predominate. With Liu Hsin, the principles of Mo Tzu and Tsou

77. This is the central point of Ku's "Chan-kuo Ch'in Han chien jen te ts'ao wei yü pien wei" [The Criticism and Creation of Spurious Literature], *KSP,* VII, part 1; see also Ku's *Tang-tai Chung-kuo shih-hsüeh* [Contemporary Chinese Historiography] (Shanghai, 1945), p. 136.

78. Ku repeatedly lamented that "The Warring States era destroyed the hierarchic [social system], but by the time of the era of [Han Wu Ti] it begins to reconstitute itself" (*CHFSJS,* p. 19). Or, "although the end of the Warring States period took old institutions and completely overthrew them, the old ideas were perpetuated by way of the Confucianists" (*ibid.,* p. 50).

Cf. Liang Ch'i-ch'ao, *Intellectual Trends,* p. 103; and Liang's *History of Chinese Political Thought During the Early Tsin Period,* trans. by L. T. Chen (London, 1930), p. 31.

Yen suffered their final corruption. And with that, Liu Hsin's Golden Age became history; so did Ku Chieh-kang's.

Concluding Remarks on Ku Chieh-kang's Historiography

In the Penumbra of Confucianism

Ku Chieh-Kang argued that it was impossible to understand the nature of the Confucian thought and institutions that occupied the center (if not all) of the stage in conventional historiography without exploring the rival schools and traditions which were obscured or destroyed and covered over by Confucianism, or incorporated into its resilient body. Ku was among the first of the moderns to explore seriously and in depth what Peter Boodberg has called the "penumbra of Confucianism"—that dark (because orthodoxy kept the shades drawn) and exotic realm where the esoteric traditions of Chinese civilization flourished throughout the length of Chinese history. Here, among others, were the Alchemists, the Astronomers, and the counter-canon of the apocrypha. All of these traditions, Ku argued, were intimately involved with the growth and development of Confucianism; they existed together in a state of tension and even symbiosis. They all comprised a system; and therefore to ignore the esoteric tradition was to ignore an essential part of the system and distort the nature of historical reality.

A significant historical fact remains, however. The esoteric traditions (and less esoteric traditions such as that of the Mohists) all in themselves failed to become the substance of that ethos around which the vast and complex Chinese imperium organized itself. All of these traditions were too narrow, too brittle, too exclusive to encompass the quantitative and qualitative problems of a massive society over long spans of time. The singular ability of 'Confucianism' to do this was alluded to by Ku when he described its ability to absorb other traditions or to compromise with them. But he nevertheless made himself insensitive to its sociological accomplishments, and to its ability to foster political harmony and hold together the united empire. (And this was a unity of which he explicitly approved.) He never did consider how such a unity could have been achieved with an alternative ethos.

THE PROBLEM OF DESPOTISM

Some of Ku's historical analyses, growing out of his study of the corruption of the intellectuals after the Warring States era, have important implications for what was later known as the debate on Oriental Despotism.[79] Broadly, proponents of the theory of Oriental Despotism posit a 'hydraulic' mode of production for Chinese civilization—that is, a peculiar mode derived from the extensive use of large-scale irrigation. Based on the quantitative and qualitative problems brought about by this mode of production, a totalitarian monarchy, employing a large and servile bureaucracy, was made possible and persisted in various degrees throughout Chinese history down to the modern era. The debate has centered on the nature and actuality of an 'Asiatic mode of production,' and on the question of whether, or to what degree, the central Chinese state could usefully be called a despotism.

Ku's historiography makes important contributions to the latter question where it outlines the development of subtle means for political remonstrance and elaborate ritual institutions that played important roles in the legitimization and transmission of political power. Perhaps the greatest single limitation on his history was his inability or lack of desire to recognize the persistence of at least some of the ancient institutions which acted as checks on despotism. (Wolfram Eberhard, who has made extensive critiques of the theory of Oriental Despotism in China, has done research related to Ku's work which demonstrates how astronomy and attendant institutions at the Chinese

79. See Karl Wittfogel, *Oriental Despotism: A Comparative Study of Total Power* (New Haven, 1957); Wolfram Eberhard, *Conquerors and Rulers: Social Forces in Medieval China* (Leyden, 1952); and F. W. Mote, "The Growth of Chinese Despotism: A Critique of Wittfogel's Theory of Oriental Despotism as Applied to China," *Oriens Extremus,* 8 (1961), 1–41.

court were used during the Han dynasty for political remonstrance.[80])

Ku confuses and distorts the political realities of China after the Ch'in unification largely through his terrible simplification of the intelligentsia as parasites of the aristocracy, while 'aristocracy' remains a vague and diffuse epithet for the ruling class. Ku shows no sensitivity to the tensions which began even in the Han dynasty (if not earlier) to develop between the monarchy and its personally-created aristocracy, and the monarchy and the bureaucracy. This bureaucracy ultimately became the arbiters and protectors of 'Confucian' culture.[81] Ku's conclusions all suggest that from the Han dynasty forward, the ruling class was a monolith, and that politically the educated elite, the clerics, were a politically undifferentiated part of the monolith. But the evidence he adduces in his most serious and careful studies points in quite the other direction—that is, toward a monarchy perennially forced to rely on and compromise with forces outside itself and represented by the philosophies and world-views of Confucianism or one of its 'rivals.'

If it is true that the 'intelligentsia' were in the stranglehold of politics during the reign of the first Ch'in emperor; and if it is true that this regime did co-opt and use to its own advantage those institutions meant to inhibit despotism—it may also be true that the regime was short-lived and incapable of governing the empire it had forged for just these same reasons. If Confucianism (in its Han dynasty formulation) advocated a 'return' to class division and particularism (as opposed to the universalism of Mo Tzu), nowhere did Ku elaborate on the exact nature of this society. Instead, he imputed to Confucianism the broadest and vaguest of social evils—the oppression of the masses. He would not attribute the original success of the Confucian ethos to its suitability to the widest contemporary social needs, but rather he said its success was due to the 'sell-out' of its advocates to the interests of (evil-intentioned) rulers.

80. Wolfram Eberhard, "The Political Function of Astronomy and Astronomers in Han China," in J. K. Fairbank, ed., *Chinese Thought and Institutions* (Chicago, 1957), pp. 33–71

81. See Levenson, *CCMF,* II.

Thus in Ku's historiography there sometimes occurs a marked descent from the most sophisticated analyses of the origins and functions of various thought systems to a new kind of 'praise and blame' historiography. Occasionally his controlled and balanced studies deteriorate into morality plays in which an evil ruling class and weak-willed and greedy intellectuals confront 'the people.'

During the period under our consideration here, Ku lacked capable critics. He was most often criticized for petty errors, and usually his critics were those stung or stunned by his secularism and his slaughter of sacred cows. However, the group of self-styled Marxists and historical materialists who were known as the Social Historians did begin to provide a more solid critique of Ku's scholarship in the late twenties and early thirties. The Social Historians admitted that Ku's work, especially in the *Critiques,* seemed to have been the logical starting point for a "scientific social history" of China.[82] But they repeatedly excoriated him for his ignorance of the social base of the eras whose intellectual history he wrote. I suspect that if he had taken some of the same pains with social history that he did with his study of ancient historical thought, he might have been less cavalier and superficial in his judgments of the role of Confucianism in Han China, and in his evaluation of the post-unification polity in general.

MYTH AND IDEOLOGY

It is when Ku Chieh-kang's history came under the fire of the Social Historians that a peculiar tendency of his scholarship became more evident (to his readers and perhaps to himself as well). To the dismay of the Social Historians, among others, Ku preoccupied himself with the study of 'ideology' at the cost of 'myth': these two concepts, as I am using them here, have a special meaning (derived from their usage over time in Western

82. See Wang I-ch'ang, "Chung-kuo she-hui shih-lün shih" [A History of the Chinese Society Debate], *Tu-shu tsa-chih* [Readers' Miscellany], II:2–3 (March 1932), 5. This journal was one of the major forums of the Social Historians, and it should not be confused with the supplement to the *Nu-li chou-pao* [Endeavor].

thought) and an important relationship to each other.[83] Broadly, 'mythological' beliefs are those which serve to integrate the individual and the group, or to bind together social groups as wholes and establish consensus. The function of 'ideological' beliefs "(in terms of individual and group interests) is to procure advantages for specific social positions and (in terms of social structure) to segregate and consolidate competing groups around rival ideas." [84]

Ideology in its segregating and group-consolidating function is logically subsequent to Myth as a force integrating and organizing the individual and the group. And likewise, from the point of view of origins, the 'origin of ideology' is a topic logically subsequent to the 'origin of myth.' This would be so because the analysis of the origin of ideology begins when socially determined 'interests' are taken into account for the analysis of beliefs, along with more primordial factors such as the nature of the symbolic expression of experience and the 'poetic' character of languages, or the 'instinctive' urges of Man in the generic sense. An analysis which takes *special* factors into account (e.g., class interests) begins at a level where generic factors (the nature of symbolism as such, the generic constitution of man) have already had some effect.[85]

These distinctions are perhaps more useful to the historian than those of ideology as 'reflection' and 'mask,' for they suggest that beliefs, at all times, are related organically with social structures, and that their functional relationship changes over time as the fundamental structure of society changes. This is not to say that 'ideology' and 'myth' do not distort (which is not to say 'mask') experience. It rather suggests that they distort in different fashions according to their respective origins: *Ideology* expresses "particular experiences under the distorting influences (consciously or not) of 'interested' motives—that is, of motives whose functional meaning is the maintenance of a

83. Here I am drawing heavily on Ben Halpern's essay " 'Myth' and 'Ideology' in Modern Usage," *History and Theory,* I:2 (1961), 129–150.

84. *Ibid.,* p. 136.

85. *Ibid.*

particular social role." [86] *Myth,* on the other hand, is subject to the distorting influences which typically have bearing upon the symbolic expression of experience.

Ku Chieh-kang's preoccupation with ideology disturbed the Social Historians along two avenues of concern. In its tendency to see beliefs as masks of social situations, Ku's historiography ultimately tended to discourage the investigation of social structures—the main concern of the Social Historians—via the study of the beliefs.[87] And by stressing the ideological (segregating) functions of legends and historical lore in the post-feudal era, rather than their mythical (integrating) functions in earlier periods, Ku took attention away from those primordial, formative stages of Chinese civilization which were, for a time, of fundamental interest to the Social Historians. Where Ku persistently found evidence of class conflict, invidious social distinctions, and special group interests, the Social Historians sought some clues for social system and coherence.

It was not that the Social Historians were shy of the Marxist *ex cathedra* about history and class conflict. It was rather that they seemed to live more easily with that notion, and were capable of putting it aside as a historical commonplace in order to get down to more 'fundamental' problems—such as the periodization of Chinese history along the lines of classic Marxist historiography. In order to accomplish this, first things had to be done first. The modes of production of each era had to be established; which is to say, the Marxist sequential modes of production had to be discovered in China's history. The goal, it seems clear enough, was to demonstrate that China and the West had parallel historical developments. From this observation on China's past (China had passed through the primitive communist, slave, and feudal stages), sanguine extrapolations about China's future could also be made (regarding not merely

86. *Ibid.*

87. For example, see Wang I-ch'ang, "Chung-kuo she-hui shih-lün shih"; and Hu Ch'iu-yüan, "P'in-k'un te che-hsüeh [Impoverished Philosophy], *Tu-shu tsa-chih,* I:3 (June 1931); Li Chi, "Tui-yü Chung-kuo she-hui lün chan kung-hsien yü p'i-p'ing" [Contributions and Critiques of the Controversy Over Chinese Society], *ibid.,* II:2–3 (March 1932).

socialism and communism in China, but about the survival of China in the twentieth century as well).

But the Social Historians were even more complex than this. Not merely did they display a passionate desire to elaborate a historical scheme which would guarantee the survival and progress of Chinese society—but in the example of a scholar like Li Chi, there was also an attempt to discover a developmental pattern that might be unique to China, or at least distinguish it from the West (e.g., the Asiatic Mode of Production).[88]

The Social Historians therefore sought to employ the historical lore and legends of antiquity as clues to modes of social organization and institutional and economic developments that marked China's progress, from those primitive beginnings which Ku Chieh-kang ignored, along variations on the scheme of Marxian evolution. Li Chi, one of the strongest critics of Ku's 'indirect' and 'stratified' history of the Golden Age, interpreted the legend of Yü, in its earliest form, as an expression of the development of primitive tribal leadership—that is, as one of the earliest forms of social organization and integration in Chinese civilization.[89] He approached it 'mythologically,' whereas Ku Chieh-kang, observing the legend's later stages, treated it as ideology. Though Ku did allude in passing to the integrative role of the legend of Yü (in its primordial habitat among the Southern tribes, and perhaps even in its service to the Mohists), he chose to emphasize its role in setting up sectional interests (the Central Region vs. the barbarians) or political factions (Wang Mang vs. the Han ruling house).

The Social Historians did not establish a dialogue with Ku Chieh-kang, and when they and he did respond to each other they talked past one another, refusing to see not only the legitimacy of the other's point of view, but, more importantly, failing to see that they were all dealing with the same problem (the nature of Chinese civilization as indicated by antiquity) and focusing on different parts of the same historical continuum.

From the other end of the political spectrum, the Kuomin-

88. Li Chi, "Tui-yü Chung-kuo she-hui lün," pp. 19–21.
89. *Ibid.*

tang intellectuals also criticized Ku's emphasis on an ideological rather than a mythological interpretation of ancient beliefs. When Ku exposed the unhistoricity of the lore of Yü and the Golden Age, the Kuomintang criticized him because Ku undermined the party's desire to employ this lore in a fundamentally mythic fashion—that is, as an element in a new ethos designed to integrate, unify, and produce consensus where there was thus far only a fragmented, inchoate nation. Ku's emphasis on class conflict and on the ideological origins of the lore of antiquity likewise conflicted with Kuomintang efforts (evident from 1928 with increasing clarity) to steer the consciousness and social development of the new nation away from the fundamental social changes that could be achieved only at the cost of greater internal strife. However, with the invasion and occupation of China by Japan, Ku's writings made a rather dramatic reversal. From the late thirties, virtually all of his work focused on the problem of national unity, and with that he noticeably eschewed discussions of China's past which recalled issues of class or sectional conflict. His writing even drew on lore from antiquity which dramatized problems of cultural unification and of 'national' unity.

THE IMAGE OF THE WARRING STATES EPOCH

In keeping with his emphasis on class division and conflict in his pre-war writings, Ku gave considerable attention, and usually positive appraisal, to the chaos, flux, and disequilibrium that generally characterized the Warring States epoch. The Wang Mang era undoubtedly represented for Ku's historiography the consummation of those intellectual problems which were his main interest. However, according to his understanding, these problems were conceived and defined in the earlier epoch of the Warring States.

Ku's adulation of and emphasis on this epoch were not merely acts of contrariness in his design to overthrow the traditional historiography (for which the Warring States epoch was a running sore). For those traditional thinkers with whom Ku was most intimate, the epoch was the archetype of one of the two most terrifying historical eras of Chinese history. The other, its obverse in conventional social criticism, was the Ch'in dynasty. The former epitomized chaos; the latter epitomized stasis imposed by uncompromising force. Melodramatic violence was done to the perennial Confucian values of harmony, compromise, and mediation in both of these eras, which became the inexhaustible source of negative examples for the conventional moralizing historian. Ku's concentration on this epoch makes good historical sense, if only because the period is so basic to the development of that 'Confucian' world outlook which anathematized it. Though we may not agree with all of his analyses and evaluations, Ku's argument is sound where it suggests that it is impossible to understand the origins and functions of Confucianism without seeing it as a product of the dialectical relationship between the chaos of the Warring States and the ruthless imposition of order under the Ch'in.

Ku, and many of his contemporaries, saw something in the Warring States era that was vital to all future Chinese history. Contemporary Western historians, exploring the nature of twentieth-century Chinese revolutionary processes, agree with this point of view, though they have developed it well beyond Ku's suggestions and implications: the massive social changes of the Warring States epoch (as the link between a feudal-decentralized society and a monarchical-bureaucratic-centralized empire) are characterized as having no counterpart in Chinese history until the nineteenth and twentieth centuries.[90] This is far from saying that there were no changes or alterations in Chinese society during the interim. But it does suggest that from the point of view of fundamental political, social, and economic arrangements, what changes occurred did so within structures that evolved out of trends begun during the immediate post-Warring States era. In a word, the Warring States was a period of revolution, in the fullest sense, that culminated in the Han polity.

In Ku Chieh-kang's writings, analogies are sometimes made between the Warring States epoch and twentieth-century China.

90. For example, see *CCMF,* II; Etienne Balazs, *Chinese Civilization and Bureaucracy* (New Haven, 1964), chap. 11; and Franz Schurmann, *Ideology and Organization in Communist China* (Berkeley and Los Angeles, 1966), p. xl.

When he is explicit about the similarity between them, he usually emphasizes turbulence, violence, and the suffering wreaked by 'warlords' upon the masses. Less explicitly, an analogy is also made between the intellectuals of each era, whose tendency it is to give themselves up to politics or sell themselves to the ruling class, which is understood to be corrupt and exploitive. Implicit, but most significant, is the analogy between the "liberation of thought" in the Warring States and in modern China. In the respective free competitions of ideas and values and in the open clash of beliefs, Ku saw the raw potential for progress. In the conflict and instability of both periods, he saw fertile soil to start roots for a worthy civilization. His emphasis on flux, becoming, and potential provides the fundamental link between the two eras.

In Ku's telling, the Warring States' opportunities and potentials for progress were lost when, under the Ch'in-Han unification, chaos and flux were resolved into fixity. If this is so, how did such an inflexible and even petrified post-Warring States Chinese culture survive in a universe that demanded of society constant, though evolutionary, change and adaptation? Ku answered this question by suggesting that, in fact, Chinese culture in its Ch'in-Han formulation did not manage to survive on its own power. Instead, over the course of the Han dynasty, Chinese civilization grew effete and moribund and survived only via the chance occurrence, from the outside, of the barbarians.

Part Four: The Barbarians

VIII

Historical Notions in a Time of National Crisis

> *It is true that the physical condition of our people is weak, but with better educational methods and with higher standards of eugenics, it is reasonable to expect that we can develop a sturdier type of manhood. There is hope for the future of China if we see to it that all racial elements are given educational advantages, by the aid of which they can work out their own salvation.*—Ku Chieh-kang, 1926

Ku Chieh-kang's writings of the 1930s and 1940s yielded, with increasing frequency, to the temptation of melding past and present. In his serious historical writings, the Warring States period became a world just on the other side of the looking glass, before which stood the Warlord era of modern China. In his propagandistic historical essays, twentieth-century China, suffering Japanese invasions in the North, was a *dejà vu*: the Sung, the Liao, the Chin, once again. Scholars and warriors radiated their skullduggery, genius, or bravery over the millennia and lived again in different times but, seemingly, equivalent situations. Ku Chieh-kang's historical scholarship and propaganda complemented each other as the former devoted itself more and more to the question of the formation of the Chinese people while the latter pleaded with countrymen to defend modern China from annihilation. His interest and understanding of both of these problems were nourished each time he was drawn or driven, physically or intellectually, to China's inner Asian frontiers. It was a time of suddenly expanded experience and heightened awareness.

Barbarians and Chinese History

During the decades after the publication of his *Alchemists and Confucianists,* Ku Chieh-kang's scholarship and personal sentiments were dominated by a peculiar motif, present in his earlier thought, though restricted then to a subordinate position. The *barbarian motif,* as I shall call it, presents a most dramatic illustration of Ku's deep concern for the continuity of Chinese culture and the survival of the Chinese people. However undeveloped and erratically employed by Ku and other Chinese scholars of the time, this motif did become central to their study of the developmental processes of Chinese civilization.

There seem to have been three broad questions that concerned Ku and many others regarding the place of culturally or racially non-*Han* peoples in Chinese history. (The concepts of *nation, race,* and *culture* were constantly interchanged and confused.)[1] What was their actual role in the formation of earliest Chinese culture? What was their contribution to the continuity of Chinese culture? What were the potential contribu-

1. The confusion seems to have begun during the anti-Manchu revolutionary period between 1900 and 1911. Michael Gasster reports that the T'ung-meng-hui writers used the terms "nation" and "race" interchangeably; "It was their aim to portray the Chinese as a distinct racial group, to identify race with nation and nation with state, and to argue that a state composed of one race was best." (*Chinese Intellectuals and the Revolution of 1911* [Seattle, 1969], pp. 78–79.)

In the text below, I employ a number of terms traditionally used to distinguish 'Chinese' from non-Chinese peoples (or barbarians) living on China's borders or completely outside the imperium: (1) *Han* is the general term used by northerners, and during the modern period by all Chinese, to designate Chinese. It is derived from the name of the first dynasty to reign over the imperium in its classic formulation. (Southerners have identified themselves with the second of the great imperial dynasties, the T'ang.) Thus, 'men of Han' differentiate themselves from the Hui (Moslem) or Fan (Tibetan), etc. (2) The terms *Hua* and *Hsia* are of an earlier vintage, and were used to designate the first cultural conglomerate which evolved continuously into the later civilization of the Han empire. The term Hsia was applied to the 'dynastic' era just preceding the Shang.

tions which the non-*Han* peoples of China could make toward the future of Chinese culture?

The role that non-*Han* peoples played in the formative years of Chinese civilization was a question to which Ku addressed himself in the late 1920s. Though he did not devote a good deal of time specifically to the problem, it nevertheless occupied the highest place on his earliest programs of historical reorganization. In 1923 he wrote to Hu Shih and Ch'ien Hsüan-t'ung that of all the distorted Chinese historical outlooks on antiquity, perhaps the first needing correction was the viewpoint that the various peoples of China had a common source of origin and had been a homogeneous whole during the Golden Age. (Some legends had it that the Yellow Emperor was the original progenitor of all the peoples of China.)[2] This myth, he felt, was companion to the one which suggested that all of China (that is, the equivalent of the twentieth-century geopolitical unit) had been united and governed as one unit in high antiquity. Ku resisted the notion of early racial or ethnic homogeneity because it obscured and often obliterated the diversity of ancient China and the special contributions which distinct social groups had made.

In the late 1920s, this issue of racial unity in antiquity became entangled with current Kuomintang ideology. In their effort to bring China's multi-ethnic population into some kind of viable political unit, the Nationalists employed what Ku said were the same intellectual ploys that had been used in the Warring States epoch to foster political unity. Contemporary Western observers suggested, in corroboration of Ku's point of view, that the Kuomintang was fostering a policy of "Pan-Hanism" or "Secondary Imperialism," the effect of which was the absorption of the ethnic minorities.[3] By 1926 the Nationalists had begun to use the motto "The Five Races In Unity" (*Wu tsu kung-ho*), and their spokesmen sometimes suggested that all the racial groups in contemporary China (the Mongols,

2. *KSP*, I, 96–102.

3. Edgar Snow, *Red Star Over China* (New York: Random House, 1944), pp. 342 ff.; and Owen Lattimore, *Inner Asian Frontiers of China* (New York, 1940), p. 193.

Manchus, Tibetans, Muslims, etc.) were descendents of the Yellow Emperor, Yao, Shun, and Yü. Nationalist ideologues also went so far as to claim that Mongolia, Manchuria, and the other border political units had been amalgamated with the central Chinese state from the time of the Yellow Emperor, and evermore thereafter. This great geopolitical entity, it was said, was the great ecumene (*T'ien Hsia*) of traditional literature.[4]

Ku had no quarrel with Nationalist desires to unify the country, nor with their desire to improve *Han* and non-*Han* relations, which were often so terrible during the Republican period. However, he could not see the necessity of sacrificing historical truth even to that worthy goal. He believed that the real story of barbarian participation in Chinese culture would better contribute to understanding and mutual respect between *Han* and other peoples. He feared that China's crucial need of unity could ill afford to base itself on lies. It is best, he wrote in 1936, to rely on the real, natural roots of racial unity, such as the amalgamation of various stocks of people over the long span of Chinese history. "If lies are used," he queried, "what is to keep our people from breaking apart when they discover the truth? Our racial self-confidence must be based on reason. We must break off every kind of unnatural bond and unite on a basis of reality." [5] Ku personally tried to ameliorate certain aspects of this problem in the mid-1930s.

From another, and less politically engaged, area of contemporary thought, the general problem of early racial heterogeneity received further challenges and more complex treatment. Latter-day Chinese Social Darwinists criticized Ku's arguments by invoking Darwin's "common parent" thesis which hypothesized a common ancestor for members of the same species. This, of course, laid all emphasis on the purely physical

4. See Ku's "Ch'in Han t'ung-i yu-lai ho Chan-kuo jen tui-yü shih-chieh te hsiang-hsiang" [The Sources of Ch'in-Han Unification and the Conception of the World During the Warring States Period], *KSP*, II (dated 1926), 5; and Chiang Kai-shek, *China's Destiny and Chinese Economic Theory* (New York, 1947), for the most widely circulated official formulation of these themes.

5. Ku's preface to *SHK* (dated 1936), p. 25.

aspects of Ku's historical argument, and it completely ignored the central argument which stated that, whatever the racial identity (in the strict physical sense) of ancient China's diverse social groupings, they assuredly possessed distinct cultural characteristics. (In Owen Lattimore's discussions of the early differentiation of *Chinese* from *barbarians,* he emphasized that "on the whole, these barbarians are not described even at later periods as different 'races,' but as people who had not yet adopted the complex of economic practices and social organization that the Chinese were carrying with them.")[6] Only when these cultural factors melded did there come about the culture of *China* (the *Hua* or *Hsia*), a derivative and composite culture.

The Social Darwinian rebuttal of Ku's hypothesis was intent on ignoring questions of culture; it persisted in driving its point well beyond the issues at hand by asserting that not only did all of the human species derive from one common source, but further, that common source might assuredly have been located in East Asia. These were the days when the anthropologists' perennial search for human beginnings was focusing on North China and Mongolia. To some Chinese it would have been a source of considerable pride (and a somewhat perverse corroboration of traditional ethnocentric notions) to have it known that man's beginnings were in the Central Kingdom. Since the twenties, of course, Professor Leakey's discoveries in sub-Saharan Africa have made such claims the property of Black Culturalists—gathering a history, like some Chinese Social Darwinists, where they might.[7]

When, in the early 1930s, Chinese Marxist historiography proliferated into the Social History controversy, the physical and cultural aspects of primordial Chinese civilization were given sustained and exhaustive attention. Though Ku Chieh-

6. Lattimore, *Inner Asian Frontiers,* p. 56.

7. Lu Mao-te, "P'ing Ku Chieh-kang Ku-shih pien." [Criticism of Ku Chieh-kang's Critiques], *KSP,* II. To substantiate his arguments about "common parents" and homo sapiens origins in China, Lu Mao-te cited the following: (1) J. McCabe, *Evolution of Civilization* (New York, 1922); (2) H. F. Osborn, "Mongolia Might Be the Home of Primitive Man," *Peking Leader* (Peking, Oct. 10, 1923); (3) R. C. Andrews, *On the Trail of Ancient Man* (New York, 1926).

kang was not a participant in the Social History debates, they were responsible for lifting his original concern (for a proper appreciation of the role of non-'Chinese' culture in the formation of China) into a larger ambiance, and this concern was made the initial question in a dynamic view of Chinese history. When Ku originally considered the question, he did so from the point of view of historical consciousness, not from the standpoint of social history. He had primarily been concerned with righting a misconception of historical reality perpetuated by the Chou militarists and the Han obscurantists. Marxist and materialist historians now simply ignored the traditional legends or turned them into fodder for their anthropological theories. They set about describing the nature of antiquity as a prelude to their schematization of all of Chinese history.

BARBARIAN CONTRIBUTIONS TO CHINESE CULTURE

A dynamic view of Chinese history was, of course, not foreign to the non-Marxist historiography of National Studies. However, the mechanisms that moved Chinese history received only desultory consideration, for the Chinese New Historians seldom sought a synoptic view of Chinese history and they always approached comprehensive schemes with extreme skepticism. A case in point was the question of the role which barbarian peoples and cultures played in the development and continuity of Chinese civilization after the Ch'in-Han unification in the third century B.C. Ku Chieh-kang's scattered observations on this question were quite consistent: Non-Chinese peoples and cultures were the primary forces that permitted a periodically moribund Chinese culture to resuscitate itself and to persist. It is not clear in many instances whether Ku attributed this sustaining role of the barbarians to cultural infusions, like Buddhism, or to actual physical amalgamation through intermarriage. In his 1923 *Elementary National History,* he had rather straightforwardly said that during the dark days of the Latter-Han dynasty, it was Buddhism, derived from Hindu civilization, that had rescued a collapsing Chinese culture.[8] There is ambi-

8. Ku Chieh-kang, *Pen Kuo Shih* [Elementary National History] (Shanghai, 1923), I, 90.

guity, however, in the following kind of statement, which he made in the *Autobiography*:

In the period of the Warring Kingdoms, when there was an influx of many new racial elements, China was unusually vigorous and powerful; but in the Han dynasty, the arbitrary power of the monarchy, and the exclusiveness of Confucian teaching, brought Chinese culture to the verge of extinction. The reduced physical stamina of the people, their intellectual mediocrity, their lack of enthusiasm and will-power, all signified that the end was near. Had it not been for the infusion of new blood from the Five Barbarian groups (*Wu Hu*) of the Chin dynasty, from the Khitan, from the Jürched and Mongols, I fear that the *Han* race could not have survived.[9]

Whether or not Ku was speaking metaphorically here, when he spoke of "new blood," is not evident. However, he clearly did emphasize the potential physical contributions of non-*Han* peoples when, from the late 1920s, he became preoccupied with their future role in an again-failing Chinese civilization.

From the point of view of cultural history, some prominent scholars agreed with Ku's attitude, some disagreed, and some wavered. Hu Shih, representing the latter category, had very early in his career attributed a positive role in Chinese history to the influence of Indian art. At that time he said that "fresh impetus from the religious art of India" was responsible for moving Chinese art from its long and unnaturally arrested state.[10] In later writings, Hu Shih seems consistently to have given a negative appraisal of the influence of Indian civilization. "After the Wei and the Tsin dynasties," he wrote in 1924, "there occurred a confusion of various peoples, and the encroachments of the Hindu religion produced a dark medieval period." [11] Hu Shih most often seems to have written about the Indian influence from a hypersensitive, chauvinistic point of

9. *ACH,* p. 166.

10. Hu Shih, *The Development of the Logical Method in China* (Shanghai, 1922), p. 77. Hu was referring to an "arrested development" from the Warring States period down to the first century A.D., which he partly attributed to the influence of Mohism.

11. *HSWT,* II (dated 1924), 74.

view; and particularly in his English-language essays, he increasingly found Indianization to have been a catastrophe for China. "It was those religions of defeatism [like Buddhism] that sank the whole civilized world under the universal deluge of Medievalism," he wrote in Charles Beard's *Whither Mankind?*[12] In Hu's *The Chinese Renaissance,* Buddhism was that "imported religion from India" and that "foreign religion" under which the Chinese had suffered "humiliating domination." [13] Han Yü (768–824) and other adamant anti-Buddhists of the T'ang and Sung periods would have approved of Hu Shih's rhetoric—especially his 1937 piece "The Indianization of China," the longest and most dramatic of the lot.[14]

Still, Hu Shih did not completely reject those aspects of Chinese culture undeniably associated with non-*Han* influences. In his writings on literary history, the eras of strongest foreign domination of China were given a high place, for during these epochs 'vernacular literature' flourished. He wrote that in the centuries during which the Khitan, the Jürched, and then the Mongols held sway over China, China's literature possessed a new freshness and managed to cleanse itself of the "putrid odor of Southern classicism." In particular, he felt that Yüan drama was a singular contribution to what he called a spontaneous and appropriate literature.[15] If he made any detailed efforts to elaborate the relationship of these important literary phenomena to barbarian culture, I do not know of them.

Hu Shih was not the first scholar in modern China to give a new and elevated status to the literature of Mongol-dominated China. Wang Kuo-wei wrote earlier, more, and better on the subject, and though he was not in quest of 'vernacular literature,' he too remarked on the freshness, vigor, and spontaneity of Yüan drama. Beyond that, however, Wang's attitude toward foreign cultural influences in general, and Buddhism in partic-

12. "The Civilizations of East and West," in C. Beard, ed., *Whither Mankind?* (New York, 1928), pp. 30–31.

13. Hu Shih, *The Chinese Renaissance* (Chicago, 1933), pp. 84–88.

14. "The Indianization of China: A Case Study of Cultural Borrowing," in *Independence, Convergence and Borrowing* (Cambridge, Mass., 1937).

15. "Yüan jen te ch'ü-tzu" [Yüan Drama], *HSWT,* III (dated 1922), p. 652.

ular, contrasted with those of Hu Shih. Wang welcomed foreign thought on China, much as Hu Shih did; but his rationale was that all great philosophy was the product of cross-fertilization. He saw Buddhism as essentially a productive force in early Chinese society. "When Buddhism first reached China," he wrote, "the Chinese mind had lost its vigor." From China's point of view, Wang called the influx of contemporary Western culture "the second Buddhism." [16]

At the beginning of the National Studies movement, Liang Ch'i-ch'ao's seminal writings on Chinese historiography prominently advocated the study of "the origins of the Chinese people." His outline of future historical research included such topics as the ethnic mixture from which the Han nation was precipitated. Cognate issues, Liang felt, were the roles played by the "outer barbarians" and by discrete cultures outside of China in the formation of Chinese civilization.[17] His program had to wait over a decade for significant responses, but in the interim his own studies of Buddhism[18] and Wang Kuo-wei's studies of Mongol history[19] provided important examples for its implementation.

BARBARIAN CONTRIBUTIONS TO CHINA'S FUTURE

In the *Autobiography*'s more somber pages, Ku Chieh-kang, openly fearing the imminent extinction of China, clutched at the straws of race and eugenics. "Instead of saying that such elements of our population as the Mohammedans and the Tibetans have reached a stage of decline," he wrote,

It is truer to say that they are still primitive peoples scarcely removed from the nomadic, hunting, and fishing epochs. And even within the confines of southwestern China there are aboriginal tribes such as

16. Chester Wang, "Wang Kuo-wei, His Life and His Scholarship," doctoral thesis (University of Chicago, 1967), p. 56.

17. Liang Ch'i-ch'ao, *CKLSYCF,* part 1 (dated 1923), p. 5.

18. *Fo-hsüeh yen-chiu shih-pa p'ien* [Eighteen Studies of Buddhism] (Taipei, 2nd printing 1966).

19. See Chester Wang, "Wang Kuo-wei," pp. 160–177, for bibliography and discussion; also see Ku Chieh-kang, *Tang-tai Chung-kuo shih-hsüeh* (Hong Kong, 1964), p. 115.

the Miao, Yao, T'ung, and P'o, which, despite the policy of the Ming and Ch'ing emperors to "bring them within the range of Chinese culture," have not yet been truly assimilated. Instead of saying that these races have declined, one should say that they have not yet reached their maturity. And while it is true that the culture of the purely Chinese, or Han, clans is certainly old, it must be remembered that under centuries of autocratic domination "the rules of ceremony did not apply to the common people," so that education was never widespread, and higher culture had only a limited influence on the masses. When one views Chinese culture in terms of the educated classes, one cannot avoid the conclusion that it is old and decrepit, but looked at from the standpoint of the population as a whole, it is still immature. The condition which one finds in China today points to a country that is weak and diseased rather than one that is old and decayed. True education will take cognizance of this state of affairs and stimulate the people to rejuvenate themselves and inject a new potency into our national life.[20]

Ku's speculations were very much in keeping with a crude Social Darwinism that had punctuated many areas of Chinese thought since the turn of the century. Liang Ch'i-ch'ao had been concerned about the debilitation of the Chinese race and the subsequent jeopardy of the nation. He had recommended "racial strengthening" (through improved medical and hygienic practices) for survival.[21] Even closer to Ku's formulations were those made by Li Ta-chao just before the May Fourth Movement. According to Maurice Meisner, "Li believed that backwardness was a positive advantage—that the very backwardness of nations like China and Russia held the seeds of youth and progress—whereas the material maturity of the West was a prelude to decline and decay." [22]

Beyond these isolated speculations during the 1920s, there

20. *ACH*, pp. 167–168.

21. Ralph C. Croizier, *Traditional Medicine in Modern China: Science, Nationalism, and the Tensions of Cultural Change* (Cambridge, Mass., 1968), pp. 60–61.

22. Maurice Meisner, *Li Ta-chao and the Origins of Chinese Marxism* (Cambridge, Mass., 1967), pp. 65–67.

emerged a body of literature devoted to establishing theories of eugenics and advocating their application to modern China.[23] By 1930, casual usage of eugenic arguments had become so common in Chinese scholarly circles that the historians leading the Social History debates chose such arguments as one of their first targets. Genetic theories which reduced historical processes to factors of inheritance ran counter to the burgeoning new concerns for the historical roles of physical environment and social structures. However, the thoroughness and accuracy of this criticism notwithstanding, vulgar eugenics maintained its appeal throughout the 1930s. In the last analysis, it quite often signified a temporary failure of nerve and a loss of faith in China's ability to control its destiny and work its way out of its dilemmas through direct human action. The Social Historians who criticized Chinese eugenic thought argued (rather cogently) that a theory of society based on eugenics ("nature" as opposed to "nurture") was ultimately a conservative and defeatist theory, for it was a deterministic scheme which robbed man's social creations and his will to social action of any primary significance.[24]

In twentieth-century China an important clue to major social changes has been the change in attitudes displayed toward the idea of *race* or toward those peoples who traditionally were known as the barbarians (*inner, outer, Northern, Southern,* etc.). The range of new attitudes can be marked, for our purposes, by the thought of Ku's erstwhile hero, Chang T'ai-yen, and, at the other pole, by Ku's own thought. Considerations of race were important to both scholars' thought at critical times of their lives. But where Chang's racism was exclusive, Ku's was inclusive. Chang's nationalism, like that of Sun Yat-sen, grew from a rejection of the Manchus as an alien race. By extension, no other ethnic group or *race* should have had or should

23. For a detailed description of the literature, see Ju Sung's "P'ing yu-sheng hsüeh yü huan-ching-lün te lün-ch'eng" [A Critique of the Debates Between the Theory of Eugenics and the Theory of Environment], *Erh-shih shih-chi* [The Twentieth Century], I:1 (Feb. 1931), 57–124.

24. *Ibid.* The key practitioners of eugenic analysis here were Chou Chien-jen, Sun Pen-wen, and P'an Hsien-tan.

have more than a subordinate place in the Chinese (*Han*) nation. Indeed, it is questionable whether or not, according to the logic of Chang's and Sun's predominant early polemics, the new Chinese nation had *any* place for non-*Han* Chinese (though Chang thought that, despite racial differences, assimilation was possible if the Chinese held political power).[25] For Chang, the immediate historical and cultural reaction was to renew interest in and respect for the Ming dynasty, which had been ruled by *Han* Chinese.[26]

On the other hand, Ku Chieh-kang's adult years were lived decades past the time when the Manchus were a threat. It was easy for Ku to abstract them not as alien conquerors but as a racial group *per se* (and at that, just the lesser of many others in contemporary China). But in Ku's historiography, the monarchy itself was now abstracted as well, so that (Chinese) Ming and (Manchu) Ch'ing were merely variations on the same evil themes—intellectual corruption and social repression. Hence, for Ku Chieh-kang, the Ming, Chinese or not, did its considerable bit for the corruption of scholarship and high culture (witness the literary straitjacket of the "Eight-Legged Essay"). His few remarks on the Ming dynasty were limited to observing the literary persecutions which it sponsored[27] and to haranguing the upper-class way of life responsible for the oppression of the common people during its tenure. The tyranny of the *Li-chiao* (the orthodox social codes and institutions) became too great for the common folk, he said, and he applauded their rebellions in the late sixteenth and early seventeenth centuries against the decadent, oppressive institutions that robbed them of their freedom. Out of their reputed suffering and bravery came the folksongs and poetry that were so treasured in Ku's circles.[28]

And so, where Chang T'ai-yen condemned the Ch'ing and

25. Gasster, *Chinese Intellectuals* (n. 1, above), p. 203.

26. See Chang T'ai-yen, *T'ai-yen hsien-sheng tzu-ting nien-p'u* [Autobiography of Chang *T'ai-yen*] (Hong Kong, 1965), pp. 8–9.

27. Ku Chieh-kang, "A Study of Literary Persecutions During the Ming," trans. by L. C. Goodrich, *Harvard Journal of Asiatic Studies*, no. 3–4 (Dec. 1938), pp. 254–311.

28. Ku's preface to Cheng Chen-to, ed., *Feng Meng-lung, Shan-ke* [Hill Songs by Feng Meng-lung] (Shanghai, 1935), pp. 5a–6b.

celebrated the Chinese purity of the Ming, Ku mourned the corruption of the scholar's intellect, condemned all monarchy, and celebrated the purity of the *people's culture.* Yet both Chang and Ku made major and complementary contributions to the transformation of many traditional notions about the role of the barbarians in Chinese culture. Chang's target was the monarchy specifically. Like Ming Loyalists and Taiping ideologues before him, he did his share in making ethnicity, not cultural practices and political functions, the prime source of monarchical, indeed all political, legitimacy. Only Chinese should rule Chinese. It no longer mattered that the Manchus had carefully sought out and then cultivated factors that traditionally comprised Chinese identity. Chang T'ai-yen, however, was apparently caught in a dilemma when he saw that, in the process of shifting from *culturalism* to ethnic or national identity, prized literary and scholarly traditions (once protected by the despised Manchus) crumbled. For all his initial zeal, Chang could not enter into what J. R. Levenson describes as the *new cosmopolitanism.*[29] Though Chang had been responsible, through his early nationalism, for taking the first steps toward the great and comprehensive leveling that has since followed throughout Chinese thought and institutions, Chang would not himself consciously foster the leveling. He did not appreciate the post-May Fourth extensions of his own nationalistic logic.

When class analysis was added to early nationalist arguments, a peculiar twist subtly turned the original argumentation in on itself. The post-May Fourth iconoclasts began to characterize Chinese history as a battleground between oppressor and oppressed, aristocracy and people. Yes, the Manchus *as monarchs* were bad; they were conquerors; they had had to be removed. But their being Manchus was only a melodramatic side issue on the list of evils that could have been applied to any monarchy. It was not the Chinese, as such, who had been under the

29. See J. R. Levenson, "The Province, the Nation and the World: The Problem of Chinese Identity," in Albert Feuerwerker *et al.*, eds., *Approaches to Modern Chinese History* (Berkeley and Los Angeles, 1967), pp. 268–288.

thumbs of monarchs and their aristocratic accomplices, but it had been the *people,* the *oppressed.* And in the eyes of historians like Ku Chieh-kang, non-*Han* peoples suffered as much or more than did the *Han* people. The concept of class oppression forged a new bond that identified the new Chinese nation not with the *Han* Chinese, per se, but with the great and long-suffering, heterogeneous masses—a group that cut across the *Han* people, the Moslems, the Tibetans, the Miaos, the Mongols, the Yaos, and yes, even the Manchus.

The *old cosmopolitanism* of China had resulted from a bond among ruling-class bureaucrats, local gentry, and monarchy. The great *Tao T'ung* was the cultural substance and source of continuity of the old cosmopolitanism, and it expressed itself in the history books, in philosophy, poetry, and painting. It flourished in the great capital cities, and it transcended local language and culture; indeed, it claimed to transcend time itself. The narrowly focused ephemera of folk culture, the diversity of language and style of life among the peasantry—these had been the substance of the *old provincialism.* Now, seen from the 1920s and 1930s, the culture of the old gentry and literati and their contemporary vestiges represented the narrow view of a minority class. What now was truly comprehensive, what really was universal, it was claimed, was the enduring, ever-renewing people's culture. From Ku Chieh-kang's vantage point in the 1930s, those who were once generically categorized as barbarians or as non-*Han* Chinese were all an intimate part of the new, cosmopolitan people's culture—perhaps its most vital and seminal element.

At the same time that this new cosmopolitanism was taking shape in the thought of Ku Chieh-kang, it was being pushed to further extremes by Chinese Marxists, whose tendency it was to see the Chinese historical experience as merely a local variation of a universal historical pattern. For these Marxist thinkers, China's popular culture (*proletarian* culture) was cosmopolitan because it represented the situation of an international social class: a commonly oppressed group that was common heir to the next stage of history.

The issues of race, ethnicity, and Chinese national identity gained in immediacy for Ku Chieh-kang as China approached the war with Japan. In 1926 Ku expressed a strong interest in the historical aspects of what he called "racial survival," and he indicated a great need for scholarship to attack the issue immediately. Ku said that, lacking an aptitude for politics, he felt he could realize his patriotic desires best by helping to solve this problem. "In all other problems," he said, "I do not care to have anything to do with practical aims," but in this special instance he would engage himself. After investigating textual materials and the "living conditions of the people," he planned to submit his findings to politicians, educationalists, and social reformers.[30] Lack of funds, and then personal obligations, prevented him from implementing his program of investigation before the mid-1930s. By that time China's international political situation had deteriorated even further, and Ku's program became for him a dramatic quest and crusade that led him to abandon his nonpolitical ethos.

The Tribute of Yü: Nationalism and Historical Geography

The 'Eastern neighbor' harbors ideas of encroachment and wants to call our eighteen provinces their headquarters. It darkly suggests that our frontier lands are not ours; and we bunch of oafs naturally are intoxicated by this, and our geography books call the same tune. Is this not to our disgrace?—from the editorial introduction to the first issue of *Tribute of Yü*, March, 1934

One of Ku Chieh-kang's most highly individual contributions to the historical scholarship of this period was a journal of Chinese historical geography which he entitled the *Tribute of Yü* (*Yü Kung*) after that chapter in the *Book of Documents* which dealt with the geography of high antiquity.[31] This journal was a response to the intellectual milieu precipitated by the Social History controversy and to the Japanese invasion of

30. *ACH*, p. 169.

31. The *Yü Kung* began on March 1, 1934. The final issue is numbered VII:10 (July 17, 1937). It was a fortnightly. There was a total of 82 issues, including ten special numbers. Ku Chieh-kang and T'an Ch'i-hsiang were co-editors from the first issue to the fall of 1934. Thereafter, Ku was co-editor with Feng Chia-sheng.

North China. In his frequent editorial comments in the journal from 1934 to 1937, Ku wrote that the journal's *raison d'étre* was the Japanese absorption of Chinese territory and the subsequent need to stimulate Chinese national self-awareness. Perhaps, he thought, in this way he and the journal could "assist with the work of national revival." [32]

The sources of the *Tribute of Yü,* however, are not to be found solely in the Japanese threat. As early as 1923, Ku's *Elementary National History* had dwelt at length on the importance of historical geography to a sound knowledge of Chinese history. The book devoted a considerable portion of its limited space to the subject.[33] Ku's personal interest in the subject was stimulated at National Sun Yat-sen University, where he began to study the *Book of Documents* in depth for the first time in 1927, and later at Yenching, where he became deeply involved in the question of the geopolitical structure of antiquity. Yet another significant stimulus for the establishment of the jounral was the current trend in scholarship, growing out of the Social History debates, toward an active interest in the material aspects of China's history, including demography and physical geography. It was no accident that the journals *Economics* (*Shih-huo*) and *Geographical Studies* (*Ti-li hsüeh-pao*) were also launched in 1934. Thus, the Japanese crisis was used by Ku Chieh-kang to lend a sense of urgency and emotional appeal to an academic subject that was already quite in the making by the time of the Mukden Incident in 1931. We might add that Ku seems purposefully to have infused the journal with some of the nationalistic sentiment of the day in order to give more dramatic significance and audience appeal to its sometimes extremely dry and esoteric subject matter.[34]

32. His impassioned rhetoric on the subject may be seen from issue I:1 (March 1, 1934), pp. 2–5 and thereafter; Association News section in IV:6 (Nov. 1935), 1; V:5 (May 31, 1936), 56; VII:1–2–3 (March 1937), 3.

33. See esp. the apologia in the Introduction and, in the text, see the attempt to identify ancient place names and geopolitical divisions with their modern equivalents.

34. The early issues of the journal were widely criticized as being too narrow and esoteric. See Ku's Afterword to the first volume of *YK,* and "Letters to the Editor" section in IV:6 (Nov. 1935). Issues from 1936 and 1937 are noticeably more diversified.

There is a noticeable change in tone and content of the *Tribute of Yü* between Volume One and Volume Four (in 1935). The earlier issues were dominated by Ku Chieh-kang and his immediate associates, and they were concerned with meticulous textual studies aimed at deciphering the meaning of ancient geopolitical terms and geographical place names. From Volume Four on, the journal was more heterogeneous both in subject matter and contributors. In addition, Ku's initial scholastic orientation to antiquity became balanced with ethnographic and demographic studies, often based on recently-gathered data. China's inner-Asian frontiers and the Moslem peoples who were to be found within them became the overwhelming concern of the journal. Owen Lattimore's writings were translated in the journal's pages, and many articles by Chinese authors displayed a growing awareness of the importance to Chinese history of the ecology of the frontier.[35]

RACE AND NATION

As the *Tribute of Yü* shifted to these concerns, it became an important forum for the systematic reevaluation of the ideas of *race* and *nation* and of the related problem, the role of the barbarians in China's past and future. In the journal the transformation of China's ethnic minorities—from inner or outer barbarians to *Chinese*—was carried a very long way. (The issue was developed later, in Chinese Communist intellectual circles, under the rubric of *national minorities*.)[36] The journal focused largely on the Moslem peoples of north central and northwest China, but the attitudes expressed toward them were exemplary of the journal's policies toward all of China's non-*Han* elements. The Moslems were of special interest because they were China's largest ethnic minority, and because in the

35. It is useful to compare the contents of the *YK* with those of *Ti-li hsüeh pao* in order to appreciate the special role the *YK* filled. *Ti-li hsüeh-pao* was founded in Nanking by the Chinese Geographical Society in Feb. 1934, and devoted itself largely to cartography, geology (soils, petroleum), population studies, meteorology, transportation, and general macro-economic data.

36. See George Mosely, *The Party and the National Quesiton* (Cambridge, Mass., 1966).

period 1934 to 1937 their homes along the northern frontiers lay in the general area of China's current territorial crises. In addition, the Chinese Moslems were in particular prominence due to the stimulating effects of the Islamic Revival pulsating outward from the Near Eastern cultural centers. Even before the full impact of Islamic Nationalism was felt in China, the Chinese Moslems had been the object of considerable attention both from the Manchus and from more recent Warlord regimes. Moslem rebellions in the nineteenth and twentieth centuries were answered with sustained and often brutal military reactions. Finally, Chinese Moslems, like the Tibetans, occupied strategic border areas that for long periods of time had been schemed after by Imperial Russia, England, and then Soviet Russia.

Contributors to the *Tribute of Yü* found it of prime necessity to cut through the tangled intellectual legacies of San Yat-sen, Chang T'ai-yen, and others who in recent decades had made prominent statements about *race* and *nation*. The pre-1911 legacy of Sun and Chang was often narrow, exclusive racism that gave little practical consideration to the place of groups like the Chinese Moslems in the new Chinese nation-state.[37] Later, in statements like his 1924 *Three Principles of the People* (*San min chu-i*), Sun offered a definition of nation which he felt was applicable to peoples such as the Chinese Moslems. He noted that just as Islamic nations around the world (in Arabia, Persia,

37. Ch'i Ssu-ho, "Min-tsu yü chung-tsu" [Race and Nation], *YK*, VII: 1–2–3 (1937), 25–27.

See Gasster, *Chinese Intellectuals* (n. 1, above), for discussion of pre-Republican debates over the issue of assimilation of minority peoples (p. 82). Chang T'ai-yen "explicitly recognized that Moslems in China might have the same hatred for the Chinese that the Chinese had for the Manchus" (*ibid.*, p. 203). Further, Gasster reports, "Chang was certainly not in favor of permitting minorities to split away from China and establish independent nations, partly because he believed that they were not ready for independence and partly because he hoped for the reestablishment of China's borders as they were under the Former-Han dynasty. Nevertheless, he was willing to regard China's relationship with Sinkiang as an 'alliance' in which the two would act as 'complementary wings to cut off Russia's right arm.' He hoped the Moslems would see that it was in their own interest to assimilate with the Chinese, but he clearly recognized that they might not" (*ibid.*).

North India, Afganistan, etc.) had great anti-imperialist potential, just so did the Chinese Moslems constitute an essential element in the Chinese nation's fight against imperialism. China's anti-imperialist success would depend on the unified aid of her minority peoples, the largest segment of which was the Moslems.[38] Precisely how these minority nations fit into *the* Chinese nation, and precisely what their relation was to have been with the *Han* nation, Sun did not elaborate. And so, even in the *Tribute of Yü* more than a decade after the publication of the *Three Principles of the People,* the confusion continued. Defenders of Islam in China proudly demonstrated how well the Chinese Moslems (the *Hui* people) met Sun's criteria for nationhood (common blood, economy, language, religion, and style of life).[39] But in designating the *Hui* people as a nation, it seemed that the overall unity of the Chinese polity was suffering yet another setback—this time with the sanction of ex cathedras from the nation's father himself.[40]

In a major policy statement in the *Tribute of Yü* Ch'i Ssu-ho set about to survey these problems derived from earlier attempts to conceptualize nationalism, and he hoped to correct the misguided Chinese tendencies set in motion by Sun Yat-sen's pronouncements.[41] Ch'i Ssu-ho recognized that Sun had made a major shift in his nationalistic thought: from exclusive racism to ideas aimed at giving national status to the various peoples on the inner-Asian frontiers. Sun's purpose apparently had been to grant these peoples a concrete political identity and a significant role in stabilizing the growth of the new Chinese state. Nevertheless, in the 1930s it seems that the Nationalist government was following a policy of absorption of border peoples

38. See Ma Sung-t'ing, "Chung-kuo Hui-chiao yü Ch'eng-ta Shih-fan Hsüeh-hsiao" [Chinese Islam and Ch'engta Normal University], *YK,* V:11, p. 14.

39. *San Min Chu-i* [Three Principles of the People], lecture one. The source of Sun's definition of a nation was probably Wang Ching-wei, who made this same formulation before 1911. (See Gasster, *Chinese Intellectuals,* p. 79.)

40. See Chin Chi-t'ang, "Hui-chiao min-tsu shuo" [Islamic Nationalism], *YK,* V:11, pp. 31 ff.

41. Ch'i, "Min-tsu yü chung-tsu."

more than one of federal cooperation between the *Han* nation and minority nations.[42] Yet Sun's ideas on nationalism were still prominent, and they constituted a thorn in the side of scholars who were interested in clearing the air on this crucial subject.

Ch'i Ssu-ho designated the clarification of the concepts of 'race' and 'nation' a primary purpose of the journal. His own considerable contribution was, first, to demolish Sun Yat-sen's popular definition of nation. It was not difficult for him to upset Sun's sketchy, contradictory set of factors: for example, *common religion* (what about the American nation with a multiplicity of religions—or China, without any single universally shared religion?); *common blood* (again, what of America, or the complexity of the English national background?); and so on.[43] Drawing widely on contemporary Western discussions of nationalism, Ch'i Ssu-ho instructed his readers that it would be most profitable to consider the structure of modern nationalism from what he called a subjective and spiritual point of view: Nationalism was structured basically by ideas and feelings, not necessarily by objective and concrete factors like Sun's notions of common blood or common ways of life. Nationalism was the feeling or the idea of unity or common bond possessed by a group of people who had shared a common historical experience and who had shared pressures (oppression perhaps) from the outside.[44]

At the same time that it was necessary to grasp the true nature of nationalism, Ch'i Ssu-ho wrote, it was also necessary to disabuse the Chinese intellectual world of the myths of race which had for so long been prevalent and which had been confused with the concept of nation by such prominent figures as Sun Yat-sen. Ch'i explained that 'race' was a concept declining

42. Snow, *Red Star Over China*, pp. 342–344; Lattimore, *Inner Asian Frontiers*, p. 193.

43. Ch'i, "Min-tsu yü chung-tsu," pp. 28–30.

44. *Ibid.*, p. 30. Ch'i was drawing on Arthur M. Holcomb, *The Foundation of the Modern Commonwealth*; H. Laski, *Grammar of Politics*; C. Hayes, *Essays on Nationalism*; Muir, *Nationalism and Internationalism*; Gooch, *Nationalism*; and C. Hayes, *The Evolution of Modern Nationalism*.

in use in Western scholarship. Not only were scholars growing weary of the scientifically unproved and potentially dangerous theories of race, but some were now actively engaged in demonstrating that human characteristics once thought to be racial (that is, inherited) changed or disappeared with changed environment.[45] He also brought color theories of race under his able criticism.

The concern and confusion over the ideas of race and nation were reflected in essays in the *Tribute of Yü* which were devoted to the Moslem problem.[46] Realizing full well now the potential political implications of their writings, contributors to the journal revealed the glories of the Chinese Moslems' past and their unique and vital place in contemporary China. Writers told of the importance of Islam to the study of world history and reviewed the link with the west that Islam had provided for China from the T'ang dynasty in the tenth century down into the Ming dynasty, five centuries later. It was a major contention that Islamic people and culture had been an intimate part of Chinese civilization until the Manchus came to power in the seventeenth century. On their accession, the latter had beaten down and suppressed an antagonistic Islamic populace; and, the Manchus' preoccupation thereafter with the cultivation of *Han* culture resulted in a continuing weak position and low status for such minorities as the Moslems. The journal's implication was that due to Manchu prejudice, the Moslem peoples were excluded from Chinese culture and their former place in it was forgotten. One aspect of the contemporary movement to revive Chinese Islam was thus an effort to restore Islam to its historic place *within* Chinese society.

At this point there was again raised the problem of the nature

45. Here, Ch'i drew on the work of Franz Boas, *Changes in Bodily Form of Descendants of Immigrants* (New York, 1912), and A. Ivanovsky, "Physical Modification of the Population of Russia Under Famine," *American Journal of Physical Anthropology,* VI:4 (1923).

46. The following summary is drawn largely from these pieces in *YK*: (1) Ma Sung-t'ing, "Chung-kuo Hui-chiao yü Ch'eng-ta"; (2) Chin Chi-t'ang, "Hui-chiao min-tsu shuo"; (3) a series of short pieces in *YK,* VII:4 (1936), 183–193; (4) Nei Chung, *"Hui-chiao yü A-la-pa wen-ming hsü-mu,"* [Preface to Islam and Arabic Civilization], *YK,* VIII:10, pp. 47–52.

of the Moslem people's role in the modern Chinese nation-state. Sun Yat-sen's approach was attractive, for it encouraged the integrity and independence of Moslem society. Contributors to the journal repeatedly implied, however, that it would be the *Han* people who would profit most from the incorporation of an active Moslem community into the new body politic of China. In those areas where Moslem and *Han* lived in close proximity, it was observed, the Moslems possessed "greater vitality and spirit." The vigorously enforced ethics of their communities and their tight social organization buoyed up their morale and made it possible for them, for example, to eliminate opium from their communities. Meanwhile, it was said, opium was debilitating the spirit of their Chinese neighbors. The Moslems were considered to be physically more fit and able than the Chinese living under similar conditions.[47]

Ultimately, in the 1930s, the Moslem problem resolved itself into these issues: Should the Moslems be classified as a *nation,* and hence receive some quantum of political autonomy? Or should they be considered merely as a religious group strictly within the political purview of the central government of the Chinese state? All contributors to the *Tribute of Yü* desired that the Moslem peoples, whatever their formal status, be permitted —indeed, be encouraged—to practice and perpetuate their own traditions. There was the implicit fear, however, that the Moslems as a *nation* would be best in, but not of, the new China. At the same time, there was also the fear that the Moslem people's thirst for cultural autonomy (perhaps attainable only through political autonomy) would weaken their resistance to the seductions of the Japanese, who now promised to lift the yoke of Chinese oppression.[48]

Ku Chieh-Kang as Propagandist

Another notable addition to the *Tribute of Yü* format came with Volume Four (September 1935 to February 1936), in which a new section was added—"News Of Our Nation's Geographical

47. See esp. Chin Chi-t'ang," Hui-chiao min-tsu shuo."
48. Nei Chung, "Hui-chiao yü A-la-pa wen-ming," p. 51.

World." In spite of Ku Chieh-Kang's blatantly chauvinistic editorials, this section was the closest the journal came to an active concern with the Japanese advances in the north; and this was a restrained and often indirect concern at that. For example, the section charted the moves of the Japanese (as reported by on-the-scene correspondents or by newspapers in the areas) and their absorption of northern railroads, public roads, and productive capacity of raw material. The mood of these reports was factual and non-inflammatory.

Ku Chieh-Kang's editorials in the journal were the most circumspect of his reactions to the Japanese invasion of North China. Shortly after the September Eighteenth Incident of 1931, when the Japanese seized Mukden, he began to devote considerable time to an anti-Japanese propaganda organization. By 1936 he was editor of an anti-Japanese journal whose success soon necessitated his flight from the Japanese southern advance.

Ku wrote that Yenching University made it possible for him in the early thirties to travel widely throughout Honan, Hopei, Shensi, and Shantung. However, it was not merely old monuments and ruins that he saw. He became aware at the same time of the "exhaustion of the peasantry and the enfeeblement of the People." "I cried to see what I saw," he wrote, "for not only was the nation perishing, but so were the minority peoples." [49] Returning to Peking, Ku discussed the border peoples with his friends in politics, seeking in vain some sort of immediate ameliorative efforts. Shortly, Manchuria fell, and Ku saw the situation as "so close to that of the Sung and Liao" eras when North China was conquered and occupied by nomadic peoples.

To vent his anger and despair at the spread of what he called the Japanese poison, he became the editor of the *Popular Readings* (*T'ung-su tu-wu*), a propaganda series aimed at the North China public and designed to stir up hostility to the Japanese.[50] The series, employing the techniques of the old story hawkers, published stories of the exploits of young heroes who fought against the barbarian founders of the Chin, Yüan, and Ch'ing dynasties. The tales were written in the vernacular and dis-

49. *HPKCJC,* pp. 1a–1b.
50. *Ibid.; SLTC,* p. 2.

tributed with the intention that they be read aloud to the illiterate public. Stories were also written in the form of "short ditties accompanied with suitable pictures." [51] These techniques Ku attributed to his earlier work in the Folksong Research Society and to his experience during the May Thirtieth Movement. (Ku had briefly joined his friends in the writing of anti-English and anti-Japanese propaganda billets at that time. His special contribution was the writing of some propaganda folksongs which were performed in the city crowds. In this fashion, he said, he had hoped to reach the illiterate masses with the intended political message.)[52] He reported wide success with his propaganda of the thirties. So successful was he that he was ordered by Ch'en Li-fu, speaking for the Nationalist government in Nanking, and later by the Japanese puppet government in North China, to close down the enterprise or be arrested.[53] Nevertheless, he managed to continue this activity with impunity until the Japanese were on their way to Peking in mid-1937.

The efforts of the Popular Readings Society were typical of the political reactions of many of the students and teachers in Peking. When the Kuomintang crushed student activities at Peking University in 1935, the Yenching student body became a storm center of hostility to the Japanese and a leader in calling for a hasty military confrontation.[54] The brief "rural crusade" of January 1936, in which Peking students attempted to politicize the countryside of northern Hopei, employed techniques much like those of Ku Chieh-kang's society.[55]

Near March of 1936, Ku lent his prestige to the students' activities and went on public record as a supporter of the Student National Salvation Movement which called for China to prepare

51. Ku, "Ts'ung wo tzu-chi k'an Hu Shih" [A Personal Look at Hu Shih], *Ta Kung Pao* (Dec. 24, 1951), p. 3.

52. *Ibid.*

53. *Ibid.* I have not been able to find any examples of the propaganda published by the T'ung-su tu-wu she before 1936. The 1936–37 journal, discussed below in the text, was a later product of the organization.

54. John Israel's *Student Nationalism in China, 1927–1937* (Stanford, 1966), gives a portrait of this; for example pp. 48–49, 113 ff.; also see Dwight Edwards, *Yenching University* (New York, 1959), p. 338.

55. Israel, *Student Nationalism,* pp. 134 ff.

for war and to end appeasement of the Japanese.[56] With the same goals in mind, he launched *The Peoples' Intelligence* (*Ta-chung chih-shih*), through the auspices of the Popular Readings Society, 1936.[57] This propaganda forum was tastefully, simply, and intelligently written, and even informative in its articles dealing with major political events in China, Europe, and the United States. It could be read comfortably by an audience of many levels of literacy, though it obviously was aimed at such politically important readers as businessmen and students. Its political orientation was clearly enunciated: in articles discussing contemporary Spain, Germany, and Italy, it was anti-Fascist.[58] Japanese politics were characterized as Fascist and described as an analogue to the European type. There was no hard sell. The case was built up with accurate information on the political parties and key events shaping European politics. Spain, in an article written before the outbreak of the civil war there, was seen as a preview to the future politics of Europe. Roosevelt's New Deal was given a favorable press.

In *The Peoples' Intelligence,* the Japanese were directly treated in long first-person narrative articles based on personal observation in the Northeast. Japanese military expansion was detailed, and special note was made of the Japanese mistreatment of Chinese and Korean nationals. A typical article ended with an exhortation to fight for Suiyuan; however, it chided that if one did not want to fight, he need not cooperate and make it easier for the Japanese to succeed.

Heroes abounded. Throughout the essays, no matter what their subject, there was a wide sampling of Chinese historical

56. *Ibid.,* p. 146.

57. Consulting American libraries, I was only able to find four issues of the journal—in the Hoover Institution. Issue I:2 is dated Nov. 5, 1936; I:6 is dated Jan. 5, 1937.

58. It seems that as late as the Sian Incident of Dec. 9, 1937, Chiang's public relations men had failed to make any clear dissociation between his regime and Fascism. Shortly after Chiang's release, "the official broadcasting station carried an address by a Central University student, who appealed to his colleagues to support the government and oppose all front organizations." "China's students," the speaker said, "must follow the example of the youth in Hitler's Germany, Mussolini's Italy, and Stalin's Russia." (Israel, *Student Nationalism,* p. 173.)

figures. Ordinarily, one would not group the Sung political reformers Fang Chung-yen and Wang An-shih with Mo Tzu, Hsuan Ts'ang (a T'ang dynasty Buddhist pilgrim), and "a young Mongol maiden heroine." The common denominator of the group was little more than a heroic stance at a time of crisis—Fang and Wang advocated fending off, not appeasing, the Khitan and the Hsi Hsia barbarians of the Northern steppes; Mo Tzu balanced his philosophy of universal love with realpolitik in an age of political chaos and usurpation. The Mongol Jeanne d'Arc evoked the need for *all* Chinese to give themselves to *the cause;* the Buddhist, perhaps, was an abstraction of Chinese fortitude and daring.

Ku Chieh-kang's special contribution to the journal was a series of effusive essays which display a great finesse with the rhetorical techniques of the demagogue.[59] A pair of these essays, for example, dealt with traitors (*han-chien*) at the time of the Khitan threat to China's Northeast, during the Five Dynasties period. Factually, the narratives are sound enough; but they were embroidered with imagined dialogue which was used to dramatize important political and military decisions. (They are in good Peking vernacular.) The success of the Khitan was attributed to a handful of Chinese collaborators who made it possible for these crude barbarians to take over Northeast China. The essay concluded meaningfully with a statement that the Khitan ultimately were unable to cope with the problems of governing North China.[60]

In a special series of seven essays in *The Peoples' Intelligence,* Ku Chieh-kang exhorted his readers to develop the inner virtues

59. These essays were reprinted in book form in 1937 by the T'ung-su tu-wu she, with a preface by Ku's old friend Wang Po-hsiang: *Ku Chieh-kang t'ung-su lün-chi* [An Anthology of Popular Essays by Ku Chieh-kang] (Shanghai, 3rd printing, 1947).

60. See Ku's "Shih Ching-t'an ho Chao Te-chun, Wu-tai shih te liang-ke han-chien" [Shih Ching-t'an and Chao Te-chun, Two Traitors of the Five Dynasties Period], *Ta-chung chih-shih* [People's Intelligence], I:5 (Dec. 20, 1936), 55–59; and "Chao Yen-shou ho Tu Chung-wei, yu shih liang-ke Wu-tai shih te han-chien chieh-kuo to kei Ch'i-t'an-jen lung-le i-ch'ang" [Chao Yen-shou and Tu Chung-wei, Two More Traitors of the Five Dynasties Period Who Were Both Taken by the Khitan], *ibid.,* I:6 (Jan. 5, 1937), 50–54.

and outer attitudes which were needed to promote national unity and to sustain an optimistic belief in China's ability to expel the invaders. In the essay "Two Kinds of Thinking Which Are Most Desirable to Eliminate," the subjects were *decadent pleasures* and *fear,* and Yüeh Fei, Han Wu Ti, Kuo Tzu-i, and Kou Chun were used as exemplars.[61] In the essay "Trust," Ku explained the need to follow *one suitable leader,* and the dangerous national consequences for the failure to do so. Turkey's experience with Kemal Pasha was cited as an illustration, as was the unrealized Five-Year Plan in Russia (attributed to the "Soviet people—who did not trust their leaders").[62] The essays entitled "Sacrifice," "Create," "Determination," and "Render Mutual Assistance" elaborated the message of their titles by way of other exemplary figures (Aristotle, Dante, Newton, Moses, Tseng Kuo-fan, Kropotkin) and negative examples (T'ao Yüan-ming and Robinson Crusoe).[63]

According to some Western studies of Chinese youth of the 1930s, young nationalists were attracted to an interminable array of Chinese and Western heroes who shared little if anything in common but their success in uniting their nation or defending it against foreign invasions.[64] Ku Chieh-kang's essays were thus employing common currency and appealing to a

61. Probably in *ibid.,* I:1 (Oct. 1936); reprinted in *Ku Chieh-kang t'ung-su lün-chi,* pp. 1–7.

Yüeh Fei was a Southern Sung leader of the movement to regain North China from the nomad Chin invaders; Emperor Wu Ti of Han expanded China's borders and settled the Hsiung Nu problem; Kuo Tzu-i, in the eighth century, defended the T'ang dynasty against An Lu-shan—who is often depicted in the traditional histories as a villain of barbarian origins; and Kou Chun was a hero of the Northern Sung who defended the dynasty against the Khitan in the eleventh century.

John Israel notes that Chiang Kai-shek compared himself to Yüeh Fei before an audience of anxious students that petitioned him in Nov. 1931, to meet the Japanese seizure of Manchuria with force (*Student Nationalism,* p. 61).

62. Original in *Ta-chung chih-shih,* I:2 (Nov. 5, 1936).

63. T'ao Yüan-ming is condemned here for his egoism and escapism, and Crusoe for his anti-social inclinations.

64. Israel, *Student Nationalism,* pp. 98, 173 for examples; also see Olga Lang, *Chinese Family and Society* (New Haven, 1946), whose findings on this subject are summarized by Israel on p. 180.

broad, emotionally volatile public. This no doubt contributed greatly to the success he reported for his propaganda journal, and to his very high place on the Kwantung Army's "Most Wanted" list in July of 1937.

A Journey to the West

Within two weeks of the Marco Polo Bridge Incident (July 7, 1937), rumors had begun circulating in Peking that Ku Chieh-kang would be in grave danger from the Japanese once they entered the city. A close friend confirmed this on July 21, and that night Ku fled with three pieces of luggage "and no books." The diary which he kept during the following months, *The Northwest Studies Diary* (*Hsi-pei k'ao-ch'a jih-chi*) provides an account as intimate as the *Autobiography*.[65]

On July 15, Ku Chieh-kang had signed his name with twenty others from the Peking area to a telegram which urged General Sung Che-yüan to resist the Japanese movement into the Tien-tsin area.[66] Sung had been one of the first generals, along with Fu Tso-yi, to clash with the Japanese in North China.[67] This provides an explanation of the fact that on his flight from Peking, Ku's earliest stopover was in Kueisui, the capital of Suiyuan, where his first social call was paid to Fu Tso-yi.[68] During his week in Kueisui, Ku requested from the General and the Provincial Government the permission to carry on the propa-

65. The *HPKCJC,* proper, covers the period of Sept. 1937 to Dec. 1938. Its preface is a brief sketch of Ku's life, and it provides details for the events leading up to his flight in July and for his sojourn in the Northwest in September. Though Ku describes himself as a prolific journal-keeper, this diary is the only one of his to have been published.

66. *HPKCJC,* p. 1b.

67. See F. F. Liu, *A Military History of Modern China, 1924–1949* (Princeton, 1956), p. 114.

68. Fu Tso-yi as well as Sung Che-yuan was popular with the university community of Peking. (See Israel, *Student Nationalism,* pp. 165–167.) General Fu, who repulsed the Japanese invasion of Suiyuan in the fall of 1936, was a member of the 'non-central' military group which was not a direct follower of Chiang Kai-shek at this time. (Liu, *Military History,* pp. 114, 128.)

ganda activities of the Popular Reading Society. Their assent was no doubt encouraged by the nature of his first project—a popular song whose lyrics would commemorate the battle of Pailingmiao, at which Fu Tso-yi had recaptured a strategic holding from the Japanese on November 24, 1936.[69] After another dinner with General Fu, on the night of the 26th, Ku left Kueisui, heading south to Chengchow by way of Taiyuan. Then, after a week and a half of lurching travel across central China, he arrived in Soochow.

The air of the Shanghai area was filled with panic and pessimism. As they speculated on the southern progress of the Japanese, Ku's friends predicted that Soochow would fall as Tientsin had fallen. In his diary, Ku described the trains and stations in Shanghai as crammed with crushing, frightened crowds. And by the 16th his diary recorded the sounds of the Japanese advancing on Shanghai. He soon ordered his terrified relatives to dig storage pits to protect their belongings.[70]

On September 21, Ku received a formal invitation from the Board of Directors of the Boxer Indemnity Education Fund to visit Kansu, Chinghai, and Ninghsia provinces for the purpose of investigating and reforming Moslem education. Since he began publishing the *Tribute of Yü,* Ku had become deeply interested in the Chinese Moslems, and in the two years preceding this invitation he had made a conspicuous effort to increase his own knowledge of their situation and to promote a nationwide awareness of 'the Moslem problem.' In addition to the medium of the journal, Ku stirred up interest in the subject by way of the Borderland Research Society, which in 1936 held weekly colloquia that were often attended by guests visiting Peking from the border areas.[71]

Ku's personal contact with Moslem students and educators increased rapidly during 1936. He even came to know representatives of Egypt's al Azhar University, the great academic center of the contemporary movement to revive Islamic cul-

69. *HPKCJC,* p. 2a; Liu, *Military History,* p. 114.
70. *HPKCJC,* p. 2b.
71. Preface to *ibid.,* p. 1b.

ture.[72] He was then given more opportunities to observe the efforts being made in Peking to educate young Moslems, particularly at the newly-established Ch'eng-ta Normal College in Peking. The hope was that students educated in such institutions would return to the Northwest to assist their people.[73] Articles which Ku Chieh-kang published on the subject cast the problem in a nationalistic light: Writing less than a decade after the horrific Moslem rebellion in Feng Yü-hsiang's bailiwick,[74] Ku said that the primary issue regarding the Moslems was one of national unity; the Chinese nation could not afford any internal cleavages. In tracing the recent history of the Moslems in China, he charged the Ch'ing dynasty with gross mistreatment of this minority group; and he laid the blame for contemporary Chinese-Moslem antagonism on Chinese ignorance and bigotry.

The first step toward helping the Moslems was therefore the education of Chinese about Islamic history and culture. (Obviously, this came to be one of the major purposes of the *Tribute of Yü*.) He publicly proposed that major Chinese universities teach courses on Moslem culture, and that chapters in history books be devoted to the subject. Government aid would be necessary, he said, to accelerate the "Moslem renaissance" in Moslem schools, and to provide a Chinese education to Moslem youth. Ku argued that once Chinese understood Moslem culture, and once the Moslems understood their own culture better, Chinese and Moslems would recognize that they belonged to one nation, and that their only (and merely superficial) difference was that of religion. He further warned that helping

72. *Ibid.*, p. 2a.

73. *Ibid.* For a general survey of the Moslems in China, see Fu T'ung-hsien, *Chung-kuo Hui-chiao shih* [A History of Chinese Islam] (Shanghai, 1940, and Taipei, 1969), esp. pp. 210 ff., for discussion of educational developments in the 1930s.

74. See James E. Sheridan, *Chinese Warlord: The Career of Feng Yü-hsiang* (Stanford, 1966), pp. 249–252. See also Wang Hsü-huai, *Hsien, T'ung Yünnan Hui-min shih-pien* [The Mohammedan Uprising in Yünnan, 1856–1873] (Taipei: Academia Sinica, 1968). The latter publication has a comprehensive bibliography on Chinese–Moslem–Manchu relations in the nineteenth and twentieth centuries.

Chinese Moslems was a Chinese imperative: It would be a dangerous situation if "other nations" were permitted to carry out a properly Chinese role.[75]

THE NORTHWEST EDUCATIONAL MISSION

The invitation from the Boxer Educational Commission was accepted. An excursion to the Northwest seemed to offer safety from the Japanese advance and a firsthand opportunity to see if the Moslem peoples were all that they seemed to be. Ku's diary recorded that before departing he spent three more weeks in Soochow completing unfinished business and preparing cases of his father's books, maps, and antiquities for safe storage in a great pit in the earth.[76] (The diary records that Ku's father, then living in Soochow, was apparently quite old and infirm.)

On September 15, Ku Chieh-kang set out for Lanchow, the capital city of Kansu, by way of Wuhan and Hsian. Friends entertained and banqueted him all along the difficult two-week journey, which included his first airplane trip. In Lanchow, though ill from travel and apprehensive about his family's welfare (the Japanese were already intercepting the mail), Ku followed a heavy routine devoted to speaking with Moslem educators, lecturing, and visiting schools.[77]

Two weeks after his arrival in Lanchow, Ku was asked by the editor of a local newspaper to write a propaganda piece in the style of his Popular Readings essays. He accepted the request in order "to stir up the people," and he "extemporized a four-thousand-word essay." [78] It was just after this that Ku was sought out by a group of students, from the Peking area perhaps, who had been wandering from province to province in the North. They had established a propaganda organization modeled on Ku's Popular Readings Society, which they called The Common

75. Ku, "Hui Han wen-t'i ho mu-ch'ien ying-yu te kung-tso" [The Chinese-Moslem Question and the Work Before Us], *YK,* VII:4 (April 1937), 179–181; also see his article in the Tientsin-Shanghai *Ta Kung Pao* (March 7, 1937), reprinted in *YK,* VII:4.

76. *HPKCJC,* p. 3b. This is the only other source, outside of the *ACH,* in which Ku mentions his father.

77. *Ibid.*

78. *Ibid.,* p. 8b.

People (*Lao-pai-hsing*). The journal they published was comprised of a series of folksongs, freshly composed for anti-Japanese propaganda. The students asked Ku Chieh-kang to take charge of the organization. Just then, Ku wrote, "the new officials arrived [in Lanchow] and attempted to gain control over the thought of the people of the entire province." [79]

The "new officials," no doubt representatives of the Nanking government, were contemptuously criticized in his diary for their immediate efforts to reorganize and control the school system. Ku was quickly asked by these officials to act as intermediary between themselves and the teachers and students. When he refused, he wrote, "they began to have doubts [about me] and to make slanderous accusations against me." [80] Then they suppressed The Common People on the grounds that its journal had applauded the victory of the Communist Eighth Route Army over the Japanese in an article entitled "The Great Battle at P'ing-hsing Pass." [81] Ku then recorded the following encounter:

> Here, [the officials] said, was ironclad evidence that The Common People was supporting the 'other party.' When I heard this, I laughed and said: "In fighting this war, the Kuomintang and the Communists are working together. But according to your [thinking], since the Eighth Route Army is completely controlled by the Communist Party, [it appears that] its troops cannot be patriotic! And thus, the victory at P'ing-hsing Pass is not a victory for our nation! Now, if there is not sufficient cause for you to indict me as a member of the Communist Party—and hence to execute me—then how dare you still accuse me of the crime of being a traitor?" [82]

The officials then reported Ku to civil and military authorities higher up, and also demanded that the Boxer organization dismiss him. All responses from the authorities were tolerant; but Ku, nevertheless, discreetly absented himself from Lanchow to permit the loess to settle.

79. *Ibid.,* Preface, pp. 2a–2b.
80. *Ibid.*
81. The battle was fought in Eastern Shansi in September, 1937, under the leadership of Lin Piao. (Liu, *Military History* (n. 67, above), p. 201.)
82. *HPKCJC,* Preface, pp. 2a–2b.

In the following weeks, Ku Chieh-kang explored the area, of great archaeological interest, between Lanchow and Hsining, the capital of Ch'inghai. When he arrived in Hsining, he visited with Ma Lin, president of the provincial government, and with General Ma Pu-fang, both Moslems.[83] For the remainder of the year, he continued to visit the isolated Moslem communities and their schools scattered about the great ancient spaces between the two provincial capitals.

In the autumn, Ku had received a letter from his father and wife. It caused him to reflect in his diary that a year earlier he had received an invitation from Szechwan University which would have given him a long-hoped-for opportunity to travel in the West. However, his wife and father had contended with him about the trip, his father saying that since Ku was his only son, he should not go far away. Although he wanted to go, Ku "persistently restrained" himself, and finally refused the invitation. "Now," his diary continued, "I have become a vagabond" because of the advances of the enemy; and "if I do not keep moving, then I shall die; if I do not die, then I am disgraced [for leaving my family]." [84] Ku's family was forced to flee Peking when it was learned that the Japanese would hold them responsible for his propaganda activities. By the beginning of winter, he had learned of this and of the fall of Peking and Soochow. Return was now impossible. Before the year was out, Taiyuan was taken. Lanchow could now be bombed, and it endured air attack for almost three weeks in December, during which time the roof was blown off of Ku's residence, while he was on tour.[85] Shortly after, he received a strong invitation from National Yünnan University to become a visiting lecturer. The proximity of the Japanese made even Yünnan a welcome prospect, and he accepted for the following fall.[86]

Letters from Soochow then made it clear to Ku that his father

83. The latter was one of the "Four Mas" described by Edgar Snow in *Red Star Over China* (part 9, section 3). Snow wrote that Ma Pu-fang was Nanking-appointed Pacification Commissioner of Kansu, "while his brother, Ma Pu-ching, helps out in Chinghai."

84. *HPKCJC,* pp. 9a–9b.

85. *Ibid.,* p. 12b.

86. *Ibid.,* p. 13a.

was extremely ill and unwilling to accompany Ku's wife to such a distant place as Yünnan. Ku senior's last letter to his son explained that he had become concerned that Chieh-kang be in Soochow for his funeral; now he realized that this was impossible: "You are oppressed by conditions of the time. You cannot but be like such wayfarers as Fan Pang and Chang Chien."[87] Ku replied to his father with a poem:

How I admire the Hengyang goose,
  When spring comes, it flies North again.
Flowers return to their former beauty,
  But human affairs turn bad indeed.
I did not expect to be diverted to such far-flung places;
  My soul is called and seeks everywhere a way.
Life or death, who can tell,
  Do not ask me to return home.[88]

During the spring and summer of 1938, Ku Chieh-kang continued and completed his investigation of Moslem education. His missions took him to more primitive and isolated communities, and his side trips, for personal research, became longer. The notebooks which he kept bristled with the historical data he gathered while exploring along the T'ao, Huang, and Hsi Ch'ing rivers in southeast Kansu.[89] There he was able to trace remnants of the Great Wall from the Ch'in era, and to relate places mentioned in the "Tribute of Yü" chapter of the *Book of Documents* to his surroundings.[90] Undaunted by a toothache from an unaccustomed diet of lamb, Ku added remarks on Buddhism to his personal notebook, and Lamaist temples to his itinerary.

87. *Ibid.,* p. 15a. Fang Pang (Meng-po) (A.D. 137–169) subdued the Ch'iang tribes in the Northwest. Chang Chien (d. 651 A.D.) was the T'ang dynasty conqueror of the Northwest.

88. *Ibid.* This is one illegible ideograph in the text of the poem.

89. These notes comprise a good part of Ku's serial "Lan-k'o ts'un sui-pi" [Notes from Lankow Village], which appeared in the *Tse-shan pan-yüeh k'an* [Exhortations to Virtuous Deeds]—hereinafter referred to as *TS*—throughout the 1940s. They are almost all collected and expanded in Ku's book *Shih-lin tsa-chih* (Shanghai, 1963).

90. "Chu Nan" [Southern Chu], *TS,* I:2 (April 1, 1940), p. 15; *HPKCJC,* passim.; *SLTC,* introduction, pp. 2–3, 77–78.

His notes swelled with newly learned Lamaist schemes of reincarnation, temple customs, doctrinal terminology, observations on the Buddhist canon, and data about past relations of the area and people to the central government. He was awed at the sophistication of the Buddhist libraries, and the knowledge of Chinese classical learning displayed by the monks.[91] On May 20, Ku gave a guest lecture to a joint meeting of all of the Buddhists in the area. Speaking through an interpreter (he feared that the monks would not understand his "Southern accent"), Ku stressed the propinquity, historically speaking, of the *Han* and the *Fan* (Tibetan) peoples, and he asked his audience to appreciate the fundamental unity of the two peoples.[92]

A concern for national unity threaded its way through the summaries and final reports on Northwest education which Ku Chieh-kang submitted to the Boxer Commission. Within the plethora of technical details and descriptive materials, there ran the thesis that it was a combination of Western-style technical and Chinese humanistic education that would provide the answer to the two basic problems he observed: economic underdevelopment (the resources were there, he felt, but unexploited), and disunity and hostility. His report stressed that he had developed a great respect for the Lamaist scholars, among others, and therefore that he had no intention of suggesting that the indigenous culture of the Northwest he supplanted by *Han* culture:[93]

If the Chinese (*Han*), the Moslem, and the Tibetan are able to have a similar education, then they will be able to think alike. And because they can think alike, their feelings will coalesce. Because their feelings coalesce, they will cohere and form a single body.[94]

The suggestions which Ku Chieh-kang offered were not merely designed to benefit the Moslems and the Tibetans. His observations in the Northwest convinced him that he was right

91. *HPKCJC*, pp. 23a ff.; *TS*, I:9 (July 16, 1940), 21, and I:23 (Feb. 16, 1941), 15.
92. *HPKCJC*, pp. 29a–29b.
93. *Ibid.*, pp. 19a–20b, 39a–40b.
94. *Ibid.*, p. 40b.

in looking to the frontiers for a revitalization of all of China. The Mohammedans were even more virile than he had imagined, and his diary proclaimed admiration for their rugged, equestrian militia. The Tibetans, whom he had always imagined to be quite primitive, provided further, unexpected confirmation.[95] It was the intellectual vitality of their Buddhism, as well as their vigorous life, that attracted him.

We can now see that Ku Chieh-kang employed polar conceptions of the *barbarian* according to his varying needs and moods. For propaganda purposes, he exploited the stereotypes of traditional Chinese history: When he wished to use them in his attacks on the Japanese, the barbarians were symbols of national catastrophe. But to salve the despair that came from contemplating cultural extinction, Ku committed himself as well to positions antithetical to traditional thought. He easily shifted his stance so as to see the barbarians as minority races which could revitalize China in the present as they had reputedly done in the past. This was the context of his great interest in the Moslems, an interest aroused from the time that the Japanese entered North China. At that time, it had been with special attention that he observed the "strength of [the Moslem] militia, the difficulty of their life, their bravery and daring." And it was then that he "realized that in the revival of the Chinese race, the Moslems would have a large responsibility." [96]

ACADEME IN EXILE

The trip to Kunming and the National University of Yünnan was a leisurely one, leading to Chengtu, Chungking, and then down the Yangtze. A report to the Boxer Commission in Chungking and an excursion into Lo Lo country were the only notable events along the way. The Lo Lo tribes provided Ku further opportunity to pursue his unflagging interest in the relationship of barbarian culture (the Lo Lo were one of the *I* barbarians) to that of the Chinese. In his observations of Lo Lo temples, language, and legends, Ku remarked on the many points of obvi-

95. *Ibid.*
96. *YK,* VII:4 (March 1937).

ous relationship with the Mongols and the Manchus as well as the Chinese.[97]

Yünnan was miserable. In the early winter Ku senior died in Soochow. Even if it had been safe for him to go back, Ku Chieh-kang was too ill to travel, and thus his wife had to return east to manage the funeral, even though she had only arrived in Kunming in November.[98] (Ku's writings give no indication when or if husband and wife rejoined each other.) At about the same time, the Japanese began to bomb Kunming. The incessant night raids reactivated Ku's insomnia—apparently a chronic problem for him—and for a little peace of mind he was finally forced to move six miles outside the city to Lang-k'o village. It was a swampy, out-of-the-way place, surrounded on three sides by the Coiling Dragon River. Visitors were few, and Ku only went into the pummeled city twice a week to teach classes.[99] His only luxury was leisure time to read and think about his recent excursions in the North, and about a score of wide-ranging historical and textual problems.[100]

When the academic year mercifully ended, Ku Chieh-kang took himself to Chengtu and his new teaching position at Cheeloo University, which had itself recently come to Szechwan from Tsinan, Shantung. It took him almost half a year to recover from an illness he had developed in Yünnan, and he was not able to resume his usual pace until mid-1940. By that time, he had assumed his teaching duties and the directorship of the newly organized Research Academy[101] and the editorship of the Academy's new journal, the *Tse-shan* (Admonitions to Virtuous Deeds).[102]

The journal was a forum for most of the many scholars-in-exile in Szechwan, and its contents ranged widely over the best

97. *HPKCJC*, p. 41a; *TS*, I:3 (April 16, 1940), 16.

98. *HPKCJC*, p. 2a.

99. *SLTC*, pp. 2–3.

100. These comprise the "Lang-k'o ts'un sui-pi."

101. *TS*, I:5 (May 16, 1940), 5; *Tu-shu t'ung-hsun*, no. 9 (Sept. 1, 1940), 8.

102. The *TS* was published in two volumes and 48 numbers. It ran from March 1940 through Nov. 1942. The Lung Meng Bookstore, Hong Kong, published a complete new printing during the 1960s.

of contemporary Chinese scholarship. Before the journal had run its course in November 1942, Ku had turned over its management to Ch'ien Mu. Ku supplied the journal, throughout its short life, with a serialization of his notes from his Northwest expedition and his miscellaneous studies in Yünnan.[103] Ku's prestige at the University is suggested by the front page of the student bulletin,[104] which in traditional fashion was inscribed with his name. The bulletin, from time to time, recorded his hectic activities and gives evidence that his interest in China's frontier cultures was unabated throughout his stay in the West.[105] Other publications reveal that his interest in Chinese Buddhists and in the Chinese Mohammedans also continued.[106]

Within the period we are considering, Ku was responsible for two further noteworthy publications. A periodical, *Literature and History* (*Wen-shih tsa-chih*), was begun under Ku's editorship in March of 1941 and persisted until 1948.[107] Ch'ien Mu alternated with Ku in administering the periodical, a rather nondescript production, much more heterogeneous than the *Tse-shan*. While the latter represented a full range of the academic disciplines traditionally associated with historiography in China, the former went further and also encompassed literary criticism and contemporary fiction, drama, and poetry. *Ch'in Shih Huang-ti*, a short monograph, was the second work produced by Ku Chieh-kang while in Szechwan during the war.[108] The subject matter and methodology displayed by Ku Chieh-kang in his publications of the 1940s were distinct departures from his previous scholarly work. They deserve our attention because they illustrate his most immediate intellectual and emo-

103. That is, the "Lang-k'o ts'un sui-pi."

104. *Ch'i-lu ta-hsüeh-hsiao k'an* [Cheeloo University Bulletin]. Bulletin no. 1 is dated Dec. 1938; no. 33 is dated May 1943.

105. For example, no. 16 (Oct. 15, 1941), 4, reports that Ku flew to Chungking "in response to an invitation from the Chungking Borderlands Association."

106. For example, *TS*, I:9 (July 16, 1940), 21; and I:24 (Jan. 3, 1941), 13–14.

107. The journal was published in Chungking and went to a total of 63 numbers in 42 issues. The last issue was VI:3 (Oct. 1948). The Lung Meng Bookstore, Hong Kong, reprinted this journal during the 1960s.

108. Ku Chieh-kang, *Ch'in Shih Huang-ti* (Chungking, 1944).

tional response to his Northwest excursion and to the unrelenting problems of the Sino-Japanese war.

History in the 1940s: National and Popular

Ku Chieh-kang's historical essays in *Literature and History* and his monograph on the first Ch'in emperor are narratives, written in a simple, crystalline prose style with all technical apparatus tucked quietly away in Western-style footnotes. Format, style, and subject matter are all evidence that it was for a popular audience (as opposed to professional scholars) that they were written. And an editorial in *Literature and History* made this orientation explicit.[109] There were two dominant and interacting themes: the formation of the Chinese people, and the perennial problem of political unity.

Within the small formats of his essays, his footnotes reveal that he assembled mounds of facts tested and proved by his own research as well as by Fu Ssu-nien, Wang Kuo-wei, and others. But the facts, arranged and set in motion, were transformed by Ku into the details of an epic drama of the Chinese people. His first essay, "The Rise to Eminence of the Chou and Their Conquest of the Shang," will in some passages remind the Western reader of the Biblical account of the Israelites' journey to the Promised Land.

In the third essay, "The Imperial Epoch of the Western Chou," [110] Ku focused on one heroic figure, Duke Mu of Chao (Chao Mu-kung). Ku Chieh-kang felt that in the history of the Chou dynasty, Duke Mu's preeminence was second only to the Duke of Chou himself. Duke Mu earned this tribute because of his reputed devotion and sacrifice to the unity of the Chou realm—his lifelong work "to unify the clans and nobility of Chou into one body." [111] This essay was not, however, merely the recounting of an incident in ancient history. The narrative was carefully shaped to evoke a comparison between contemporary Chinese politics and those of Duke Mu's times. It was a

109. *Wen-shih tsa-chih,* I:2 (April 16, 1941), 70.
110. *Ibid.,* I:9 (Aug. 1941), 38–43.
111. *Ibid.,* pp. 39–40.

not overly subtle criticism of the Chungking regime, delivered as a parable based on materials in ancient texts.

The body of this essay began with the reign of King Li (ca. 878 B.C.), who, we are told, was a most autocratic, haughty, and harsh ruler. The King relied on officials who sought out monopolies for themselves and thereby caused the people to suffer. The people of course complained. It was only Duke Mu who confronted the King with the truth and who warned him that the people would not tolerate the situation much longer. Furious, the King ordered local sorcerers to spy out the critics and kill them. The people were intimidated and soon sublimated their criticism—but their faces showed the hatred their hearts still bore. Now, Ku's essay continued, the King recalled Duke Mu and harangued, "You see! Have I not put a stop to this rubbish, this chatter? Now they certainly will not open their mouths!" The good Duke told the King that he was only fooling himself and that one day the people would not contain themselves. And sure enough, within three years, King Li was dethroned by collective action of the discontented people.[112]

An interregnum followed under the leadership of Duke Mu. At a crucial juncture, the Duke chose to sacrifice the life of his own son in order that the Chou heir apparent, under his loyal protection, could live to take the throne. The period is known in the *Tso Commentary* as the Unified Harmony (*Kung ho*) reign. ("*Kung Ho*," as a modern compound word, is also the common word for "Republic.") According to Ku's exposition, it was during this period, and on the occasion of strengthening the militia of the Chou nobility, that Duke Mu wrote a famous poem exhorting brothers to forget their differences and unite against their common foe. Ku Chieh-kang wrote this essay a few months after the New Fourth Army Incident, wherein the Chungking regime reopened hostilities with the Chinese Communists.

This third essay on the Chou epoch ended on a familiar note: Disunity means disaster. The catastrophes occasioning the east-

112. *Ibid.*, p. 39. Ku Chieh-kang's source for this material was the "Chou yü" section of the *Kuo Yü*.

ward shift of the Chou capital in the eighth century B.C. he laid at the feet of rulers too incompetent and selfish to maintain a centralized realm. The theme was picked up again and further embellished in the last of his series in *Literature and History,* a 1943 essay on the first of the Hegemons (*Pa*). This was Duke Huan of Ch'i (Ch'i Huan-kung), who flourished in the mid-seventh century B.C.[113] It was yet another heroic portrait that Ku painted, using much of the same palette that he employed in his earlier propaganda pieces. Duke Huan earned his pedestal not only because he successfully stopped the feudalizing tendencies of his day, but also because he decisively routed the aggressive barbarians on the northern and western frontiers.

Ku Chieh-kang's last noteworthy publication of the war period was *Ch'in Shih Huang-ti.* It was published in 1944 by the Victory Company as one of the many titles in a popular series entitled "Stories of Our Nation's Great Men." From the context in which we are viewing it, the monograph can be understood as Ku's final statement on the problem of political unity. Although it did fail to offer any sophisticated analysis of the Ch'in unification, it was more than merely a good survey. The fact that the first Ch'in emperor was taken for granted as a 'Great Man' was in itself significant. Ch'in Shih Huang-ti had been for the Confucian historical tradition the arch-political villain who "burned the books and buried the scholars," in every Chinese history book from the time of Ssu-ma Ch'ien. The new departure in Chinese historiography which this monograph represented is to be seen in Ku's attempt to give a balanced appraisal of the short-lived Ch'in dynasty. Far from being the loathsome abortion depicted in traditional history, the Ch'in dynasty in this presentation made the positive and lasting contribution of unity and standardization to all areas of Chinese life. It was the Ch'in that made China possible. Like some traditional historians, Ku was quick to balance the ledger, and to tabulate the costs of Ch'in's immense achievements: The Great Wall, the palaces, the fabulous wars against the Hsiung Nu nomads—all of these were *not* worth the equally immense costs in human life

113. "Ch'i Huan-kung te pa-yeh" [The Hegemony of Duke Huan of Ch'i], *Wen-shih tsa-chih,* III:1–2 (Jan. 1, 1944), 73–88.

and resources. It is not clear whether Ku considered the price of unification itself also too high.

The monograph returned to the spirit of his *Literature and History* essays when it described the destruction of the remaining independent states by Ch'in. Here, Ku Chieh-kang was at his narrative best. There was a moral ambiguity and a division of sympathies on his part that makes it clear that he could not value the unification of the empire more than the integrity of any one of the independent states. He did not cheer at the sidelines whenever Ch'in swallowed up another state. On the contrary, the demise of each one was treated as a tragedy—sometimes minor, but complete nevertheless. If there was a hero to the piece, it was the Queen of Ch'i, who was depicted as the wise old counsellor of the contending states when she advised that if they did not unite "like the jade ring" against Ch'in, they would all perish. And indeed they did perish, one by one, each with its own brave deeds and sordid tales of treachery and ignorance.

Each time Ku's narrative completed the story of one of the defeated feudal states, it employed a simple coda: *"Kuo wang"* —the state perished. But there is no resolution. The reader has been coaxed into sympathy with each individual state. Yet, when those final words were knelled, Ku Chieh-kang also raised the spectre of the destruction of China in the twentieth century, and we are repeatedly reminded that it was the brutal absorption of those states in antiquity which made China possible. It is this historical double vision, this ambiguity of sentiments and of symbols, that rescued *Ch'in Shih Huang-ti* from being just another survey of a perennial historical problem and transformed it into a dramatic statement on China's fate in mid-century.

By 1944, the charged words *"kuo wang"* had for over a decade possessed the terrifying immediacy which they had had for Ku's predecessors at the beginning of the century. Now, however, the long Japanese occupation, combined with vicious civil war, promised little hope for China's future. Ku Chieh-kang's despair over his nation's fate was expressed in his overlapping concern with China's ethnic minorities and China's political unity. Up to the early 1930s, Ku's work had been devoted to finding ways to insure the historical continuity of Chinese culture. With the increasing Japanese presence in China, he shifted his concern to a much less sophisticated and intellectually cruder preoccupation with the mere physical survival of China. His interest in barbarian culture began as a part of his optimistic quest to find cultural alternatives to unacceptable traditions of the past; but in the end, his interest in the barbarians had become the major symptom of a despair that, in the future, China's reorganized past would find no China to dwell in. Two decades before the great civil war, Ku had already written, in the *Autobiography,* of his fears that foreign encroachment and civil war would exterminate the Chinese by poverty and the sword. "When one looks at the problem from this angle," he wrote, "one is almost forced to conclude that our race has deteriorated, and that its extinction is so near that all we can do is to sit pessimistically waiting for the end." [114]

114. *ACH,* p. 167.

EPILOGUE

Ku Chieh-kang in The People's Republic: Contributions of an Un-Marxist Historian to Revolution

> *Nationalism, being a jealous mistress, demands the creation of a particularistic history, a private affair, as it were, between the state and the people. This is all very well in the privacy of the sovereign realm, but it is awkward in the vestibule of the new ecumeni. For Marxism, too, is jealous and demands of her historians universality.*[1]

The pessimism which Ku Chieh-kang expressed during the heights of Warlord conflict and civil war, and during the Japanese invasion, was a function of real threats to the survival and continuity of Chinese culture. His concerns and fears here were the most personal links between himself and those thinkers who came before and after him; those who asked how it was possible to be Chinese in the twentieth century. The wonder is that the expressions of Ku's despair were so few and far between. His thought was more prominently characterized by a cautious but persistent optimism that China's internal problems could be identified and eliminated by men of scientific intellect.

1. Harold Kahn and Albert Feuerwerker, "The Ideology of Scholarship: China's New Historiography," in Albert Feuerwerker, ed., *History in Communist China* (Cambridge, Mass., 1968), p. 1.

If we succumb to Ku's overly narrow conception of politics, then it must be said that he sought his solutions in the realm of nonpartisan scholarship which focused on what Hu Shih had called cultural reform. But in twentieth-century China, even the thinking of a historian of antiquity has had potentially weighty and dramatic significance for more conventionally defined political activities. Breaking with the past ways of thinking and acting—in any realm of the society—could constitute a political statement; and all such breaks have contributed to a broad, cumulative, revolutionary process which only in recent decades has come to channel itself primarily through considerations of power and the construction of a new political economy. Thought about the past in particular, especially from the time of the Nationalist government's accession to power in the early 1930s, has often been inseparable from political doctrine and party line.

In Ku Chieh-kang's thought about the past, he confronted questions which intellectuals in the generation before him had started to ask and which continued to be asked by the generation which has overlapped with his under the People's Republic. When J. R. Levenson wrote of Liang Ch'i-ch'ao, he suggested that Liang—mentor of Ku Chieh-kang's generation—could better be understood if we attempted to see him as part of a coherent twentieth-century Chinese intellectual world. Coherence, it was suggested, could be found among the central questions being asked, if not in the answers being given. Liang and the Communists were compatible to the degree that the latter continued to ask Liang's questions; and to that same degree we can begin to understand what has held together this fragmented Chinese intellectual world whose chief characteristics seem to be ambiguity and contradiction.

From the time of Liang Ch'i-ch'ao through the current decade, Chinese intellectuals have continued to explore and implement modes of strengthening China which have resulted in jarring social and intellectual changes. At the same time, there has been a compulsion to maintain the continuity of Chinese history. A national identity has been sought which would be equivalent to any other (and particularly Western) nation, different enough and different in such a way as to be called Chinese, and whose value would be defensible beyond the borders of China. Ku Chieh-kang, like Liang and the Chinese Communists, perennially experienced the tensions generated by the confrontation of personal satisfaction and universal validity, of Chinese and modern.

In the realm of historical thought, formal and informal, where the relation of China's past, present, and future has been considered, the questions and tensions have provoked a search for schemes of universal historical development or cultural growth, for the fundamental processes of change and the indicators of progress. In some instances, this search has ended with crude attempts at cultural equivalency between China and the West. In others, schemes of necessary historical development have acted as rationalizations of China's absorption into the Western cultural sphere; and, in effect, they have also acted as guarantors of the survival and progress of Chinese civilization.

During the time of Ku Chieh-kang's early intellectual development, a great variety of such historical notions were current. However, the most prevalent of them did not yet derive from Marxism. There was the dramatic utopianism of K'ang Yu-wei, the Social Darwinian legacies transmitted by Yen Fu and Liang Ch'i-ch'ao, and the historical groping and hoping of the *journal of National Essence* and *New Tide*. When Ku began to write as a professional historian, he was faced essentially with two questions precipitated from this intellectual potpourri: What is history? and What is China? Ku and his associates in the National Studies Movement addressed themselves to the latter, and thereby saved themselves some of the anguish that has often resulted from embracing a scheme of universal historical progress which has the effect of leveling civilizations: historical equality at the cost of cultural uniqueness. It was thus the second question that bound together Ku, his associates, and the generations that came before and after them. Indeed, the answers which National Studies and Ku's other enterprises offered already began to prepare the way for the later answers of the

Chinese Communists. The manner in which Ku formulated his central questions seems to be the most useful indicator of where his scholarship has torn away from the outlooks of pre-modern Chinese thought; his answers best reveal where his scholarship is engaged with the problems of post-Confucian Chinese life. Together, they indicate the intellectual symptoms of his modernity.

It is remarkable that Ku could sustain what optimism he did express for China in his writing and in his activities without adopting the kinds of universal historical schemes that sprang up all about him. He explicitly eschewed even such systems as historical materialism, whose potential usefulness to scholarship he did acknowledge. He roundly mocked those of his colleagues who even suggested the possibility of grasping ultimate principles, and he had no use for those who wanted to find in man's life some all-pervading unity or some underlying, connecting patterns. He was a skeptic; but his skepticism was directed at inherited knowledge of the past—and the values, still in use, based on such knowledge. His optimism was derived from the belief that he could get at the reality of what had happened in the past, and thereby make the appropriate corrections of the present: his judgment of what China is and should be was based on his discoveries of what it really had been. Ku refused the opportunity to see some salvation for China in a scheme which placed the realities of China's past into a predetermined and global developmental pattern. His satisfaction came from contemplating the possibilities for historical continuity and progress based on the internal workings and unique products of Chinese civilization, as he interpreted them.

The only universal which Ku permitted in his intellectual repertory was science. But he understood science quite narrowly, as a universally valid method to get at uniqueness and particularity. Ku's younger contemporaries (such as the Social Historians) and his later Chinese Communist critics (who were sometimes his erstwhile students) all argued that he was not really scientific precisely because his scholarship was preoccupied with the accidental and not the universal; Ku did not try to formulate laws from his studies. And further, while Ku's critics did acknowledge the value of his devotion to the destruction of historical fantasy, he was decried for his failure to establish concrete historical verities in their place. The latter criticism, if my analysis of Ku's historiography is correct, is at best a half-truth; for Ku, quite explicitly and with some success, did demonstrate how historical fantasy could be transformed into verity. His critics were persistent, however, and they went on to challenge the "mere idealism" that was the product of such scholarship: Ku was merely dealing with ideas and values, instead of the social structures which ultimately generated them—a further demonstration, it was insisted, that Ku's scholarship was unscientific.[2]

Such criticism is useful in bringing attention to the pattern and ramifications of Ku's interests in the particular, as opposed to the universal. It was indeed China, and not history in general, that preoccupied him; he expressed a bias for the empirical and analytic modes of scholarship, but suspicion and near-contempt for the deductive; and he advocated the confrontation of individual scholarly minds (which he contrasted to schools or political parties) with the facts. By the early 1930s, Ku seemed to stand between two kinds of scholarship and their attendant approaches to the past: the branch of Academia Sinica under Fu Ssu-nien, and the Social Historians. In the late twenties, the former, emphasizing the most conservative aspects of Ku's scholarship, began to cling tenaciously to the so-called individual facts and, as a matter of principle, to avoid interpretation, elucidation, hypothesis, and deductive procedures in general. Fu Ssu-nien argued that the narrow goal of modern historical scholarship in China was to preserve and then learn to use the great masses of new historical data discovered in recent decades. And he emphasized an approach which would let the data speak for itself, as it were, expressing a fear of "repairing" or "tampering"

2. See T'ung Shu-yeh, "Ku-shih pien p'ai te chieh-chi pen-chih" [The Class Character of the *Critiques* Clique], *Wen shih che* [History, Literature, and Philosophy], LII:3 (Jan. 1952), 32–34; and Yang Hsiang-k'uei, "Ku-shih pien p'ai te hsüeh-shu-ssu-hsiang p'i-pan" [A Criticism of the Scholarly Thought of the *Critiques* Clique], *ibid.*, pp. 34–37.

with the new data.[3] Meanwhile, the Social Historians plunged into quite ambitious applications of European sociological theory—especially the theories of classical Marxism.

The imagery which John Dewey used in one of his descriptions of the "new empiricism" in the West seems to point to the broader implications of what has often enough been mistaken (in China and elsewhere) as an autonomous mode of perception. In *Reconstruction in Philosophy,* Dewey wrote of "the substitution of a democracy of individual facts for the feudal state of an ordered gradation of general classes [of ideas] of unequal rank." [4] The Academia Sinica notwithstanding, Ku Chieh-kang understood the empirical mode of inquiry to be quite broad enough so that this democracy of individual facts could be organized at least to the extent of revealing past realities and the process through which they evolved. He was committed, like the rest of his fellow New Historians (who once included Fu Ssu-nien), to revealing not only what had been, but how it came to be. Dewey's imagery points to what was clear enough in the scholarship of Ku and his circle; that is, once having discovered *what was,* and *how it came to be,* one should move on to consider what *ought to be.* And what ought to be was suggested in Dewey's evocation of the egalitarian, democratic society.

Beyond this, an overview of Ku's historiography reveals some significant deviations from his explicit concern for the particular. His interest in how things came to be was expressed repeatedly in his characterization of process and flux in specific eras, and he was no cautious empiricist when he found evidence of progress (or lack of it). Though he expressed mistrust of deductive thinking, Ku certainly was not noticeably inhibited from implementing, from time to time, Hu Shih's early call for "bold hypotheses."

Two inchoate schemes of historical process, each intimately involved with his notion of positive or negative progress in

3. See Fu's editorial introduction to *Li-shih yü-yen yen-chiu-so chou-k'an* [Journal of the Historical and Philological Research Institute], I:1 (Oct. 1928), reprinted in *FSNHC,* III, 484.

4. John Dewey, *Reconstruction in Philosophy* (Boston, 1957), p. 66.

Chinese civilization, are evident in Ku's historical writings. He perceived a series of social and intellectual tendencies during the epoch of the Warring States which resulted in great advances for China. When these tendencies were arrested, there followed a great expanse of generally ill-favored history (which Ku did not discuss) that seemed to end with the intellectual ferment of the twentieth century. Another configuration of Chinese history which emerges from Ku's writings takes on the shape of a cycle —a rising and falling motivated by the periodic decay of Chinese civilization and its revivification by the barbarians.

In neither of these schemes do individual actors play a basic role. In the first, progressive developments were manifested in individual behavior; the tendency of Ku's thought, however, was to characterize individual behavior as a reflection of larger, impersonal social phenomena, and ultimately to characterize human thought and action as a collective (class) phenomenon. None of the scholars or philosophers he described escaped for long the characterization of being a product of his times—not even himself. Nor did any, including himself, escape being explained as the member of a class. The only historical actors to whom he really ascribed any autonomy or will (those who cause, rather than merely reflect other causes) were the social parasites and militant defenders of class privilege who oppressed the masses and inhibited general social progress. Just as Ku often felt his own ambitions as a scholar frustrated and dictated by the unpredictable and tortuous course of his times, just so were his favored historical actors overwhelmed by the current of their own history. Only evil men seemed to be free.

Ku's tendency to minimize the role of individuals in the basic processes of history is all the more evident in the cyclical configuration with which he explained the role of the barbarians. Here was a collective, nameless force to which he attributed the survival and perpetuation of Chinese civilization in the past, and on which he sometimes pinned hopes for the future. For all his admiration of individual scholars of the past, and for all his promotion of the autonomy of individual scholars in the present, in the crush Ku's hopes for China were lodged in an untutored collectivity.

In the new contexts provided by the growth of the People's Republic, Ku's questions and answers, his historiography and his proposals for alternative traditions—all have taken on new meanings and have revealed some of their most powerful potentials. As the Marxist legacy has been shaped into a viable Chinese political doctrine and tool of social organization, it seems that the answers which Ku and his colleagues had given to central questions have been reiterated; but far-reaching political implications have been more acutely perceived and exploited. The utility of an alternative view of tradition; the contemporary and historical role of vernacular literature and folk culture; the relationship of the intellectual to the masses—all of these have persisted and have been important considerations in post-1949 China. However, each of these issues has been greatly elaborated and then fused with the others into a rather systematic political doctrine, self-conscious and ambitiously goal-oriented.

Between 1949 and 1963 (when Ku's last work seems to have been published), Ku's voice has been a quiet one and seldom heard. More or less, Ku seems to belong to that "older generation of non-Marxist scholars" whose reputations and whose expertise had, at least until the mid-1960s, "spared them from excessive criticism." But unlike many of his scholarly contemporaries who stayed on the mainland after 1949, he seems not to have been shunted off into "the obscurity of local historical commissions and boards where they are tolerated, neutralised and counted as curios from a bygone age." [5] Nor do I find any evidence, as has been suggested, that Ku has had to undertake demeaning work as some kind of punishment for his previous life outside of the Marxist fold.[6] Notably, however, Ku did not

5. Kahn and Feuerwerker, "The Ideology of Scholarship," p. 8. In addition to the Feuerwerker anthology, cited in note 1 above, I find these items most useful for discussing Chinese Communist historiography: Levenson, *CCMF,* I, chap. 10, and II, part 3; Benjamin Schwartz, "A Marxist Controversy on China," *Far Eastern Quarterly* (Feb. 1954); Albert Feuerwerker and S. Cheng, eds., *Chinese Communist Studies of Modern Chinese History* (Cambridge, Mass., 1961); James R. Pusey, *Wu Han: Attacking the Present Through the Past* (Cambridge, Mass., 1969).

6. The *BDRC* (II, p. 247) observes that under the People's Republic, ca. 1958, "Ku . . . took the humble position of punctuator and annotator of the by now familiar 'Yü-kung' chapter of the *Book of History* as part of

participate in any of the prolific debates on Chinese history that packed the 1950s. His publications, three books and a number of substantial articles, have been for the most part reprints of his earlier scholarly works (sometimes accompanied by ritual self-criticism essays), or works of scholarship which show a marked continuation of his interests of the late thirties (especially in the realm of textual criticism of ancient documents).[7]

In 1955, Ku's *Alchemists and Confucianists* was reprinted, virtually unchanged from the 1934 original, but prefaced by lengthy self-criticism which illustrates some points of compatibility and incompatibility between Ku's thought and that of the Communists—from the latter's point of view. Or perhaps

---

the anthology . . . prepared under the supervision of one of his former disciples, Hou Jen-chih." The reference is to Ku's rather impressive essay—his crowning study of the "Tribute of Yü"—"Yü-kung, ch'uan wen chu-shih" [A Commentary on the Complete Text of the Yü-Kung Chapter of the Book of Documents], in Hou Jen-chih, ed., *Chung-kuo ku-tai ti-li ming-chu* [An Anthology of Famous Authors on Chinese Ancient Geography] (Hong Kong, 1963; first ed. prob. Peking, 1958). If Ku was somehow forced to take the job of dealing with this text as a form of humiliation, there is no evidence for it. There is in fact no reason to believe that this lively and commanding study of this document, so long a favorite subject of his, is anything but the result of Ku's cumulative experience and personal interest. In the 1920s and 1930s, when he repeatedly annotated and punctuated various sections of the *Book of Documents,* he did so with the idea of setting an example of how a canonical work could be made into historical data, and how this historical data could in turn be made available to the broadest reading public.

7. Ku's major post-1949 publications are: *CHFSJS,* a 1955 reprint of the 1934 original; *Ku chi k'ao-pien ts'ung-k'an* [An Anthology of Critical Studies of Ancient Documents] (Shanghai, 1955), an expanded one-volume edition of the series *Symposium on the Critiques of Spurious Literature;* "Hsi jang k'ao" [A Study of the Concept of Productive Soil], *Wen shih che,* LVII:10 (Oct. 1957), 43–47; "Yü-kung ch'uan wen chu-shih" cited in note 6 above; "Shang shu ta-k'ao chin shih" [A Contemporary Annotation of the Great Announcement Chapter of the Book of Documents], *Li-shih yen-chiu* [Historical Studies], LXII:4 (Aug. 1962), 26–51; "I-chou shu, shih-fu pien chiao-chu, hsieh-ting yü p'ing-lun" [A Textual Analysis, Authentication, and Criticism of the Shih-fu Chapter of the Book of Chou], *Wen shih* [Literature and History], no. 2 (1963), pp. 1–43; *Shih-lin tsa-chih* [A Historical Miscellany] (Peking, 1963). The latter book is an anthology of updated and expanded essays which Ku originally published serially, during the 1940s, under the title of "Liang-k'ou ts'un sui-pi" [Miscellaneous Notes from Liang-k'ou Village], in the journal *Tse-shan* [Exhortations to Virtuous Action].

it would be better to say that it reveals the strains put on contemporary Chinese thought by the particular demands of nationalism and the universalistic pretensions of Marxism. In this preface, Ku apologized primarily for his earlier failure to adopt and use historical materialism as the structure for his historiography. But more important was Ku's need to apologize for being overly critical of China's past. He had damned the ruling class of antiquity, he confessed, and had let himself be carried away to the point of criticizing all who came under their influence. His sin, heavy but redeemable, he categorized with the aid of one of Mao's aphorisms: "If one does not have historical materialism's spirit of criticism, what is called bad is considered absolutely bad, completely bad; what is considered good is absolutely good, completely good."

Ku's book, valuable to the Communists for its devastating characterization of the intelligentsia and ruling class of antiquity, at the same time seemed to clash with the so-called historicist tendency which was aimed at discovering what might be "positively inherited" from the past. Thus, Ku said that he had come to see that this book of his was severely limited where it failed to derive the scholarly thought of the Han period from an economic substructure. In addition, it failed to show that though such intellectual systems as the Five Elements had "produced an opium cloud," they in simplified form "contain some of the ideas of materialism . . . which must occupy an important place in the history of our nation's science." [8]

A year after Ku composed this prefatory essay, there appeared a handsome one-volume edition of his *Symposium on Critiques of Spurious Literature*. It was accompanied by a new preface, dated 1955, which presented, in his syntax of the 1920s, a strong and confident argument for the modern relevance of the scholars in the *Symposium*. Notably, there was no self-criticism. (Apparently, a rite of passage had been negotiated with the earlier essay, and Ku was now purged of his previous sins and placed in his proper niche. Self-criticism does not seem to have accompanied any of his published writings from this point.) The *Symposium* worked comfortably into the Chinese Communists'

8. *CHFSJS,* 1954 Introduction, pp. 14–15.

search for an indigenous scientific heritage for China and into their general but erratic efforts to acquire a "positive inheritance" from the past. These efforts took hold for a while, especially in the early sixties, after the prevalence of the so-called class viewpoint which yielded "an anonymous history of dynasties without 'feudal' emperors or bureaucrats, literature minus landlord-scholar-official literature and nameless peasant rebellions as the central matter of China's history." [9]

The "class viewpoint," whatever its fluctuations, has provided foundations for the Chinese Communists' evaluations of the past and for much of their reconstruction of that part of universal history which is Chinese. This is particularly in evidence in their treatment of popular history and culture—peasant rebellions, vernacular literature, folk poetry, and drama. The intensity with which the historical role of the masses has been attended to has rendered "the People" a virtual *ideé fixe*. The People, through their periodic rebellions of the past, have become the main motive force in Chinese history, each peasant rebellion potentially pushing China, from the *inside,* further along toward a new and more advanced stage of history. Ku's notion of the role of the barbarians makes for an interesting contrast, where it relies on an 'outside force' to maintain Chinese civilization. Had Ku formulated this notion more systematically, he might well have had to recant it under the new dispensation, for it had become a cardinal principle that China was autonomously evolving according to the universal pattern already traced by the capitalist West. Too seminal a role for the barbarians of the past raises questions about the purely negative or negligible role assigned by Chinese Communist historiography to the West in recent times.

Despite this potential deviation from the mass line of Chinese Communist historiography, Ku's cultural populism was, and was perceived to be, the most significant area of overlap with the intellectual trends of post-1949 China. In what appears to have been his first published statement under the new regime,

9. Albert Feuerwerker, "China's Modern Economic History in Communist Chinese Historiography," in Feuerwerker, ed., *History in Communist China,* p. 216.

Ku, in 1951, established his legitimate place in the People's Republic on grounds of his previous excursions into the realm of popular culture (via the Folklore Movement) and popular politics (via his anti-imperialist propaganda). This 1951 piece was primarily devoted to explaining away Ku's earlier intimacy with Hu Shih, who had become the *bête noire* of Chinese Communist intellectuals. Ku exorcised Hu Shih from his past with a rather mechanical denunciation of his former teacher and colleague as a political and intellectual enemy of China, and justified his own un-Marxist presence in contemporary China primarily by demonstrating that he and Hu Shih had differed significantly on the basic issues of cultural and political populism.[10]

Ku's legacy to the emerging idea of the People's culture was dramatized in the period of the Great Leap Forward and the Hundred Flowers. In 1957, two of Ku's longtime close associates, Yü P'ing-po and Chung Ching-wen, were caught up in the "blooming and contending" of the time; the scholarship of both was denounced as contrary to the interests of People and party. Yü came under a critical barrage (also directed at Hu Shih, in absentia) for his interpretations of the *Dream of the Red Chamber*; Chung was impeached for being a salesman of capitalist folklore and for insisting on the separation of scientific studies of folklore from its use as socialist propaganda.[11] (Ku was moved to come to the defense of Yü P'ing-po, and he was able to publish a rare public statement on the subject.)[12]

These two incidents dramatize the stark political side of Chinese Communist cultural populism, which is fully intelligible only if we recognize its roots in the less politicized intellectual world of the 1920s. Of all those cultural alternatives ex-

10. Ku Chieh-kang, "Ts'ung wo tzu-chi k'an Hu Shih" [A Personal Look at Hu Shih], *Ta Kung Pao* [The Impartial] (Dec. 24, 1951).

11. See Jerome B. Grieder, "The Communist Critique of the *Hung Lou Meng*," *Papers on China*, X (Cambridge, Mass., 1956); and D. W. Fokkema, *Literary Doctrine in China and Soviet Influence, 1956–1960* (The Hague, 1965). Also see Richard Dorson's Foreword to Wolfram Eberhard, ed., *Folktales of China* (Chicago, 1965), p. xiv.

12. See interview with Ku Chieh-kang reported in the *Kuang-ming jih-pao*, April 21, 1957, as cited in Fokkema, *Literary Doctrine in China*, p. 136.

plored and promoted by Ku Chieh-kang, surely that of popular culture was the most immediately relevant to the culture of the People's Republic. By the late 1950s, particularly during the Great Leap, Ku's Folk Culture—and Hu Shih's Vernacular Literature as well—had in effect found a central place in the Chinese Communist view of the cultural heritage of the past.

When Hu Shih and Yü P'ing-po were bombarded in the debates on the *Dream of the Red Chamber,* the chief issue was the interpretation of the novel. The novel itself and the literary tradition which it represented were nevertheless acknowledged as most valuable for building an alternative Chinese literary tradition. Suffice it to note that however vilified Hu Shih might have been over the past two decades, the great vernacular novels which he promoted (but which had not been acceptable to Ch'ü Ch'iu-pai) have become standard elements in the Chinese Communist version of Chinese literary history. And Hu Shih's argument for the fundamental role of the folk and of popular literature in all literary innovation is quite compatible with post-1949 ideas about the Chinese literary tradition.[13]

Nor is the legacy of the Folklore Movement obscure. *The Book of Odes* is the standard point of departure for the Chinese People's literary tradition; and in some recent literary histories, its former role as a member of the Classical canon is never mentioned at all. More dramatically, the idea of Folk Culture—especially from the time of the Great Leap era—has taken on rather awesome proportions. It can be argued that the Chinese Communists parodied the 1920s idea of spontaneous, pure folk

13. In addition to the studies of Fokkema and Grieder, cited in note 11, above, the place of Vernacular Literature in the Chinese Communist conception of China's literary heritage may be directly seen in the English-language translations published by the Peking Foreign Languages Press. For example, Feng Yuan-chun, *A Short History of Classical Chinese Literature* (Peking, 1958); *The Courtesan's Jewelbox: Chinese Stories of the Tenth–Eighteenth Centuries* (Peking, 1957); Wu Ching-tzu, *The Scholars* (Peking, 1957). Also see the spate of general literary histories published during the late fifties and early sixties which conventionally give a prominent place to Vernacular Literature: e.g., Liu Ta-chieh, *Chung-kuo wen-hsüeh fa-chan shih* [A History of the Development of Chinese Literature] (Shanghai, 1957); Peking University, *Chung-kuo wen-hsüeh shih* [A History of Chinese Literature], 4 vols. (Peking, 1959); Literature Section of the Chinese Academy of Sciences, *Chung-kuo wen-hsüeh shih* (Peking, 1962).

culture, and that folk poetry produced on demand to meet quotas has little to do with the interest of the Folksong Research Society. The Great Leap Forward in folk poetry (like that in industry or agriculture) may well have been a sad burlesque of the needs and goals of modern China, but its excesses should not obscure our recognition of the continuous modes in which central cultural problems have been approached since the 1920s: It was not the Communists, but scholars of a reformist mentality, who first explored the utility of folk poetry to the new national heritage; and it was men of similarly moderate political leanings who first suggested that aspects of folk culture would serve well as a medium for social reform. If the Rice Sprout Dramas were first systematically used for political education in the People's Republic, their use for "educational purposes" was first proposed by the American-trained sociologists of Ting Hsien experimental village, decades earlier.[14]

The broad continuity I am suggesting here wants considerable elucidation, for it is not clear just where the lines of transmission lie over the battered decade of the 1940s. But it is evident that the need to destroy *and* conserve traditions—so strongly felt by Ku Chieh-kang in the 1920s and 1930s—was no less forceful a guide to thought in the 1950s and 1960s. However, the answers which Ku's New History and National Studies offered had powerful political potentials, of which Ku seemed aware

14. Red China's cultural populism has received some diverse and illuminating attention: e.g., Clarence Moy, "Communist China's Use of the Yang-ko [Rice Sprout Dramas]," *Papers on China,* VI (Cambridge, Mass., 1952), 112–148; "Folklore," *China News Analysis,* no. 7 (Hong Kong, Oct. 9, 1953), p. 7; "Folk Songs and Folk Tales: Methods and Results," *ibid.,* no. 353 (Hong Kong, Dec. 16, 1960), pp. 1–7; S. H. Chen, "Multiplicity in Uniformity: Poetry and the Great Leap Forward," *China Quarterly,* no. 3 (July–Sept. 1960), 1–16; Alsace C. Yen, "Red China's Use of Folklore," *Literature East and West,* VII:2–3 (1964), 72–86.

The role of the *Book of Poetry* is described in S. H. Chen's essay, and this former classic's new status is evident in all of the literary histories listed in note 13. Also see these examples of new literary studies devoted just to folk literature: T'an Ta-hsien, *Min-chien wen-hsüeh san-lün* [Essays on Folk Literature] (Canton, 1959), and Mai Chih, *Min-chien wen-hsüeh lun-chi* [Anthology of Discussions on Folk Literature] (Peking, 1963). Cheng Chen-to's synthesis of the literature of folk culture studies of the 1920s and 1930s, *Chung-kuo su-wen-hsüeh shih* [A History of China's Common Literature], was reprinted in a two-volume edition, Peking, 1954.

only on occasion. It has been the special genius of the leaders of Chinese Communism to perceive and imaginatively employ these potentials for the purposes of constructing a new and highly organized society and an attendant ideology.

This has been most fully evidenced in the Communists' treatment of the relationship of the intellectuals and society, a perennial problem in Ku's circles before 1949. The attitudes of the young men who shouted "To the People" in the 1920s, as well as the early populist tendencies of Ku and his colleagues, have taken on a Kafkesque dimension in the Downward Transfer (*Hsia-fang*) movements dating from the mid-1950s. Herein, the question of "the intellectuals' separation from the people" has been fully acknowledged as a major contemporary problem. By the application of ingenuity, ruthlessness, and force, the Chinese Communists have been able to carry Ku Chieh-kang's earlier reasoning on the Chinese intellectual to its logical conclusion: If China's progress requires the propinquity of intelligentsia and People, then the former must be *made* to draw near the latter. In the process of bringing the two together, the Maoist regime has discovered a potent device for political control and social change. Ku Chieh-kang could not have imagined such ramifications, three decades earlier, when he urged his colleagues to draw near the masses and to recognize that the intellectuals too were but common people.[15]

Ku Chieh-kang's preoccupations with the People, the intellectuals, and the past were all aspects of his passionate concern for China's present and future. All along, his most persistent fear was that the chaos and brutality of the twentieth century would destroy those vestiges of the past that were necessary for an intelligible Chinese history, and hence for appropriate change and progress. The Chinese, he lamented in the 1930s, ostensibly so deeply involved with their past, have been and continued to be the most wanton destroyers of its remnants; thus their continued need to rely on legend. He believed that the strength of the new Chinese nation-state would be a function of the soundness of its historical vision. But Ku did not foresee that a successful

15. See T. A. Hsia, *A Terminological Study of the Hsia-fang Movement* (Berkeley, 1963).

form of Nationalism could both foster the preservation of vestiges of the past and still obscure the realities of history. He lived to see Chinese nationalism, in its more strident moods, make such impossible demands of history that legend frequently has been found more useful than historical truth.

The Chinese Communists have never had to bother with the historicity of that legend of legends, the Golden Age—on that subject Ku Chieh-kang had done all that needed doing; and besides, such a notion is anathema to the Marxist historiography which seeks Primitive Communism and Slave Society in those distant times. But the Chinese Communists, as Chinese, have had special intellectual needs; and so, Ku Chieh-kang notwithstanding, the Great Yü, the Golden Age hero who tamed the deluge, has become the first of China's hydraulic engineers, with a statue in the historical museum in Peking.[16]

16. A fact cited in A.F.P. Hulsewé, "Origins and Foundations of the Chinese Empire," in Feuerwerker, ed., *History in Communist China,* p. 122.

Bibliography

Biographical Dictionary of Republican China, Howard L. Boorman, ed., 2 vols., New York, 1967–1968.

Burne, Charlotte Sophia, *Handbook of Folklore*, London, 1914.

Cheng Chen-to 鄭振鐸, "Ch'ieh man t'an so-wei Kuo-hsüeh" 且慢談所謂國學 [Not So Fast with this Talk About So-called National Studies], *Hsiao-shuo yüeh-pao* 小說月報 [Fiction Monthly], XX:1 (Jan. 1929), 8–13.

———. *Chung-kuo su-wen-hsüeh shih* 中國俗文學史 [A History of China's Common Literature], 2 vols., Peking, 1954.

———. ed., *Feng Meng-lung, Shan ke* 馮夢龍山歌 [Feng Meng-lung's Hill Songs], Shanghai, 1935. Preface by Ku Chieh-kang.

Ch'eng Fang-wu 成仿吾 "Kuo-hsüeh yün-tung te wo chien" 國學運動的我見 [My View of the National Studies Movement], *Ch'uang-tsao chou-pao* 創造週報 [Creation Weekly], I:28 (Nov. 25, 1923), 1–3.

Ch'i Ssu-ho 齊思和 "Hsien-tai Chung-kuo shih-hsüeh p'ing-lün" 現代中國史學評論 [A Critique of Contemporary Chinese Historical Scholarship], *Ta Chung* 大中 [Great China] I:1 (Jan. 1946), 33–38.

———. "Chin pai nien lai Chung-kuo shih-hsüeh te fa-chan" 今百年來中國史學的發展 [The Development of Chinese Historical Scholarship in the Past Century], *Yen-ching she-hui k'o-hsüeh* 燕京社會科學 [Yenching Journal of Social Science], II (1949), 1–35.

———. "Min-tsu yü chung-tsu" 民族与種族 [Race and Nation], *Yü Kung* 禹貢 [The Tribute of Yü], VII:1–2–3 (1937), 1–33.

Ch'ien Hsüan-t'ung 錢玄同 "Chung lün chin-ku wen-hsüeh wen-t'i" 重論今古文學問題 [A Recapitulation of the Arguments on the Question of the Classical Old-New Text Scholarship], appendix to K'ang Yu-wei 康有為 *Hsin-hsüeh wei-ching k'ao* 新學偽經考 [The False Classics of the New School], Ch'ien Hsüan-t'ung, ed., Peking, 1956.

Chou Tso-jen 周作人 *I-shu yü sheng-huo* 藝術与生活 [Art and Life], Peking, 1931.

———. *T'an Hu Chi* 談虎集 [Speaking to the Tiger], 2 vols., n.p., 1929.

———. *Tzu-chi te yüan-ti* 自己的園地 [Our Own Garden], np., 1923.

Chow Tse-tsung, *The May Fourth Movement*, Cambridge, Mass., 1960.

Ch'ü Ch'iu-pai 瞿秋白 *Ch'ü Ch'iu-pai wen-chi* 瞿秋白文集 [Collected Writings of Ch'ü Ch'iu-pai], 4 vols., Peking, 1953–1954.

———. *Luan T'an* 亂彈 [Vulgar Music], Shanghai, 1939.

———. *Lün Chung-kuo wen-hsüeh ke-ming* 論中國文學革命 [Discussions on the Chinese Literary Revolution], Hong Kong, 1949.

Chung Ching-wen, ed., 鍾敬文 *Ke-yao lün-chi* 歌謠論集 [A Symposium on Folksongs], Shanghai, Peking, 1928.

———. Lou Tze-k'uang 婁子匡 eds., *Min-su-hsüeh chi-chien* 民俗學集鐫 [Anthology of Folklore Studies], No. 2 (Aug. 1932).

Dewey, John, "Historical Judgements," in Hans Meyerhoff, ed., *The Philosophy of History in Our Time*, New York, 1959, pp. 163–173. Originally in John Dewey, *Logic: The Theory of Inquiry*, New York, 1938.

———. *Reconstruction in Philosophy*, Boston, 1957.

———. "The Need for Recovery of Philosophy," in John Dewey, et al., *Creative Intelligence: Essays in the Pragmatic Attitude*, New York, 1917.

Eberhard, Wolfram, *Folktales of China*, rev. ed., Chicago, 1965. Foreword by Richard M. Dorson.

Fu Ssu-nien 傅斯年 *Fu Ssu-nien hsüan-chi* 傅斯年選集 [Selected Works of Fu Ssu-nien], 7 vols., Taipei, 1967.

Fung Yu-lan, *A History of Chinese Philosophy*, Derk Bodde, trans., 2 vols., Princeton, 1953.

Gasster, Michael, *Chinese Intellectuals and the Revolution of 1911: The Birth of Modern Chinese Radicalism*, Seattle, 1969.

Grieder, Jerome B., "Hu Shih and Liberalism: A Chapter in the Intellectual Modernization of China, 1917–1930," unpublished PhD dissertation, Harvard University, 1963.

Halpern, Ben, " 'Myth' and 'Ideology' in Modern Usage," *History and Theory*, I:2 (1961), 129–150.

Ho Ping-sung 何炳松 trans., *Hsin shih-hsüeh* 新史學 [The New History], Shanghai, 1925. A translation of James Harvey Robinson, *The New History*.

———. "Lün so-wei 'Kuo hsüeh' " 論所謂國學 [On the So-called National Studies], *Hsiao-shuo yüeh-pao*, XX:1 (1929).

Hsia Mien-tsun 夏丏尊 "Chih-shih chieh-chi te yün-ming" 知識階級的運命 [The Fate of the Intelligentsia], *I-pan* 一般 [In General], No. 5 (Shanghai, 1928), pp. 100–110.

Hsin-ch'ao 新潮 [The New Tide], Peking, 1919–1922.

Hsin-ju 心如 "Ts'ung ta-tao chih-shih chieh-chi' i k'ou-hao chung so jen-shih te" 從打倒知識階級一口號中所認識的 [What I Understand by the Slogan 'Overthrow the Intelligentsia'], *I-pan*, No. 3 (Shanghai, 1927), pp. 35–41.

Hu Ch'iu-yuan 胡秋原 "P'in-k'un te che-hsüeh" 貧困的哲學 [The Impoverished Philosophy], *Tu-shu tsa-chih* 讀書雜誌 [Readers' Miscellany], I:3 (June 1931), I:6 (Sept. 1931).

Hu Huai-shen 胡懷琛 *Chung-kuo min-ke yen-chiu* 中國民歌研究 [A Study of Chinese Folksongs], Shanghai, 1925.

Hu Shih 胡適 *The Chinese Renaissance*, Chicago, 1933.

———. *The Development of the Logical Method in China*, Shanghai, 1922.

———. "Hsin wen-hua yün-tung yü Kuo-min-tang" 新文化運動与國民黨 [The New Culture Movement and the Kuomintang], *Hsin-yüeh* 新月 [The Crescent Moon], II:6–7 (Sept. 10, 1929), 1–15.

———. *Hu Shih wen-ts'un* 胡適文存 [Collected Writings of Hu Shih], 12 vols. in 6, Shanghai, 1922–1940.

———. *Pai-hua wen-hsüeh shih* 白話文學史 [A History of Vernacular Literature], I, Shanghai, 1929.

———. "Wang Mang, the Socialist Emperor of Nineteen Centuries Ago," *Journal of the North China Branch of the Royal Asiatic Society*, LIX (1928), 218–230.

———. "Wen-hsüeh kai-liang ch'u-i" 文學改良芻議 [Tentative Proposals for Literary Reform], *Hsin ch'ing-nien* 新青年 [New Youth], II:5 (Jan. 1917), 1–11.

Hummel, Arthur W., trans. *The Autobiography of a Chinese Historian*, Leyden, 1931.

———. ed., *Emminent Chinese of the Ch'ing Period,* 2 vols., Washington, D. C., 1943.

Israel, John, *Student Nationalism in China, 1927–1937*, Stanford, 1966.

Ju-sung 如松 "P'ing yu-sheng-hsüeh yü huan-ching lün te lün-cheng" 評優生學与環境論的論爭 [A Critique of the Debate Between the Theory of Eugenics and the Theory of Environment], *Erh-shih shih-chi* 二十世紀 [Twentieth Century], I:1 (Feb. 1, 1931), 57–124.

Jung Chao-tsu 容肇祖 *Chung-kuo wen-hsüeh shih ta-kang* 中國文學史大綱 [A Survey of Chinese Literary History], Peking, 1935.

———. "Pei-ta ke-yao yen-chiu hui chi feng-su tiao-ch'a hui te ching-kuo" 北大歌謠研究會及風俗調查會的經過 [The Vicissitudes of the Peking Folksong Study Society and the Folklore Research Society], *Min-su* 民俗 [Folklore], No. 15–16 (July 1928), pp. 1–10, No. 17–18 (July 1928), pp. 14–30.

Karlgren, Bernard, "Legends and Cults in Ancient China," *Bulletin of the Museum of Far Eastern Antiquities,* No. 18 (1946), pp. 199–367.

Ke-yao chou-k'an 歌謠週刊 [Folksong Weekly], Shanghai, Dec. 1922–June 1925; April 1936–Jan. 1937.

Ku Chieh-kang 顧頡剛 "Cheng Ch'iao chuan" 鄭樵傳 [Biography of Cheng Ch'iao], *Kuo-hsüeh chi-k'an* 國學季刊 [Journal of National Studies], I:2 (1923), 309–332.

———. "Cheng Ch'iao chu-shu k'ao" 鄭樵著述考 [On the Writings of Cheng Ch'iao], *Kuo-hsüeh chi-k'an,* I:1 (1923), 96–138.

———. "Cheng Ch'iao tui-yü ke-tz'u yü ku-shih te chien-chieh" 鄭樵對於歌詞与故事的見解 [Cheng Ch'iao's Views on Folksongs and Legend], *Hsiao-shuo yüeh-pao,* XIV:11 (Nov. 1923).

———. *Ch'in Han te Fang-shih yü Ju-sheng* 秦漢的方士与儒生 [The Alchemists and Confucianists of the Ch'in-Han Era], Shanghai, 1955. Originally published as *Han-tai hsüeh-shu shih-lüeh* 漢代學術史略 [An Outline History of Scholarship of the Han Era], Peking (?), 1935, Chengtu, 1944.

———. *Ch'in Shih Huang-ti* 秦始皇帝 [The First Emperor of the Ch'in Dynasty], Chungking, 1944, Taipei, 1953.

———. and Shih Nien-hai 史念海 *Chung-kuo chiang-yü yen-ko shih* 中國疆域沿革史 [A History of the Changes of China's Frontiers], Shanghai, 1938.

———. *Chung-kuo hsüeh-shu nien-piao te shuo-ming* 中國學術年表的說明 [A Chronological Table of Chinese Scholarship], Peking, 1924.

———. and Wang Chung-ch'i 王鍾麒 *Pen Kuo Shih* 本國史 [Elementary National History], I, Shanghai, 1923.

———. *Hsi-pei k'ao-ch'a jih-chi* 西北考察日記 [Northwest Studies Diary], Peking, 1949.

———. "Hsü" 序 [Preface], *Kuo-li Chung-shan ta-hsüeh yü-yen li-shih-hsüeh yen-chiu so chou-k'an* 國立中山大學語言歷史學研究所週刊 [Journal of the National Sun Yat-sen University Institute of Advanced Philological and Historical Studies], VI: 62–63–64 (Jan. 16, 1929), 1–6.

———. "Hsü," *Pei-ching ta-hsüeh kuo-hsüeh-men chou-k'an* 北京大學國學門週刊 [Peking University National Studies Weekly] I:1 (Jan. 1, 1926).

———. et al., eds., *Ku-shih pien* 古史辨 [Critiques of Ancient History], 7 vols., 1926–1941.

———. ed., *Ku chi k'ao-pien ts'ung-k'an* 古籍考辨叢刊 [An Anthology of Critical Studies of Ancient Documents], Shanghai, 1955.

———. *Ku Chieh-kang t'ung-su lün-chu-chi* 顧頡剛通俗論著集 [An Anthology of Popular Essays by Ku Chieh-kang], Wang Po-hsiang 王伯祥 ed., 3rd printing, Shanghai, 1947.

———. "Lün K'ang Yu-wei pien-wei ch'eng-chi" 論康有為辨偽之成績 [On K'ang Yu-wei's Accomplishments in Critiques of Spurious Literature], *Kuo-li Chung-shan ta-hsüeh yü-yen li-shih-hsüeh yen-chiu so chou-k'an,* XI: 123–124 (March 26, 1930), 13–14.

———. ed., *Meng-chiang ku-shih: yen-chiu chi* 孟姜故事研究集 [The Legend of Lady Meng-chiang: An Anthology of Studies], Canton, 1929.

———. "Meng-chiang nü ku-shih chih li-shih te hsi-t'ung" 孟姜女故事之歷史的系統 [An Historical Filiation of the Lady Meng-chiang Legend], *Hsien-tai p'ing-lün* 現代評論 [The Contemporary Critic], III: 75, 76, 77 (May 1926).

———. *Miao Feng Shan* 妙峯山 [Mt. Miao Feng], Canton, 1928.

———. and T'ung Shu-yeh 童書業 "Mo Tzu hsing-shih pien" 墨子姓氏辨 [Discussions of the Name "Mo Tzu"], *Shih-hsüeh chi-k'an* 史學集刊 [The Historical Journal], I:2 (1936), 151–175.

———. ed., Pien-wei ts'ung-k'an 辨偽叢刊 [Symposium on the Critique of Spurious Literature], 8 vols., Peking, 1928–1935.

———. "Pu mei" 不寐 [Insomnia], in *Wo-men te liu yüeh* 我們的六月 [Our Sixth Month], "OM" ed., Shanghai, 1925.

———. and Yang Hsiang-k'uei 楊向奎 *San Huang k'ao* 三皇考 [A Study of The Three Emperors], Peking, 1936.

———. ed., *Shang-shu yen-chiu chiang-i* 尚書研究講義 [Commentaries on the Study of the Book of Documents], Peking, 1933.

———. "Sheng-hsien wen-hua yü min-chung wen-hua" 聖賢文化与民衆文化 [Culture of the Sages and Culture of the Masses], *Min-su,* I:5 (April 17, 1928).

———. ed., *Shih-hsüeh chi-k'an* 史學集刊 [Subtitled in English: Historical Journal], Peking, April 1936–Dec. 1947.

———. *Shih-lin tsa-chih* 史林雜識 [An Historical Miscellany], Peking, 1963.

———. "A Study of Literary Persecutions During the Ming Dynasty," L. C. Goodrich, trans., *Harvard Journal of Asiatic Studies,* No. 3–4 (Dec. 1938), 254–311.

———. and Liu Wan-chang 劉萬章 *Su-Yüeh te hun sang* 蘇粵的婚喪 [Marriage and Mourning Customs in Soochow and Canton], Canton, 1928.

———. ed., *Ta-chung chih-shih* 大衆知識 [The Peoples' Intelligence], Peking, Oct. (?) 1936–Jan. 1937.

———. *Tang-tai Chung-kuo shih-hsüeh* 當代中國史學 [Contemporary Chinese Historical Scholarship], Nanking, 1947, Hong Kong, 1964.

———. "Tao Wang Ching-an hsien-sheng" 悼王靜安先生 [Obituary for Wang Kuo-wei], *Wen-hsüeh chou-pao* 文學週報 [Literary Journal], V (Feb. 1928), 1–11.

———. and Ch'ien Mu 錢穆 eds., *Tse-shan pan-yüeh k'an* 責善半月刊 [Exhortations to Virtuous Action], Chengtu, March 1940–Nov. 1942.

———. ed., *Ts'ui Tung-pi i-shu* 崔東壁遺書 [The Collected Works of Ts'ui Shu], 7 vols., Peking, 1936.

———. "Ts'ung wo tzu-chi k'an Hu Shih" 從我自己看胡適 [A Personal Look at Hu Shih], *Ta Kung Pao* 大公報 [The Impartial], Dec. 24, 1951.

———. "Tung Chung-shu ssu-hsiang chung te Mo-chiao ch'eng-fen" 董仲舒思想中的墨教成分 [Mohist Elements in the Thought of Tung Chung-shu], *Wen-lan hsüeh-pao* 文瀾學報 [The Literary Wave], III:1 (March 1937).

———. ed., *Wen-shih tsa-chih* 文史雜誌 [Literature and History], Chungking, March 1941–Oct. 1948.

———. and Hu Shih, et al., "*Yeh yu szu chün* chih t'ao-lün" 野有死麕之討論 [A Symposium on the Book of Odes Poem 'A Dead Doe in the Field'], *Yü-ssu* 語絲 [Threads of Conversation], No. 31 (1925), 17–18.

———. "*Yü Kung:* ch'üan wen chu-shih" 禹貢全文注釋 [A Commentary on the Complete Text of the 'Yü Kung' Chapter of the Book of Documents], in Hou Jen-chih 侯仁之 ed., *Chung-kuo ku-tai ti-li ming-chu hsüan tu* 中國古代地理名著選讀 [An Anthology of Famous Authors on Chinese Ancient Geography], Hong Kong, 1963.

———. and T'an Ch'i-hsiang 譚其驤 and Feng Chia-sheng eds., *Yü Kung pan-yüeh k'an* 禹貢半月刊 [Subtitled in English: Chinese Historical Geography], Peking, March 1934–July 1937.

Kuo-hsüeh chi-k'an 國學季刊 [Subtitled in English: Journal of Sinological Studies], Hu Shih, et al., eds., Peking, 1923–1936.

Kuo-ku t'ao-lün chi 國故討論集 [An Anthology of Discussions on the National Heritage], Hsü Hsiao-t'ien 許嘯天 ed., 4 vols., Shanghai, 1927.

Kuo-ts'ui hsüeh-pao 國粹學報 [Journal of National Essence] Liu Shih-p'ei 劉師培 et al., eds., Shanghai, 1905–1911.

Kwok, Daniel, *Scientism in Chinese Thought, 1900–1950,* New Haven, 1965.

Levenson, Joseph R., *Confucian China and Its Modern Fate,* 3 vols., Berkeley, 1958–1965.

———. *Liang Ch'i-ch'ao and the Mind of Modern China,* Cambridge, Mass., 1959.

———. "The Province, the Nation and the World: The Problem of Chinese Identity," in Albert Feuerwerker, et al., eds., *Approaches to Modern Chinese History,* Berkeley, 1967, pp. 268–288.

Li Ching-han 李景漢 *Ting-hsien she-hui kai-k'uang tiao-ch'a* 定縣社會概況調查 [A General Investigation of Ting Hsien Society], n.p., 1933.

Li Tiao-yüan 李調元 *Yüeh Feng* 粵風 [Airs of Kwangtung], Chung Ching-wen, ed., foreword by Ku Chieh-kang, Peking, 1927.

Liang Ch'i-ch'ao 梁啓超 *Chung-kuo li-shih yen-chiu fa* 中國歷史研究法 Taipei, 1967.

———. *Kuo-hsüeh yen-tu fa san chung* 國學研讀法三種 [Three Pieces on Readings in National Studies], Taipei, 1968.

———. *Intellectual Trends in the Ch'ing Period,* I. C. Y. Hsü, trans., Cambridge, Mass., 1959

Liang Shih-ch'iu 梁實秋 "Ke-yao yü hsin-shih" 歌謠与新詩 [Folksong and the New Poetry], *Ke-yao* n.s., II:9 (May 30, 1936), 1–3.

Lichtheim, George, "The Concept of Ideology," *History and Theory,* IV:2 (1965), 164–195.

Liu, C. J., *Controversies in Modern Chinese Intellectual History,* Cambridge, Mass., 1964.

Liu P'u 劉樸 "Pi wen-hsüeh fen kuei-tsu p'ing-min chih-wei" 闢文學分貴族平民之謬 [Criticism of the

Division of Literature into Aristocratic and Popular] *Hsüeh Heng* 學衡 No. 32 (Aug. 1924).

Lou Tze-k'uang 婁子匡 "Chung-kuo min-su-hsüeh yün-tung te tso-yeh ho chin-ch'en" 中國民俗學運動的昨夜和今晨 [The Past Night and Present Dawn of the Chinese Folklore Movement], *Min-chien yüeh-k'an* 民間月刊 [The People], II:5 (1933), 1–17.

Mao Tse-tung, *Report on an Investigation of the Peasant Movement in Hunan,* Peking, 1965.

———. *Talks at the Yenan Forum on Literature,* Peking, 1959.

Mao Tzu-shui 毛子水 "Kuo ku ho k'o-hsüeh te ching-shen" 國故和科學的精神 [The Spirits of the National Heritage and of Science], *Hsin-ch'ao,* I:5 (1919), 733–747.

———. "Po Hsin-ch'ao, Kuo-ku ho k'o-hsüeh te ching-shen pien ting-wu" 駁新潮國故和科學的精神篇訂誤 [Arguments Against a Critique of New Tide, National Heritage and the Spirit of Science], *Hsin-ch'ao,* II:1 (1919), 37–57.

Maspero, Henri, "Legendes mythologiques de le *Chou Ching,*" *Journal Asiatique,* CCIV:1 (1924), 1–100.

Meisner, Maurice, *Li Ta-chao and the Origins of Chinese Marxism,* Cambridge, Mass., 1967.

Min-chien wen-i 民間文藝 [Peoples' Literature and Art], Canton, Nov. 1, 1927–Jan. 10, 1928.

Min-chien yüeh-k'an 民間月刊 [The People], Lou Tze-k'uang, Chung Ching-wen, et al., eds., Shao-hsing, Chekiang, 1931–1934.

Min-chung chiao-yü chi-k'an 民衆教育季刊 [Subtitled in English: Adult Education Quarterly], III:1 (Chekiang, Feb. 1922).

Min-su chou-k'an 民俗週刊 [Folklore], Chung Ching-wen, ed., Canton, March 21, 1928–April 30, 1930; 1933; 1936–1937.

Nivison, David, *The Life and Thought of Chang Hsüeh-ch'eng,* Stanford, 1966.

———. "The Problem of Knowledge and Action Since Wang Yang-ming," in A. F. Wright, ed., *Studies in Chinese Thought,* Chicago, 1953, pp. 112–146.

Nu-li chou-pao 努力週報 [Subtitled in English: The Endeavor], Hu Shih, ed., Peking, 1922–1925 (?).

Pipes, Richard, ed., *The Russian Intelligentsia,* New York, 1961.

Pocock, J. G. A., "Time, Institutions and Action: An Essay on Traditions and their Understanding," in *Politics and Experience: Essays Presented to Professor Michael Oakeshott on the Occasion of His Retirement,* Cambridge, England, 1968, pp. 209–237.

Pollard, A. P., "The Russian Intelligentsia: The Mind of Russia," *California Slavic Studies,* III (Berkeley, 1964).

Robinson, James Harvey, *The New History,* New York, 1965.

Schwartz, Benjamin, *Chinese Communism and the Rise of Mao,* Cambridge, Mass., 1952.

———. *In Search of Wealth and Power, Yen Fu and the West,* Cambridge, Mass., 1964.

———. "Some Polarities in Confucian Thought," in A. F. Wright and David Nivison, eds., *Confucianism in Action,* Stanford, 1959, pp. 50–63.

Sun Yat-sen, *The Three Principles of the People,* Frank W. Price, trans., L. T. Chen, ed., Chungking, 1943.

Teng Shih 鄧實 "Kuo-hsüeh chen lün" 國學真論 [A True Critique of National Studies], *Kuo-ts'ui hsüeh-pao,* III:2 (Feb. 1907).

———. "Kuo-hsüeh wu yung pien" 國學無用辨 [A Critique of the Idea that National Studies are Useless], *Kuo-ts'ui hsüeh-pao,* III:5 (May 1907).

T'ien Han 田漢 "Tao min-chien ch'ü" 到民間去 [To the People], in *T'ien Han san-wen chi* 田漢散文集 [Collected Writings of T'ien Han], Shanghai, 1936.

Ts'ao Mu-kuan 曹慕管 "Lün wen-hsüeh wu hsin chiu chih i" 論文學無新舊之異 [Literature Does Not Have an Old and New], *Hsüeh Heng* [The Critical Review], No. 32 (Aug. 1924).

T'ung Shu-yeh 童書業 "Ku-shih pien p'ai te chieh-chi pen-chih" 古史辨派的階級本質 [The Class Disposition of the Ku-shih pien Clique], *Wen shih che* 文史哲 [Literature, History, Philosophy], LII:3 (Peking, Jan. 1952), 32–34.

van Gennep, Arnold, *Le folklore,* Paris, 1924.

Venturi, Franco, *Roots of Revolution: A History of the Populist and Socialist Movements in Nineteenth Century Russia,* New York, 1960.

Wang, Chester C., "Wang Kuo-wei, His Life and His Scholarship," unpub. doctoral dissertation, University of Chicago, 1967.

Wang I-ch'ang 王宜昌 "Chung-kuo she-hui shih-lün shih" 中國社會史論史 [A History of the Chinese Society Debate], *Tu-shu tsa-chih,* II:2–3 (March 1932).

Wang Li-hsi 王禮錫 "Huo wen-hsüeh-shih chih szu" 活文學史之死 [The Death of the History of Living Literature], *Tu-shu tsa-chih,* I:3 (June 1931).

Wang Yi-t'ung, "Biographic Sketches of 29 Classical Scholars of the Late Manchu and Early Republican Era," unpub. ms., Columbia University, 1963.

Woodbridge, Frederick J. E., *The Purpose of History,* New York, 1916.

Wright, Mary C., ed., *China in Revolution: The First Phase, 1900–1913,* New Haven, 1968.

Wu Fang-chi 吳芳吉 "San lün wu-jen yen-chung chih hsin chiu wen-hsüeh kuan" 三論吾人眼中之新舊文學觀 [Third Discussion Regarding the Viewpoints on Old and New Literature], *Hsüeh Heng,* No. 31 (July 1924).

Yang Hsiang-k'uei 楊向奎 "Ku-shih pien p'ai te hsüeh-shu ssu-hsiang 'p'i-p'an" 古史辨派的學術思想批判 [A Criticism of the Thought and Scholarship of the Ku-shih pien Clique], *Wen shih che,* LII:3 (Peking, Jan. 1952), 34–37.

Index